OSDMLAHTBLRHS

From the painting by G. F. Watts, R. A.

ROBERT BROWNING

1865

THE
READER'S BROWNING

SELECTED POEMS

*Edited, with Introduction,
Bibliography, and Notes by*

WALTER GRAHAM
PROFESSOR OF ENGLISH,
UNIVERSITY OF ILLINOIS

AMERICAN BOOK COMPANY
*New York · Cincinnati · Chicago
Boston · Atlanta*

PREFACE

THE poems of Browning included in the following pages are selected to reveal, as well as possible, to men and women of the twentieth century, the lasting beauty of this poet's work. John Drinkwater, A. Allen Brockington, Frances Theresa Russell, Geo. R. Elliott, and other well known contemporary critics have, within the last two decades, shown us that Browning is the one poet of Victorian England whose influence is strongly felt today. Because of the changing critical values of the past half century, the editor of this book has attempted to derive from the abundant comment of the 1880's and 1890's only that small critical residuum which has relevance and meaning for modern students. It has seemed to him more important to supply what is lacking in nearly all existing editions of Browning's poetry—a summary of the scholarly findings of the last thirty years, along with a bibliography of the valuable studies which have been published within this period. It has also been the purpose of the editor to offer students a large-print text of the best poems—a text based upon that of the 1888-9 edition of Browning's *Works,* published by Smith, Elder and Company, which incorporates the poet's last revisions and his own punctuation. The Notes at the end of the book are intended to offer not explication of word or phrase (for which the student can in many cases go to a dictionary) but rather a hint of what Browning's poems may mean to a reader of today. It is easy to bury Browning in footnotes, and not at all necessary. The average reader wishes to get delight from the poems rather than to acquire information regarding the Italian Renaissance. Moreover, there are plenty of guides and commentaries, with the help of which Browning's work may be minutely dissected—if one so desires.

I have departed from the practice of nearly all editors of Browning in giving the poems a strictly chronological arrangement, according to date of first publication. For the aid of the many readers of Browning who are not familiar with the Italian language, I have appended to the Notes a list (with indicated pronunciation) of the most troublesome Italian names that are to be found in the poems.

W. G.

CONTENTS

Preface III

Introduction
    I. Some Facts about Browning IX
   II. Browning and Modern Poetry XIX

Selected Bibliography
    I. Standard Editions XXVI
   II. Letters XXVI
  III. Handbooks and Commentaries XXVII
  IV. Valuable Recent Books and Articles for the
        Browning Student XXVII

Selected Poems
Pippa Passes 3 (455)*
Cavalier Tunes
    I. Marching Along 56 (456)
   II. Give a Rouse 57 (456)
  III. Boot and Saddle 58 (456)
My Last Duchess 58 (456)
Soliloquy of the Spanish Cloister 60 (456)
Rudel to the Lady of Tripoli 62 (457)
Cristina 63 (457)
Through the Metidja to Abd-el-Kadr 65 (457)
The Pied Piper of Hamelin 67 (457)
Nationality in Drinks 76 (458)
The Flower's Name 78 (458)
Pictor Ignotus 79 (458)

*Numbers in parentheses indicate the pages on which notes may be found.

The Italian in England 81 (459)

The Lost Leader 86 (459)

The Lost Mistress 87 (459)

Home-Thoughts, from Abroad 88 (459)

Home-Thoughts, from the Sea 88 (459)

The Bishop Orders His Tomb at St. Praxed's Church 89 (460)

The Confessional 92 (460)

The Flight of the Duchess 95 (460)

Earth's Immortalities (460)

    Fame 122

    Love 122

Song 122 (460)

Meeting at Night 123 (461)

Parting at Morning 123 (461)

Saul 123 (461)

The Glove 142 (461)

Love among the Ruins 148 (462)

A Lovers' Quarrel 150 (462)

Evelyn Hope 155 (462)

Up at a Villa—Down in the City 157 (462)

A Woman's Last Word 161 (463)

Fra Lippo Lippi 162 (463)

A Toccata of Galuppi's 173 (463)

By the Fireside 176 (464)

Any Wife to Any Husband 185 (464)

My Star 189 (464)

Instans Tyrannus 190 (465)

"Childe Roland to the Dark Tower Came" 192 (465)

Respectability 199 (465)

A Light Woman 200 (466)

The Statue and the Bust 202 (466)

Love in a Life   211   (466)

Life in a Love   212   (466)

How It Strikes a Contemporary   213   (466)

The Last Ride Together   216   (467)

Master Hugues of Saxe-Gotha   220   (467)

Bishop Blougram's Apology   225   (467)

Memorabilia   254   (468)

Andrea del Sarto   255   (469)

Before   263   (469)

After   264   (469)

In Three Days   265   (470)

In a Year   266   (470)

Old Pictures in Florence   269   (470)

"De Gustibus—"   278   (470)

Women and Roses   279   (471)

Protus   281   (471)

Cleon   283   (471)

Popularity   293   (471)

Two in the Campagna   295   (472)

A Grammarian's Funeral   298   (472)

Misconceptions   302   (472)

One Word More: To E. B. B.   302   (472)

May and Death   309   (472)

The Worst of It   310   (473)

Too Late   314   (473)

Abt Vogler   318   (473)

Rabbi Ben Ezra   323   (474)

Caliban upon Setebos; or, Natural Theology in the
    Island   330   (474)

Confessions   339   (475)

Prospice   340   (475)

Youth and Art   341   (475)

Apparent Failure   344   (475)

The Ring and the Book   346   (346, 476)
   [The Finding of the Yellow Book]   351
   [The Contents of the Yellow Book]   354
   [Dedication to Elizabeth Barrett Browning]   370
   [Caponsacchi's Reply to the Judges]   371
   [Caponsacchi's Story of the Flight]   377
   [Pompilia's Story of Her Life]   406
   [Pompilia's Tribute to Caponsacchi—Her Death]
   433
   [The Pope's Praise of Pompilia and Caponsacchi]
   435
   [Browning's Address to the British Public]   441
Hervé Riel   443   (477)
Helen's Tower   448   (477)
Why I Am a Liberal   449   (477)
Development   449   (477)
Epilogue to Asolando   453   (478)
Notes on the Poems   455
Pronunciation of Some Italian Names   479
Index of Titles and First Lines   481

INTRODUCTION

I. Some Facts about Browning

"FATHER, Mother, only son, and only daughter, formed a most united, harmonious and intellectual family," wrote Alfred Domett, referring to the exceptionally congenial domestic group of which the elder Robert Browning was the head. Robert, the father of the poet, was a clerk in the Bank of England, in easy circumstances, whose wide range of interests and aptitudes unquestionably influenced the tastes and the achievements of his famous son. Writer of humorous verses, caricaturist with pencil, collector of Hogarth prints, lover of out-of-the-way literature, Robert Browning, senior, possessed a splendid, though curiously selected library, in which Robert, junior, was able to make himself one of the most broadly learned of English writers. That library in the home on Southampton Street, Camberwell, London, was certainly one of our poet's universities, if, as he declared, Italy was another. The elder Browning's interests extended even to the enthusiastic following of celebrated criminal cases, which is significant indeed in a parent of the author of *The Ring and the Book*. The mother of the poet (Sarah Anna Wiedemann) was a talented woman, of German and Scotch ancestry, who transmitted to her son some of her love of music. Sarianna, the sister, two years his junior, lived to be the poet's companion after the death of Elizabeth Barrett Browning. Unmarried, she survived her brother, and died in Venice, April 22, 1903.

Robert Browning, the poet, was born May 7, 1812. Reared in an atmosphere of gentle affection and sensible,

Cavalier Tunes.

if somewhat conservative, religious feeling, the young poet's earliest impressions were happy and conducive to the formation of that optimistic outlook upon life which was reflected in his thought. Like his father, Robert enjoyed bodily health and mental vigor of no ordinary sorts. His energy of mind made him a swift learner. After elementary lessons at home, he was prepared for the neighboring school of the Reverend Thomas Ready, under whose care he remained, as a day-boarder, until he was fourteen years old. Before he left the school—practically the only regular education he ever had—he was probably getting far more from his father's library than from his schoolbooks. Byron captured him for a time— his manuscript volume of non-extant juvenilia, *Incondita,* was said to have been written under that poet's influence. Then in 1826 he met the work of Shelley, dramatically enough, in a pirated volume of Benbow, but certainly not first in the "atheistical" and unrepresentative *Queen Mab,* as almost every authority on Browning has asserted. (See note on "Memorabilia," p. 468). Shelley's influence appears most strikingly in *Pauline* and *Paracelsus.* "It was Shelley's special function to fling an aërial bridge from reality, as we commonly understand that word, to the higher reality which we name the ideal." This was the "function" that impressed Browning when he read Shelley, the quality in Shelley which he celebrated in the lines of "Memorabilia," and in the later *Essay on Shelley.* Shelley was to him a "climbing spirit." Like Shelley, he resolved to point the way and follow the way toward the unattainable best in life. If later Browning thought less of Shelley as a poet or man, it is hard to believe that he was not permanently indebted to him for spiritual direction and for his high conception of the poet's office.

Since Oxford and Cambridge were not open to conscientious dissenters (the Brownings were members of an Independent congregation) and the newly established London University (1828), to which his father subscribed one hundred pounds, could hold his interest for little more than one term, the poet virtually quitted his formal education at the age of fourteen. The time came, however, when he was obliged to make some choice of a future career. With the full consent of his understanding parents, Browning, like Milton, chose to be a poet. He had always known that he wanted to be an artist; the question which was really decided in the family councils was what kind of an artist he should be. His interest in all the other forms of art—music, painting, architecture, sculpture—is illustrated in his later poems. No English writer has approached the art of poetry with a wider knowledge or more catholic taste in the sister arts. Throughout his life he did much modeling; he was truly "the musician's poet"; and it is not without significance that his only son, Robert Wiedemann Barrett Browning, became a distinguished painter.

As poet, Browning served an apprenticeship long and trying, in spite of the encouragement of such friends as Alfred Domett, Joseph Arnould, the Rev. William Johnson Fox, Eliza and Sarah Flower (daughters of Benjamin Flower); of his Aunt Christiana Silverthorne, who financed his earliest published work, _Pauline, 1833_; and of his father, who paid the cost of _Paracelsus, 1835_, and _Sordello, 1840_. These early poems showed great poetic abilities and brought him the friendship of John Forster, Carlyle, Leigh Hunt, "Barry Cornwall," Richard Hengist Horne, Dickens, Wordsworth, Landor, and other writers of the day; but they left the general reading public untouched.

As a bid for public notice, consequently, Browning followed the suggestion of his publisher, Moxon, and between 1841 and 1846 issued eight numbers of what he called *Bells and Pomegranates* ("sound with sense, poetry with thought"). These inexpensive pamphlets, *Pippa Passes*, 1841, *King Victor and King Charles*, 1842, *Dramatic Lyrics*, 1842, *The Return of the Druses*, 1843, *A Blot in the 'Scutcheon*, 1843, *Colombe's Birthday*, 1844, *Dramatic Romances and Lyrics*, 1845, and *Luria*, 1846, did not immediately increase his fame. But they showed the world the real Browning: not the introspective and difficult poet of *Pauline* and *Paracelsus*, but the poet whose natural instinct was dramatic, who combined the dramatic and lyric, the romantic and the realistic, in poetry in an unprecedented way.

Browning had appeared before the public as a writer of plays, in May 1837, when Macready produced and acted *Strafford*, a drama which he had induced Browning to write (based to some extent on John Forster's *Thomas Wentworth, Earl of Strafford*,[1] 1836). His experience as the author of *Strafford* had taught Browning that his genius was better adapted to writing plays for the closet than for the stage. *A Blot in the 'Scutcheon*, which, owing to a quarrel with Macready, Browning got printed in twenty-four hours and published before its actual first appearance at Drury Lane, was (later, when revived at Sadler's Wells) a moderate success on the stage, while *Colombe's Birthday* appeared at the Haymarket in 1853 with unquestioned credit to the author. Nevertheless, it is true, in the main, that the dramatic talent of Browning was of the static kind. Dowden has pointed out that the poet showed with extraordinary skill and subtlety char-

[1] In *Lives of Eminent British Statesmen*, vol. II.

acter in position, but attained only a labored success with character in movement.[2]

Travel had much to do with Browning's development as a writer, in that it broadened his interests and discovered to him fields for poetic cultivation neglected by other English poets. During the winter of 1833-34, he spent three months in Russia, nominally in the character of secretary to the Russian consul-general, Chevalier George de Benkhausen. Browning may have harbored for a time some thoughts of a diplomatic career as a result of this, but it seems to have left almost no traces in his poetry. The effect was quite otherwise a few years later when, in the summer of 1838, the young poet saw Italy for the first time. A visit of a month included a fortnight in Venice, four days in Asolo, and shorter stays in Padua, Verona, and Tyrol, and the Rhine country. The most direct and best known results of this journey are, perhaps, *Sordello* and *Pippa Passes;* but the effects of it were felt throughout his career. Italy became his spiritual as well as later, for fifteen years, his real home. Years after, in "De Gustibus—," he could write his own epitaph—

> "Open my heart and you will see
> Graved inside of it, 'Italy.' "

A second journey in 1844 confirmed his love of Italy, and became a brief prelude to his great romance. Landing at Naples, he traveled in the leisurely and fruitful manner of the time to Rome. The first experiences and impressions of the "Eternal City" are to be found abundantly reflected in the pages of his subsequent works. With his marriage and removal to the Continent in 1846,

[2] Dowden, *Life of Robert Browning* (Everyman Edition), p. 53.

Browning's association with Italy became for fifteen years almost continuous. The spirit and content and very life of his poetry, much of it later written in England, were derived from the land to which he had given his heart.

Browning's love of Elizabeth Barrett must be regarded as the crowning influence upon his career. More than any other experiences, those of love and marriage made him a great poet. Many of the most important of his poems (those published as *Men and Women,* 1855, and *Dramatis Personæ,* 1864, as well as *The Ring and the Book,* 1868-9) were written after he had wed the invalid poetess of Wimpole Street. In fact, of the sixty-four "love" poems in his works, only seven were written before he met Elizabeth Barrett. "My Star," "By the Fireside," "One Word More," "Love Among the Ruins," "Prospice," and the beautiful apostrophe, "O Lyric Love," in *The Ring and the Book,* are only a few of the poems of Browning in which her influence is most obvious. After 1846, it can be said to permeate and transform his poetry. Many of Browning's women, like Pompilia, partake of the character of Elizabeth Barrett.

In 1841 Browning, then almost unknown, mentioned to his elderly good friend, John Kenyon, the gratification he felt to find his own works praised in a poem called "Lady Geraldine's Courtship." The author of this poem, Elizabeth Barrett Moulton-Barrett (born March 6, 1806) had been well known to the reading public for several years (*The Seraphim and Other Poems,* 1838). Kenyon, a wealthy gentleman who had been a schoolfellow of Browning's father, was a second cousin of the poetess. Kenyon suggested that Browning write to the lady, who was a semi-invalid and confined to her home. On January 10, 1845, after she had issued a very successful new volume of poems (*Poems*, 1844), Browning wrote his famous letter—"I love your verses with all my heart, dear Miss Barrett." A few months later they met. Under circumstances unique in the annals of romance, Browning swept the almost bedridden poetess, six years his senior, into one of the strangest and happiest marriages ever recorded. Her father, Edward Moulton-Barrett, was obdurately opposed to the marriage of any one of his large family of children. He successively disowned Elizabeth, Henrietta, and Alfred, because they defied him by elopements. Browning and Elizabeth Barrett were married secretly at the Marylebone Church on September 12, 1846, with James Silverthorne and Miss Barrett's maid Wilson for witnesses. A week later they slipped away to Italy.[3] The emotional experiences of courtship and marriage were idealized by Mrs. Browning in *Sonnets from the Portuguese,* first published privately in 1847, as *Sonnets by E. B. B.* After a few years, Florence became their more or less permanent home, and Browning's several poems about Florentine artists, as well as Mrs. Browning's *Casa Guidi Windows,* were direct results of this change of residence. Many details of their life in Italy are to be found in Henry James's *William Wetmore Story and His Friends;* for the American sculp-

[3] The story of this celebrated romance is best told, of course, in the *Letters of Robert Browning and Elizabeth Barrett Barrett, 1845-46,* edited by the son. The following books, however, are of interest to modern students who wish to know more of the affair: *The Brownings* by Osbert Burdett, London, 1928; *Andromeda in Wimpole Street* by Dorothy J. Baynes ("Dormer Creston"), London, 1929; Mrs. C. Lenanton's novel, *Miss Barrett's Elopement,* New York, 1930; Rudolf Besier's play, *The Barretts of Wimpole Street,* New York, 1931; Oliver Elton's *The Brownings,* London, 1924; and Chapter VIII, "Browning's Reputation as a Lover," in A. A. Brockington's *Browning and the Twentieth Century,* London, 1932.

tor and his family were among the Brownings' inner circle of acquaintances.[4]

Although Browning himself had little income to live on, Mrs. Browning had £360 a year, a bequest from an uncle. John Kenyon, her kinsman, who had been responsible for their meeting, continued to be the best of friends. After the birth of their one child in 1849, Kenyon insisted on giving the Brownings an allowance of one hundred pounds a year, and on his death in 1856 they received a generous legacy of eleven thousand pounds, which thenceforth removed from them any necessity of financial worry. During Kenyon's life, they had always been welcome guests at his house in Wimbledon when they were in England. They were visiting him in West Cowes, Isle of Wight, when the last pages of Mrs. Browning's longest poem, *Aurora Leigh*, 1856, were written. She dedicated the work to him as "This poor sign of esteem, gratitude, and affection, from your unforgetting E. B. B."

Fifteen years of married happiness brought Mrs. Browning a new lease of health and activity, and likewise brought the talented pair a host of friendships with notable men and women. Mary Russell Mitford had long been an intimate of Elizabeth Barrett. Joseph Milsand, a Frenchman, met them through his critical appreciations of their work, and became one of Browning's most valued correspondents. Alfred Tennyson and his older brother Frederick, Countess Ossoli (Margaret Fuller), Miss Isa Blagden, who was to be one of their dearest friends (see *Letters of Robert Browning to Miss Isa Blagden*), Thomas

[4] See also Mabel Major, "Browning and the Florentine Renaissance," in *Texas Christian University Quarterly*, Fort Worth, Texas, July, 1924 (I, nos. 2-3).

and Jane Welsh Carlyle, Charles Kingsley, Mazzini, the Italian patriot, Ruskin, George Sand, and Dante Gabriel Rossetti, were among the congenial callers at "Casa Guidi," their apartment in Florence, or among those whom they met on their frequent visits to England.

With the constant stimuli of his great and abiding love for Elizabeth Barrett, of devoted friendships, and of the artistic culture of his loved Italy, Browning's genius carried him on to success—such success in poetry that he lived to see Browning Societies established in England and America to do him honor. The first step in the direction of general fame was the publication of a collected edition of his works in 1849. It was followed by the *Men and Women* of 1855, the *Dramatis Personæ* of 1864, and finally by the widely acclaimed *The Ring and the Book,* his greatest poem, in 1868-9. Browning was by this time recognized generally as a great poet. The last two works appeared after the profoundest sorrow of his life, the death of Mrs. Browning in 1861. After this date, he could not longer bear to live in Florence, but returned to England, to establish himself at 19 Warwick Crescent, London. But Italy remained the country of his soul, and poems of Italy continued to appear from his pen.

The closing period of Browning's life was crowded with interests and occupations. He became something of an oracle. He became Henry James's "accomplished, saturated, sane, sound man of the London world and the world of culture." He was a celebrated conversationalist, a man of affairs, a man who savored "the best of life for which the first was made." That he was not the "hero of all the handbooks and gospels" which the too-enthusiastic members of the Browning cult tried to make him, we have Edmund Gosse's trustworthy word for. He wrote many poems which are now little read—in such volumes as *Prince Hohenstiel-Schwangau,* 1871, *Fifine at the Fair,* 1872, *Red Cotton Night-Cap Country,* 1873, *The Inn Album,* 1875, *La Saisiaz,* 1878, *Dramatic Idyls,* 1879, second series, 1880, *Jocoseria,* 1883, *Ferishtah's Fancies,* 1884, *Parleyings with Certain People of Importance,* 1887, and *Asolando,* 1889. Later Greek studies resulted in *Balaustion's Adventure,* 1871, *Aristophanes' Apology,* 1875, and a translation of the *Agamemnon* of Æschylus, 1877, and revealed an interesting and original attitude toward Greek art and thought. Honors came to him, along with general fame. By 1881 Browning Societies were formed. The London Society was the joint creation of Dr. F. J. Furnivall and Miss Emily Hickey, and the parent of many other societies throughout the English-speaking world. America, which had early liked Browning's works, gave him before 1881 far more praise than his own country.[5] These later years brought honorary degrees from Cambridge University (1879), Oxford (1882), and Edinburgh University (1884).

Browning's absence of seventeen years from Italy did not in any sense mean alienation. His heart was still in the land where he had found his highest happiness, although he could never bring himself to revisit Florence and the "Casa Guidi." His London life had been varied by many journeyings to French seacoast towns, to Wales, and to Scotland. In 1878, he once more set foot on Italian shores, going with his sister Sarianna to Venice and Asolo,

[5] For records and other materials regarding the Browning Societies in America, see the volumes of *Poet-Lore,* Philadelphia, 1889 ff. Sixteen reviews of Browning's works had appeared in American magazines and literary journals by the year 1855.

the two places which in these later years gave him the most pleasure. His son, whose professional painting was now becoming widely known, spent the autumn of 1885 with his father in Venice, and later (1888) brought to this city his bride of 1887, an American girl (Miss Fannie Coddington) for whom he purchased the Rezzonico Palace on the Grand Canal. The story of Browning's last (they had become "annual") visits to Venice is told well by Mrs. Katherine Bronson.[6] Mrs. Bronson entertained Browning and his sister at her own home in Venice and also at "La Mura," her summer home in the small town of Asolo. It was shortly after a stay in "delicious Asolo," which he found even more beautiful than it had been when he first saw it fifty years before, that Browning returned to his son's home in Venice to die, on the 12th of December, 1889. His last task was that of correcting the proofs of his volume, *Asolando,* which was issued in London on the very day of his death. It is impossible not to associate his noble "Epilogue" to *Asolando* and the quiet confidence with which he gave up his long and happy life. Although Mrs. Browning had been buried, and still lies, in the English cemetery at Florence, Browning's body was brought back to England and appropriately interred in Westminster Abbey. "Poet's Corner received one poet more."

II. Browning and Modern Poetry

TENNYSON AND BROWNING are now usually regarded as the two considerable poets of the Victorian Period. The former showed his contemporaries the still fresh and

[6] "Browning in Venice," *Century Magazine,* Feb. 1902 (N.S. XLI, 572-84.)

vital possibilities of a great traditional manner; the latter showed them what were the likeliest methods of departure and revolt from that manner. Tennyson's example influenced the versification and spirit of many poets in his own age; while Browning's influence, far less immediate or direct in its effect, proved to be a more durable one.[7]

Browning's reputation for obscurity, although it is rapidly diminishing and was always greatly exaggerated, cannot be ignored. Such poems as *Prince Hohenstiel-Schwangau* and *Fifine at the Fair,* products of his later years, lead the reader into metaphysical realms where few care to go. Likewise, one can hardly be expected to get immediate satisfaction from the early poems, *Paracelsus* and *Sordello,* any more than Browning's bewildered contemporaries did. But in the thirty years following *Pippa Passes* (1841) Browning produced poems that any reader of intelligence and sympathy may enjoy. This span of years was his golden period.[8] His range of interests was wide, his instinct for the appropriate poetic garb of his ideas was remarkable. The poet who wrote "Popularity" could also write "Love Among the Ruins" and "Saul" and *The Ring and the Book.*

In diction and manner Browning abandoned the traditions adhered to with more or less fidelity by his contemporaries. The elevated manner seemed to him to be exhausted. He was dissatisfied with the habit of verse as he found it in common use. He created for himself a new complex of the conversational idiom, a realistic

[7] John Drinkwater, *Victorian Poetry* (People's Library ed.), p. 81.

[8] With a few exceptions, the selected poems in this volume were written between 1841 and 1870. The date of each poem is given in the Notes (pp. 455 ff.). The arrangement is chronological by date of first publication.

language lifted bodily (not always with success) into poetry—an alert and personal manner, which avoided at once the elevation of the Tennysonian style and the flat commonplaceness of the pure colloquial. Browning's idiom was sometimes ennobled and intensified, as in "O lyric Love, half angel and half bird," and sometimes vexed into what may be called verbal antics, as in "Hobbs hints blue—straight he turtle eats." His subject matter, form, and temper, were determined by the effects he wished to produce. It must not be forgotten that Browning was always the deliberate artist, making his material subservient to his purpose. Although he could write in the traditional manner, he was seldom content to do so. Language and prosody were never Browning's masters; they were his servants.

It is important to note that Browning's poetry is essentially dramatic in principle—it is objective rather than subjective. His early efforts to find success as a dramatist only confirmed his natural tendency. The very titles of his *Men and Women* and *Dramatis Personæ* volumes indicate his main interest—human nature. Only the "soul" was worth study, he wrote in a letter to Milsand, apropos of *Sordello*. Outside the nine or ten works which he called dramas, Browning's dramatic instinct found play in poems about people—his dramatic lyrics, as he called such poems as "Saul," "Any Wife to Any Husband," or "Master Hugues of Saxe-Gotha"; his dramatic romances, the poems like "The Glove," "The Flight of the Duchess," or "The Statue and the Bust"; or his later dramatic idyls, like "Pheidippides" or "Echetlos." Practically all the poems he wrote in his really great period (1841-1870) are inclusively referred to as *dramatic monologues;* that is, one speaker only is employed to be the mouthpiece of the poet. Obviously, the first question a reader must decide for himself is that of the identity of the monologuist. As soon as this point has been settled (and it is seldom a difficult one) most of the so-called obscurity of Browning disappears. It has been remarked [9] that part of the difficulty of Browning is inherent in the form he invented. Browning himself warns the reader not to regard his dramatic lyrics as expressive of his own thoughts and feelings. "Though often lyric in expression," he says, "these poems are always dramatic in principle, and so many utterances of so many imaginary persons, *not mine*." Browning's poems (with certain notable exceptions, of course, like "Prospice" or the "Epilogue" to *Asolando*, are lyrical, and therefore subjective, *only* in the sense that they convey to the reader the feelings and thoughts of an imaginary speaker, whether Cleon or Mr. Sludge, Guido, Pompilia, or any one of his unnamed lovers.

More important than these considerations to the modern reader of Browning, however, is the forward-looking nature of his work. Like Whitman in America, Browning in England cultivated the "natural" emotion of the "modern man"—a rich field for tillage in the nineteenth century. Whitman and Browning, intense individualists, turned away more definitely than their predecessors from the old principles of art, and marked out the main course which poetry was to follow in our time. "Browning, in spite of his now despised Victorianism, ought to have even more credit than Whitman as a grandfather of our 'New Poetry.' For under cover of his Victorian propriety he was able to foster in the breast of solid Brit-

[9] A. A. Brockington, *Browning and the Twentieth Century*, London, 1932, p. 120.

ish and American citizenry that was cold to Whitman, a thirst for sheer temperamentalism in art."[10] Whitman sang the glories of the body—he had nothing left for the soul. Browning sang of the soul, but his real theme was how "flesh helps soul," and how soul helps to the enjoyment of the pleasures of this flesh. Browning's contemporaries could find in his poetry the kind of religion they had been brought up on, nicely accommodated to urgent human desires. This point was long ago touched upon by E. J. Bailey in a study of Browning's love poetry.[11] He found in Browning's conception of love a sensuousness wholly modern, no disembodied spirituality; he found in his poetry that touch of brutality recommended by Synge and developed by Kipling and Masefield. What Bailey first hinted, recent critics of Browning have insisted upon. In a realistic attitude toward human life, its passions and individual problems of living, Browning's poetry is in temper more closely akin to the poetry of our day than that of any of his contemporaries. With a life-span that practically comprehended the creative years of Tennyson, Rossetti, Arnold, Clough, Swinburne, and Morris, Browning, of all the Victorians, may be said with certainty to have exerted a powerful influence upon the writers of the twentieth century—an influence which is still potent. To be thoroughly convinced of the modern obligation to Browning's experiments in versification and diction, his individualist and realist view-point, his temperamentalism, one needs only to read together Kipling's "Jobson's Amen," Hardy's

[10] G. R. Elliott, "Browning's Whitmanism," *Sewanee Review*, 1929 (XXXVII, 165).

[11] "Browning's Theory of Love," *Arena*, Mar., 1909 (XLI, 274-284). Compare Louis Wann, "Browning's Theory of Love," *Personalist*, 1925 (VI, 23-35).

"The Dead Quire," Housman's "Reveille," John David-son's "A Frosty Morning," T. S. Eliot's "Rhapsody on a Windy Night," Brooke's "The Fish," and Masefield's "Everlasting Mercy," and then go back to a score of the best known poems of Browning. It is true and important that Browning had no real predecessors; it is equally true and significant that the best of our modern poets are indebted to him for manner and theme.

When the Victorians finally took Browning to their hearts, in the 'seventies and 'eighties, they did so because they saw in him a teacher and moralist rather than an artist. No further proof of this is necessary than a glance through the Browning Society publications. It is doubt-ful whether they ever discovered his peculiar genius. They certainly could not understand his forward-looking aims. Probably much of the apathy toward Browning today is the result of this older emphasis on the "mes-sage" of his poetry; for his religious speculations and moral disputations are no longer of general interest to readers. Browning suffered more than most writers from the universal tendency of readers to make their poets the receptacles of other men's thoughts. For this reason, it is necessary to clear away the rubbish of later Victorian criticism of Browning, before this poet's most enduring qualities can be clearly descried. When such a house-cleaning has been accomplished, however, the poet of "A Toccata of Galuppi's," "Abt Vogler," "Love Among the Ruins," and *The Ring and the Book* is seen to deserve a high rank. He is not the greatest, perhaps, but the most singular and original of later English poets. He surprised and repelled his earlier contemporaries by his mannerisms, language, and liking for the baroque; but we of a later day find that by virtue of these very qualities

he is the "father of modern experimental verse," the
"forerunner of that type of romantic realism" which
Masefield has made popular. We see that the bulk of his
poetry is "concerned just as avidly and concretely with
the facts of everyday living" as that of the modern
Georgian.[12] Like the post-war Georgians, Browning had
a flair for feelings, and a zest for the bizarre, the eccentric,
and the seamy sides of life. Like them he was a "great
lover." Like them he had a passionate belief in ordinary men and women.

Perhaps Browning can never be regarded as a profound
thinker. Poets seldom are. As far as I know, his disciples have never claimed such distinction for him. He
was an artist, and his artistic aim was to present, as he
saw them, what he called eternal truths. These he presented with courage and joy and beauty. He looked on
men and women and saw that they were good, and capable of becoming better. He saw in what the world
calls failure, often a higher success. He expressed the
wisdom of the ages when he declared the greatest human
fault was the "unlit lamp and the ungirt loin"—sluggish-
ness, indifference, sloth of living. He preached (if we
must use that term) a doctrine of individual development,
and asserted the necessity of the will to effort. He studied
the same common humanity that has engaged the attention of Kipling and Hardy, Masefield or Housman or
Synge. With makers of literature in all ages of human
history, Browning attempted to find for the facts and
conditions of life an interpretation favorable to the
human species.

[12]Arthur Compton-Rickett, *Robert Browning: Humanist,* London,
1924, p. 18.

SELECTED BIBLIOGRAPHY

I. STANDARD EDITIONS

Complete Works, ed. with introductions and notes by Charlotte Porter and Helen A. Clarke. 12 vols. New York, 1898.

The Works of Robert Browning, with introductions by F. G. Kenyon (Centenary Edition). 9 vols. London, 1912.

New Poems of Robert Browning and Elizabeth Barrett Browning, ed. by F. G. Kenyon. London, 1914.

The Ring and the Book, ed. by Charlotte Porter and Helen A. Clarke. New York, 1898.

The Ring and the Book, ed. by F. M. Padelford. New York, 1917. (A good inexpensive edition.)

The Ring and the Book, ed. by M. J. Moses and Helen A. Clarke. New York, 1927.

II. LETTERS

The Letters of Robert Browning and Elizabeth Barrett Barrett, 1845-46, ed. by R. B. Browning. 2 vols. New York, 1899.

Letters of Robert Browning to Miss Isa Blagden, ed. by A. J. Armstrong. Waco, Texas, 1923.

"Some Letters from Matthew Arnold to Robert Browning," in *A Book for Bookmen,* ed. by John Drinkwater. London, 1926.

Robert Browning and Alfred Domett, ed. by F. G. Kenyon. London, 1906.

Letters to Her Sister by Elizabeth Barrett Browning, 1846-59, ed. by Leonard Huxley. London, 1929.

Letters of Robert Browning, collected by Thomas J. Wise, ed. by Thurman L. Hood. New Haven, 1933.

III. HANDBOOKS AND COMMENTARIES

Berdoe, Edward. *The Browning Cyclopædia*. London, 1891. (Many times reprinted, last 1928.)

Berdoe, Edward. *A Primer of Browning*. New York, 1904.

Cook, A. K. *A Commentary on The Ring and the Book*. London, 1920.

Cooke, George Willis. *A Guide-Book to the Poetic and Dramatic Works of Robert Browning*. Boston, 1891, 1919.

Corson, Hiram. *An Introduction to the Study of Browning's Poetry*. Boston, 1898.

Orr, Mrs. S. *A Handbook to the Works of Robert Browning*. London, 1885. (Many editions, last 1930.)

Phelps, W. L. *Robert Browning, How to Know Him*. Indianapolis, 1915. (Also new edition, 1932, with seven additional chapters.)

IV. VALUABLE RECENT BOOKS AND ARTICLES
FOR THE BROWNING STUDENT

Aikat, A. *On the Poetry of Matthew Arnold, Robert Browning, and Rabindranath Tagore*. Calcutta, 1921.

Bailey, E. J. "Browning's Theory of Love," in *Arena,* Mar., 1909 (XLI, 274-284).

Bates, Margaret H. *Browning Critiques*. Chicago, 1921.

Baylor Browning Interests, Series 1-7. Waco, Texas, 1927-33. (A series of Browning Studies published by the Library and the English Department of Baylor University.)

Baynes, Dorothy J. *Andromeda in Wimpole Street; the Romance of Elizabeth Barrett Browning*. London, 1929.

Bitzkat, F. "Robert Browning's 'A Toccata of Galuppi's,'" in *Englische Studien,* 1923 (LVII, 196); 1925, (LIX, 316).

Bleier, Karl. *Die Technik Rob. Browning's in seinen 'dramatischen Monologen.'* Marburg, 1910.

Brinton, Daniel G. "New Poetic Form as Shown in Browning," in *Poet-Lore,* 1890 (II, 234-246).

Brockington, A. A. *Browning and the Twentieth Century.* London, 1932.

Bronson, Katherine. "Browning in Asolo," in *Century Magazine,* Apr., 1900 (LIX, 920-31); "Browning in Venice," in *Cornhill Magazine,* 1902 (LXXXV, 145-71); also in *Century Magazine,* Feb., 1902 (N. S. XLI, 572-84).

Brooke, Stopford A. *The Poetry of Robert Browning.* New York, 1902.

Brooks, A. E. *Browningiana in Baylor University.* Waco, Texas: Baylor Univ. Press, 1921. (Catalogue of a very rich and important collection, probably the largest in America.)

Broughton, Leslie N. and Stelter, B. F. *Concordance to the Poetical Works of Robert Browning.* 2 vols. New York, 1924-5.

Browning, Fannie Barrett. *Some Memories of Robert Browning.* Boston, 1928. (By Browning's daughter-in-law.)

Burdett, Osbert. *The Brownings.* Boston, 1928.

Campbell, Lily Bess. *The Grotesque in the Poetry of Robert Browning.* Austin, Texas, 1907.

Chancellor, E. Beresford. "Browning in London," in *Living Age,* 1912 (273: 755-757).

Chesterton, G. K. *Robert Browning.* New York, 1903.

Clarke, Helen A. *Browning and His Century.* Garden City, N. Y., 1912.

Compton-Rickett, A. *Robert Browning: Humanist.* London, 1924. (A book of selections with an important introductory essay.)

Crawford, A. W. "Browning's 'Cleon,'" in *Journal of English and Germanic Philology,* 1927 (XXVI, 485-90).

Crawford, A. W. "Browning's 'Saul,'" in *Queen's Quarterly,* Apr.-June, 1927 (XXXIV, 448-54).

Cunliffe, J. W. "Browning and the Marathon Race," in *Pub. Mod. Lang. Assn.,* March, 1909 (XXIV, 154-63).

DeVane, Wm. Clyde. *Browning's "Parleyings"; the Autobiography of a Mind.* New Haven, 1927.

DeVane, Wm. Clyde. "The Landscape of 'Childe Roland to the Dark Tower Came,'" in *Pub. Mod. Lang. Assn.,* 1925 (XL, 426).

Dickson, Arthur. "Browning's Source for 'The Pied Piper of Hamelin,'" in *Studies in Philology,* July, 1926 (XXIII, 327-36).

Dowden, Edward. *The Life of Robert Browning.* New York, 1915. (Everyman's Library.)

Drachmann, A. G. "Alloy and Gold," in *Studies in Philology,* July, 1925 (XXII, 418-24).

Drinkwater, John. *Victorian Poetry.* London, n.d. (People's Library.)

Duckworth, F. R. G. *Browning: Background and Conflict.* London, 1931.

Duclaux, Mary. *Robert Browning: Étude sur sa pensée et sa vie.* Paris, 1922.

Elliott, G. R. "Browning's Whitmanism," in *Sewanee Review,* April, 1929 (XXXVII, 164-70).

Elliott, G. R. "Shakespeare's Significance for Browning," in *Anglia,* Jan., 1909 (XXXII, 90-162).

Elton, Oliver. *The Brownings.* London, 1924.

Fehr, Bernard. "Über Robert Brownings 'Love Among the Ruins,'" in *Archiv,* Dec., 1921 (CXLII, 260).

Flower, B. O. "Browning's 'Rabbi Ben Ezra,'" in *Arena,* Oct., 1908 (XL, 334-41).

Fonblanque, Ethel. "The Influence of Italy on the Poetry of the Brownings," in *Fortnightly Review,* Aug., 1909 (XCII, 327-44).

Gaylord, Harriet. *Pompilia and Her Poet.* New York, 1931.

Gest, John Marshall. *The Old Yellow Book: A new translation*. Boston, 1925.

Gleason, K. F. *The Dramatic Art of Robert Browning*. Boston, 1927.

Glicksman, Harry. "The Legal Aspect of Browning's *The Ring and the Book*," in *Mod. Lang. Notes,* Dec., 1920 (XXV, 473-79).

Golder, Harold. "Browning's 'Childe Roland,'" in *Pub. Mod. Lang. Assn.,* 1924 (XXXIX, 963).

Goodrich, A. F. *Caponsacchi*. New York, 1927. (Play.)

Goodrich-Freer, A. "Robert Browning the Musician," in *Nineteenth Century,* Apr., 1901 (XLIX, 648-58).

Graham, David. *Pompilia*. New York, 1928. (Play.)

Griffin, W. Hall, and Minchin, H. C. *The Life of Robert Browning*. London, 1910. (The most important biographical work.)

Hatcher, Harlan H. *The Versification of Robert Browning*. Columbus, O., 1928.

Herford, C. H. *Robert Browning*. New York, 1905.

Hodell, Charles W. (tr.) *The Old Yellow Book*. London and New York, 1911. (Everyman's Library.)

Hogrefe, Pearl. *Browning and Italian Art and Artists*. (*Univ. of Kansas Humanistic Studies,* No. 3.) Lawrence, Kansas, 1914.

Hood, T. L. "Browning's Ancient Classical Sources," *Harvard Studies in Classical Philology,* 1922 (XXXIII, 79-188).

Hood, T. L. "The Meaning of 'Childe Roland,'" in *New England Magazine,* 1912 (N. S. XLVI, 130).

Ker, W. P. "Browning," in *Essays and Studies of the English Association,* No. 1, pp. 70-84. Oxford, 1910.

Law, Robert Adger. "The Background of Browning's 'Love Among the Ruins,'" in *Mod. Lang. Notes,* May, 1922 (XXXVII, 312).

Ley, Wilfred Rooke. "The Brownings in Paris," in *American Review,* 1933 (I, 308-12).

Loth, David. *The Brownings: A Victorian Idyll.* New York, 1929.

Lounsbury, T. R. *The Early Literary Career of Robert Browning.* New York, 1911.

Major, Mabel. "Browning and the Florentine Renaissance," in *Texas Christian University Quarterly,* 1924 (I, 3-74).

Masson, David. "Browning in Edinburgh," in *Living Age,* 1909 (260: 653 ff.).

Mayne, Ethel Colburn. *Browning's Heroines.* London, 1913.

More, Paul Elmer. "Why Is Browning Popular?" in *Shelburne Essays,* Third Series, 143-165.

Orr, Mrs. S. *Life and Letters of Robert Browning,* rev. and ed. by F. G. Kenyon. New York, 1908.

Phelps, Wm. Lyon. "Robert Browning as Seen by His Son," in *Century Magazine,* 1912-13 (LXXXV, 417-20).

Phelps, Wm. Lyon. "Notes on Browning's *Pauline,*" in *Mod. Lang. Notes,* May, 1932 (XLVII, 292-99).

Pottle, F. A. *Shelley and Browning: A Myth and Some Facts.* Chicago, Pembroke Press, 1924.

Raymond, W. O. "Light on the Genesis of *The Ring and the Book,*" in *Mod. Lang. Notes,* June, 1928 (XLIII, 357-68. Cf. XLIII, 445-50).

Raymond, W. O. "Browning and the Higher Criticism," in *Pub. Mod. Lang. Assn.,* June, 1929 (XLIV, 590-621).

Rea, John D. "My Last Duchess," in *Studies in Philology,* 1932 (XXIX, 120-22).

Russell, Frances Theresa. *One Word More on Browning.* Stanford Univ. Press, 1927. (Valuable for criticism and for annotated bibliography.)

Russell, Frances Theresa. "Gold and Alloy," in *Studies in Philology,* July, 1924 (XXI, 467-79).

Somervell, D. C. "The Reputation of Robert Browning," in *Essays and Studies of the English Association,* No. 15, 122-38. Oxford, 1929.

Thompson, S. P. (ed.) *The Pied Piper.* (With an inquiry into the sources.) New York, 1905.

Treves, Sir F. *The Country of "The Ring and the Book."* London, 1913.

Wann, Louis. "Browning's Theory of Love," in *Personalist,* Jan., 1925 (VI, 23-35).

Watkin, Ralph Granger. *Robert Browning and the English Pre-Raphaelites.* Breslau, 1905.

Wenger, Christian. *The Æsthetics of Robert Browning.* Ann Arbor, Mich., 1924.

Wise, T. J. *A Complete Bibliography of the Writings in Prose and Verse of Robert Browning.* Privately printed. London, 1897.

Wise, T. J. *A Browning Library.* Privately printed. London, 1929.

Woolf, Virginia. *Flush.* New York, 1933. (The biography of a dog, with side-lights on the love story of Robert Browning and Elizabeth Barrett.)

SELECTED POEMS

BY ROBERT BROWNING

PIPPA PASSES

A DRAMA

PERSONS

PIPPA.	PHENE.
OTTIMA.	Austrian Police.
SEBALD.	BLUPHOCKS.
Foreign Students.	LUIGI and his mother.
GOTTLIEB.	Poor Girls.
SCHRAMM.	MONSIGNOR and his attend-
JULES.	ants.

INTRODUCTION

NEW YEAR'S DAY AT ASOLO IN THE TREVISAN

A large mean airy chamber.   A girl, PIPPA, *from the
silk-mills, springing out of bed.*

DAY!
Faster and more fast,
O'er night's brim, day boils at last:
Boils, pure gold, o'er the cloud-cup's brim
Where spurting and suppressed it lay,
For not a froth-flake touched the rim
Of yonder gap in the solid gray
Of the eastern cloud, an hour away;
But forth one wavelet, then another, curled,
Till the whole sunrise, not to be suppressed,
Rose, reddened, and its seething breast
Flickered in bounds, grew gold, then overflowed the
world.

Oh Day, if I squander a wavelet of thee,
A mite of my twelve-hours' treasure,

The least of thy gazes or glances,
 (Be they grants thou art bound to or gifts above measure)
One of thy choices or one of thy chances,
 (Be they tasks God imposed thee or freaks at thy pleasure)
—My Day, if I squander such labor or leisure,
Then shame fall on Asolo, mischief on me!

Thy long blue solemn hours serenely flowing,
Whence earth, we feel, gets steady help and good—
Thy fitful sunshine-minutes, coming, going,
As if earth turned from work in gamesome mood—
All shall be mine!   But thou must treat me not
As prosperous ones are treated, those who live
At hand here, and enjoy the higher lot,
In readiness to take what thou wilt give,
And free to let alone what thou refusest;
For, Day, my holiday, if thou ill-usest
Me, who am only Pippa,—old-year's sorrow,
Cast off last night, will come again to-morrow:
Whereas, if thou prove gentle, I shall borrow
Sufficient strength of thee for new-year's sorrow.
All other men and women that this earth
Belongs to, who all days alike possess,
Make general plenty cure particular dearth,
Get more joy one way, if another, less:
Thou art my single day, God lends to leaven
What were all earth else, with a feel of heaven,—
Sole light that helps me through the year, thy sun's!
Try now!   Take Asolo's Four Happiest Ones—
And let thy morning rain on that superb
Great haughty Ottima; can rain disturb
Her Sebald's homage?   All the while thy rain
Beats fiercest on her shrub-house window-pane
He will but press the closer, breathe more warm
Against her cheek; how should she mind the storm?
And, morning past, if mid-day shed a gloom

O'er Jules and Phene,—what care bride and groom
Save for their dear selves? 'Tis their marriage-day;
And while they leave church and go home their way,
Hand clasping hand, within each breast would be
Sunbeams and pleasant weather spite of thee.
Then, for another trial, obscure thy eve
With mist,—will Luigi and his mother grieve—
The lady and her child, unmatched, forsooth,
She in her age, as Luigi in his youth,
For true content? The cheerful town, warm, close
And safe, the sooner that thou art morose,
Receives them. And yet once again, outbreak
In storm at night on Monsignor, they make
Such stir about,—whom they expect from Rome
To visit Asolo, his brothers' home,
And say here masses proper to release
A soul from pain,—what storm dares hurt his peace?
Calm would he pray, with his own thoughts to ward
Thy thunder off, nor want the angels' guard.
But Pippa—just one such mischance would spoil
Her day that lightens the next twelvemonth's toil
At wearisome silk-winding, coil on coil!
   And here I let time slip for naught!
Aha, you foolhardy sunbeam, caught
With a single splash from my ewer!
You that would mock the best pursuer,
Was my basin over-deep?
One splash of water ruins you asleep,
And up, up, fleet your brilliant bits
Wheeling and counterwheeling,
Reeling, broken beyond healing:
Now grow together on the ceiling!
That will task your wits.
Whoever it was quenched fire first, hoped to see
Morsel after morsel flee
As merrily, as giddily . . .

Meantime, what lights my sunbeam on,
Where settles by degrees the radiant cripple?
Oh, is it surely blown, my martagon?
New-blown and ruddy as St. Agnes' nipple,
Plump as the flesh-bunch on some Turk bird's poll!
Be sure if corals, branching 'neath the ripple
Of ocean, bud there,—fairies watch unroll
Such turban-flowers; I say, such lamps disperse
Thick red flame through that dusk green universe!
I am queen of thee, floweret!
And each fleshy blossom
Preserve I not— (safer
Than leaves that embower it,
Or shells that embosom)
—From weevil and chafer?
Laugh through my pane then; solicit the bee;
Gibe him, be sure; and, in midst of thy glee,
Love thy queen, worship me!

—Worship whom else? For am I not, this day,
Whate'er I please? What shall I please today?
My morn, noon, eve and night—how spend my day?
Tomorrow I must be Pippa who winds silk,
The whole year round, to earn just bread and milk:
But, this one day, I have leave to go,
And play out my fancy's fullest games;
I may fancy all day—and it shall be so—
That I taste of the pleasures, am called by the names
Of the Happiest Four in our Asolo!

See! Up the hillside yonder, through the morning,
Some one shall love me, as the world calls love:
I am no less than Ottima, take warning!
The gardens, and the great stone house above,
And other house for shrubs, all glass in front,

Are mine; where Sebald steals, as he is wont,
To court me, while old Luca yet reposes:
And therefore, till the shrub-house door uncloses,
I . . . what now?—give abundant cause for prate
About me—Ottima, I mean—of late,
Too bold, too confident she'll still face down
The spitefullest of talkers in our town.
How we talk in the little town below!
   But love, love, love—there's better love, I know!
This foolish love was only day's first offer;
I choose my next love to defy the scoffer:
For do not our Bride and Bridegroom sally
Out of Possagno church at noon?
Their house looks over Orcana valley:
Why should not I be the bride as soon
As Ottima? For I saw, beside,
Arrive last night that little bride—
Saw, if you call it seeing her, one flash
Of the pale snow-pure cheek and black bright tresses,
Blacker than all except the black eyelash;
I wonder she contrives those lids no dresses!
—So strict was she, the veil
Should cover close her pale
Pure cheeks—a bride to look at and scarce touch,
Scarce touch, remember, Jules! For are not such
Used to be tended, flower-like, every feature,
As if one's breath would fray the lily of a creature?
A soft and easy life these ladies lead:
Whiteness in us were wonderful indeed.
Oh, save that brow its virgin dimness,
Keep that foot its lady primness,
Let those ankles never swerve
From their exquisite reserve,
Yet have to trip along the streets like me,
All but naked to the knee!
How will she ever grant her Jules a bliss

So startling as her real first infant kiss?
Oh, no—not envy, this!

—Not envy, sure!—for if you gave me
Leave to take or to refuse,
In earnest, do you think I'd choose
That sort of new love to enslave me?
Mine should have lapped me round from the beginning;
As little fear of losing it as winning:
Lovers grow cold, men learn to hate their wives,
And only parents' love can last our lives.
At eve the Son and Mother, gentle pair,
Commune inside our turret: what prevents
My being Luigi?   While that mossy lair
Of lizards through the winter-time is stirred
With each to each imparting sweet intents
For this new-year, as brooding bird to bird—
 (For I observe of late, the evening walk
Of Luigi and his mother, always ends
Inside our ruined turret, where they talk,
Calmer than lovers, yet more kind than friends)
—Let me be cared about, kept out of harm,
And schemed for, safe in love as with a charm;
Let me be Luigi!   If I only knew
What was my mother's face—my father, too!
   Nay, if you come to that, best love of all
Is God's; then why not have God's love befall
Myself as, in the palace by the Dome,
Monsignor?—who tonight will bless the home
Of his dead brother; and God bless in turn
That heart which beats, those eyes which mildly burn
With love for all men!   I, tonight at least,
Would be that holy and beloved priest.

Now wait!—even I already seem to share
In God's love: what does New-year's hymn declare?
What other meaning do these verses bear?

All service ranks the same with God:
If now, as formerly he trod
Paradise, his presence fills
Our earth, each only as God wills
Can work—God's puppets, best and worst,
Are we; there is no last nor first.

Say not "a small event!" Why "small"?
Costs it more pain that this, ye call
A "great event," should come to pass,
Than that? Untwine me from the mass
Of deeds which make up life, one deed
Power shall fall short in or exceed!

And more of it, and more of it!—oh yes—
I will pass each, and see their happiness,
And envy none—being just as great, no doubt,
Useful to men, and dear to God, as they!
A pretty thing to care about
So mightily, this single holiday!
But let the sun shine!   Wherefore repine?
—With thee to lead me, O Day of mine,
Down the grass path gray with dew,
Under the pine-wood, blind with boughs,
Where the swallow never flew
Nor yet cicala dared carouse—
No, dared carouse!   [*She enters the street.*

I. MORNING

Up the Hillside, inside the Shrub-house. LUCA'S *Wife*
   OTTIMA, *and her Paramour, the German* SEBALD.

Sebald. [*sings.*] *Let the watching lids wink!*
               Day's ablaze with eyes, think!
               Deep into the night, drink!

Ottima. Night? Such may be your Rhineland nights,
    perhaps;
But this blood-red beam through the shutter's chink
—We call such light, the morning: let us see!
Mind how you grope your way, though! How these tall
Naked geraniums straggle! Push the lattice
Behind that frame!—Nay, do I bid you?—Sebald,
It shakes the dust down on me! Why, of course
The slide-bolt catches. Well, are you content,
Or must I find you something else to spoil?
Kiss and be friends, my Sebald! Is't full morning?
Oh, don't speak then!

   Seb.   Ay, thus it used to be!
Ever your house was, I remember, shut
Till mid-day; I observed that, as I strolled
On mornings through the vale here; country girls
Were noisy, washing garments in the brook,
Hinds drove the slow white oxen up the hills:
But no, your house was mute, would ope no eye!
And wisely: you were plotting one thing there,
Nature, another outside. I looked up—
Rough white wood shutters, rusty iron bars,
Silent as death, blind in a flood of light.
Oh, I remember!—and the peasants laughed
And said, "The old man sleeps with the young wife."
This house was his, this chair, this window—his.

   Otti. Ah, the clear morning! I can see Saint Mark's;
That black streak is the belfry. Stop: Vicenza
Should lie . . . there's Padua, plain enough, that blue!
Look o'er my shoulder, follow my finger!

   Seb.   Morning?
It seems to me a night with a sun added.
Where's dew, where's freshness? That bruised plant, I
    bruised
In getting through the lattice yestereve,
Droops as it did. See, here's my elbow's mark

I' the dust o' the sill.

Otti.   Oh, shut the lattice, pray!

Seb. Let me lean out. I cannot scent blood here,
Foul as the morn may be.

                                   There, shut the world out!
How do you feel now, Ottima? There, curse
The world and all outside! Let us throw off
This mask: how do you bear yourself? Let's out
With all of it!

Otti.   Best never speak of it.

Seb. Best speak again and yet again of it,
Till words cease to be more than words. "His blood,"
For instance—let those two words mean, "His blood"
And nothing more. Notice, I'll say them now,
"His blood."

Otti.   Assuredly if I repented
The deed—

Seb. Repent? Who should repent, or why?
What puts that in your head? Did I once say
That I repented?

Otti.   No; I said the deed . . .

Seb. "The deed" and "the event"—just now it was
"Our passion's fruit"—the devil take such cant!
Say, once and always, Luca was a wittol,
I am his cut-throat, you are . . .

Otti.   Here's the wine;
I brought it when we left the house above,
And glasses too—wine of both sorts. Black? White
     then?

Seb. But am not I his cut-throat? What are you?

Otti. There trudges on his business from the Duomo
Benet the Capuchin, with his brown hood
And bare feet; always in one place at church,
Close under the stone wall by the south entry.
I used to take him for a brown cold piece
Of the wall's self, as out of it he rose

To let me pass—at first, I say, I used:
Now, so has that dumb figure fastened on me,
I rather should account the plastered wall
A piece of him, so chilly does it strike.
This, Sebald?
   Seb. No, the white wine—the white wine!
Well, Ottima, I promised no new year
Should rise on us the ancient shameful way;
Nor does it rise. Pour on! To your black eyes!
Do you remember last damned New Year's day?
   Otti. You brought those foreign prints. We looked
     at them
Over the wine and fruit. I had to scheme
To get him from the fire. Nothing but saying
His own set wants the proof-mark, roused him up
To hunt them out.
   Seb.   'Faith, he is not alive
To fondle you before my face.
   Otti.   Do you
Fondle me then! Who means to take your life
For that, my Sebald?
   Seb.   Hark you, Ottima!
One thing to guard against. We'll not make much
One of the other—that is, not make more
Parade of warmth, childish officious coil,
Than yesterday: as if, sweet, I supposed
Proof upon proof were needed now, now first,
To show I love you—yes, still love you—love you
In spite of Luca and what's come to him
—Sure sign we had him ever in our thoughts,
White sneering old reproachful face and all!
We'll even quarrel, love, at times, as if
We still could lose each other, were not tied
By this: conceive you?
   Otti.   Love!
   Seb.   Not tied so sure!

Because though I was wrought upon, have struck
His insolence back into him—am I
So surely yours?—therefore forever yours?

Otti.   Love, to be wise, (one counsel pays another,)
Should we have—months ago, when first we loved,
For instance that May morning we two stole
Under the green ascent of sycamores—
If we had come upon a thing like that
Suddenly . . .

Seb.   "A thing"—there again—"a thing!"

Otti.   Then, Venus' body, had we come upon
My husband Luca Gaddi's murdered corpse
Within there, at his couch-foot, covered close—
Would you have pored upon it? Why persist
In poring now upon it? For 't is here
As much as there in the deserted house:
You cannot rid your eyes of it. For me,
Now he is dead I hate him worse: I hate . . .
Dare you stay here? I would go back and hold
His two dead hands, and say, "I hate you worse,
Luca, than" . . .

Seb.   Off, off—take your hands off mine,
'T is the hot evening—off! oh, morning is it?

Otti.   There's one thing must be done: you know what
          thing.
Come in and help to carry. We may sleep
Anywhere in the whole wide house tonight.

Seb. What would come, think you, if we let him lie
Just as he is? Let him lie there until
The angels take him! He is turned by this
Off from his face beside, as you will see.

Otti.   This dusty pane might serve for looking-glass.
Three, four—four gray hairs! Is it so you said
A plait of hair should wave across my neck?
No—this way.

Seb.   Ottima, I would give your neck,

Each splendid shoulder, both those breasts of yours,
That this were undone! Killing! Kill the world,
So Luca lives again!—ay, lives to sputter
His fulsome dotage on you—yes, and feign
Surprise that I return at eve to sup,
When all the morning I was loitering here—
Bid me dispatch my business and begone.
I would . . .

    Otti.   See!

    Seb.   No, I'll finish. Do you think
I fear to speak the bare truth once for all?
All we have talked of, is, at bottom, fine
To suffer; there's a recompense in guilt;
One must be venturous and fortunate:
What is one young for, else? In age we'll sigh
O'er the wild reckless wicked days flown over;
Still, we have lived: the vice was in its place.
But to have eaten Luca's bread, have worn
His clothes, have felt his money swell my purse—
Do lovers in romances sin that way?
Why, I was starving when I used to call
And teach you music, starving while you plucked me
These flowers to smell!

    Otti.   My poor lost friend!

    Seb.   He gave me
Life, nothing less: what if he did reproach
My perfidy, and threaten, and do more—
Had he no right? What was to wonder at?
He sat by us at table quietly:
Why must you lean across till our cheeks touched?
Could he do less than make pretence to strike?
'T is not the crime's sake—I'd commit ten crimes
Greater, to have this crime wiped out, undone!
And you—O how feel you? Feel you for me?

    Otti. Well then, I love you better now than ever,
And best (look at me while I speak to you)—

Best for the crime; nor do I grieve, in truth,
This mask, this simulated ignorance,
This affectation of simplicity,
Falls off our crime; this naked crime of ours
May not now be looked over: look it down!
Great? let it be great; but the joys it brought,
Pay they or no its price?   Come: they or it!
Speak not!   The past, would you give up the past
Such as it is, pleasure and crime together?
Give up that noon I owned my love for you?
The garden's silence: even the single bee
Persisting in his toil, suddenly stopped,
And where he hid you only could surmise
By some campanula chalice set a-swing.
Who stammered—"Yes, I love you?"
 Seb.   And I drew
Back; put far back your face with both my hands
Lest you should grow too full of me—your face
So seemed athirst for my whole soul and body!
 Otti. And when I ventured to receive you here,
Made you steal hither in the mornings—
 Seb.   When
I used to look up 'neath the shrub-house here,
Till the red fire on its glazed windows spread
To a yellow haze?
 Otti.   Ah—my sign was, the sun
Inflamed the sere side of yon chestnut-tree
Nipped by the first frost.
 Seb.   You would always laugh
At my wet boots: I had to stride through grass
Over my ankles.
 Otti.   Then our crowning night!
 Seb. The July night?
 Otti.   The day of it too, Sebald!
When heaven's pillars seemed o'erbowed with heat,
Its black-blue canopy suffered descend

Close on us both, to weigh down each to each,
And smother up all life except our life.
So lay we till the storm came.
 Seb.   How it came!
 Otti. Buried in woods we lay, you recollect;
Swift ran the searching tempest overhead;
And ever and anon some bright white shaft
Burned through the pine-tree roof, here burned and there,
As if God's messenger through the close wood screen
Plunged and replunged his weapon at a venture,
Feeling for guilty thee and me: then broke
The thunder like a whole sea overhead—
 Seb. Yes!
 Otti. —While I stretched myself upon you, hands
To hands, my mouth to your hot mouth, and shook
All my locks loose, and covered you with them—
You, Sebald, the same you!
 Seb.   Slower, Ottima!
 Otti. And as we lay—
 Seb.   Less vehemently! Love me!
Forgive me! Take not words, mere words, to heart!
Your breath is worse than wine. Breathe slow, speak
 slow!
Do not lean on me!
 Otti.   Sebald, as we lay,
Rising and falling only with our pants,
Who said, "Let death come now! 'T is right to die!
Right to be punished! Naught completes such bliss
But woe!" Who said that?
 Seb.   How did we ever rise?
Was't that we slept? Why did it end?
 Otti.   I felt you
Taper into a point the ruffled ends
Of my loose locks 'twixt both your humid lips.
My hair is fallen now: knot it again!
 Seb. I kiss you now, dear Ottima, now and now!

This way?   Will you forgive me—be once more
My great queen?
    Otti.   Bind it thrice about my brow;
Crown me your queen, your spirit's arbitress,
Magnificent in sin.   Say that!
    Seb.   I crown you
My great white queen, my spirit's arbitress,
Magnificent . .
       [From without is heard the voice of PIPPA *singing—*

> The year's at the spring
> And day's at the morn;
> Morning's at seven;
> The hillside's dew-pearled;
> The lark's on the wing;
> The snail's on the thorn:
> God's in his heaven—
> All's right with the world!

                            [PIPPA *passes.*

    Seb.   God's in his heaven!   Do you hear that?   Who
      spoke?
You, you spoke!
    Otti.   Oh—that little ragged girl!
She must have rested on the step: we give them
But this one holiday the whole year round.
Did you ever see our silk-mills—their inside?
There are ten silk-mills now belong to you.
She stoops to pick my double heartsease . . . Sh!
She does not hear: call you out louder!
    Seb.   ·   Leave me!
Go, get your clothes on—dress those shoulders!
    Otti.   Sebald?
    Seb.   Wipe off that paint!   I hate you.
    Otti.   Miserable!
    Seb.   My God, and she is emptied of it now!

Outright now!—how miraculously gone
All of the grace—had she not strange grace once?
Why, the blank cheek hangs listless as it likes,
No purpose holds the features up together,
Only the cloven brow and puckered chin
Stay in their places: and the very hair,
That seemed to have a sort of life in it,
Drops, a dead web!

    Otti.   Speak to me—not of me!

    Seb.—That round great full-orbed face, where not an
      angle
Broke the delicious indolence—all broken!

    Otti. To me—not of me! Ungrateful, perjured cheat!
A coward too: but ingrate's worse than all!
Beggar—my slave—a fawning, cringing lie!
Leave me! Betray me! I can see your drift!
A lie that walks and eats and drinks!

    Seb.   My God!
Those morbid olive faultless shoulder-blades—
I should have known there was no blood beneath!

    Otti. You hate me then? You hate me then?

    Seb.   To think
She would succeed in her absurd attempt,
And fascinate by sinning, show herself
Superior—guilt from its excess superior
To innocence! That little peasant's voice
Has righted all again. Though I be lost,
I know which is the better, never fear,
Of vice or virtue, purity or lust,
Nature or trick! I see what I have done,
Entirely now! Oh I am proud to feel
Such torments—let the world take credit thence—
I, having done my deed, pay too its price!
I hate, hate—curse you! God's in his heaven!

    Otti.   —Me!
Me! no, no, Sebald, not yourself—kill me!

Mine is the whole crime. Do but kill me—then
Yourself—then—presently—first hear me speak!
I always meant to kill myself—wait, you!
Lean on my breast—not as a breast; don't love me
The more because you lean on me, my own
Heart's Sebald! There, there, both deaths presently!
   Seb. My brain is drowned now—quite drowned: all
     I feel
Is . . . is, at swift-recurring intervals,
A hurry-down within me, as of waters
Loosened to smother up some ghastly pit:
There they go—whirls from a black fiery sea!
   Otti. Not me—to him, O God, be merciful!

Talk by the way, while PIPPA *is passing from the hillside to Orcana. Foreign Students of painting and
sculpture, from Venice, assembled opposite the house
of* JULES, *young French statuary, at Possagno.*

1*st Student.* Attention! My own post is beneath this
window, but the pomegranate clump yonder will hide
three or four of you with a little squeezing, and Schramm
and his pipe must lie flat in the balcony. Four, five—
who's a defaulter? We want everybody, for Jules must
not be suffered to hurt his bride when the jest's found
out.
   2*d Stud.* All here! Only our poet's away—never
having much meant to be present, moonstrike him! The
airs of that fellow, that Giovacchino! He was in violent
love with himself, and had a fair prospect of thriving in
his suit, so unmolested was it,—when suddenly a woman
falls in love with him, too; and out of pure jealousy he
takes himself off to Trieste, immortal poem and all:
whereto is this prophetical epitaph appended already, as
Bluphocks assures me,—*"Here a mammoth-poem lies,
Fouled to death by butterflies."* His own fault, the

simpleton! Instead of cramp couplets, each like a knife
in your entrails, he should write, says Bluphocks, both
classically and intelligibly.—*Æsculapius, an Epic. Catalogue of the drugs: Hebe's plaister—One strip Cools your
lip. Phœbus' emulsion—One bottle Clears your throttle.
Mercury's bolus—One box Cures* . . .

3d Stud. Subside, my fine fellow! If the marriage was
over by ten o'clock, Jules will certainly be here in a
minute with his bride.

2d Stud. Good!—only, so should the poet's muse have
been universally acceptable, says Bluphocks, *et canibus
nostris* . . . and Delia not better known to our literary
dogs than the boy Giovacchino!

1st Stud. To the point, now. Where's Gottlieb, the
new-comer? Oh,—listen, Gottlieb, to what has called
down this piece of friendly vengeance on Jules, of which
we now assemble to witness the winding-up. We are all
agreed, all in a tale, observe, when Jules shall burst out
on us in a fury by and by: I am spokesman—the verses
that are to undeceive Jules bear my name of Lutwyche—
but each professes himself alike insulted by this strutting
stone-squarer, who came along from Paris to Munich, and
thence with a crowd of us to Venice and Possagno here,
but proceeds in a day or two alone again—oh, alone in-
dubitably!—to Rome and Florence. He, forsooth, take
up his portion with these dissolute, brutalized, heartless
bunglers!—so he was heard to call us all. Now, is Schramm
brutalized, I should like to know? Am I heartless?

Gottlieb. Why, somewhat heartless; for, suppose Jules
a coxcomb as much as you choose, still, for this mere
coxcombry, you will have brushed off—what do folks style
it?—the bloom of his life. Is it too late to alter? These
love-letters now, you call his—I can't laugh at them.

4th Stud. Because you never read the sham letters of
our inditing which drew forth these.

Gott. His discovery of the truth will be frightful.

4th Stud. That's the joke. But you should have joined us at the beginning: there's no doubt he loves the girl—loves a model he might hire by the hour!

Gott. See here! "He has been accustomed," he writes, "to have Canova's women about him, in stone, and the world's women beside him, in flesh; these being as much below, as those above, his soul's aspiration: but now he is to have the reality." There you laugh again! I say, you wipe off the very dew of his youth.

1st Stud. Schramm! (Take the pipe out of his mouth, somebody!) Will Jules lose the bloom of his youth?

Schramm. Nothing worth keeping is ever lost in this world: look at a blossom—it drops presently, having done its service and lasted its time; but fruits succeed, and where would be the blossom's place could it continue? As well affirm that your eye is no longer in your body, because its earliest favorite, whatever it may have first loved to look on, is dead and done with—as that any affection is lost to the soul when its first object, whatever happened first to satisfy it, is superseded in due course. Keep but ever looking, whether with the body's eye or the mind's, and you will soon find something to look on! Has a man done wondering at women?—there follow men, dead and alive, to wonder at. Has he done wondering at men?—there's God to wonder at: and the faculty of wonder may be, at the same time, old and tired enough with respect to its first object, and yet young and fresh sufficiently, so far as concerns its novel one. Thus . . .

1st Stud. Put Schramm's pipe into his mouth again! There, you see! Well, this Jules . . . a wretched fribble—oh, I watched his disportings at Possagno, the other day! Canova's gallery—you know: there he marches first resolvedly past great works by the dozen without vouchsafing an eye: all at once he stops full at the *Psiche-fanciulla*—cannot pass that old acquaintance without a nod of encouragement—"In your new place, beauty?

Then behave yourself as well here as at Munich—I see
you!" Next he posts himself deliberately before the un-
finished *Pietà* for half an hour without moving, till up
he starts of a sudden, and thrusts his very nose into—I
say, into—the group; by which gesture you are informed
that precisely the sole point he had not fully mastered in
Canova's practice was a certain method of using the drill
in the articulation of the knee-joint—and that, likewise,
has he mastered at length! Good-by, therefore, to poor
Canova—whose gallery no longer needs detain his successor Jules, the predestinated novel thinker in marble!

5th Stud. Tell him about the women: go on to the
women!

1st Stud. Why, on that matter he could never be super-
cilious enough. How should we be other (he said) than
the poor devils you see, with those debasing habits we
cherish? He was not to wallow in that mire, at least: he
would wait, and love only at the proper time, and meanwhile put up with the *Psiche-fanciulla*. Now, I happened
to hear of a young Greek—real Greek girl at Malamocco;
a true Islander, do you see, with Alciphron's "hair like
sea-moss"—Schramm knows!—white and quiet as an ap-
parition, and fourteen years old at farthest,—a daughter
of Natalia, so she swears—that hag Natalia, who helps us
to models at three *lire* an hour. We selected this girl for
the heroine of our jest. So first, Jules received a scented
letter—somebody had seen his Tydeus at the Academy,
and my picture was nothing to it: a profound admirer
bade him persevere—would make herself known to him
ere long. (Paolina, my little friend of the *Fenice,* tran-
scribes divinely.) And in due time, the mysterious corre-
spondent gave certain hints of her peculiar charms—the
pale cheeks, the black hair—whatever, in short, had struck
us in our Malamocco model: we retained her name, too—
Phene, which is, by interpretation, sea-eagle. Now, think
of Jules finding himself distinguished from the herd of

us by such a creature! In his very first answer he proposed marrying his monitress: and fancy us over these
letters, two, three times a day, to receive and dispatch!
I concocted the main of it: relations were in the way—
secrecy must be observed—in fine, would he wed her on
trust, and only speak to her when they were indissolubly
united? St—st—Here they come!

6th Stud. Both of them! Heaven's love, speak softly,
speak within yourselves!

5th Stud. Look at the bridegroom! Half his hair in
storm and half in calm,—patted down over the left
temple,—like a frothy cup one blows on to cool it: and
the same old blouse that he murders the marble in.

2d Stud. Not a rich vest like yours, Hannibal
Scratchy!—rich, that your face may the better set it off.

6th Stud. And the bride! Yes, sure enough, our
Phene! Should you have known her in her clothes? How
magnificently pale!

Gott. She does not also take it for earnest, I hope?

1st Stud. Oh, Natalia's concern, that is! We settle
with Natalia.

6th Stud. She does not speak—has evidently let out no
word. The only thing is, will she equally remember the
rest of her lesson, and repeat correctly all those verses
which are to break the secret to Jules?

Gott. How he gazes on her! Pity—pity!

1st Stud. They go in: now, silence! You three,—not
nearer the window, mind, than that pomegranate: just
where the little girl, who a few minutes ago passed us
singing, is seated!

II. NOON

Over Orcana. The house of JULES, *who crosses its threshold with* PHENE: *she is silent, on which* JULES *begins—*

Do not die, Phene! I am yours now, you

Are mine now; let fate reach me how she likes,
If you'll not die: so, never die! Sit here—
My work-room's single seat. I over-lean
This length of hair and lustrous front; they turn
Like an entire flower upward: eyes, lips, last
Your chin—no, last your throat turns: 't is their scent
Pulls down my face upon you. Nay, look ever
This one way till I change, grow you—I could
Change into you, beloved!

                You by me,
And I by you; this is your hand in mine,
And side by side we sit: all's true. Thank God!
I have spoken: speak you!

                O my life to come!
My Tydeus must be carved that's there in clay;
Yet how be carved, with you about the room?
Where must I place you? When I think that once
This room-full of rough block-work seemed my heaven
Without you! Shall I ever work again,
Get fairly into my old ways again,
Bid each conception stand while, trait by trait,
My hand transfers its lineaments to stone?
Will my mere fancies live near you, their truth—
The live truth, passing and repassing me,
Sitting beside me?

                Now speak!

                Only first,
See, all your letters! Was't not well contrived?
Their hiding-place is Psyche's robe; she keeps
Your letters next her skin: which drops out foremost?
Ah,—this that swam down like a first moonbeam
Into my world!

              Again those eyes complete
Their melancholy survey, sweet and slow,
Of all my room holds; to return and rest
On me, with pity, yet some wonder too:

As if God bade some spirit plague a world,
And this were the one moment of surprise
And sorrow while she took her station, pausing
O'er what she sees, finds good, and must destroy!
What gaze you at? Those? Books, I told you of;
Let your first word to me rejoice them, too:
This minion, a Coluthus, writ in red,
Bistre and azure by Bessarion's scribe—
Read this line . . . no, shame—Homer's be the Greek
First breathed me from the lips of my Greek girl!
This Odyssey in coarse black vivid type
With faded yellow blossoms 'twixt page and page,
To mark great places with due gratitude;
"He said, and on Antinous directed
A bitter shaft" . . . a flower blots out the rest!
Again upon your search? My statues, then!
—Ah, do not mind that—better that will look
When cast in bronze—an Almaign Kaiser, that,
Swart-green and gold, with truncheon based on hip.
This, rather, turn to! What, unrecognized?
I thought you would have seen that here you sit
As I imagined you,—Hippolyta,
Naked upon her bright Numidian horse.
Recall you this then? "Carve in bold relief"—
So you commanded—"carve, against I come,
A Greek, in Athens, as our fashion was,
Feasting, bay-filleted and thunder-free,
Who rises 'neath the lifted myrtle-branch.
'Praise those who slew Hipparchus!' cry the guests,
'While o'er thy head the singer's myrtle waves
As erst above our champion: stand up, all!' "
See, I have labored to express your thought.
Quite round, a cluster of mere hands and arms
 (Thrust in all senses, all ways, from all sides,
Only consenting at the branch's end
They strain toward) serves for frame to a sole face,

The Praiser's, in the centre: who with eyes
Sightless, so bend they back to light inside
His brain where visionary forms throng up,
Sings, minding not that palpitating arch
Of hands and arms, nor the quick drip of wine
From the drenched leaves o'erhead, nor crowns cast off,
Violet and parsley crowns to trample on—
Sings, pausing as the patron-ghosts approve,
Devoutly their unconquerable hymn.
But you must say a "well" to that—say "well!"
Because you gaze—am I fantastic, sweet?
Gaze like my very life's-stuff, marble—marbly
Even to the silence!   Why, before I found
The real flesh Phene, I inured myself
To see, throughout all nature, varied stuff
For better nature's birth by means of art:
With me, each substance tended to one form
Of beauty—to the human archetype.
On every side occurred suggestive germs
Of that—the tree, the flower—or take the fruit,—
Some rosy shape, continuing the peach,
Curved beewise o'er its bough; as rosy limbs,
Depending, nestled in the leaves; and just
From a cleft rose-peach the whole Dryad sprang.
But of the stuffs one can be master of,
How I divined their capabilities!
From the soft-rinded smoothening facile chalk
That yields your outline to the air's embrace,
Half-softened by a halo's pearly gloom;
Down to the crisp imperious steel, so sure
To cut its one confided thought clean out
Of all the world.   But marble!—'neath my tools
More pliable than jelly—as it were
Some clear primordial creature dug from depths
In the earth's heart, where itself breeds itself,
And whence all baser substance may be worked;

Refine it off to air, you may,—condense it
Down to the diamond;—is not metal there,
When o'er the sudden speck my chisel trips?
—Not flesh, as flake off flake I scale, approach,
Lay bare those bluish veins of blood asleep?
Lurks flame in no strange windings where, surprised
By the swift implement sent home at once,
Flushes and glowings radiate and hover
About its track?
                    Phene? what—why is this?
That whitening cheek, those still dilating eyes!
Ah, you will die—I knew that you would die!

PHENE *begins, on his having long remained silent.*

Now the end's coming; to be sure, it must
Have ended sometime!   Tush, why need I speak
Their foolish speech?   I cannot bring to mind
One half of it, beside; and do not care
For old Natalia now, nor any of them.
Oh, you—what are you?—if I do not try
To say the words Natalia made me learn,
To please your friends,—it is to keep myself
Where your voice lifted me, by letting that
Proceed: but can it?   Even you, perhaps,
Cannot take up, now you have once let fall,
The music's life, and me along with that—
No, or you would!   We'll stay, then, as we are:
Above the world.
                    You creature with the eyes!
If I could look forever up to them,
As now you let me,—I believe, all sin,
All memory of wrong done, suffering borne,
Would drop down, low and lower, to the earth
Whence all that's low comes, and there touch and stay
—Never to overtake the rest of me,

All that, unspotted, reaches up to you,
Drawn by those eyes!   What rises is myself,
Not me the shame and suffering; but they sink,
Are left, I rise above them.   Keep me so,
Above the world!
               But you sink, for your eyes
Are altering—altered!   Stay—"I love you, love" . . .
I could prevent it if I understood:
More of your words to me: was't in the tone
Or the words, your power?
                 Or stay—I will repeat
Their speech, if that contents you!   Only change
No more, and I shall find it presently
Far back here, in the brain yourself filled up.
Natalia threatened me that harm should follow
Unless I spoke their lesson to the end,
But harm to me, I thought she meant, not you.
Your friends,—Natalia said they were your friends
And meant you well,—because, I doubted it,
Observing (what was very strange to see)
On every face, so different in all else,
The same smile girls like me are used to bear,
But never men, men cannot stoop so low;
Yet your friends, speaking of you, used that smile,
That hateful smirk of boundless self-conceit
Which seems to take possession of the world
And make of God a tame confederate,
Purveyor to their appetites . . . you know!
But still Natalia said they were your friends,
And they assented though they smiled the more,
And all came round me,—that thin Englishman
With light lank hair seemed leader of the rest;
He held a paper—"What we want," said he,
Ending some explanation to his friends—
"Is something slow, involved and mystical,
To hold Jules long in doubt, yet take his taste

And lure him on until, at innermost
Where he seeks sweetness' soul, he may find—this!
—As in the apple's core, the noisome fly:
For insects on the rind are seen at once,
And brushed aside as soon, but this is found
Only when on the lips or loathing tongue."
And so he read what I have got by heart:
I'll speak it,—"Do not die, love! I am yours" . . .
No—is not that, or like that, part of words
Yourself began by speaking? Strange to lose
What cost such pains to learn! Is this more right?

> *I am a painter who cannot paint;*
> *In my life, a devil rather than saint;*
> *In my brain, as poor a creature too:*
> *No end to all I cannot do!*
> *Yet do one thing at least I can—*
> *Love a man or hate a man*
> *Supremely: thus my lore began.*
> *Through the Valley of Love I went,*
> *In the lovingest spot to abide,*
> *And just on the verge where I pitched my tent,*
> *I found Hate dwelling beside.*
> *(Let the Bridegroom ask what the painter meant,*
> *Of his Bride, of the peerless Bride!)*
> *And further, I traversed Hate's grove,*
> *In the hatefullest nook to dwell;*
> *But lo, where I flung myself prone, couched Love*
> *Where the shadow threefold fell.*
> *(The meaning—those black bride's-eyes above,*
> *Not a painter's lip should tell!)*

"And here," said he, "Jules probably will ask,
'You have black eyes, Love,—you are, sure enough,
My peerless bride,—then do you tell indeed
What needs some explanation! What means this?'"
—And I am to go on, without a word—

So, I grew wise in Love and Hate,
From simple that I was of late.
Once, when I loved, I would enlace
Breast, eyelids, hands, feet, form and face
Of her I loved, in one embrace—
As if by mere love I could love immensely!
Once, when I hated, I would plunge
My sword, and wipe with the first lunge
My foe's whole life out like a sponge—
As if by mere hate I could hate intensely!
But now I am wiser, know better the fashion
How passion seeks aid from its opposite passion:
And if I see cause to love more, hate more
Than ever man loved, ever hated before—
And seek in the Valley of Love
The nest, or the nook in Hate's Grove
Where my soul may surely reach
The essence, naught less, of each,
The Hate of all Hates, the Love
Of all Loves, in the Valley or Grove,—
I find them the very warders
Each of the other's borders.
When I love most, Love is disguised
In Hate; and when Hate is surprised
In Love, then I hate most: ask
How Love smiles through Hate's iron casque,
Hate grins through Love's rose-braided mask,—
And how, having hated thee,
I sought long and painfully
To reach thy heart, nor prick
The skin but pierce to the quick—
Ask this, my Jules, and be answered straight
By thy bride—how the painter Lutwyche can hate!

JULES *interposes.*

Lutwyche!   Who else?   But all of them, no doubt,
Hated me: they at Venice—presently
Their turn, however!   You I shall not meet:
If I dreamed, saying this would wake me.

                                        Keep
What's here, the gold—we cannot meet again,
Consider! and the money was but meant
For two years' travel, which is over now,
All chance or hope or care or need of it.
This—and what comes from selling these, my casts
And books and medals, except . . . let them go
Together, so the produce keeps you safe
Out of Natalia's clutches!   If by chance
(For all's chance here) I should survive the gang
At Venice, root out all fifteen of them,
We might meet somewhere, since the world is wide.
    [*From without is heard the voice of* PIPPA, *singing—*

Give her but a least excuse to love me!
When—where—
How—can this arm establish her above me,
If fortune fixed her as my lady there,
There already, to eternally reprove me?
("Hist!"—said Kate the Queen;
But "Oh!" cried the maiden, binding her tresses,
" 'Tis only a page that carols unseen,
Crumbling your hounds their messes!")

Is she wronged?—To the rescue of her honor,
My heart!
Is she poor?—What costs it to be styled a donor?
Merely an earth to cleave, a sea to part.
But that fortune should have thrust all this upon her!
("Nay, list!"—bade Kate the Queen;
And still cried the maiden, binding her tresses,

" 'Tis only a page that carols unseen,
Fitting your hawks their jesses!")

[PIPPA *passes.*

JULES *resumes.*

What name was that the little girl sang forth?
Kate?   The Cornaro, doubtless, who renounced
The crown of Cyprus to be lady here
At Asolo, where still her memory stays,
And peasants sing how once a certain page
Pined for the grace of her so far above
His power of doing good to, "Kate the Queen—
She never could be wronged, be poor," he sighed,
"Need him to help her!"

　　　　　　　　Yes, a bitter thing
To see our lady above all need of us;
Yet so we look ere we will love; not I,
But the world looks so.   If whoever loves
Must be, in some sort, god or worshipper,
The blessing or the blest one, queen or page,
Why should we always choose the page's part?
Here is a woman with utter need of me,—
I find myself queen here, it seems!

　　　　　　　　How strange!
Look at the woman here with the new soul,
Like my own Psyche,—fresh upon her lips
Alit, the visionary butterfly,
Waiting my word to enter and make bright,
Or flutter off and leave all blank as first.
This body had no soul before, but slept
Or stirred, was beauteous or ungainly, free
From taint or foul with stain, as outward things
Fastened their image on its passiveness:
Now, it will wake, feel, live—or die again!
Shall to produce form out of unshaped stuff

Be Art—and further, to evoke a soul
From form be nothing?   This new soul is mine!

Now, to kill Lutwyche, what would that do?—save
A wretched dauber, men will hoot to death
Without me, from their hooting.   Oh, to hear
God's voice plain as I heard it first, before
They broke in with their laughter!   I heard them
Henceforth, not God.
                              To Ancona—Greece—some isle!
I wanted silence only; there is clay
Everywhere.   One may do whate'er one likes
In Art: the only thing is, to make sure
That one does like it—which takes pains to know.
  Scatter all this, my Phene—this mad dream!
Who, what is Lutwyche, what Natalia's friends,
What the whole world except our love—my own,
Own Phene?   But I told you, did I not,
Ere night we travel for your land—some isle
With the sea's silence on it?   Stand aside—
I do but break these paltry models up
To begin Art afresh.   Meet Lutwyche, I—
And save him from my statue meeting him?
Some unsuspected isle in the far seas!
Like a god going through his world, there stands
One mountain for a moment in the dusk,
Whole brotherhoods of cedars on its brow:
And you are ever by me while I gaze
—Are in my arms as now—as now—as now!
Some unsuspected isle in the far seas!
Some unsuspected isle in far-off seas!

Talk by the way, while PIPPA *is passing from Orcana to
   the Turret.   Two or three of the Austrian Police loitering with* BLUPHOCKS, an English vagabond, *just in view
   of the Turret.*

Bluphocks.[1] So, that is your Pippa, the little girl who
passed us singing? Well, your Bishop's Intendant's money
shall be honestly earned:—now, don't make me that sour
face because I bring the Bishop's name into the business;
we know he can have nothing to do with such horrors:
we know that he is a saint and all that a bishop should be,
who is a great man beside. *Oh were but every worm a
maggot, Every fly a grig, Every bough a Christmas fagot,
Every tune a jig!* In fact, I have abjured all religions;
but the last I inclined to was the Armenian: for I have
travelled, do you see, and at Koenigsberg, Prussia Improper (so styled because there's a sort of bleak hungry
sun there), you might remark, over a venerable house-
porch, a certain Chaldee inscription; and brief as it is, a
mere glance at it used absolutely to change the mood of
every bearded passenger. In they turned, one and all;
the young and lightsome, with no irreverent pause, the
aged and decrepit, with a sensible alacrity: 't was the
Grand Rabbi's abode, in short. Struck with curiosity,
I lost no time in learning Syriac— (these are vowels, you
dogs,—follow my stick's end in the mud—*Celarent, Darii,
Ferio!*) and one morning presented myself, spelling-book
in hand, a, b, c,—I picked it out letter by letter, and what
was the purport of this miraculous posy? Some cherished
legend of the past, you'll say—"*How Moses hocus-pocussed
Egypt's land with fly and locust,*"—or, "*How to Jonah
sounded harshish, Get thee up and go to Tarshish,*"—or
"*How the angel meeting Balaam, Straight his ass returned
a salaam.*" In no wise! "*Shackabrack—Boach—somebody or other—Isaach, Re-cei-ver, Pur-cha-ser and Ex-
chan-ger of—Stolen Goods!*" So, talk to me of the religion
of a bishop! I have renounced all bishops save Bishop
Beveridge!—mean to live so—and die—*As some Greek dog-
sage, dead and merry, Hellward bound in Charon's*

[1] "He maketh his sun to rise on the evil and on the good, and
sendeth rain on the just and on the unjust."

*wherry, With food for both worlds, under and upper,
Lupine-seed and Hecate's supper, And never an obolus*
. . . (though thanks to you, or this Intendant through
you, or this Bishop through his Intendant—I possess a
burning pocket-full of *zwanzigers*) . . . *To pay the Stygian
Ferry!*

1*st Policeman.* There is the girl, then; go and deserve
them the moment you have pointed out to us Signor
Luigi and his mother. [*To the rest.*] I have been notic-
ing a house yonder, this long while: not a shutter un-
closed since morning!

2*d Pol.* Old Luca Gaddi's, that owns the silk-mills
here: he dozes by the hour, wakes up, sighs deeply, says
he should like to be Prince Metternich, and then dozes
again, after having bidden young Sebald, the foreigner,
set his wife to playing draughts. Never molest such a
household, they mean well.

Blup. Only, cannot you tell me something of this little
Pippa, I must have to do with? One could make something of that name. Pippa—that is, short for Felippa—
rhyming to *Panurge consults Hertrippa—Believest thou,
King Agrippa?* Something might be done with that
name.

2*d Pol.* Put into rhyme that your head and a ripe
muskmelon would not be dear at half a *zwanziger!* Leave
this fooling, and look out; the afternoon's over or nearly
so.

3*d Pol.* Where in this passport of Signor Luigi does
our Principal instruct you to watch him so narrowly?
There? What's there beside a simple signature? (That
English fool's busy watching.)

2*d Pol.* Flourish all round—"Put all possible obstacles
in his way;" oblong dot at the end—"Detain him till
further advices reach you;" scratch at bottom—"Send him
back on pretence of some informality in the above:"
ink-spirt on right-hand side (which is the case here)—

"Arrest him at once." Why and wherefore, I don't concern myself, but my instructions amount to this: if Signor Luigi leaves home to-night for Vienna—well and good, the passport deposed with us for our *visa* is really for his own use, they have misinformed the Office, and he means well; but let him stay over to-night—there has been the pretence we suspect, the accounts of his corresponding and holding intelligence with the Carbonari are correct, we arrest him at once, to-morrow comes Venice, and presently Spielberg. Bluphocks makes the signal, sure enough! That is he, entering the turret with his mother, no doubt.

III. EVENING

Inside the Turret on the Hill above Asolo. LUIGI *and his* MOTHER *entering.*

> *Mother.* If there blew wind, you'd hear a long sigh, easing
> The utmost heaviness of music's heart.
> *Luigi.* Here in the archway?
> *Mother.*   Oh no, no—in farther,
> Where the echo is made, on the ridge.
> *Luigi.*   Here surely, then.
> How plain the tap of my heel as I leaped up!
> Hark—"Lucius Junius!" The very ghost of a voice
> Whose body is caught and kept by . . . what are those?
> Mere withered wallflowers, waving overhead?
> They seem an elvish group with thin bleached hair
> That lean out of their topmost fortress—look
> And listen, mountain men, to what we say,
> Hand under chin of each grave earthy face.
> Up and show faces all of you!—"All of you!"
> That's the king dwarf with the scarlet comb; old Franz,
> Come down and meet your fate? Hark—"Meet your fate!"

Mother. Let him not meet it, my Luigi—do not
Go to his City! Putting crime aside,
Half of these ills of Italy are feigned:
Your Pellicos and writers for effect,
Write for effect.
    Luigi.   Hush! Say A writes, and B.
    Mother. These A's and B's write for effect, I say.
Then, evil is in its nature loud, while good
Is silent; you hear each petty injury,
None of his virtues; he is old beside,
Quiet and kind, and densely stupid. Why
Do A and B kill not him themselves?
    Luigi.   They teach
Others to kill him—me—and, if I fail,
Others to succeed; now, if A tried and failed,
I could not teach that: mine's the lesser task.
Mother, they visit night by night . . .
    Mother.   You, Luigi?
Ah, will you let me tell you what you are?
    Luigi. Why not? Oh, the one thing you fear to hint,
You may assure yourself I say and say
Ever to myself! At times—nay, even as now
We sit—I think my mind is touched, suspect
All is not sound: but is not knowing that,
What constitutes one sane or otherwise?
I know I am thus—so, all is right again.
I laugh at myself as through the town I walk,
And see men merry as if no Italy
Were suffering; then I ponder—"I am rich,
Young, healthy; why should this fact trouble me,
More than it troubles these?" But it does trouble.
No, trouble's a bad word: for as I walk
There's springing and melody and giddiness,
And old quaint turns and passages of my youth,
Dreams long forgotten, little in themselves,
Return to me—whatever may amuse me:

And earth seems in a truce with me, and heaven
Accords with me, all things suspend their strife,
The very cicala laughs "There goes he, and there!
Feast him, the time is short; he is on his way
For the world's sake: feast him this once, our friend!"
And in return for all this, I can trip
Cheerfully up the scaffold-steps. I go
This evening, mother!
  Mother.   But mistrust yourself—
Mistrust the judgment you pronounce on him!
  Luigi. Oh, there I feel—am sure that I am right!
  Mother. Mistrust your judgment then, of the mere
   means
To this wild enterprise: say, you are right,—
How should one in your state e'er bring to pass
What would require a cool head, a cool heart,
And a calm hand? You never will escape.
  Luigi. Escape? To even wish that, would spoil all.
The dying is best part of it. Too much
Have I enjoyed these fifteen years of mine,
To leave myself excuse for longer life:
Was not life pressed down, running o'er with joy,
That I might finish with it ere my fellows
Who, sparelier feasted, make a longer stay?
I was put at the board-head, helped to all
At first; I rise up happy and content.
God must be glad one loves his world so much.
I can give news of earth to all the dead
Who ask me:—last year's sunsets, and great stars
Which had a right to come first and see ebb
The crimson wave that drifts the sun away—
Those crescent moons with notched and burning rims
That strengthened into sharp fire, and there stood,
Impatient of the azure—and that day
In March, a double rainbow stopped the storm—
May's warm slow yellow moonlit summer nights—

Gone are they, but I have them in my soul!
   Mother. (He will not go!)
   Luigi.   You smile at me? 'T is true,—
Voluptuousness, grotesqueness, ghastliness,
Environ my devotedness as quaintly
As round about some antique altar wreathe
The rose festoons, goats' horns, and oxen's skulls.
   Mother. See now: you reach the city, you must cross
His threshold—how?
   Luigi.   Oh, that's if we conspired!
Then would come pains in plenty, as you guess—
But guess not how the qualities most fit
For such an office, qualities I have,
Would little stead me, otherwise employed,
Yet prove of rarest merit only here.
Every one knows for what his excellence
Will serve, but no one ever will consider
For what his worst defect might serve: and yet
Have you not seen me range our coppice yonder
In search of a distorted ash?—I find
The wry spoilt branch a natural perfect bow.
Fancy the thrice-sage, thrice-precautioned man
Arriving at the palace on my errand!
No, no! I have a handsome dress packed up—
White satin here, to set off my black hair;
In I shall march—for you may watch your life out
Behind thick walls, make friends there to betray you;
More than one man spoils everything. March straight—
Only, no clumsy knife to fumble for,
Take the great gate, and walk (not saunter) on
Through guards and guards— I have rehearsed it all
Inside the turret here a hundred times.
Don't ask the way of whom you meet, observe!
But where they cluster thickliest is the door
Of doors; they'll let you pass—they'll never blab
Each to the other, he knows not the favorite,

Whence he is bound and what's his business now.
Walk in—straight up to him; you have no knife:
Be prompt, how should he scream?   Then, out with you!
Italy, Italy, my Italy!
You're free, you're free!   Oh mother, I could dream
They got about me—Andrea from his exile,
Pier from his dungeon, Gualtier from his grave!
   Mother.   Well, you shall go.   Yet seems this patriotism
The easiest virtue for a selfish man
To acquire: he loves himself—and next, the world—
If he must love beyond,—but naught between:
As a short-sighted man sees naught midway
His body and the sun above.   But you
Are my adored Luigi, ever obedient
To my least wish, and running o'er with love:
I could not call you cruel or unkind.
Once more, your ground for killing him!—then go!
   Luigi.   Now do you try me, or make sport of me?
How first the Austrians got these provinces . . .
 (If that is all, I'll satisfy you soon)
—Never by conquest but by cunning, for
That treaty whereby . . .
   Mother.   Well?
   Luigi.   (Sure, he's arrived,
The tell-tale cuckoo: spring's his confidant,
And he lets out her April purposes!)
Or . . . better go at once to modern time.
He has . . . they have . . . in fact, I understand
But can't restate the matter; that's my boast:
Others could reason it out to you, and prove
Things they have made me feel.
   Mother.   Why go tonight?
Morn's for adventure.   Jupiter is now
A morning-star.   I cannot hear you, Luigi!
   Luigi.   "I am the bright and morning-star," saith God—
And, "to such an one I give the morning-star."

The gift of the morning-star!   Have I God's gift
Of the morning-star?
   Mother.   Chiara will love to see
That Jupiter an evening-star next June.
   Luigi. True, mother.   Well for those who live through
    June!
Great noontides, thunder-storms, all glaring pomps
That triumph at the heels of June the god
Leading his revel through our leafy world.
Yes, Chiara will be here.
   Mother.   In June: remember,
Yourself appointed that month for her coming.
   Luigi. Was that low noise the echo?
   Mother.   The night-wind.
She must be grown—with her blue eyes upturned
As if life were one long and sweet surprise:
In June she comes.
   Luigi.   We were to see together
The Titian at Treviso. There, again!

[*From without is heard the voice of* PIPPA, *singing—*

   A king lived long ago,
   In the morning of the world,
   When earth was nigher heaven than now;
   And the king's locks curled,
   Disparting o'er a forehead full
   As the milk-white space 'twixt horn and horn
   Of some sacrificial bull—
   Only calm as a babe new-born:
   For he was got to a sleepy mood,
   So safe from all decrepitude,
   Age with its bane, so sure gone by,
   (The gods so loved him while he dreamed)
   That, having lived thus long, there seemed
   No need the king should ever die.

Luigi.   No need that sort of king should ever die!

> *Among the rocks his city was:*
> *Before his palace, in the sun,*
> *He sat to see his people pass,*
> *And judge them every one*
> *From its threshold of smooth stone.*
> *They haled him many a valley-thief*
> *Caught in the sheep-pens, robber-chief*
> *Swarthy and shameless, beggar-cheat,*
> *Spy-prowler, or rough pirate found*
> *On the sea-sand left aground;*
> *And sometimes clung about his feet,*
> *With bleeding lip and burning cheek,*
> *A woman, bitterest wrong to speak*
> *Of one with sullen thickset brows:*
> *And sometimes from the prison-house*
> *The angry priests a pale wretch brought,*
> *Who through some chink had pushed and pressed*
> *On knees and elbows, belly and breast,*
> *Worm-like into the temple,—caught*
> *He was by the very god,*
> *Who ever in the darkness strode*
> *Backward and forward, keeping watch*
> *O'er his brazen bowls, such rogues to catch!*
> *These, all and every one,*
> *The king judged, sitting in the sun.*

Luigi.   That king should still judge sitting in the sun!

> *His councillors, on left and right,*
> *Looked anxious up,—but no surprise*
> *Disturbed the king's old smiling eyes*
> *Where the very blue had turned to white.*
> *'T is said, a Python scared one day*
> *The breathless city, till he came,*

With forky tongue and eyes on flame,
Where the old king sat to judge alway;
But when he saw the sweepy hair
Girt with a crown of berries rare
Which the god will hardly give to wear
To the maiden who singeth, dancing bare
In the altar-smoke by the pine-torch lights,
At his wondrous forest rites,—
Seeing this, he did not dare
Approach that threshold in the sun,
Assault the old king smiling there.
Such grace had kings when the world begun!

[PIPPA *passes.*

Luigi. And such grace have they, now that the world
ends!
The Python at the city, on the throne,
And brave men, God would crown for slaying him,
Lurk in by-corners lest they fall his prey.
Are crowns yet to be won in this late time,
Which weakness makes me hesitate to reach?
'T is God's voice calls: how could I stay? Farewell!

Talk by the way, while PIPPA *is passing from the Turret
to the Bishop's Brother's House, close to the Duomo
S. Maria. Poor* GIRLS *sitting on the steps.*

  1*st Girl.* There goes a swallow to Venice—the stout
seafarer!
Seeing those birds fly, makes one wish for wings.
Let us all wish; you, wish first!
  2*d Girl.*   I? This sunset
To finish.
  3*d Girl.* That old—somebody I know,
Grayer and older than my grandfather,
To give me the same treat he gave last week—
Feeding me on his knee with fig-peckers,

Lampreys and red Breganze-wine, and mumbling
The while some folly about how well I fare,
Let sit and eat my supper quietly:
Since had he not himself been late this morning
Detained at—never mind where,—had he not . . .
"Eh, baggage, had I not!"—
  2d Girl.   How she can lie!
  3d Girl.   Look there—by the nails!
  2d Girl.   What makes your fingers red?
  3d Girl.   Dipping them into wine to write bad words
  with
On the bright table: how he laughed!
  1st Girl.   My turn.
Spring's come and summer's coming. I would wear
A long loose gown, down to the feet and hands,
With plaits here, close about the throat, all day;
And all night lie, the cool long nights, in bed;
And have new milk to drink, apples to eat,
Deuzans and junetings, leather-coats . . . ah, I should say,
This is away in the fields—miles!
  3d Girl.   Say at once
You'd be at home: she'd always be at home!
Now comes the story of the farm among
The cherry orchards, and how April snowed
White blossoms on her as she ran. Why, fool,
They've rubbed the chalk-mark out, how tall you were,
Twisted your starling's neck, broken his cage,
Made a dung-hill of your garden!
  1st Girl.   They destroy
My garden since I left them? well—perhaps
I would have done so: so I hope they have!
A fig-tree curled out of our cottage wall;
They called it mine, I have forgotten why,
It must have been there long ere I was born:
Cric—cric—I think I hear the wasps o'er head
Pricking the papers strung to flutter there

And keep off birds in fruit-time—coarse long papers,
And the wasps eat them, prick them through and through.
   3d Girl. How her mouth twitches! Where was I?—
     before
She broke in with her wishes and long gowns
And wasps—would I be such a fool!—Oh, here!
This is my way: I answer every one
Who asks me why I make so much of him—
(If you say, "you love him"—straight "he'll not be
     gulled!")
"He that seduced me when I was a girl
Thus high—had eyes like yours, or hair like yours,
Brown, red, white,"—as the case may be: that pleases!
See how that beetle burnishes in the path!
There sparkles he along the dust: and, there—
Your journey to that maize-tuft spoiled at least!
   1st Girl. When I was young, they said if you killed one
Of those sunshiny beetles, that his friend
Up there, would shine no more that day nor next.
   2d Girl. When you were young? Nor are you young,
     that's true.
How your plump arms, that were, have dropped away!
Why, I can span them. Cecco beats you still?
No matter, so you keep your curious hair.
I wish they'd find a way to dye our hair
Your color—any lighter tint, indeed,
Than black: the men say they are sick of black,
Black eyes, black hair!
   4th Girl.   Sick of yours, like enough
Do you pretend you ever tasted lampreys
And ortolans? Giovita, of the palace.
Engaged (but there's no trusting him) to slice me
Polenta with a knife that had cut up
An ortolan.
   2d Girl. Why, there! Is not that Pippa
We are to talk to, under the window,—quick!—

Where the lights are?
    1st Girl. That she? No, or she would sing,
For the Intendant said . . .
    3d Girl.   Oh, you sing first!
Then, if she listens and comes close . . . I'll tell you,—
Sing that song the young English noble made,
Who took you for the purest of the pure,
And meant to leave the world for you—what fun!
    2d Girl. [*Sings.*]

> *You'll love me yet!—and I can tarry*
>   *Your love's protracted growing:*
> *June reared that bunch of flowers you carry,*
>   *From seeds of April's sowing.*
>
> *I plant a heartfull now: some seed*
>   *At least is sure to strike,*
> *And yield—what you'll not pluck indeed,*
>   *Not love, but, may be, like.*
>
> *You'll look at least on love's remains,*
>   *A grave's one violet:*
> *Your look?—that pays a thousand pains.*
>   *What's death? You'll love me yet!*

    3d Girl. [*To* PIPPA *who approaches.*] Oh, you may
come closer—we shall not eat you! Why, you seem the
very person that the great rich handsome Englishman has
fallen so violently in love with. I'll tell you all about it.

IV. NIGHT

Inside the Palace by the Duomo. MONSIGNOR, *dismissing
his Attendants.*

    Monsignor. Thanks, friends, many thanks! I chiefly
desire life now, that I may recompense every one of you.
Most I know something of already. What, a repast pre-

pared? *Benedicto benedicatur* . . . ugh, ugh! Where
was I? Oh, as you were remarking, Ugo, the weather is
mild, very unlike winter-weather: but I am a Sicilian,
you know, and shiver in your Julys here. To be sure,
when 't was full summer at Messina, as we priests used to
cross in procession the great square on Assumption Day,
you might see our thickest yellow tapers twist suddenly
in two, each like a falling star, or sink down on themselves in a gore of wax. But go, my friends, but go! [*To
the* Intendant.] Not you, Ugo! [*The others leave the
apartment.*] I have long wanted to converse with you,
Ugo.

Intendant. Uguccio—

Mon. . . . 'guccio Stefani, man! of Ascoli, Fermo and
Fossombruno;—what I do need instructing about, are
these accounts of your administration of my poor
brother's affairs. Ugh! I shall never get through a third
part of your accounts: take some of these dainties before
we attempt it, however. Are you bashful to that degree?
For me, a crust and water suffice.

Inten. Do you choose this especial night to question
me?

Mon. This night, Ugo. You have managed my late
brother's affairs since the death of our elder brother:
fourteen years and a month, all but three days. On the
Third of December, I find him . . .

Inten. If you have so intimate an acquaintance with
your brother's affairs, you will be tender of turning so
far back: they will hardly bear looking into, so far back.

Mon. Ay, ay, ugh, ugh,—nothing but disappointments
here below! I remark a considerable payment made to
yourself on this Third of December. Talk of disappointments! There was a young fellow here, Jules, a foreign
sculptor I did my utmost to advance, that the Church
might be a gainer by us both: he was going on hopefully
enough, and of a sudden he notifies to me some marvel-

lous change that has happened in his notions of Art. Here's his letter,—"He never had a clearly conceived Ideal within his brain till today. Yet since his hand could manage a chisel, he has practised expressing other men's Ideals; and, in the very perfection he has attained to, he foresees an ultimate failure: his unconscious hand will pursue its prescribed course of old years, and will reproduce with a fatal expertness the ancient types, let the novel one appear never so palpably to his spirit. There is but one method of escape: confiding the virgin type to as chaste a hand, he will turn painter instead of sculptor, and paint, not carve, its characteristics,"—strike out, I dare say, a school like Correggio: how think you, Ugo?

Inten. Is Correggio a painter?

Mon. Foolish Jules! and yet, after all, why foolish? He may—probably will—fail egregiously; but if there should arise a new painter, will it not be in some such way, by a poet now, or a musician (spirits who have conceived and perfected an Ideal through some other channel), transferring it to this, and escaping our conventional roads by pure ignorance of them; eh, Ugo? If you have no appetite, talk at least, Ugo!

Inten. Sir, I can submit no longer to this course of yours. First, you select the group of which I formed one,—next you thin it gradually,—always retaining me with your smile,—and so do you proceed till you have fairly got me alone with you between four stone walls. And now then? Let this farce, this chatter end now: what is it you want with me?

Mon. Ugo!

Inten. From the instant you arrived, I felt your smile on me as you questioned me about this and the other article in those papers—why your brother should have given me this villa, that *podere,*—and your nod at the end meant,—what?

Mon. Possibly that I wished for no loud talk here.
If once you set me coughing, Ugo!—

Inten. I have your brother's hand and seal to all I
possess: now ask me what for! what service I did him—
ask me!

Mon. I would better not: I should rip up old disgraces,
let out my poor brother's weaknesses. By the way,
Maffeo of Forli, (which, I forgot to observe, is your true
name,) was the interdict ever taken off you for robbing
that church at Cesena?

Inten. No, nor needs be: for when I murdered your
brother's friend, Pasquale, for him . . .

Mon. Ah, he employed you in that business, did he?
Well, I must let you keep, as you say, this villa and that
podere, for fear the world should find out my relations
were of so indifferent a stamp? Maffeo, my family is the
oldest in Messina, and century after century have my
progenitors gone on polluting themselves with every
wickedness under heaven: my own father . . . rest his
soul!—I have, I know, a chapel to support that it may
rest: my dear two dead brothers were,—what you know
tolerably well; I, the youngest, might have rivalled them
in vice, if not in wealth: but from my boyhood I came
out from among them, and so am not partaker of their
plagues. My glory springs from another source; or if
from this, by contrast only,—for I, the bishop, am the
brother of your employers, Ugo. I hope to repair some
of their wrong, however; so far as my brother's ill-gotten
treasure reverts to me, I can stop the consequences of his
crime: and not one *soldo* shall escape me. Maffeo, the
sword we quiet men spurn away, you shrewd knaves pick
up and commit murders with; what opportunities the
virtuous forego, the villanous seize. Because, to pleasure
myself apart from other considerations, my food would
be millet-cake, my dress sackcloth, and my couch straw,—
am I therefore to let you, the off-scouring of the earth,

seduce the poor and ignorant by appropriating a pomp
these will be sure to think lessens the abominations so
unaccountably and exclusively associated with it? Must
I let villas and *poderi* go to you, a murderer and thief,
that you may beget by means of them other murderers
and thieves? No—if my cough would but allow me to
speak!

Inten. What am I to expect? You are going to punish
me?

Mon. Must punish you, Maffeo. I cannot afford to
cast away a chance. I have whole centuries of sin to
redeem, and only a month or two of life to do it in.
How should I dare to say . . .

Inten. "Forgive us our trespasses"?

Mon. My friend, it is because I avow myself a very
worm, sinful beyond measure, that I reject a line of conduct you would applaud perhaps. Shall I proceed, as it
were, a-pardoning?—I?—who have no symptom of reason
to assume that aught less than my strenuousest efforts
will keep myself out of mortal sin, much less keep others
out. No: I do trespass, but will not double that by allow-
ing you to trespass.

Inten. And suppose the villas are not your brother's
to give, nor yours to take? Oh, you are hasty enough
just now!

Mon. 1, 2—No. 3!—ay, can you read the substance of a
letter, No. 3, I have received from Rome? It is precisely
on the ground there mentioned, of the suspicion I have
that a certain child of my late elder brother, who would
have succeeded to his estates, was murdered in infancy
by you, Maffeo, at the instigation of my late younger
brother—that the Pontiff enjoins on me not merely the
bringing that Maffeo to condign punishment, but the
taking all pains, as guardian of the infant's heritage for
the Church, to recover it parcel by parcel, howsoever,
whensoever, and wheresoever. While you are now gnaw-

ing those fingers, the police are engaged in sealing up your papers, Maffeo, and the mere raising my voice brings my people from the next room to dispose of yourself. But I want you to confess quietly, and save me raising my voice. Why, man, do I not know the old story? The heir between the succeeding heir, and this heir's ruffianly instrument, and their complot's effect, and the life of fear and bribes and ominous smiling silence? Did you throttle or stab my brother's infant? Come now!

Inten. So old a story, and tell it no better? When did such an instrument ever produce such an effect? Either the child smiles in his face; or, most likely, he is not fool enough to put himself in the employer's power so thoroughly: the child is always ready to produce—as you say—howsoever, wheresoever, and whensoever.

Mon. Liar!

Inten. Strike me? Ah, so might a father chastise! I shall sleep soundly tonight at least, though the gallows await me tomorrow; for what a life did I lead! Carlo of Cesena reminds me of his connivance, every time I pay his annuity; which happens commonly thrice a year. If I remonstrate, he will confess all to the good bishop—you!

Mon. I see through the trick, caitiff! I would you spoke truth for once. All shall be sifted, however—seven times sifted.

Inten. And how my absurd riches encumbered me! I dared not lay claim to above half my possessions. Let me but once unbosom myself, glorify Heaven, and die!

Sir, you are no brutal dastardly idiot like your brother I frightened to death: let us understand one another. Sir, I will make away with her for you—the girl—here close at hand; not the stupid obvious kind of killing; do not speak—know nothing of her nor of me! I see her every day—saw her this morning: of course there is to be no killing; but at Rome the courtesans perish off every three years, and I can entice her thither—have indeed begun operations already. There's a certain lusty blue-eyed florid-complexioned English knave, I and the Police employ occasionally. You assent, I perceive—no, that's not it—assent I do not say—but you will let me convert my present havings and holdings into cash, and give me time to cross the Alps? 'T is but a little black-eyed pretty singing Felippa, gay silk-winding girl. I have kept her out of harm's way up to this present; for I always intended to make your life a plague to you with her. 'T is as well settled once and forever. Some women I have procured will pass Bluphocks, my handsome scoundrel, off for somebody; and once Pippa entangled!— you conceive? Through her singing? Is it a bargain?

[*From without is heard the voice of* PIPPA, *singing—*

> *Overhead the tree-tops meet,*
> *Flowers and grass spring 'neath one's feet;*
> *There was naught above me, naught below,*
> *My childhood had not learned to know:*
> *For, what are the voices of birds*
> *—Ay, and of beasts,—but words, our words,*
> *Only so much more sweet?*
> *The knowledge of that with my life begun.*
> *But I had so near made out the sun,*
> *And counted your stars, the seven and one,*
> *Like the fingers of my hand:*
> *Nay, I could all but understand*
> *Wherefore through heaven the white moon ranges;*
> *And just when out of her soft fifty changes*
> *No unfamiliar face might overlook me—*
> *Suddenly God took me.*

[PIPPA *passes.*

Mon. [*Springing up.*] My people—one and all—all— within there! Gag this villain—tie him hand and foot!

He dares . . . I know not half he dares—but remove him—
quick! *Miserere mei, Domine!* Quick, I say!

PIPPA's *Chamber again. She enters it.*

The bee with his comb,
The mouse at her dray,
The grub in his tomb,
While winter away;
But the fire-fly and hedge-shrew and lob-worm, I pray,
How fare they?
Ha, ha, thanks for your counsel, my Zanze!
"Feast upon lampreys, quaff Breganze"—
The summer of life so easy to spend,
And care for tomorrow so soon put away!
But winter hastens at summer's end,
And fire-fly, hedge-shrew, lob-worm, pray,
How fare they?
No bidding me then to . . . what did Zanze say?
"Pare your nails pearlwise, get your small feet shoes
More like" . . . (what said she?)—"and less like canoes!"
How pert that girl was!—would I be those pert
Impudent staring women! It had done me,
However, surely no such mighty hurt
To learn his name who passed that jest upon me:
No foreigner, that I can recollect,
Came, as she says, a month since, to inspect
Our silk-mills—none with blue eyes and thick rings
Of raw-silk-colored hair, at all events.
Well, if old Luca keep his good intents,
We shall do better, see what next year brings!
I may buy shoes, my Zanze, not appear
More destitute than you perhaps next year!
Bluph . . . something! I had caught the uncouth name
But for Monsignor's people's sudden clatter
Above us—bound to spoil such idle chatter

As ours: it were indeed a serious matter
If silly talk like ours should put to shame
The pious man, the man devoid of blame,
The . . . ah but—ah but, all the same,
No mere mortal has a right
To carry that exalted air;
Best people are not angels quite:
While—not the worst of people's doings scare
The devil; so there's that proud look to spare
    Which is mere counsel to myself, mind! for
I have just been the holy Monsignor:
And I was you too, Luigi's gentle mother,
And you too, Luigi!—how that Luigi started
Out of the turret—doubtlessly departed
On some good errand or another,
For he passed just now in a traveller's trim,
And the sullen company that prowled
About his path, I noticed, scowled
As if they had lost a prey in him.
And I was Jules the sculptor's bride,
And I was Ottima beside,
And now what am I?—tired of fooling.
Day for folly, night for schooling!
New Year's day is over and spent,
Ill or well, I must be content.
    Even my lily's asleep, I vow:
Wake up—here's a friend I've plucked you!
Call this flower a heart's-ease now!
Something rare, let me instruct you,
Is this, with petals triply swollen,
Three times spotted, thrice the pollen;
While the leaves and parts that witness
Old proportions and their fitness,
Here remain unchanged, unmoved now;
Call this pampered thing improved now!
Suppose there's a king of the flowers

And a girl-show held in his bowers—
"Look ye, buds, this growth of ours,"
Says he, "Zanze from the Brenta,
I have made her gorge polenta
Till both cheeks are near as bouncing
As her . . . name there's no pronouncing!
See this heightened color too,
For she swilled Breganze wine
Till her nose turned deep carmine;
'T was but white when wild she grew.
And only by this Zanze's eyes
Of which we could not change the size,
The magnitude of all achieved
Otherwise, may be perceived."

Oh what a drear dark close to my poor day!
How could that red sun drop in that black cloud?
Ah Pippa, morning's rule is moved away,
Dispensed with, never more to be allowed!
Day's turn is over, now arrives the night's.
Oh lark, be day's apostle
To mavis, merle and throstle,
Bid them their betters jostle
From day and its delights!
But at night, brother owlet, over the woods,
Toll the world to thy chantry;
Sing to the bats' sleek sisterhoods
Full complines with gallantry:
Then, owls and bats,
Cowls and twats,
Monks and nuns, in a cloister's moods,
Adjourn to the oak-stump pantry!
                    [*After she has begun to undress herself.*
Now, one thing I should like to really know:
How near I ever might approach all these
I only fancied being, this long day:

—Approach, I mean, so as to touch them, so
As to . . . in some way . . . move them—if you please,
Do good or evil to them some slight way.
For instance, if I wind
Silk tomorrow, my silk may bind
                                    [*Sitting on the bedside.*
And border Ottima's cloak's hem.
Ah me, and my important part with them,
This morning's hymn half promised when I rose!
True in some sense or other, I suppose.
                                    [*As she lies down.*
God bless me! I can pray no more tonight.
No doubt, some way or other, hymns say right.

> *All service ranks the same with God—*
> *With God, whose puppets, best and worst,*
> *Are we; there is no last nor first.*
>   [*She sleeps.*

CAVALIER TUNES

I. MARCHING ALONG

KENTISH Sir Byng stood for his King,
Bidding the crop-headed Parliament swing:
And, pressing a troop unable to stoop
And see the rogues flourish and honest folk droop,
Marched them along, fifty-score strong,
Great-hearted gentlemen, singing this song.

God for King Charles! Pym and such carles
To the Devil that prompts 'em their treasonous parles!
Cavaliers, up! Lips from the cup,
Hands from the pasty, nor bite take nor sup
Till you're—
    CHORUS.—Marching along, fifty-score strong,
                Great-hearted gentlemen, singing this song.

Hampden to hell, and his obsequies' knell
Serve Hazelrig, Fiennes, and young Harry as well!
England, good cheer! Rupert is near!
Kentish and loyalists, keep we not here,
    CHO.—Marching along, fifty-score strong,
        Great-hearted gentlemen, singing this song?

Then, God for King Charles! Pym and his snarls
To the Devil that pricks on such pestilent carles!
Hold by the right, you double your might;
So, onward to Nottingham, fresh for the fight,
    CHO.—March we along, fifty-score strong,
        Great-hearted gentlemen, singing this song!

II. GIVE A ROUSE

King Charles, and who'll do him right now?
King Charles, and who's ripe for fight now?
Give a rouse: here's, in hell's despite now,
King Charles!

Who gave me the goods that went since?
Who raised me the house that sank once?
Who helped me to gold I spent since?
Who found me in wine you drank once?
   CHO.—King Charles, and who'll do him right now?
      King Charles, and who's ripe for fight now?
     Give a rouse: here's, in hell's despite now,
     King Charles!

To whom used my boy George quaff else,
By the old fool's side that begot him?
For whom did he cheer and laugh else,
While Noll's damned troopers shot him?
   CHO.—King Charles, and who'll do him right now?
      King Charles, and who's ripe for fight now?
     Give a rouse: here's, in hell's despite now,
     King Charles!

III. BOOT AND SADDLE

Boot, saddle, to horse, and away!
Rescue my castle before the hot day
Brightens to blue from its silvery gray.
   CHO.—Boot, saddle, to horse, and away!

Ride past the suburbs, asleep as you'd say;
Many's the friend there, will listen and pray
"God's luck to gallants that strike up the lay—
   CHO.—Boot, saddle, to horse, and away!"

Forty miles off, like a roebuck at bay,
Flouts Castle Brancepeth the Roundheads' array:
Who laughs, "Good fellows ere this, by my fay,
   CHO.—Boot, saddle, to horse, and away!"

Who? My wife Gertrude; that, honest and gay,
Laughs when you talk of surrendering, "Nay!
I've better counsellors; what counsel they?
   CHO.—Boot, saddle, to horse, and away!"

MY LAST DUCHESS

FERRARA

THAT's my last Duchess painted on the wall,
Looking as if she were alive. I call
That piece a wonder, now: Fra Pandolf's hands
Worked busily a day, and there she stands.
Will 't please you sit and look at her? I said
"Frà Pandolf" by design, for never read
Strangers like you that pictured countenance,
The depth and passion of its earnest glance,
But to myself they turned (since none puts by
The curtain I have drawn for you, but I)
And seemed as they would ask me, if they durst,

How such a glance came there; so, not the first
Are you to turn and ask thus. Sir, 't was not
Her husband's presence only, called that spot
Of joy into the Duchess' cheek: perhaps
Frà Pandolf chanced to say "Her mantle laps
Over my lady's wrist too much," or "Paint
Must never hope to reproduce the faint
Half-flush that dies along her throat:" such stuff
Was courtesy, she thought, and cause enough
For calling up that spot of joy. She had
A heart—how shall I say?—too soon made glad,
Too easily impressed: she liked whate'er
She looked on, and her looks went everywhere.
Sir, 't was all one! My favor at her breast,
The dropping of the daylight in the West,
The bough of cherries some officious fool
Broke in the orchard for her, the white mule
She rode with round the terrace—all and each
Would draw from her alike the approving speech,
Or blush, at least. She thanked men,—good! but thanked
Somehow—I know not how—as if she ranked
My gift of a nine-hundred-years-old name
With anybody's gift. Who'd stoop to blame
This sort of trifling? Even had you skill
In speech— (which I have not)—to make your will
Quite clear to such an one, and say, "Just this
Or that in you disgusts me; here you miss,
Or there exceed the mark"—and if she let
Herself be lessoned so, nor plainly set
Her wits to yours, forsooth, and made excuse,
—E'en then would be some stooping; and I choose
Never to stoop. Oh sir, she smiled, no doubt,
Whene'er I passed her; but who passed without
Much the same smile? This grew; I gave commands;
Then all smiles stopped together. There she stands
As if alive. Will 't please you rise? We'll meet

The company below, then. I repeat,
The Count your master's known munificence
Is ample warrant that no just pretence
Of mine for dowry will be disallowed;
Though his fair daughter's self, as I avowed
At starting, is my object. Nay, we'll go
Together down, sir. Notice Neptune, though,
Taming a sea-horse, thought a rarity,
Which Claus of Innsbruck cast in bronze for me!

SOLILOQUY OF THE SPANISH CLOISTER

GR-R-R—there go, my heart's abhorrence!
    Water your damned flower-pots, do!
If hate killed men, Brother Lawrence,
    God's blood, would not mine kill you!
What? your myrtle-bush wants trimming?
    Oh, that rose has prior claims—
Needs its leaden vase filled brimming?
    Hell dry you up with its flames!

At the meal we sit together:
    Salve tibi! I must hear
Wise talk of the kind of weather,
    Sort of season, time of year:
Not a plenteous cork-crop: scarcely
    Dare we hope oak-galls, I doubt:
What's the Latin name for "parsley"?
    What's the Greek name for Swine's Snout?

Whew! We'll have our platter burnished,
    Laid with care on our own shelf!
With a fire-new spoon we're furnished,
    And a goblet for ourself,
Rinsed like something sacrificial
    Ere 't is fit to touch our chaps—

Marked with L for our initial!
  (He-he!   There his lily snaps!)

Saint, forsooth!   While brown Dolores
  Squats outside the Convent bank
With Sanchicha, telling stories,
  Steeping tresses in the tank,
Blue-black, lustrous, thick like horsehairs,
  —Can't I see his dead eye glow,
Bright as 't were a Barbary corsair's?
  (That is, if he'd let it show!)

When he finishes refection,
  Knife and fork he never lays
Cross-wise, to my recollection,
  As do I, in Jesu's praise.
I the Trinity illustrate,
  Drinking watered orange-pulp—
In three sips the Arian frustrate;
  While he drains his at one gulp.

Oh, those melons!   If he's able
  We're to have a feast! so nice!
One goes to the Abbot's table,
  All of us get each a slice.
How go on your flowers?   None double?
  Not one fruit-sort can you spy?
Strange!—And I, too, at such trouble
  Keep them close-nipped on the sly!

There's a great text in Galatians,
  Once you trip on it, entails
Twenty-nine distinct damnations,
  One sure, if another fails:
If I trip him just a-dying,
  Sure of heaven as sure can be,
Spin him round and send him flying
  Off to hell, a Manichee?

Or, my scrofulous French novel
  On gray paper with blunt type!
Simply glance at it, you grovel
  Hand and foot in Belial's gripe:
If I double down its pages
  At the woeful sixteenth print,
When he gathers his greengages,
  Ope a sieve and slip it in't?

Or, there's Satan!—one might venture
  Pledge one's soul to him, yet leave
Such a flaw in the indenture
  As he'd miss till, past retrieve,
Blasted lay that rose-acacia
  We're so proud of! *Hy, Zy, Hine* . . .
'St, there's Vespers! *Plena gratiâ,*
  Ave, Virgo! Gr-r-r—you swine!

RUDEL TO THE LADY OF TRIPOLI

I

I KNOW a Mount, the gracious Sun perceives
First, when he visits, last, too, when he leaves
The world; and, vainly favored, it repays
The day-long glory of his steadfast gaze
By no change of its large calm front of snow.
And underneath the Mount, a Flower I know,
He cannot have perceived, that changes ever
At his approach; and, in the lost endeavor
To live his life, has parted, one by one,
With all a flower's true graces, for the grace
Of being but a foolish mimic sun,
With ray-like florets round a disk-like face.
Men nobly call by many a name the Mount
As over many a land of theirs its large
Calm front of snow like a triumphal targe

Is reared, and still with old names, fresh names vie,
Each to its proper praise and own account:
Men call the Flower the Sunflower, sportively.

II

Oh, Angel of the East, one, one gold look
Across the waters to this twilight nook,
—The far sad waters, Angel, to this nook!

III

Dear Pilgrim, art thou for the East indeed?
Go!—saying ever as thou dost proceed,
That I, French Rudel, choose for my device
A sunflower outspread like a sacrifice
Before its idol. See! These inexpert
And hurried fingers could not fail to hurt
The woven picture; 't is a woman's skill
Indeed; but nothing baffled me, so, ill
Or well, the work is finished. Say, men feed
On songs I sing, and therefore bask the bees
On my flower's breast as on a platform broad:
But, as the flower's concern is not for these
But solely for the sun, so men applaud
In vain this Rudel, he not looking here
But to the East—the East! Go, say this, Pilgrim dear!

CRISTINA

SHE should never have looked at me
    If she meant I should not love her!
There are plenty . . . men, you call such,
    I suppose . . . she may discover
All her soul to, if she pleases,
    And yet leave much as she found them:
But I'm not so, and she knew it
    When she fixed me, glancing round them.

What?   To fix me thus meant nothing?
   But I can't tell (there's my weakness)
What her look said!—no vile cant, sure,
   About "need to strew the bleakness
Of some lone shore with its pearl-seed,
   That the sea feels"—no "strange yearning
That such souls have, most to lavish
   Where there's chance of least returning."

Oh, we're sunk enough here, God knows!
   But not quite so sunk that moments,
Sure though seldom, are denied us,
   When the spirit's true endowments
Stand out plainly from its false ones,
   And apprise it if pursuing
Or the right way or the wrong way,
   To its triumph or undoing.

There are flashes struck from midnights,
   There are fire-flames noondays kindle,
Whereby piled-up honors perish,
   Whereby swollen ambitions dwindle,
While just this or that poor impulse,
   Which for once had play unstifled,
Seems the sole work of a lifetime,
   That away the rest have trifled.

Doubt you if, in some such moment,
   As she fixed me, she felt clearly,
Ages past the soul existed,
   Here an age 'tis resting merely,
And hence fleets again for ages,
   While the true end, sole and single,
It stops here for is, this love-way,
   With some other soul to mingle?

Else it loses what it lived for,
  And eternally must lose it;
Better ends may be in prospect,
  Deeper blisses (if you choose it),
But this life's end and this love-bliss
  Have been lost here.   Doubt you whether
This she felt as, looking at me,
  Mine and her souls rushed together?

Oh, observe!   Of course, next moment,
  The world's honors, in derision,
Trampled out the light forever:
  Never fear but there's provision
Of the devil's to quench knowledge
  Lest we walk the earth in rapture!
—Making those who catch God's secret
  Just so much more prize their capture!

Such am I: the secret's mine now!
  She has lost me, I have gained her;
Her soul's mine: and thus, grown perfect,
  I shall pass my life's remainder.
Life will just hold out the proving
  Both our powers, alone and blended:
And then, come the next life quickly!
  This world's use will have been ended.

THROUGH THE METIDJA TO
ABD-EL-KADR

  As I ride, as I ride,
  With a full heart for my guide,
  So its tide rocks my side,
  As I ride, as I ride,
  That, as I were double-eyed,
  He, in whom our Tribes confide,

Is descried, ways untried,
As I ride, as I ride.

As I ride, as I ride
To our Chief and his Allied,
Who dares chide my heart's pride
As I ride, as I ride?
Or are witnesses denied—
Through the desert waste and wide
Do I glide unespied
As I ride, as I ride?

As I ride, as I ride,
When an inner voice has cried,
The sands slide, nor abide
(As I ride, as I ride)
O'er each visioned homicide
That came vaunting (has he lied?)
To reside—where he died,
As I ride, as I ride.

As I ride, as I ride,
Ne'er has spur my swift horse plied,
Yet his hide, streaked and pied,
As I ride, as I ride,
Shows where sweat has sprung and dried,
—Zebra-footed, ostrich-thighed—
How has vied stride with stride
As I ride, as I ride!

As I ride, as I ride,
Could I loose what Fate has tied,
Ere I pried, she should hide
(As I ride, as I ride)
All that's meant me—satisfied
When the Prophet and the Bride
Stop veins I'd have subside
As I ride, as I ride!

THE PIED PIPER OF HAMELIN

A CHILD'S STORY

(Written for, and inscribed to, W. M. the Younger.)

I

HAMELIN Town's in Brunswick,
By famous Hanover city;
  The river Weser, deep and wide,
  Washes its wall on the southern side;
  A pleasanter spot you never spied;
But, when begins my ditty,
  Almost five hundred years ago,
  To see the townsfolk suffer so
    From vermin, was a pity.

II

Rats!
They fought the dogs and killed the cats,
  And bit the babies in the cradles,
And ate the cheeses out of the vats,
  And licked the soup from the cooks' own ladles,
Split open the kegs of salted sprats,
Made nests inside men's Sunday hats,
And even spoiled the women's chats
  By drowning their speaking
  With shrieking and squeaking
In fifty different sharps and flats.

III

At last the people in a body
  To the Town Hall came flocking:
" 'T is clear," cried they, "our Mayor's a noddy;
  And as for our Corporation—shocking
To think we buy gowns lined with ermine
For dolts that can't or won't determine

What's best to rid us of our vermin!
You hope, because you're old and obese,
To find in the furry civic robe ease?
Rouse up, sirs! Give your brains a racking
To find the remedy we're lacking,
Or, sure as fate, we'll send you packing!"
At this the Mayor and Corporation
Quaked with a mighty consternation.

IV

An hour they sat in council;
  At length the Mayor broke silence:
"For a guilder I'd my ermine gown sell,
  I wish I were a mile hence!
It's easy to bid one rack one's brain—
I'm sure my poor head aches again,
I've scratched it so, and all in vain.
Oh for a trap, a trap, a trap!"
Just as he said this, what should hap
At the chamber-door but a gentle tap?
"Bless us," cried the Mayor, "what's that?"
(With the Corporation as he sat,
Looking little though wondrous fat;
Nor brighter was his eye, nor moister
Than a too-long-opened oyster,
Save when at noon his paunch grew mutinous
For a plate of turtle green and glutinous)
"Only a scraping of shoes on the mat?
Anything like the sound of a rat
Makes my heart go pit-a-pat!"

V

"Come in!"—the Mayor cried, looking bigger:
And in did come the strangest figure!
His queer long coat from heel to head
Was half of yellow and half of red,

And he himself was tall and thin,
With sharp blue eyes, each like a pin,
And light loose hair, yet swarthy skin,
No tuft on cheek nor beard on chin,
But lips where smiles went out and in;
There was no guessing his kith and kin:
And nobody could enough admire
The tall man and his quaint attire.
Quoth one: "It's as my great-grandsire,
Starting up at the Trump of Doom's tone,
Had walked this way from his painted tombstone!"

VI

He advanced to the council-table:
And, "Please your honors," said he, "I'm able,
By means of a secret charm, to draw
All creatures living beneath the sun,
That creep or swim or fly or run,
After me so as you never saw!
And I chiefly use my charm
On creatures that do people harm,
The mole and toad and newt and viper;
And people call me the Pied Piper."
(And here they noticed round his neck
A scarf of red and yellow stripe,
To match with his coat of the self-same cheque;
And at the scarf's end hung a pipe;
And his fingers, they noticed, were ever straying
As if impatient to be playing
Upon this pipe, as low it dangled
Over his vesture so old-fangled.)
"Yet," said he, "poor piper as I am,
In Tartary I freed the Cham,
Last June, from his huge swarms of gnats;
I eased in Asia the Nizam
Of a monstrous brood of vampire-bats:

And as for what your brain bewilders,
If I can rid your town of rats
Will you give me a thousand guilders?"
"One? fifty thousand!"—was the exclamation
Of the astonished Mayor and Corporation.

VII

Into the street the Piper stept,
   Smiling first a little smile,
As if he knew what magic slept
   In his quiet pipe the while;
Then, like a musical adept,
To blow the pipe his lips he wrinkled,
And green and blue his sharp eyes twinkled,
Like a candle-flame where salt is sprinkled;
And ere three shrill notes the pipe uttered,
You heard as if an army muttered;
And the muttering grew to a grumbling;
And the grumbling grew to a mighty rumbling;
And out of the houses the rats came tumbling.
Great rats, small rats, lean rats, brawny rats,
Brown rats, black rats, gray rats, tawny rats,
Grave old plodders, gay young friskers,
   Fathers, mothers, uncles, cousins,
Cocking tails and pricking whiskers,
   Families by tens and dozens,
Brothers, sisters, husbands, wives—
Followed the Piper for their lives.
From street to street he piped advancing,
And step for step they followed dancing,
Until they came to the river Weser,
Wherein all plunged and perished!
—Save one who, stout as Julius Cæsar,
Swam across and lived to carry
(As he, the manuscript he cherished)
To Rat-land home his commentary:

Which was, "At the first shrill notes of the pipe,
I heard a sound as of scraping tripe,
And putting apples, wondrous ripe,
Into a cider-press's gripe:
And a moving away of pickle-tub-boards,
And a leaving ajar of conserve-cupboards,
And a drawing the corks of train-oil-flasks,
And a breaking the hoops of butter-casks:
And it seemed as if a voice
(Sweeter far than bý harp or bý psaltery
Is breathed) called out, 'Oh rats, rejoice!
The world is grown to one vast drysaltery!
So munch on, crunch on, take your nuncheon,
Breakfast, supper, dinner, luncheon!'
And just as a bulky sugar-puncheon,
All ready staved, like a great sun shone
Glorious scarce an inch before me,
Just as methought it said, 'Come, bore me!'
—I found the Weser rolling o'er me."

VIII

You should have heard the Hamelin people
Ringing the bells till they rocked the steeple.
"Go," cried the Mayor, "and get long poles,
Poke out the nests and block up the holes!
Consult with carpenters and builders,
And leave in our town not even a trace
Of the rats!"—when suddenly, up the face
Of the Piper perked in the market-place,
With a, "First, if you please, my thousand guilders!"

IX

A thousand guilders! The Mayor looked blue;
So did the Corporation too.
For council dinners made rare havoc
With Claret, Moselle, Vin-de-Grave, Hock;

And half the money would replenish
Their cellar's biggest butt with Rhenish.
To pay this sum to a wandering fellow
With a gypsy coat of red and yellow!
"Beside," quoth the Mayor with a knowing wink,
"Our business was done at the river's brink;
We saw with our eyes the vermin sink,
And what's dead can't come to life, I think.
So, friend, we're not the folks to shrink
From the duty of giving you something for drink,
And a matter of money to put in your poke;
But as for the guilders, what we spoke
Of them, as you very well know, was in joke.
Beside, our losses have made us thrifty.
A thousand guilders!   Come, take fifty!"

X

The Piper's face fell, and he cried,
"No trifling!   I can't wait, beside!
I've promised to visit by dinner time
Bagdat, and accept the prime
Of the Head-Cook's pottage, all he's rich in,
For having left, in the Caliph's kitchen,
Of a nest of scorpions no survivor:
With him I proved no bargain-driver,
With you, don't think I'll bate a stiver!
And folks who put me in a passion
May find me pipe after another fashion."

XI

"How?" cried the Mayor, "d'ye think I brook
Being worse treated than a Cook?
Insulted by a lazy ribald
With idle pipe and vesture piebald?
You threaten us, fellow?   Do your worst,
Blow your pipe there till you burst!"

XII

Once more he stept into the street,
   And to his lips again
Laid his long pipe of smooth straight cane;
   And ere he blew three notes (such sweet
Soft notes as yet musician's cunning
   Never gave the enraptured air)
There was a rustling that seemed like a bustling
Of merry crowds justling at pitching and hustling;
Small feet were pattering, wooden shoes clattering,
Little hands clapping and little tongues chattering,
And, like fowls in a farm-yard when barley is scattering,
Out came the children running.
All the little boys and girls,
With rosy cheeks and flaxen curls,
And sparkling eyes and teeth like pearls,
Tripping and skipping, ran merrily after
The wonderful music with shouting and laughter.

XIII

The Mayor was dumb, and the Council stood
As if they were changed into blocks of wood,
Unable to move a step, or cry
To the children merrily skipping by,
—Could only follow with the eye
That joyous crowd at the Piper's back.
But how the Mayor was on the rack,
And the wretched Council's bosoms beat,
As the Piper turned from the High Street
To where the Weser rolled its waters
Right in the way of their sons and daughters!
However, he turned from South to West,
And to Koppelberg Hill his steps addressed,
And after him the children pressed;
Great was the joy in every breast.
"He never can cross that mighty top!

He's forced to let the piping drop,
And we shall see our children stop!"
When, lo, as they reached the mountain-side,
A wondrous portal opened wide,
As if a cavern was suddenly hollowed;
And the Piper advanced and the children fol-
    lowed,
And when all were in to the very last,
The door in the mountain-side shut fast.
Did I say, all? No! One was lame,
And could not dance the whole of the way;
And in after years, if you would blame
His sadness, he was used to say,—
"It's dull in our town since my playmates left!
I can't forget that I'm bereft
Of all the pleasant sights they see,
Which the Piper also promised me.
For he led us, he said, to a joyous land,
Joining the town and just at hand,
Where waters gushed and fruit-trees grew
And flowers put forth a fairer hue,
And everything was strange and new;
The sparrows were brighter than peacocks here,
And their dogs outran our fallow deer,
And honey-bees had lost their stings,
And horses were born with eagles' wings:
And just as I became assured
My lame foot would be speedily cured,
The music stopped and I stood still,
And found myself outside the hill,
Left alone against my will,
To go now limping as before,
And never hear of that country more!"

XIV

Alas, alas for Hamelin!
　There came into many a burgher's pate
　A text which says that heaven's gate
　Opes to the rich at as easy rate
As the needle's eye takes a camel in!
The Mayor sent East, West, North and South,
To offer the Piper, by word of mouth,
　Wherever it was men's lot to find him,
Silver and gold to his heart's content,
If he'd only return the way he went,
　And bring the children behind him.
But when they saw 't was a lost endeavor,
And Piper and dancers were gone forever,
They made a decree that lawyers never
　Should think their records dated duly
If, after the day of the month and year,
These words did not as well appear,
"And so long after what happened here
　On the Twenty-second of July,
Thirteen hundred and seventy-six:"
And the better in memory to fix
The place of the children's last retreat,
They called it, the Pied Piper's Street—
Where any one playing on pipe or tabor
Was sure for the future to lose his labor.
Nor suffered they hostelry or tavern
　To shock with mirth a street so solemn;
But opposite the place of the cavern
　They wrote the story on a column,
And on the great church-window painted
The same, to make the world acquainted
How their children were stolen away,
And there it stands to this very day.
And I must not omit to say
That in Transylvania there's a tribe

Of alien people who ascribe
The outlandish ways and dress
On which their neighbors lay such stress,
To their fathers and mothers having risen
Out of some subterraneous prison
Into which they were trepanned
Long time ago in a mighty band
Out of Hamelin town in Brunswick land,
But how or why, they don't understand.

XV

So, Willy, let me and you be wipers
Of scores out with all men—especially pipers!
And, whether they pipe us free fróm rats or fróm mice,
If we've promised them aught, let us keep our promise!

NATIONALITY IN DRINKS

I

My heart sank with our Claret-flask,
   Just now, beneath the heavy sedges
That serve this pond's black face for mask;
   And still at yonder broken edges
O' the hole, where up the bubbles glisten,
After my heart I look and listen.

Our laughing little flask, compelled
   Through depth to depth more bleak and shady;
As when, both arms beside her held,
   Feet straightened out, some gay French lady
Is caught up from life's light and motion,
And dropped into death's silent ocean!

II

—Up jumped Tokay on our table,
Like a pygmy castle-warder,

Dwarfish to see, but stout and able,
Arms and accoutrements all in order;
And fierce he looked North, then, wheeling South,
Blew with his bugle a challenge to Drouth,
Cocked his flap-hat with the tosspot-feather,
Twisted his thumb in his red moustache,
Jingled his huge brass spurs together,
Tightened his waist with its Buda sash,
And then, with an impudence naught could abash,
Shrugged his hump-shoulder, to tell the beholder,
For twenty such knaves he should laugh but the bolder:
And so, with his sword-hilt gallantly jutting,
And dexter-hand on his haunch abutting,
Went the little man, Sir Ausbruch, strutting!

III

—Here's to Nelson's memory!
'T is the second time that I, at sea,
Right off Cape Trafalgar here,
Have drunk it deep in British Beer.
Nelson forever—any time
Am I his to command in prose or rhyme!
Give me of Nelson only a touch,
And I save it, be it little or much:
Here's one our Captain gives, and so
Down at the word, by George, shall it go!
He says that at Greenwich they point the beholder
To Nelson's coat, "still with tar on the shoulder:
For he used to lean with one shoulder digging,
Jigging, as it were, and zig-zag-zigging
Up against the mizzen-rigging!"

THE FLOWER'S NAME

(*From* GARDEN FANCIES)

HERE's the garden she walked across,
  Arm in my arm, such a short while since:
Hark, now I push its wicket, the moss
  Hinders the hinges and makes them wince!
She must have reached this shrub ere she turned,
  As back with that murmur the wicket swung;
For she laid the poor snail, my chance foot spurned,
  To feed and forget it the leaves among.

Down this side of the gravel-walk
  She went while her robe's edge brushed the box:
And here she paused in her gracious talk
  To point me a moth on the milk-white phlox.
Roses, ranged in valiant row,
  I will never think that she passed you by!
She loves you, noble roses, I know;
  But yonder, see, where the rock-plants lie!

This flower she stopped at, finger on lip,
  Stooped over, in doubt, as settling its claim;
Till she gave me, with pride to make no slip,
  Its soft meandering Spanish name:
What a name!   Was it love or praise?
  Speech half-asleep or song half-awake?
I must learn Spanish, one of these days,
  Only for that slow sweet name's sake.

Roses, if I live and do well,
  I may bring her, one of these days,
To fix you fast with as fine a spell,
  Fit you each with his Spanish phrase;

But do not detain me now; for she lingers
  There, like sunshine over the ground,
And ever I see her soft white fingers
  Searching after the bud she found.

Flower, you Spaniard, look that you grow not,
  Stay as you are and be loved forever!
Bud, if I kiss you 'tis that you blow not,
  Mind, the shut pink mouth opens never!
For while it pouts, her fingers wrestle,
  Twinkling the audacious leaves between,
Till round they turn and down they nestle—
  Is not the dear mark still to be seen?

Where I find her not, beauties vanish;
  Whither I follow her, beauties flee;
Is there no method to tell her in Spanish
  June's twice June since she breathed it with me?
Come, bud, show me the least of her traces,
  Treasure my lady's lightest footfall!
—Ah, you may flout and turn up your faces—
  Roses, you are not so fair after all!

PICTOR IGNOTUS

FLORENCE, 15—

I COULD have painted pictures like that youth's
  Ye praise so. How my soul springs up! No bar
Stayed me—ah, thought which saddens while it soothes!
  —Never did fate forbid me, star by star,
To outburst on your night with all my gift
  Of fires from God: nor would my flesh have shrunk
From seconding my soul, with eyes uplift
  And wide to heaven, or, straight like thunder, sunk
To the centre, of an instant; or around
  Turned calmly and inquisitive, to scan

The license and the limit, space and bound,
    Allowed to truth made visible in man.
And, like that youth ye praise so, all I saw,
    Over the canvas could my hand have flung,
Each face obedient to its passion's law,
    Each passion clear proclaimed without a tongue;
Whether Hope rose at once in all the blood,
    A-tiptoe for the blessing of embrace,
Or Rapture drooped the eyes, as when her brood
    Pull down the nesting dove's heart to its place;
Or Confidence lit swift the forehead up,
    And locked the mouth fast, like a castle braved,—
O human faces, hath it spilt, my cup?
    What did ye give me that I have not saved?
Nor will I say I have not dreamed (how well!)
    Of going—I, in each new picture,—forth,
As, making new hearts beat and bosoms swell,
    To Pope or Kaiser, East, West, South, or North,
Bound for the calmly satisfied great State,
    Or glad aspiring little burgh, it went,
Flowers cast upon the car which bore the freight,
    Through old streets named afresh from the event,
Till it reached home, where learned age should greet
    My face, and youth, the star not yet distinct
Above his hair, lie learning at my feet!—
    Oh, thus to live, I and my picture, linked
With love about, and praise, till life should end,
    And then not go to heaven, but linger here,
Here on my earth, earth's every man my friend,—
    The thought grew frightful, 't was so wildly dear!
But a voice changed it. Glimpses of such sights
    Have scared me, like the revels through a door
Of some strange house of idols at its rites!
    This world seemed not the world it was before:
Mixed with my loving trusting ones, there trooped
    . . . Who summoned those cold faces that begun

To press on me and judge me? Though I stooped
  Shrinking, as from the soldiery a nun,
They drew me forth, and spite of me . . . enough!
  These buy and sell our pictures, take and give,
Count them for garniture and household-stuff,
  And where they live needs must our pictures live
And see their faces, listen to their prate,
  Partakers of their daily pettiness,
Discussed of,—"This I love, or this I hate,
  This likes me more, and this affects me less!"
Wherefore I chose my portion. If at whiles
  My heart sinks, as monotonous I paint
These endless cloisters and eternal aisles
  With the same series, Virgin, Babe and Saint,
With the same cold calm beautiful regard,—
  At least no merchant traffics in my heart;
The sanctuary's gloom at least shall ward
  Vain tongues from where my pictures stand apart:
Only prayer breaks the silence of the shrine
  While, blackening in the daily candle-smoke,
They moulder on the damp wall's travertine,
  'Mid echoes the light footstep never woke.
So, die my pictures! surely, gently die!
  O youth, men praise so,—holds their praise its worth?
Blown harshly, keeps the trump its golden cry?
  Tastes sweet the water with such specks of earth?

THE ITALIAN IN ENGLAND

THAT second time they hunted me
From hill to plain, from shore to sea,
And Austria, hounding far and wide
Her blood-hounds through the country-side,
Breathed hot and instant on my trace,—
I made six days a hiding-place
Of that dry green old aqueduct

Where I and Charles, when boys, have plucked
The fire-flies from the roof above,
Bright creeping through the moss they love:
—How long it seems since Charles was lost!
Six days the soldiers crossed and crossed
The country in my very sight;
And when that peril ceased at night,
The sky broke out in red dismay
With signal fires; well, there I lay
Close covered o'er in my recess,
Up to the neck in ferns and cress,
Thinking on Metternich our friend,
And Charles's miserable end,
And much beside, two days; the third,
Hunger o'ercame me when I heard
The peasants from the village go
To work among the maize; you know,
With us in Lombardy, they bring
Provisions packed on mules, a string
With little bells that cheer their task,
And casks, and boughs on every cask
To keep the sun's heat from the wine;
These I let pass in jingling line,
And, close on them, dear noisy crew,
The peasants from the village, too;
For at the very rear would troop
Their wives and sisters in a group
To help, I knew. When these had passed,
I threw my glove to strike the last,
Taking the chance: she did not start,
Much less cry out, but stooped apart,
One instant rapidly glanced round,
And saw me beckon from the ground;
A wild bush grows and hides my crypt;
She picked my glove up while she stripped
A branch off, then rejoined the rest

With that; my glove lay in her breast.
Then I drew breath: they disappeared:
It was for Italy I feared.

An hour, and she returned alone
Exactly where my glove was thrown.
Meanwhile came many thoughts; on me
Rested the hopes of Italy;
I had devised a certain tale
Which, when 't was told her, could not fail
Persuade a peasant of its truth;
I meant to call a freak of youth
This hiding, and give hopes of pay,
And no temptation to betray.
But when I saw that woman's face,
Its calm simplicity of grace,
Our Italy's own attitude
In which she walked thus far, and stood,
Planting each naked foot so firm,
To crush the snake and spare the worm—
At first sight of her eyes, I said,
"I am that man upon whose head
They fix the price, because I hate
The Austrians over us: the State
Will give you gold—oh, gold so much!—
If you betray me to their clutch,
And be your death, for aught I know,
If once they find you saved their foe.
Now, you must bring me food and drink,
And also paper, pen and ink,
And carry safe what I shall write
To Padua, which you'll reach at night
Before the duomo shuts; go in,
And wait till Tenebræ begin;
Walk to the third confessional,
Between the pillar and the wall,

And kneeling whisper, *Whence comes peace?*
Say it a second time, then cease;
And if the voice inside returns,
From Christ and Freedom; what concerns
The cause of Peace?—for answer, slip
My letter where you placed your lip;
Then come back happy we have done
Our mother service—I, the son,
As you the daughter of our land!"

Three mornings more, she took her stand
In the same place, with the same eyes:
I was no surer of sunrise
Than of her coming. We conferred
Of her own prospects, and I heard
She had a lover—stout and tall,
She said—then let her eyelids fall,
"He could do much"—as if some doubt
Entered her heart,—then, passing out,
"She could not speak for others, who
Had other thoughts; herself she knew:"
And so she brought me drink and food.
After four days, the scouts pursued
Another path; at last arrived
The help my Paduan friends contrived
To furnish me: she brought the news.
For the first time I could not choose
But kiss her hand, and lay my own
Upon her head—"This faith was shown
To Italy, our mother; she
Uses my hand and blesses thee."
She followed down to the sea-shore;
I left and never saw her more.

How very long since I have thought
Concerning—much less wished for—aught
Beside the good of Italy,

For which I live and mean to die!
I never was in love; and since
Charles proved false, what shall now convince
My inmost heart I have a friend?
However, if I pleased to spend
Real wishes on myself—say, three—
I know at least what one should be.
I would grasp Metternich until
I felt his red wet throat distil
In blood through these two hands. And next
—Nor much for that am I perplexed—
Charles, perjured traitor, for his part,
Should die slow of a broken heart
Under his new employers. Last
—Ah, there, what should I wish? For fast
Do I grow old and out of strength.
If I resolved to seek at length
My father's house again, how scared
They all would look, and unprepared!
My brothers live in Austria's pay
—Disowned me long ago, men say;
And all my early mates who used
To praise me so—perhaps induced
More than one early step of mine—
Are turning wise: while some opine
"Freedom grows license," some suspect
"Haste breeds delay," and recollect
They always said, such premature
Beginnings never could endure!
So, with a sullen "All's for best,"
The land seems settling to its rest.
I think then, I should wish to stand
This evening in that dear, lost land,
Over the sea the thousand miles,
And know if yet that woman smiles
With the calm smile; some little farm
She lives in there, no doubt: what harm

If I sat on the door-side bench,
And, while her spindle made a trench
Fantastically in the dust,
Inquired of all her fortunes—just
Her children's ages and their names,
And what may be the husband's aims
For each of them. I'd talk this out,
And sit there, for an hour about,
Then kiss her hand once more, and lay
Mine on her head, and go my way.

So much for idle wishing—how
It steals the time! To business now.

THE LOST LEADER

Just for a handful of silver he left us,
    Just for a riband to stick in his coat—
Found the one gift of which fortune bereft us,
    Lost all the others she lets us devote;
They, with the gold to give, doled him out silver,
    So much was theirs who so little allowed:
How all our copper had gone for his service!
    Rags—were they purple, his heart had been proud!
We that had loved him so, followed him, honored him,
    Lived in his mild and magnificent eye,
Learned his great language, caught his clear accents,
    Made him our pattern to live and to die!
Shakespeare was of us, Milton was for us,
    Burns, Shelley, were with us,—they watch from
        their graves!
He alone breaks from the van and the freemen,
    —He alone sinks to the rear and the slaves!

We shall march prospering,—not through his presence;
    Songs may inspirit us,—not from his lyre;

Deeds will be done,—while he boasts his quiescence,
   Still bidding crouch whom the rest bade aspire:
Blot out his name, then, record one lost soul more,
   One task more declined, one more footpath untrod,
One more devils'-triumph and sorrow for angels,
   One wrong more to man, one more insult to God!
Life's night begins: let him never come back to us!
   There would be doubt, hesitation and pain,
Forced praise on our part—the glimmer of twilight,
   Never glad confident morning again!
Best fight on well, for we taught him—strike gallantly,
   Menace our heart ere we master his own;
Then let him receive the new knowledge and wait us,
   Pardoned in heaven, the first by the throne!

THE LOST MISTRESS

unsuccessful love

ALL's over, then: does truth sound bitter
   As one at first believes?
Hark, 't is the sparrows' good-night twitter
   About your cottage eaves!

And the leaf-buds on the vine are woolly,
   I noticed that, today;
One day more bursts them open fully
   —You know the red turns gray.

Tomorrow we meet the same then, dearest?
   May I take your hand in mine?
Mere friends are we,—well, friends the merest
   Keep much that I resign:

For each glance of the eye so bright and black
   Though I keep with heart's endeavor,—
Your voice, when you wish the snowdrops back,
   Though it stay in my soul forever!—

Yet I will but say what mere friends say,
    Or only a thought stronger;
I will hold your hand but as long as all may,
    Or so very little longer!

HOME-THOUGHTS, FROM ABROAD

OH, to be in England
Now that April's there,
And whoever wakes in England
Sees, some morning, unaware,
That the lowest boughs and the brush-wood sheaf
Round the elm-tree bole are in tiny leaf,
While the chaffinch sings on the orchard bough
In England—now!

And after April, when May follows,
And the whitethroat builds, and all the swallows!
Hark, where my blossomed pear-tree in the hedge
Leans to the field and scatters on the clover
Blossoms and dewdrops—at the bent spray's edge—
That's the wise thrush; he sings each song twice over,
Lest you should think he never could recapture
The first fine careless rapture!
And though the fields look rough with hoary dew,
All will be gay when noontide wakes anew
The buttercups, the little children's dower
—Far brighter than this gaudy melon-flower!

HOME-THOUGHTS, FROM THE SEA

NOBLY, nobly Cape Saint Vincent to the Northwest died
    away;
Sunset ran, one glorious blood-red, reeking into Cadiz
    Bay;
Bluish 'mid the burning water, full in face Trafalgar lay;

In the dimmest Northeast distance dawned Gibraltar
    grand and gray;
"Here and here did England help me: how can I help
    England?"—say,
Whoso turns as I, this evening, turn to God to praise and
    pray,
While Jove's planet rises yonder, silent over Africa.

THE BISHOP ORDERS HIS TOMB AT
SAINT PRAXED'S CHURCH

ROME, 15—

VANITY, saith the preacher, vanity!
Draw round my bed: is Anselm keeping back?
Nephews—sons mine . . . ah God, I know not! Well—
She, men would have to be your mother once,
Old Gandolf envied me, so fair she was!
What's done is done, and she is dead beside,
Dead long ago, and I am Bishop since,
And as she died so must we die ourselves,
And thence ye may perceive the world's a dream.
Life, how and what is it? As here I lie
In this state-chamber, dying by degrees,
Hours and long hours in the dead night, I ask
"Do I live, am I dead?" Peace, peace seem all.
Saint Praxed's ever was the church for peace;
And so, about this tomb of mine. I fought
With tooth and nail to save my niche, ye know:
—Old Gandolf cozened me, despite my care;
Shrewd was that snatch from out the corner South
He graced his carrion with, God curse the same!
Yet still my niche is not so cramped but thence
One sees the pulpit o' the epistle-side,
And somewhat of the choir, those silent seats,
And up into the aery dome where live
The angels, and a sunbeam's sure to lurk:

And I shall fill my slab of basalt there,
And 'neath my tabernacle take my rest,
With those nine columns round me, two and two,
The odd one at my feet where Anselm stands:
Peach-blossom marble all, the rare, the ripe
As fresh-poured red wine of a mighty pulse.
—Old Gandolf with his paltry onion-stone,
Put me where I may look at him!   True peach,
Rosy and flawless: how I earned the prize!
Draw close: that conflagration of my church
—What then? So much was saved if aught were missed!
My sons, ye would not be my death? Go dig
The white-grape vineyard where the oil-press stood,
Drop water gently till the surface sink,
And if ye find . . . Ah God, I know not, I! . . .
Bedded in store of rotten fig-leaves soft,
And corded up in a tight olive-frail,
Some lump, ah God, of *lapis lazuli,*
Big as a Jew's head cut off at the nape,
Blue as a vein o'er the Madonna's breast . . .
Sons, all have I bequeathed you, villas, all,
That brave Frascati villa with its bath,
So, let the blue lump poise between my knees,
Like God the Father's globe on both his hands
Ye worship in the Jesu Church so gay,
For Gandolf shall not choose but see and burst!
Swift as a weaver's shuttle fleet our years:
Man goeth to the grave, and where is he?
Did I say basalt for my slab, sons?   Black—
'Twas ever antique-black I meant! How else
Shall ye contrast my frieze to come beneath?
The bas-relief in bronze ye promised me,
Those Pans and Nymphs ye wot of, and perchance
Some tripod, thyrsus, with a vase or so,
The Saviour at his sermon on the mount,
Saint Praxed in a glory, and one Pan

Ready to twitch the Nymph's last garment off,
And Moses with the tables . . . but I know
Ye mark me not! What do they whisper thee,
Child of my bowels, Anselm? Ah, ye hope
To revel down my villas while I gasp
Bricked o'er with beggar's mouldy travertine
Which Gandolf from his tomb-top chuckles at!
Nay, boys, ye love me—all of jasper, then!
'Tis jasper ye stand pledged to, lest I grieve
My bath must needs be left behind, alas!
One block, pure green as a pistachio-nut,
There's plenty jasper somewhere in the world—
And have I not Saint Praxed's ear to pray
Horses for ye, and brown Greek manuscripts,
And mistresses with great smooth marbly limbs?
—That's if ye carve my epitaph aright,
Choice Latin, picked phrase, Tully's every word,
No gaudy ware like Gandolf's second line—
Tully, my masters? Ulpian serves his need!
And then how I shall lie through centuries,
And hear the blessed mutter of the mass,
And see God made and eaten all day long,
And feel the steady candle-flame, and taste
Good strong thick stupefying incense-smoke!
For as I lie here, hours of the dead night,
Dying in state and by such slow degrees,
I fold my arms as if they clasped a crook,
And stretch my feet forth straight as stone can point,
And let the bedclothes, for a mortcloth, drop
Into great laps and folds of sculptor's-work:
And as yon tapers dwindle, and strange thoughts
Grow, with a certain humming in my ears,
About the life before I lived this life,
And this life too, popes, cardinals and priests,
Saint Praxed at his sermon on the mount,
Your tall pale mother with her talking eyes,

And new-found agate urns as fresh as day,
And marble's language, Latin pure, discreet,
—Aha, ELUCESCEBAT quoth our friend?
No Tully, said I, Ulpian at the best!
Evil and brief hath been my pilgrimage.
All *lapis,* all, sons!   Else I give the Pope
My villas!   Will ye ever eat my heart?
Ever your eyes were as a lizard's quick,
They glitter like your mother's for my soul,
Or ye would heighten my impoverished frieze,
Piece out its starved design, and fill my vase
With grapes, and add a visor and a Term,
And to the tripod ye would tie a lynx
That in his struggle throws the thyrsus down,
To comfort me on my entablature
Whereon I am to lie till I must ask
"Do I live, am I dead?"   There, leave me, there!
For ye have stabbed me with ingratitude
To death—ye wish it—God, ye wish it!   Stone—
Gritstone, a-crumble!   Clammy squares which sweat
As if the corpse they keep were oozing through—
And no more *lapis* to delight the world!
Well, go!   I bless ye.   Fewer tapers there,
But in a row: and, going, turn your backs
—Ay, like departing altar-ministrants,
And leave me in my church, the church for peace,
That I may watch at leisure if he leers—
Old Gandolf—at me, from his onion-stone,
As still he envied me, so fair she was!

THE CONFESSIONAL

SPAIN

It is a lie—their Priests, their Pope,
Their Saints, their . . . all they fear or hope

Are lies, and lies—there! through my door
And ceiling, there! and walls and floor,
There, lies, they lie—shall still be hurled
Till spite of them I reach the world!

You think Priests just and holy men!
Before they put me in this den
I was a human creature too,
With flesh and blood like one of you,
A girl that laughed in beauty's pride
Like lilies in your world outside.

I had a lover—shame avaunt!
This poor wrenched body, grim and gaunt,
Was kissed all over till it burned,
By lips the truest, love e'er turned
His heart's own tint: one night they kissed
My soul out in a burning mist.

So, next day when the accustomed train
Of things grew round my sense again,
"That is a sin," I said: and slow
With downcast eyes to church I go,
And pass to the confession-chair,
And tell the old mild father there.

But when I falter Beltran's name,
"Ha!" quoth the father; "much I blame
The sin; yet wherefore idly grieve?
Despair not—strenuously retrieve!
Nay, I will turn this love of thine
To lawful love, almost divine;

"For he is young, and led astray,
This Beltran, and he schemes, men say,
To change the laws of church and state;

So, thine shall be an angel's fate,
Who, ere the thunder breaks, should roll
Its cloud away and save his soul.

"For, when he lies upon thy breast,
Thou mayest demand and be possessed
Of all his plans, and next day steal
To me, and all those plans reveal,
That I and every priest, to purge
His soul, may fast and use the scourge."

That father's beard was long and white,
With love and truth his brow seemed bright;
I went back, all on fire with joy,
And, that same evening, bade the boy
Tell me, as lovers should, heart-free,
Something to prove his love of me.

He told me what he would not tell
For hope of heaven or fear of hell;
And I lay listening in such pride!
And, soon as he had left my side,
Tripped to the church by morning-light
To save his soul in his despite.

I told the father all his schemes,
Who were his comrades, what their dreams;
"And now make haste," I said, "to pray
The one spot from his soul away;
Tonight he comes, but not the same
Will look!"   At night he never came.

Nor next night: on the after-morn,
I went forth with a strength new-born.
The church was empty; something drew
My steps into the street; I knew

It led me to the market-place:
Where, lo, on high, the father's face!

That horrible black scaffold dressed,
That stapled block . . . God sink the rest!
That head strapped back, that blinding vest,
Those knotted hands and naked breast,
Till near one busy hangman pressed,
And, on the neck these arms caressed . . .

No part in aught they hope or fear!
No heaven with them, no hell!—and here,
No earth, not so much space as pens
My body in their worst of dens
But shall bear God and man my cry,
Lies—lies, again—and still, they lie!

THE FLIGHT OF THE DUCHESS

I

YOU'RE my friend;
I was the man the Duke spoke to;
I helped the Duchess to cast off his yoke, too:
So, here's the tale from beginning to end,
My friend!

II

Ours is a great wild country:
If you climb to our castle's top,
I don't see where your eye can stop;
For when you've passed the cornfield country,
Where vineyards leave off, flocks are packed,
And sheep-range leads to cattle-tract,
And cattle-tract to open-chase,
And open-chase to the very base
Of the mountain where, at a funeral pace,

Round about, solemn and slow,
One by one, row after row,
Up and up the pine-trees go,
So, like black priests up, and so
Down the other side again
To another greater, wilder country,
That's one vast red drear burnt-up plain,
Branched through and through with many a vein
Whence iron's dug, and copper's dealt;
Look right, look left, look straight before,—
Beneath they mine, above they smelt,
Copper-ore and iron-ore,
And forge and furnace mould and melt,
And so on, more and ever more,
Till at the last, for a bounding belt,
Comes the salt sand hoar of the great sea-shore
—And the whole is our Duke's country.

III

I was born the day this present Duke was—
(And O, says the song, ere I was old!)
In the castle where the other Duke was—
(When I was happy and young, not old!)
I in the kennel, he in the bower:
We are of like age to an hour.
My father was huntsman in that day;
Who has not heard my father say
That, when a boar was brought to bay,
Three times, four times out of five,
With his huntspear he'd contrive
To get the killing-place transfixed,
And pin him true, both eyes betwixt?
And that's why the old Duke would rather
He lost a salt-pit than my father,
And loved to have him ever in call;
That's why my father stood in the hall

When the old Duke brought his infant out
To show the people, and while they passed
The wondrous bantling round about,
Was first to start at the outside blast
As the Kaiser's courier blew his horn,
Just a month after the babe was born.
"And," quoth the Kaiser's courier, "since
The Duke has got an heir, our Prince
Needs the Duke's self at his side:"
The Duke looked down and seemed to wince,
But he thought of wars o'er the world wide,
Castles a-fire, men on their march,
The toppling tower, the crashing arch;
And up he looked, and awhile he eyed
The row of crests and shields and banners
Of all achievements after all manners,
And "ay," said the Duke with a surly pride.
The more was his comfort when he died
At next year's end, in a velvet suit,
With a gilt glove on his hand, his foot
In a silken shoe for a leather boot,
Petticoated like a herald,
In a chamber next to an ante-room,
Where he breathed the breath of page and groom,
What he called stink, and they, perfume:
—They should have set him on red Berold
Mad with pride, like fire to manage!
They should have got his cheek fresh tannage
Such a day as today in the merry sunshine!
Had they stuck on his fist a rough-foot merlin!
(Hark, the wind's on the heath at its game!
Oh for a noble falcon-lanner
To flap each broad wing like a banner,
And turn in the wind, and dance like flame!)
Had they broached a white-beer cask from Berlin
—Or if you incline to prescribe mere wine

Put to his lips, when they saw him pine,
A cup of our own Moldavia fine,
Cotnar for instance, green as May sorrel
And ropy with sweet,—we shall not quarrel.

IV

So, at home, the sick tall yellow Duchess
Was left with the infant in her clutches,
She being the daughter of God knows who:
And now was the time to revisit her tribe.
Abroad and afar they went, the two,
And let our people rail and gibe
At the empty hall and extinguished fire,
As loud as we liked, but ever in vain,
Till after long years we had our desire,
And back came the Duke and his mother again.

V

And he came back the pertest little ape
That ever affronted human shape;
Full of his travel, struck at himself.
You'd say, he despised our bluff old ways?
—Not he! For in Paris they told the elf
Our rough North land was the Land of Lays,
The one good thing left in evil days;
Since the Mid-Age was the Heroic Time,
And only in wild nooks like ours
Could you taste of it yet as in its prime,
And see true castles, with proper towers,
Young-hearted women, old-minded men,
And manners now as manners were then.
So, all that the old Dukes had been, without knowing it,
This Duke would fain know he was, without being it;
'T was not for the joy's self, but the joy of his showing it,
Nor for the pride's self, but the pride of our seeing it,
He revived all usages thoroughly worn-out,

The souls of them fumed-forth, the hearts of them
    torn-out:
And chief in the chase his neck he perilled,
On a lathy horse, all legs and length,
With blood for bone, all speed, no strength;
—They should have set him on red Berold
With the red eye slow consuming in fire,
And the thin stiff ear like an abbey spire!

VI

Well, such as he was, he must marry, we heard:
And out of a convent, at the word,
Came the lady, in time of spring.
—Oh, old thoughts they cling, they cling!
That day, I know, with a dozen oaths
I clad myself in thick hunting-clothes
Fit for the chase of urochs or buffle
In winter-time when you need to muffle.
But the Duke had a mind we should cut a figure,
And so we saw the lady arrive:
My friend, I have seen a white crane bigger!
She was the smallest lady alive,
Made in a piece of nature's madness,
Too small, almost, for the life and gladness
That over-filled her, as some hive
Out of the bears' reach on the high trees
Is crowded with its safe merry bees:
In truth, she was not hard to please!
Up she looked, down she looked, round at the mead,
Straight at the castle, that's best indeed
To look at from outside the walls:
As for us, styled the "serfs and thralls,"
She as much thanked me as if she had said it,
(With her eyes, do you understand?)
Because I patted her horse while I led it;
And Max, who rode on her other hand,

Said, no bird flew past but she inquired
What its true name was, nor ever seemed tired—
If that was an eagle she saw hover,
And the green and gray bird on the field was the plover.
When suddenly appeared the Duke:
And as down she sprung, the small foot pointed
On to my hand,—as with a rebuke,
And as if his backbone were not jointed,
The Duke stepped rather aside than forward,
And welcomed her with his grandest smile;
And, mind you, his mother all the while
Chilled in the rear, like a wind to Nor'ward;
And up, like a weary yawn, with its pulleys
Went, in a shriek, the rusty portcullis;
And, like a glad sky the north-wind sullies,
The lady's face stopped its play,
As if her first hair had grown gray;
For such things must begin some one day.

VII

In a day or two she was well again;
As who should say, "You labor in vain!
This is all a jest against God, who meant
I should ever be, as I am, content
And glad in his sight; therefore, glad I will be."
So, smiling as at first went she.

VIII

She was active, stirring, all fire—
Could not rest, could not tire—
To a stone she might have given life!
(I myself loved once, in my day)
—For a shepherd's, miner's, huntsman's wife,
(I had a wife, I know what I say)
Never in all the world such an one!
And here was plenty to be done,

And she that could do it, great or small,
She was to do nothing at all.
There was already this man in his post,
This in his station, and that in his office,
And the Duke's plan admitted a wife, at most,
To meet his eye, with the other trophies,
Now outside the hall, now in it,
To sit thus, stand thus, see and be seen,
At the proper place in the proper minute,
And die away the life between.
And it was amusing enough, each infraction
Of rule— (but for after-sadness that came)
To hear the consummate self-satisfaction
With which the young Duke and the old dame
Would let her advise, and criticise,
And, being a fool, instruct the wise,
And, child-like, parcel out praise or blame:
They bore it all in complacent guise,
As though an artificer, after contriving
A wheel-work image as if it were living,
Should find with delight it could motion to strike him!
So found the Duke, and his mother like him:
The lady hardly got a rebuff—
That had not been contemptuous enough,
With his cursed smirk, as he nodded applause,
And kept off the old mother-cat's claws.

IX

So, the little lady grew silent and thin,
    Paling and ever paling,
As the way is with a hid chagrin;
    And the Duke perceived that she was ailing,
And said in his heart, " 'T is done to spite me,
But I shall find in my power to right me!"
Don't swear, friend!   The old one, many a year,
Is in hell, and the Duke's self . . . you shall hear.

X

Well, early in autumn, at first winter-warning,
When the stag had to break with his foot, of a morning,
A drinking-hole out of the fresh tender ice
That covered the pond till the sun, in a trice,
Loosening it, let out a ripple of gold,
And another and another, and faster and faster,
Till, dimpling to blindness, the wide water rolled:
Then it so chanced that the Duke our master
Asked himself what were the pleasures in season,
And found, since the calendar bade him be hearty,
He should do the Middle Age no treason
In resolving on a hunting-party.
Always provided, old books showed the way of it!
What meant old poets by their strictures?
And when old poets had said their say of it,
How taught old painters in their pictures?
We must revert to the proper channels,
Working in tapestry, paintings on panels,
And gather up woodcraft's authentic traditions:
Here was food for our various ambitions,
As on each case, exactly stated—
To encourage your dog, now, the properest chirrup,
Or best prayer to Saint Hubert on mounting your
    stirrup—
We of the household took thought and debated.
Blessed was he whose back ached with the jerkin
His sire was wont to do forest-work in;
Blesseder he who nobly sunk "ohs"
And "ahs" while he tugged on his grandsire's trunk-hose;
What signified hats if they had no rims on,
Each slouching before and behind like the scallop,
And able to serve at sea for a shallop,
Loaded with lacquer and looped with crimson?
So that the deer now, to make a short rhyme on 't,
What with our Venerers, Prickers and Verderers,

Might hope for real hunters at length and not murderers,
And oh the Duke's tailor, he had a hot time on 't!

XI

Now you must know that when the first dizziness
Of flap-hats and buff-coats and jack-boots subsided,
The Duke put this question, "The Duke's part provided,
Had not the Duchess some share in the business?"
For out of the mouth of two or three witnesses
Did he establish all fit-or-unfitnesses:
And, after much laying of heads together,
Somebody's cap got a notable feather
By the announcement with proper unction
That he had discovered the lady's function;
Since ancient authors gave this tenet,
"When horns wind a mort and the deer is at siege,
Let the dame of the castle prick forth on her jennet,
And, with water to wash the hands of her liege
In a clean ewer with a fair towelling,
Let her preside at the disembowelling."
Now, my friend, if you had so little religion
As to catch a hawk, some falcon-lanner,
And thrust her broad wings like a banner
Into a coop for a vulgar pigeon;
And if day by day and week by week
You cut her claws, and sealed her eyes,
And clipped her wings, and tied her beak,
Would it cause you any great surprise
If, when you decided to give her an airing,
You found she needed a little preparing?
—I say, should you be such a curmudgeon,
If she clung to the perch, as to take it in dudgeon?
Yet when the Duke to his lady signified,
Just a day before, as he judged most dignified,
In what a pleasure she was to participate,—
And, instead of leaping wide in flashes,

Her eyes just lifted their long lashes,
As if pressed by fatigue even he could not dissipate,
And duly acknowledged the Duke's forethought,
But spoke of her health, if her health were worth aught,
Of the weight by day and the watch by night,
And much wrong now that used to be right,
So, thanking him, declined the hunting,—
Was conduct ever more affronting?
With all the ceremony settled—
With the towel ready, and the sewer
Polishing up his oldest ewer,
And the jennet pitched upon, a piebald,
Black-barred, cream-coated and pink eye-balled,—
No wonder if the Duke was nettled!
And when she persisted nevertheless,—
Well, I suppose here's the time to confess
That there ran half round our lady's chamber
A balcony none of the hardest to clamber;
And that Jacynth the tire-woman, ready in waiting,
Stayed in call outside, what need of relating?
And since Jacynth was like a June rose, why, a fervent
Adorer of Jacynth of course was your servant;
And if she had the habit to peep through the casement,
How could I keep at any vast distance?
And so, as I say, on the lady's persistence,
The Duke, dumb-stricken with amazement,
Stood for a while in a sultry smother,
And then, with a smile that partook of the awful,
Turned her over to his yellow mother
To learn what was held decorous and lawful;
And the mother smelt blood with a cat-like instinct,
As her cheek quick whitened through all its quince-tinct.
Oh, but the lady heard the whole truth at once!
What meant she?—Who was she?—Her duty and station,
The wisdom of age and the folly of youth, at once,
Its decent regard and its fitting relation—

In brief, my friend, set all the devils in hell free
And turn them out to carouse in a belfry
And treat the priests to a fifty-part canon,
And then you may guess how that tongue of hers ran on!
Well, somehow or other it ended at last
And, licking her whiskers, out she passed;
And after her,—making (he hoped) a face
Like Emperor Nero or Sultan Saladin,
Stalked the Duke's self with the austere grace
Of ancient hero or modern paladin,
From door to staircase—oh such a solemn
Unbending of the vertebral column!

XII

However, at sunrise our company mustered;
And here was the huntsman bidding unkennel,
And there 'neath his bonnet the pricker blustered,
With feather dank as a bough of wet fennel;
For the court-yard walls were filled with fog
You might have cut as an axe chops a log—
Like so much wool for color and bulkiness;
And out rode the Duke in a perfect sulkiness,
Since, before breakfast, a man feels but queasily,
And a sinking at the lower abdomen
Begins the day with indifferent omen.
And lo, as he looked around uneasily,
The sun ploughed the fog up and drove it asunder
This way and that from the valley under;
And, looking through the court-yard arch,
Down in the valley, what should meet him
But a troop of Gypsies on their march?
No doubt with the annual gifts to greet him.

XIII

Now, in your land, Gypsies reach you, only
After reaching all lands beside;

North they go, South they go, trooping or lonely,
And still, as they travel far and wide,
Catch they and keep now a trace here, a trace there,
That puts you in mind of a place here, a place there.
But with us, I believe they rise out of the ground,
And nowhere else, I take it, are found
With the earth-tint yet so freshly embrowned:
Born, no doubt, like insects which breed on
The very fruit they are meant to feed on.
For the earth—not a use to which they don't turn it,
The ore that grows in the mountain's womb,
Or the sand in the pits like a honeycomb,
They sift and soften it, bake it and burn it—
Whether they weld you, for instance, a snaffle
With side-bars never a brute can baffle;
Or a lock that's a puzzle of wards within wards;
Or, if your colt's forefoot inclines to curve inwards,
Horseshoes they hammer which turn on a swivel
And won't allow the hoof to shrivel.
Then they cast bells like the shell of the winkle
That keep a stout heart in the ram with their tinkle;
But the sand—they pinch and pound it like otters;
Commend me to Gypsy glass-makers and potters!
Glasses they'll blow you, crystal-clear,
Where just a faint cloud of rose shall appear,
As if in pure water you dropped and let die
A bruised black-blooded mulberry;
And that other sort, their crowning pride,
With long white threads distinct inside,
Like the lake-flower's fibrous roots which dangle
Loose such a length and never tangle,
Where the bold sword-lily cuts the clear waters,
And the cup-lily couches with all the white daughters:
Such are the works they put their hand to,
The uses they turn and twist iron and sand to.
And these made the troop, which our Duke saw sally

Toward his castle from out of the valley,
Men and women, like new-hatched spiders,
Come out with the morning to greet our riders.
And up they wound till they reached the ditch,
Whereat all stopped save one, a witch
That I knew, as she hobbled from the group,
By her gait directly and her stoop,
I, whom Jacynth was used to importune
To let that same witch tell us our fortune,
The oldest Gypsy then above ground;
And, sure as the autumn season came round,
She paid us a visit for profit or pastime,
And every time, as she swore, for the last time.
And presently she was seen to sidle
Up to the Duke till she touched his bridle,
So that the horse of a sudden reared up
As under its nose the old witch peered up
With her worn-out eyes, or rather eye-holes
Of no use now but to gather brine,
And began a kind of level whine
Such as they use to sing to their viols
When their ditties they go grinding
Up and down with nobody minding:
And then, as of old, at the end of the humming
Her usual presents were forthcoming
—A dog-whistle blowing the fiercest of trebles,
(Just a sea-shore stone holding a dozen fine pebbles,)
Or a porcelain mouthpiece to screw on a pipe-end,—
And so she awaited her annual stipend.
But this time, the Duke would scarcely vouchsafe
A word in reply; and in vain she felt
With twitching fingers at her belt
For the purse of sleek pine-marten pelt,
Ready to put what he gave in her pouch safe,—
Till, either to quicken his apprehension,
Or possibly with an after-intention,

She was come, she said, to pay her duty
To the new Duchess, the youthful beauty.
No sooner had she named his lady,
Than a shine lit up the face so shady,
And its smirk returned with a novel meaning—
For it struck him, the babe just wanted weaning;
If one gave her a taste of what life was and sorrow,
She, foolish today, would be wiser tomorrow;
And who so fit a teacher of trouble
As this sordid crone bent well-nigh double?
So, glancing at her wolf-skin vesture,
(If such it was, for they grow so hirsute
That their own fleece serves for natural fursuit)
He was contrasting, 't was plain from his gesture,
The life of the lady so flower-like and delicate
With the loathsome squalor of this helicat.
I, in brief, was the man the Duke beckoned
From out of the throng, and while I drew near
He told the crone—as I since have reckoned
By the way he bent and spoke into her ear
With circumspection and mystery—
The main of the lady's history,
Her frowardness and ingratitude:
And for all the crone's submissive attitude
I could see round her mouth the loose plaits tightening,
And her brow with assenting intelligence brightening,
As though she engaged with hearty goodwill
Whatever he now might enjoin to fulfil,
And promised the lady a thorough frightening.
And so, just giving her a glimpse
Of a purse, with the air of a man who imps
The wing of the hawk that shall fetch the hernshaw,
He bade me take the Gypsy mother
And set her telling some story or other
Of hill or dale, oak-wood or fernshaw,
To while away a weary hour

For the lady left alone in her bower,
Whose mind and body craved exertion
And yet shrank from all better diversion.

XIV

Then clapping heel to his horse, the mere curveter,
Out rode the Duke, and after his hollo
Horses and hounds swept, huntsman and servitor,
And back I turned and bade the crone follow.
And what makes me confident what's to be told you
Had all along been of this crone's devising,
Is, that, on looking round sharply, behold you,
There was a novelty quick as surprising:
For first, she had shot up a full head in stature,
And her step kept pace with mine nor faltered,
As if age had foregone its usurpature,
And the ignoble mien was wholly altered,
And the face looked quite of another nature,
And the change reached too, whatever the change meant,
Her shaggy wolf-skin cloak's arrangement:
For where its tatters hung loose like sedges,
Gold coins were glittering on the edges,
Like the band-roll strung with tomans
Which proves the veil a Persian woman's:
And under her brow, like a snail's horns newly
Come out as after the rain he paces,
Two unmistakable eye-points duly
Live and aware looked out of their places.
So, we went and found Jacynth at the entry
Of the lady's chamber standing sentry;
I told the command and produced my companion,
And Jacynth rejoiced to admit any one,
For since last night, by the same token,
Not a single word had the lady spoken:
They went in both to the presence together,
While I in the balcony watched the weather.

XV

And now, what took place at the very first of all
I cannot tell, as I never could learn it:
Jacynth constantly wished a curse to fall
On that little head of hers and burn it,
If she knew how she came to drop so soundly
Asleep of a sudden and there continue
The whole time sleeping as profoundly
As one of the boars my father would pin you
'Twixt the eyes where life holds garrison,
—Jacynth forgive me the comparison!
But where I begin my own narration
Is a little after I took my station
To breathe the fresh air from the balcony,
And, having in those days a falcon eye,
To follow the hunt through the open country,
From where the bushes thinlier crested
The hillocks, to a plain where's not one tree.
When, in a moment, my ear was arrested
By—was it singing, or was it saying,
Or a strange musical instrument playing
In the chamber?—and to be certain
I pushed the lattice, pulled the curtain,
And there lay Jacynth asleep,
Yet as if a watch she tried to keep,
In a rosy sleep along the floor
With her head against the door;
While in the midst, on the seat of state,
Was a queen—the Gypsy woman late,
With head and face downbent
On the lady's head and face intent:
For, coiled at her feet like a child at ease,
The lady sat between her knees,
And o'er them the lady's clasped hands met,
And on those hands her chin was set,
And her upturned face met the face of the crone

Wherein the eyes had grown and grown
As if she could double and quadruple
At pleasure the play of either pupil
—Very like, by her hands' slow fanning,
As up and down like a gor-crow's flappers
They moved to measure, or bell clappers.
I said, "Is it blessing, is it banning,
Do they applaud you or burlesque you—
Those hands and fingers with no flesh on?"
But, just as I thought to spring in to the rescue,
At once I was stopped by the lady's expression:
For it was life her eyes were drinking
From the crone's wide pair above unwinking,
—Life's pure fire received without shrinking,
Into the heart and breast whose heaving
Told you no single drop they were leaving,
—Life, that filling her, passed redundant
Into her very hair, back swerving
Over each shoulder, loose and abundant,
As her head thrown back showed the white throat curving;
And the very tresses shared in the pleasure,
Moving to the mystic measure,
Bounding as the bosom bounded.
I stopped short, more and more confounded,
As still her cheeks burned and eyes glistened,
As she listened and she listened:
When all at once a hand detained me,
The selfsame contagion gained me,
And I kept time to the wondrous chime,
Making out words and prose and rhyme,
Till it seemed that the music furled
Its wings like a task fulfilled, and dropped
From under the words it first had propped,
And left them midway in the world:
Word took word as hand takes hand,
I could hear at last, and understand,

And when I held the unbroken thread,
The Gypsy said:—

"And so at last we find my tribe.
And so I set thee in the midst,
And to one and all of them describe
What thou saidst and what thou didst,
Our long and terrible journey through,
And all thou art ready to say and do
In the trials that remain:
I trace them the vein and the other vein
That meet on thy brow and part again,
Making our rapid mystic mark;
And I bid my people prove and probe
Each eye's profound and glorious globe
Till they detect the kindred spark
In those depths so dear and dark,
Like the spots that snap and burst and flee,
Circling over the midnight sea.
And on that round young cheek of thine
I make them recognize the tinge,
As when of the costly scarlet wine
They drip so much as will impinge
And spread in a thinnest scale afloat
One thick gold drop from the olive's coat
Over a silver plate whose sheen
Still through the mixture shall be seen.
For so I prove thee, to one and all,
Fit, when my people ope their breast,
To see the sign, and hear the call,
And take the vow, and stand the test
Which adds one more child to the rest—
When the breast is bare and the arms are wide
And the world is left outside.
For there is probation to decree,
And many and long must the trials be

Thou shalt victoriously endure,
If that brow is true and those eyes are sure;
Like a jewel-finder's fierce assay
Of the prize he dug from its mountain tomb—
Let once the vindicating ray
Leap out amid the anxious gloom,
And steel and fire have done their part
And the prize falls on its finder's heart;
So, trial after trial past,
Wilt thou fall at the very last
Breathless, half in trance
With the thrill of the great deliverance,
Into our arms forevermore;
And thou shalt know, those arms once curled
About thee, what we knew before,
How love is the only good in the world.
Henceforth be loved as heart can love,
Or brain devise, or hand approve!
Stand up, look below,
It is our life at thy feet we throw
To step with into light and joy;
Not a power of life but we employ
To satisfy thy nature's want;
Art thou the tree that props the plant,
Or the climbing plant that seeks the tree—
Canst thou help us, must we help thee?
If any two creatures grew into one,
They would do more than the world has done:
Though each apart were never so weak,
Ye vainly through the world should seek
For the knowledge and the might
Which in such union grew their right:
So, to approach at least that end,
And blend,—as much as may be, blend
Thee with us or us with thee,—
As climbing plant or propping tree,

Shall some one deck thee, over and down,
Up and about, with blossoms and leaves?
Fix his heart's fruit for thy garland-crown,
Cling with his soul as the gourd-vine cleaves,
Die on thy boughs and disappear
While not a leaf of thine is sere?
Or is the other fate in store,
And art thou fitted to adore,
To give thy wondrous self away,
And take a stronger nature's sway?
I foresee and could foretell
Thy future portion, sure and well:
But those passionate eyes speak true, speak true,
Let them say what thou shalt do!
Only be sure thy daily life,
In its peace or in its strife,
Never shall be unobserved;
We pursue thy whole career,
And hope for it, or doubt, or fear.—
Lo, hast thou kept thy path or swerved,
We are beside thee in all thy ways,
With our blame, with our praise,
Our shame to feel, our pride to show,
Glad, angry—but indifferent, no!
Whether it be thy lot to go,
For the good of us all, where the haters meet
In the crowded city's horrible street;
Or thou step alone through the morass
Where never sound yet was
Save the dry quick clap of the stork's bill,
For the air is still, and the water still,
When the blue breast of the dipping coot
Dives under, and all is mute.
So, at the last shall come old age,
Decrepit as befits that stage;
How else wouldst thou retire apart

With the hoarded memories of thy heart,
And gather all to the very least
Of the fragments of life's earlier feast,
Let fall through eagerness to find
The crowning dainties yet behind?
Ponder on the entire past
Laid together thus at last,
When the twilight helps to fuse
The first fresh with the faded hues,
And the outline of the whole,
As round eve's shades their framework roll,
Grandly fronts for once thy soul.
And then as, 'mid the dark, a gleam
Of yet another morning breaks,
And like the hand which ends a dream,
Death, with the might of his sunbeam,
Touches the flesh and the soul awakes,
Then"—
       Ay, then indeed something would happen!
But what? For here her voice changed like a bird's;
There grew more of the music and less of the words;
Had Jacynth only been by me to clap pen
To paper and put you down every syllable
With those clever clerkly fingers,
All I've forgotten as well as what lingers
In this old brain of mine that's but ill able
To give you even this poor version
Of the speech I spoil, as it were, with stammering
—More fault of those who had the hammering
Of prosody into me and syntax,
And did it, not with hobnails but tintacks!
But to return from this excursion,—
Just, do you mark, when the song was sweetest,
The peace most deep and the charm completest,
There came, shall I say, a snap—
And the charm vanished!

And my sense returned, so strangely banished,
And, starting as from a nap,
I knew the crone was bewitching my lady,
With Jacynth asleep; and but one spring made I
Down from the casement, round to the portal,
Another minute and I had entered,—
When the door opened, and more than mortal
Stood, with a face where to my mind centred
All beauties I ever saw or shall see,
The Duchess: I stopped as if struck by palsy.
She was so different, happy and beautiful,
I felt at once that all was best,
And that I had nothing to do, for the rest,
But wait her commands, obey and be dutiful.
Not that, in fact, there was any commanding;
I saw the glory of her eye,
And the brow's height and the breast's expanding,
And I was hers to live or to die.
As for finding what she wanted,
You know God Almighty granted
Such little signs should serve wild creatures
To tell one another all their desires,
So that each knows what his friend requires,
And does its bidding without teachers.
I preceded her; the crone
Followed silent and alone;
I spoke to her, but she merely jabbered
In the old style; both her eyes had slunk
Back to their pits; her stature shrunk;
In short, the soul in its body sunk
Like a blade sent home to its scabbard.
We descended, I preceding;
Crossed the court with nobody heeding;
All the world was at the chase,
The court-yard like a desert-place,
The stable emptied of its small fry;

I saddled myself the very palfrey
I remember patting while it carried her,
The day she arrived and the Duke married her.
And, do you know, though it's easy deceiving
One's self in such matters, I can't help believing
The lady had not forgotten it either,
And knew the poor devil so much beneath her
Would have been only too glad for her service
To dance on hot ploughshares like a Turk dervise,
But, unable to pay proper duty where owing it,
Was reduced to that pitiful method of showing it:
For though the moment I began setting
His saddle on my own nag of Berold's begetting,
 (Not that I meant to be obtrusive)
She stopped me, while his rug was shifting,
By a single rapid finger's lifting,
And, with a gesture kind but conclusive,
And a little shake of the head, refused me.—
I say, although she never used me,
Yet when she was mounted, the Gypsy behind her,
And I ventured to remind her,
I suppose with a voice of less steadiness
Than usual, for my feeling exceeded me,
—Something to the effect that I was in readiness
Whenever God should please she needed me,—
Then, do you know, her face looked down on me
With a look that placed a crown on me,
And she felt in her bosom,—mark, her bosom—
And, as a flower-tree drops its blossom,
Dropped me . . . ah, had it been a purse
Of silver, my friend, or gold that's worse,
Why, you see, as soon as I found myself
So understood,—that a true heart so may gain
Such a reward,—I should have gone home again,
Kissed Jacynth, and soberly drowned myself!
It was a little plait of hair

Such as friends in a convent make
To wear, each for the other's sake,—
This, see, which at my breast I wear,
Ever did (rather to Jacynth's grudgment),
And ever shall, till the Day of Judgment.
And then,—and then,—to cut short,—this is idle,
These are feelings it is not good to foster,—
I pushed the gate wide, she shook the bridle,
And the palfrey bounded,—and so we lost her.

XVI

When the liquor's out why clink the cannikin?
I did think to describe you the panic in
The redoubtable breast of our master the mannikin,
And what was the pitch of his mother's yellowness,
How she turned as a shark to snap the sparerib
Clean off, sailors say, from a pearl-diving Carib,
When she heard, what she called the flight of the feloness
—But it seems such child's play,
What they said and did with the lady away!
And to dance on, when we've lost the music,
Always made me—and no doubt makes you—sick.
Nay, to my mind, the world's face looked so stern
As that sweet form disappeared through the postern,
She that kept it in constant good-humor,
It ought to have stopped; there seemed nothing to do more.
But the world thought otherwise and went on,
And my head's one that its spite was spent on:
Thirty years are fled since that morning,
And with them all my head's adorning.
Nor did the old Duchess die outright,
As you expect, of suppressed spite,
The natural end of every adder
Not suffered to empty its poison-bladder:
But she and her son agreed, I take it,
That no one should touch on the story to wake it,

For the wound in the Duke's pride rankled fiery,
So, they made no search and small inquiry—
And when fresh Gypsies have paid us a visit, I've
Noticed the couple were never inquisitive,
But told them they're folks the Duke don't want here,
And bade them make haste and cross the frontier.
Brief, the Duchess was gone and the Duke was glad of it,
And the old one was in the young one's stead,
And took, in her place, the household's head,
And a blessed time the household had of it!
And were I not, as a man may say, cautious
How I trench, more than needs, on the nauseous,
I could favor you with sundry touches
Of the paint-smutches with which the Duchess
Heightened the mellowness of her cheek's yellowness
(To get on faster) until at last her
Cheek grew to be one master-plaster
Of mucus and fucus from mere use of ceruse:
In short, she grew from scalp to udder
Just the object to make you shudder.

XVII

You're my friend—
What a thing friendship is, world without end!
How it gives the heart and soul a stir-up
As if somebody broached you a glorious runlet,
And poured out, all lovelily, sparklingly, sunlit,
Our green Moldavia, the streaky syrup,
Cotnar as old as the time of the Druids—
Friendship may match with that monarch of fluids;
Each supples a dry brain, fills you its ins-and-outs,
Gives your life's hour-glass a shake when the thin sand
    doubts
Whether to run on or stop short, and guarantees
Age is not all made of stark sloth and arrant ease.
I have seen my little lady once more,

Jacynth, the Gypsy, Berold, and the rest of it,
For to me spoke the Duke, as I told you before;
I always wanted to make a clean breast of it:
And now it is made—why, my heart's blood, that went
    trickle,
Trickle, but anon, in such muddy driblets,
Is pumped up brisk now, through the main ventricle,
And genially floats me about the giblets.
I'll tell you what I intend to do:
I must see this fellow his sad life through—
He is our Duke, after all,
And I, as he says, but a serf and thrall.
My father was born here, and I inherit
His fame, a chain he bound his son with;
Could I pay in a lump I should prefer it,
But there's no mine to blow up and get done with:
So, I must stay till the end of the chapter,
For, as to our middle-age-manners-adapter,
Be it a thing to be glad on or sorry on,
Some day or other, his head in a morion
And breast in a hauberk, his heels he'll kick up
Slain by an onslaught fierce of hiccup.
And then, when red doth the sword of our Duke rust,
And its leathern sheath lie o'ergrown with a blue crust,
Then I shall scrape together my earnings;
For, you see, in the churchyard Jacynth reposes,
And our children all went the way of the roses:
It's a long lane that knows no turnings.
One needs but little tackle to travel in;
So, just one stout cloak shall I indue:
And for a staff, what beats the javelin
With which his boars my father pinned you?
And then, for a purpose you shall hear presently,
Taking some Cotnar, a tight plump skinful,
I shall go journeying, who but I, pleasantly!
Sorrow is vain and despondency sinful.

What's a man's age?   He must hurry more, that's all;
Cram in a day, what his youth took a year to hold:
When we mind labor, then only, we're too old—
What age had Methusalem when he begat Saul?
And at last, as its haven some buffeted ship sees,
 (Come all the way from the north-parts with sperm oil)
I hope to get safely out of the turmoil
And arrive one day at the land of the Gypsies,
And find my lady, or hear the last news of her
From some old thief and son of Lucifer,
His forehead chapleted green with wreathy hop,
Sunburned all over like an Æthiop.
And when my Cotnar begins to operate
And the tongue of the rogue to run at a proper rate,
And our wine-skin, tight once, shows each flaccid dent,
I shall drop in with—as if by accident—
"You never knew, then, how it all ended,
What fortune good or bad attended
The little lady your Queen befriended?"
—And when that's told me, what's remaining?
This world's too hard for my explaining.
The same wise judge of matters equine
Who still preferred some slim four-year-old
To the big-boned stock of mighty Berold,
And, for strong Cotnar, drank French weak wine,
He also must be such a lady's scorner!
Smooth Jacob still robs homely Esau:
Now up, now down, the world's one see-saw.
—So, I shall find out some snug corner
Under a hedge, like Orson the wood-knight,
Turn myself round and bid the world good-night;
And sleep a sound sleep till the trumpet's blowing
Wakes me (unless priests cheat us laymen)
To a world where will be no further throwing
Pearls before swine that can't value them. Amen!

EARTH'S IMMORTALITIES

FAME

SEE, as the prettiest graves will do in time,
Our poet's wants the freshness of its prime;
Spite of the sexton's browsing horse, the sods
Have struggled through its binding osier rods
Headstone and half-sunk footstone lean awry,
Wanting the brick-work promised by-and-by;
How the minute gray lichens, plate o'er plate,
Have softened down the crisp-cut name and date!

LOVE

So, the year's done with!
    (*Love me forever!*)
All March begun with,
    April's endeavor;
May-wreaths that bound me
    June needs must sever;
Now snows fall round me,
    Quenching June's fever—
        (*Love me forever!*)

SONG

NAY but you, who do not love her,
    Is she not pure gold, my mistress?
Holds earth aught—speak truth—above her?
    Aught like this tress, see, and this tress,
And this last fairest tress of all,
So fair, see, ere I let it fall?

Because you spend your lives in praising;
    To praise, you search the wide world over:

Then why not witness, calmly gazing,
    If earth holds aught—speak truth—above her?
Above this tress, and this, I touch
But cannot praise, I love so much!

MEETING AT NIGHT

THE gray sea and the long black land;
And the yellow half-moon large and low;
And the startled little waves that leap
In fiery ringlets from their sleep,
As I gain the cove with pushing prow,
And quench its speed i' the slushy sand.

Then a mile of warm sea-scented beach;
Three fields to cross till a farm appears;
A tap at the pane, the quick sharp scratch
And blue spurt of a lighted match,
And a voice less loud, through its joys and fears,
Than the two hearts beating each to each!

PARTING AT MORNING

ROUND the cape of a sudden came the sea,
    And the sun looked over the mountain's rim:
    And straight was a path of gold for him,
    And the need of a world of men for me.

SAUL

I

SAID Abner, "At last thou art come!   Ere I tell, ere thou
    speak,
Kiss my cheek, wish me well!"   Then I wished it, and did
    kiss his cheek.

And he, "Since the King, O my friend, for thy countenance sent,
Neither drunken nor eaten have we; nor until from his
tent
Thou return with the joyful assurance the King liveth
yet,
Shall our lip with the honey be bright, with the water
be wet.
For out of the black mid-tent's silence, a space of three
days,
Not a sound hath escaped to thy servants, of prayer nor
of praise,
To betoken that Saul and the Spirit have ended their
strife,
And that, faint in his triumph, the monarch sinks back
upon life.

II

"Yet now my heart leaps, O beloved! God's child with
his dew
On thy gracious gold hair, and those lilies still living
and blue
Just broken to twine round thy harp-strings, as if no
wild heat
Were now raging to torture the desert!"

III

Then I, as was meet,
Knelt down to the God of my fathers, and rose on my
feet,
And ran o'er the sand burnt to powder. The tent was
unlooped;
I pulled up the spear that obstructed, and under I
stooped;
Hands and knees on the slippery grass-patch, all withered
and gone,

That extends to the second enclosure, I groped my way on
Till I felt where the foldskirts fly open. Then once
    more I prayed,
And opened the foldskirts and entered, and was not
    afraid
But spoke, "Here is David, thy servant!" And no voice
    replied.
At the first I saw naught but the blackness: but soon I
    descried
A something more black than the blackness—the vast,
    the upright
Main prop which sustains the pavilion: and slow into
    sight
Grew a figure against it, gigantic and blackest of all.
Then a sunbeam, that burst through the tentroof,
    showed Saul.

IV

He stood as erect as that tent-prop, both arms stretched
    out wide
On the great cross-support in the centre, that goes to
    each side;
He relaxed not a muscle, but hung there as, caught in
    his pangs
And waiting his change, the king-serpent all heavily
    hangs,
Far away from his kind, in the pine, till deliverance
    come
With the spring-time,—so agonized Saul, drear and stark,
    blind and dumb.

V

Then I tuned my harp,—took off the lilies we twine round
    its chords
Lest they snap 'neath the stress of the noontide—those
    sunbeams like swords!

And I first played the tune all our sheep know, as, one
after one,
So docile they come to the pen-door till folding be done.
They are white and untorn by the bushes, for lo, they
have fed
Where the long grasses stifle the water within the stream's
bed;
And now one after one seeks its lodging, as star follows
star
Into eve and the blue far above us,—so blue and so far!

VI

—Then the tune for which quails on the cornland will
each leave his mate
To fly after the player; then, what makes the crickets
elate
Till for boldness they fight one another; and then, what
has weight
To set the quick jerboa a-musing outside his sand house—
There are none such as he for a wonder, half bird and
half mouse!
God made all the creatures and gave them our love and
our fear,
To give sign, we and they are his children, one family
here.

VII

Then I played the help-tune of our reapers, their wine-
song, when hand
Grasps at hand, eye lights eye in good friendship, and
great hearts expand
And grow one in the sense of this world's life.—And then,
the last song
When the dead man is praised on his journey—"Bear,
bear him along,

With his few faults shut up like dead flowerets! Are
    balm seeds not here
To console us? The land has none left such as he on the
    bier.
Oh, would we might keep thee, my brother!"—And then,
    the glad chaunt
Of the marriage,—first go the young maidens, next, she
    whom we vaunt
As the beauty, the pride of our dwelling.—And then, the
    great march
Wherein man runs to man to assist him and buttress an
    arch
Naught can break; who shall harm them, our friends?
    Then, the chorus intoned
As the Levites go up to the altar in glory enthroned.
But I stopped here: for here in the darkness Saul groaned.

VIII

And I paused, held my breath in such silence, and listened
    apart;
And the tent shook, for mighty Saul shuddered: and
    sparkles 'gan dart
From the jewels that woke in his turban, at once with
    a start,
All its lordly male-sapphires, and rubies courageous at
    heart.
So the head: but the body still moved not, still hung there
    erect.
And I bent once again to my playing, pursued it un-
    checked,
As I sang:—

IX

    "Oh, our manhood's prime vigor! No spirit feels
    waste,
Not a muscle is stopped in its playing nor sinew un-
    braced.

Oh, the wild joys of living! the leaping from rock up to
  rock,
The strong rending of boughs from the fir-tree, the cool
  silver shock
Of the plunge in a pool's living water, the hunt of the
  bear,
And the sultriness showing the lion is couched in his
  lair.
And the meal, the rich dates yellowed over with gold
  dust divine,
And the locust-flesh steeped in the pitcher, the full
  draught of wine,
And the sleep in the dried river-channel where bul-
  rushes tell
That the water was wont to go warbling so softly and
  well.
How good is man's life, the mere living! how fit to employ
All the heart and the soul and the senses forever in joy!
Hast thou loved the white locks of thy father, whose
  sword thou didst guard
When he trusted thee forth with the armies, for glorious
  reward?
Didst thou see the thin hands of thy mother held up as
  men sung
The low song of the nearly-departed, and hear her faint
  tongue
Joining in while it could to the witness, 'Let one more
  attest,
I have lived, seen God's hand through a lifetime, and all
  was for best'?
Then they sung through their tears in strong triumph,
  not much, but the rest.
And thy brothers, the help and the contest, the working
  whence grew
Such result as, from seething grape-bundles, the spirit
  strained true:

And the friends of thy boyhood—that boyhood of wonder
    and hope,
Present promise and wealth of the future beyond the eye's
    scope,—
Till lo, thou art grown to a monarch; a people is thine;
And all gifts, which the world offers singly, on one head
    combine!
On one head, all the beauty and strength, love and rage
    (like the throe
That, a-work in the rock, helps its labor and lets the
    gold go)
High ambition and deeds which surpass it, fame crown-
    ing them,—all
Brought to blaze on the head of one creature—King
    Saul!"

x

And lo, with that leap of my spirit,—heart, hand, harp
    and voice,
Each lifting Saul's name out of sorrow, each bidding
    rejoice
Saul's fame in the light it was made for—as when, dare
    I say,
The Lord's army, in rapture of service, strains through
    its array,
And upsoareth the cherubim-chariot—"Saul!" cried I, and
    stopped,
And waited the thing that should follow. Then Saul,
    who hung propped
By the tent's cross-support in the centre, was struck by
    his name.
Have ye seen when Spring's arrowy summons goes right
    to the aim,
And some mountain, the last to withstand her, that held
    (he alone,

While the vale laughed in freedom and flowers) on a
    broad bust of stone
A year's snow bound about for a breastplate,—leaves grasp
    of the sheet?
Fold on fold all at once it crowds thunderously down
    to his feet,
And there fronts you, stark, black, but alive yet, your
    mountain of old,
With his rents, the successive bequeathings of ages un-
    told—
Yea, each harm got in fighting your battles, each furrow
    and scar
Of his head thrust 'twixt you and the tempest—all hail,
    there they are!
—Now again to be softened with verdure, again hold the
    nest
Of the dove, tempt the goat and its young to the green
    on his crest
For their food in the ardors of summer. One long
    shudder thrilled
All the tent till the very air tingled, then sank and was
    stilled
At the King's self left standing before me, released and
    aware.
What was gone, what remained? All to traverse 'twixt
    hope and despair,
Death was past, life not come: so he waited. Awhile his
    right hand
Held the brow, helped the eyes left too vacant forthwith
    to remand
To their place what new objects should enter: 't was
    Saul as before.
I looked up and dared gaze at those eyes, nor was hurt
    any more
Than by slow pallid sunsets in autumn, ye watch from
    the shore,

At their sad level gaze o'er the ocean—a sun's slow decline
Over hills which, resolved in stern silence, o'erlap and
    entwine
Base with base to knit strength more intensely: so, arm
    folded arm
O'er the chest whose slow heavings subsided.

XI

                What spell or what charm,
(For awhile there was trouble within me,) what next
    should I urge
To sustain him where song had restored him?—Song
    filled to the verge
His cup with the wine of this life, pressing all that it
    yields
Of mere fruitage, the strength and the beauty: beyond,
    on what fields,
Glean a vintage more potent and perfect to brighten the
    eye
And bring blood to the lip, and commend them the cup
    they put by?
He saith, "It is good;" still he drinks not: he lets me
    praise life,
Gives assent, yet would die for his own part.

XII

                Then fancies grew rife
Which had come long ago on the pasture, when round
    me the sheep
Fed in silence—above, the one eagle wheeled slow as in
    sleep;
And I lay in my hollow and mused on the world that
    might lie
'Neath his ken, though I saw but the strip 'twixt the hill
    and the sky:

And I laughed—"Since my days are ordained to be passed
    with my flocks,
Let me people at least, with my fancies, the plains and
    the rocks,
Dream the life I am never to mix with, and image the
    show
Of mankind as they live in those fashions I hardly shall
    know!
Schemes of life, its best rules and right uses, the courage
    that gains,
And the prudence that keeps what men strive for."
    And now these old trains
Of vague thought came again; I grew surer; so, once more
    the string
Of my harp made response to my spirit, as thus—

XIII

                "Yea, my King,"
I began—"thou dost well in rejecting mere comforts that
    spring
From the mere mortal life held in common by man and
    by brute:
In our flesh grows the branch of this life, in our soul it
    bears fruit.
Thou hast marked the slow rise of the tree,—how its stem
    trembled first
Till it passed the kid's lip, the stag's antler; then safely
    outburst
The fan-branches all round; and thou mindest when
    these too, in turn,
Broke a-bloom and the palm-tree seemed perfect: yet more
    was to learn,
E'en the good that comes in with the palm-fruit. Our
    dates shall we slight,
When their juice brings a cure for all sorrow? or care
    for the plight

Of the palm's self whose slow growth produced them?
    Not so! stem and branch
Shall decay, nor be known in their place, while the palm-
    wine shall stanch
Every wound of man's spirit in winter. I pour thee such
    wine.
Leave the flesh to the fate it was fit for! the spirit be thine!
By the spirit, when age shall o'ercome thee, thou still
    shalt enjoy
More indeed, than at first when inconscious, the life of a
    boy.
Crush that life, and behold its wine running! Each
    deed thou hast done
Dies, revives, goes to work in the world; until e'en as the
    sun
Looking down on the earth, though clouds spoil him,
    though tempests efface,
Can find nothing his own deed produced not, must
    everywhere trace
The results of his past summer-prime,—so, each ray of
    thy will,
Every flash of thy passion and prowess, long over, shall
    thrill
Thy whole people, the countless, with ardor, till they
    too give forth
A like cheer to their sons, who in turn, fill the South
    and the North
With the radiance thy deed was the germ of. Carouse
    in the past!
But the license of age has its limit; thou diest at last:
As the lion when age dims his eyeball, the rose at her
    height,
So with man—so his power and his beauty forever take
    flight.
No! Again a long draught of my soul-wine! Look forth
    o'er the years!

Thou hast done now with eyes for the actual; begin with
  the seer's!
Is Saul dead? In the depth of the vale make his tomb—
  bid arise
A gray mountain of marble heaped four-square, till,
  built to the skies,
Let it mark where the great First King slumbers: whose
  fame would ye know?
Up above see the rock's naked face, where the record
  shall go
In great characters cut by the scribe,—Such was Saul,
  so he did;
With the sages directing the work, by the populace
  chid,—
For not half, they'll affirm, is comprised there! Which
  fault to amend,
In the grove with his kind grows the cedar, whereon they
  shall spend
 (See, in tablets 'tis level before them) their praise, and
  record
With the gold of the graver, Saul's story,—the statesman's
  great word
Side by side with the poet's sweet comment. The river's
  a-wave
With smooth paper-reeds grazing each other when
  prophet-winds rave:
So the pen gives unborn generations their due and their
  part
In thy being! Then, first of the mighty, thank God that
  thou art!"

XIV

And behold while I sang . . . but O Thou who didst
  grant me that day,
And before it not seldom hast granted thy help to essay,
Carry on and complete an adventure,—my shield and my
  sword

In that act where my soul was thy servant, thy word was
    my word,—
Still be with me, who then at the summit of human
    endeavor
And scaling the highest, man's thought could, gazed
    hopeless as ever
On the new stretch of heaven above me—till, mighty to
    save,
Just one lift of thy hand cleared that distance—God's
    throne from man's grave!
Let me tell out my tale to its ending—my voice to my
    heart
Which can scarce dare believe in what marvels last night
    I took part,
As this morning I gather the fragments, alone with my
    sheep,
And still fear lest the terrible glory evanish like sleep!
For I wake in the gray dewy covert, while Hebron up-
    heaves
The dawn struggling with night on his shoulder, and
    Kidron retrieves
Slow the damage of yesterday's sunshine.

XV

                        I say then,—my song
While I sang thus, assuring the monarch, and ever more
    strong
Made a proffer of good to console him—he slowly resumed
His old motions and habitudes kingly. The right hand
    replumed
His black locks to their wonted composure, adjusted the
    swathes
Of his turban, and see—the huge sweat that his counte-
    nance bathes,
He wipes off with the robe; and he girds now his loins
    as of yore,

And feels slow for the armlets of price, with the clasp
    set before.

He is Saul, ye remember in glory,—ere error had bent

The broad brow from the daily communion; and still,
    though much spent

Be the life and the bearing that front you, the same,
    God did choose,

To receive what a man may waste, desecrate, never quite
    lose.

So sank he along by the tent-prop till, stayed by the pile

Of his armor and war-cloak and garments, he leaned
    there awhile,

And sat out my singing,—one arm round the tent-prop,
    to raise

His bent head, and the other hung slack—till I touched
    on the praise

I foresaw from all men in all time, to the man patient
    there;

And thus ended, the harp falling forward. Then first I
    was 'ware

That he sat, as I say, with my head just above his vast
    knees

Which were thrust out on each side around me, like oak
    roots which please

To encircle a lamb when it slumbers. I looked up to
    know

If the best I could do had brought solace: he spoke not,
    but slow

Lifted up the hand slack at his side, till he laid it with
    care

Soft and grave, but in mild settled will, on my brow:
    through my hair

The large fingers were pushed, and he bent back my
    head, with kind power—

All my face back, intent to peruse it, as men do a flower.

Thus held he me there with his great eyes that scrutinized
    mine—
And oh, all my heart how it loved him! but where was
    the sign?
I yearned—"Could I help thee, my father, inventing a
    bliss,
I would add, to that life of the past, both the future and
    this;
I would give thee new life altogether, as good, ages hence,
As this moment,—had love but the warrant, love's heart
    to dispense!"

XVI

Then the truth came upon me. No harp more—no song
    more! outbroke—

XVII

"I have gone the whole round of creation: I saw and I
    spoke:
I, a work of God's hand for that purpose, received in my
    brain
And pronounced on the rest of his handwork—returned
    him again
His creation's approval or censure: I spoke as I saw:
I report, as a man may of God's work—all's love, yet all's
    law.
Now I lay down the judgeship he lent me. Each faculty
    tasked
To perceive him, has gained an abyss, where a dewdrop
    was asked.
Have I knowledge? confounded it shrivels at Wisdom
    laid bare.
Have I forethought? how purblind, how blank, to the
    Infinite Care!
Do I task any faculty highest, to image success?
I but open my eyes,—and perfection, no more and no less,

In the kind I imagined, full-fronts me, and God is seen
    God
In the star, in the stone, in the flesh, in the soul and the
    clod.
And thus looking within and around me, I ever renew
(With that stoop of the soul which in bending upraises
    it too)
The submission of man's nothing-perfect to God's all-
    complete,
As by each new obeisance in spirit, I climb to his feet.
Yet with all this abounding experience, this deity known,
I shall dare to discover some province, some gift of my
    own.
There's a faculty pleasant to exercise, hard to hoodwink,
I am fain to keep still in abeyance, (I laugh as I think)
Lest, insisting to claim and parade in it, wot ye, I worst
E'en the Giver in one gift.—Behold, I could love if I
    durst!
But I sink the pretension as fearing a man may o'ertake
God's own speed in the one way of love: I abstain for
    love's sake.
—What, my soul? see thus far and no farther? when doors
    great and small,
Nine-and-ninety flew ope at our touch, should the
    hundredth appall?
In the least things have faith, yet distrust in the greatest
    of all?
Do I find love so full in my nature, God's ultimate gift,
That I doubt his own love can compete with it? Here,
    the parts shift?
Here, the creature surpass the Creator,—the end, what
    Began?
Would I fain in my impotent yearning do all for this
    man,
And dare doubt he alone shall not help him, who yet
    alone can?

Would it ever have entered my mind, the bare will, much
  less power,
To bestow on this Saul what I sang of, the marvellous
  dower
Of the life he was gifted and filled with? to make such
  a soul,
Such a body, and then such an earth for insphering the
  whole?
And doth it not enter my mind (as my warm tears attest)
These good things being given, to go on, and give one
  more, the best?
Ay, to save and redeem and restore him, maintain at
  the height
This perfection,—succeed with life's day-spring, death's
  minute of night?
Interpose at the difficult minute, snatch Saul the mistake,
Saul the failure, the ruin he seems now,—and bid him
  awake
From the dream, the probation, the prelude, to find
  himself set
Clear and safe in new light and new life,—a new harmony
  yet
To be run, and continued, and ended—who knows?—or
  endure!
The man taught enough by life's dream, of the rest to
  make sure;
By the pain-throb, triumphantly winning intensified
  bliss,
And the next world's reward and repose, by the struggles
  in this.

XVIII

"I believe it!   'T is thou, God, that givest, 'tis I who
  receive:
In the first is the last, in thy will is my power to believe.

All's one gift: thou canst grant it moreover, as prompt to
    my prayer
As I breathe out this breath, as I open these arms to
    the air.
From thy will stream the worlds, life and nature, thy
    dread Sabaoth:
I will?—the mere atoms despise me!   Why am I not loth
To look that, even that in the face too?   Why is it I dare
Think but lightly of such impuissance?   What stops my
    despair?
This;—'tis not what man Does which exalts him, but
    what man Would do!
See the King—I would help him but cannot, the wishes
    fall through.
Could I wrestle to raise him from sorrow, grow poor to
    enrich,
To fill up his life, starve my own out, I would—knowing
    which,
I know that my service is perfect.   Oh, speak through me
    now!
Would I suffer for him that I love?   So wouldst thou—so
    wilt thou!
So shall crown thee the topmost, ineffablest, uttermost
    crown—
And thy love fill infinitude wholly, nor leave up nor
    down
One spot for the creature to stand in!   It is by no breath,
Turn of eye, wave of hand, that salvation joins issue
    with death!
As thy Love is discovered almighty, almighty be proved
Thy power, that exists with and for it, of being Beloved!
He who did most, shall bear most; the strongest shall
    stand the most weak.
'Tis the weakness in strength, that I cry for! my flesh,
    that I seek
In the Godhead!   I seek and I find it.   O Saul, it shall be

A Face like my face that receives thee; a Man like to me,
Thou shalt love and be loved by, forever: a Hand like
    this hand
Shall throw open the gates of new life to thee!   See the
    Christ stand!"

XIX

I know not too well how I found my way home in the
    night.
There were witnesses, cohorts about me, to left and to
    right,
Angels, powers, the unuttered, unseen, the alive, the
    aware:
I repressed, I got through them as hardly, as strugglingly
    there,
As a runner beset by the populace famished for news—
Life or death.   The whole earth was awakened, hell
    loosed with her crews;
And the stars of night beat with emotion, and tingled
    and shot
Out in fire the strong pain of pent knowledge: but I
    fainted not,
For the Hand still impelled me at once and supported,
    suppressed
All the tumult, and quenched it with quiet, and holy
    behest,
Till the rapture was shut in itself, and the earth sank
    to rest.
Anon at the dawn, all that trouble had withered from
    earth—
Not so much, but I saw it die out in the day's tender
    birth;
In the gathered intensity brought to the gray of the hills;
In the shuddering forests' held breath; in the sudden
    wind-thrills;

In the startled wild beasts that bore off, each with eye
    sidling still
Though averted with wonder and dread; in the birds
    stiff and chill
That rose heavily, as I approached them, made stupid
    with awe:
E'en the serpent that slid away silent,—he felt the new
    law.
The same stared in the white humid faces upturned by
    the flowers;
The same worked in the heart of the cedar and moved
    the vine-bowers:
And the little brooks witnessing murmured, persistent
    and low,
With their obstinate, all but hushed voices—"E'en so,
    it is so!"

THE GLOVE

(PETER RONSARD *loquitur.*)

"HEIGHO," yawned one day King Francis,
"Distance all value enhances!
When a man's busy, why, leisure
Strikes him as wonderful pleasure:
'Faith, and at leisure once is he?
Straightway he wants to be busy.
Here we've got peace; and aghast I'm
Caught thinking war the true pastime.
Is there a reason in metre?
Give us your speech, master Peter!"
I who, if mortal dare say so,
Ne'er am at loss with my Naso,
"Sire," I replied, "joys prove cloudlets:
Men are the merest Ixions"—
Here the King whistled aloud, "Let's

—Heigho—go look at our lions!"
Such are the sorrowful chances
If you talk fine to King Francis.

And so, to the courtyard proceeding
Our company, Francis was leading,
Increased by new followers tenfold
Before he arrived at the penfold;
Lords, ladies, like clouds which bedizen
At sunset the western horizon.
And Sir De Lorge pressed 'mid the foremost
With the dame he professed to adore most.
Oh, what a face!   One by fits eyed
Her, and the horrible pitside;
For the penfold surrounded a hollow
Which led where the eye scarce dared follow,
And shelved to the chamber secluded
Where Bluebeard, the great lion, brooded.
The King hailed his keeper, an Arab
As glossy and black as a scarab,
And bade him make sport and at once stir
Up and out of his den the old monster.
They opened a hole in the wire-work
Across it, and dropped there a firework,
And fled: one's heart's beating redoubled;
A pause, while the pit's mouth was troubled,
The blackness and silence so utter,
By the firework's slow sparkling and sputter;
Then earth in a sudden contortion
Gave out to our gaze her abortion.
Such a brute!   Were I friend Clement Marot
 (Whose experience of nature's but narrow,
And whose faculties move in no small mist
When he versifies David the Psalmist)
I should study that brute to describe you
Illum Juda Leonem de Tribu.

One's whole blood grew curdling and creepy
To see the black mane, vast and heapy,
The tail in the air stiff and straining,
The wide eyes, nor waxing nor waning,
As over the barrier which bounded
His platform, and us who surrounded
The barrier, they reached and they rested
On space that might stand him in best stead:
For who knew, he thought, what the amazement,
The eruption of clatter and blaze meant,
And if, in this minute of wonder,
No outlet, 'mid lightning and thunder,
Lay broad, and, his shackles all shivered,
The lion at last was delivered?
Ay, that was the open sky o'erhead!
And you saw by the flash on his forehead,
By the hope in those eyes wide and steady,
He was leagues in the desert already,
Driving the flocks up the mountain,
Or catlike couched hard by the fountain
To waylay the date-gathering negress:
So guarded he entrance or egress.
"How he stands!" quoth the King: "we may well swear,
(No novice, we've won our spurs elsewhere
And so can afford the confession,)
We exercise wholesome discretion
In keeping aloof from his threshold,
Once hold you, those jaws want no fresh hold,
Their first would too pleasantly purloin
The visitor's brisket or surloin:
But who's he would prove so fool-hardy?
Not the best man of Marignan, pardie!"

The sentence no sooner was uttered,
Than over the rails a glove fluttered,
Fell close to the lion, and rested:

The dame 't was, who flung it and jested
With life so, De Lorge had been wooing
For months past; he sat there pursuing
His suit, weighing out with nonchalance
Fine speeches like gold from a balance.

Sound the trumpet, no true knight's a tarrier!
De Lorge made one leap at the barrier,
Walkd straight to the glove,—while the lion
Ne'er moved, kept his far-reaching eye on
The palm-tree-edged desert-spring's sapphire,
And the musky oiled skin of the Kaffir,—
Picked it up, and as calmly retreated,
Leaped back where the lady was seated,
And full in the face of its owner
Flung the glove.

              "Your heart's queen, you dethrone her?
So should I!"—cried the King—" 't was mere vanity,
Not love, set that task to humanity!"
Lords and ladies alike turned with loathing
From such a proved wolf in sheep's clothing.

Not so, I; for I caught an expression
In her brow's undisturbed self-possession
Amid the Court's scoffing and merriment,
As if from no pleasing experiment
She rose, yet of pain not much heedful
So long as the process was needful,—
As if she had tried in a crucible,
To what "speeches like gold" were reducible,
And, finding the finest prove copper,
Felt the smoke in her face was but proper;
To know what she had *not* to trust to,
Was worth all the ashes and dust too.
She went out 'mid hooting and laughter;

Clement Marot stayed; I followed after,
And asked, as a grace, what it all meant?
If she wished not the rash deed's recallment?
"For I"—so I spoke—"am a poet:
Human nature,—behooves that I know it!"

She told me, "Too long had I heard
Of the deed proved alone by the word:
For my love—what De Lorge would not dare!
With my scorn—what De Lorge could compare!
And the endless descriptions of death
He would brave when my lip formed a breath,
I must reckon as braved, or, of course,
Doubt his word—and moreover, perforce,
For such gifts as no lady could spurn,
Must offer my love in return.
When I looked on your lion, it brought
All the dangers at once to my thought,
Encountered by all sorts of men,
Before he was lodged in his den,—
From the poor slave whose club or bare hands
Dug the trap, set the snare on the sands,
With no King and no Court to applaud,
By no shame, should he shrink, overawed,
Yet to capture the creature made shift,
That his rude boys might laugh at the gift,
—To the page who last leaped o'er the fence
Of the pit, on no greater pretence
Than to get back the bonnet he dropped,
Lest his pay for a week should be stopped.
So, wiser I judged it to make
One trial what 'death for my sake'
Really meant, while the power was yet mine,
Than to wait until time should define
Such a phrase not so simply as I,
Who took it to mean just 'to die.'

The blow a glove gives is but weak:
Does the mark yet discolor my cheek?
But when the heart suffers a blow,
Will the pain pass so soon, do you know?"

I looked, as away she was sweeping,
And saw a youth eagerly keeping
As close as he dared to the doorway.
No doubt that a noble should more weigh
His life than befits a plebeian;
And yet, had our brute been Nemean—
(I judge by a certain calm fervor
The youth stepped with, forward to serve her)
—He'd have scarce thought you did him the worst turn
If you whispered, "Friend, what you'd get, first earn!"
And when, shortly after, she carried
Her shame from the Court, and they married,
To that marriage some happiness, maugre
The voice of the Court, I dared augur.

For De Lorge, he made women with men vie,
Those in wonder and praise, these in envy;
And in short stood so plain a head taller
That he wooed and won . . . how do you call her?
The beauty, that rose in the sequel
To the King's love, who loved her a week well.
And 't was noticed he never would honor
De Lorge (who looked daggers upon her)
With the easy commission of stretching
His legs in the service, and fetching
His wife, from her chamber, those straying
Sad gloves she was always mislaying,
While the King took the closet to chat in,—
But of course this adventure came pat in.
And never the King told the story,
How bringing a glove brought such glory,

But the wife smiled—"His nerves are grown firmer:
Mine he brings now and utters no murmur."

Venienti occurrite morbo!
With which moral I drop my theorbo.

LOVE AMONG THE RUINS

WHERE the quiet-colored end of evening smiles
  Miles and miles
On the solitary pastures where our sheep
  Half-asleep
Tinkle homeward through the twilight, stray or stop
  As they crop—
Was the site once of a city great and gay,
  (So they say)
Of our country's very capital, its prince
  Ages since
Held his court in, gathered councils, wielding far
  Peace or war.

Now,—the country does not even boast a tree,
  As you see,
To distinguish slopes of verdure, certain rills
  From the hills
Intersect and give a name to, (else they run
  Into one,)
Where the domed and daring palace shot its spires
  Up like fires
O'er the hundred-gated circuit of a wall
  Bounding all,
Made of marble, men might march on nor be pressed,
  Twelve abreast.

And such plenty and perfection, see, of grass
  Never was!
Such a carpet as, this summer-time, o'erspreads

And embeds
Every vestige of the city, guessed alone,
    Stock or stone—
Where a multitude of men breathed joy and woe
    Long ago;
Lust of glory pricked their hearts up, dread of shame
    Struck them tame;
And that glory and that shame alike, the gold
    Bought and sold.

Now,—the single little turret that remains
    On the plains,
By the caper overrooted, by the gourd
    Overscored,
While the patching houseleek's head of blossom winks
    Through the chinks—
Marks the basement whence a tower in ancient time
    Sprang sublime,
And a burning ring, all round, the chariots traced
    As they raced,
And the monarch and his minions and his dames
    Viewed the games.

And I know, while thus the quiet-colored eve
    Smiles to leave
To their folding, all our many-tinkling fleece
    In such peace,
And the slopes and rills in undistinguished gray
    Melt away—
That a girl with eager eyes and yellow hair
    Waits me there
In the turret whence the charioteers caught soul
    For the goal,
When the king looked, where she looks now, breathless,
      dumb
    Till I come.

But he looked upon the city, every side,
    Far and wide,
All the mountains topped with temples, all the glades'
    Colonnades,
All the causeys, bridges, aqueducts,—and then,
    All the men!
When I do come, she will speak not, she will stand,
    Either hand
On my shoulder, give her eyes the first embrace
    Of my face,
Ere we rush, ere we extinguish sight and speech
    Each on each.

In one year they sent a million fighters forth
    South and North,
And they built their gods a brazen pillar high
    As the sky,
Yet reserved a thousand chariots in full force—
    Gold, of course.
Oh heart! oh blood that freezes, blood that burns!
    Earth's returns
For whole centuries of folly, noise and sin!
    Shut them in,
With their triumphs and their glories and the rest!
    Love is best.

A LOVERS' QUARREL

OH, what a dawn of day!
How the March sun feels like May!
    All is blue again
    After last night's rain,
And the South dries the hawthorn-spray.
    Only, my Love's away!
I'd as lief that the blue were gray.

Runnels, which rillets swell,
Must be dancing down the dell,
 With a foaming head
 On the beryl bed
Paven smooth as a hermit's cell;
 Each with a tale to tell,
Could my Love but attend as well.

Dearest, three months ago!
When we lived blocked-up with snow,—
 When the wind would edge
 In and in his wedge,
In, as far as the point could go—
 Not to our ingle, though,
Where we loved each the other so!

Laughs with so little cause!
We devised games out of straws,
 We would try and trace
 One another's face
In the ash, as an artist draws;
 Free on each other's flaws,
How we chattered like two church daws!

What's in the "Times"?—a scold
At the Emperor deep and cold;
 He has taken a bride
 To his gruesome side,
That's as fair as himself is bold:
 There they sit ermine-stoled,
And she powders her hair with gold.

Fancy the Pampas' sheen!
Miles and miles of gold and green
 Where the sunflowers blow
 In a solid glow,

And—to break now and then the screen—
      Black neck and eyeballs keen,
Up a wild horse leaps between!

Try, will our table turn?
Lay your hands there light, and yearn
      Till the yearning slips
      Through the finger-tips
In a fire which a few discern,
      And a very few feel burn,
And the rest, they may live and learn!

Then we would up and pace,
For a change, about the place,
      Each with arm o'er neck:
      'T is our quarter-deck,
We are seamen in woeful case.
      Help in the ocean-space!
Or, if no help, we'll embrace.

See, how she looks now, dressed
In a sledging-cap and vest!
      'T is a huge fur cloak—
      Like a reindeer's yoke
Falls the lappet along the breast:
      Sleeves for her arms to rest,
Or to hang, as my Love likes best.

Teach me to flirt a fan
As the Spanish ladies can,
      Or I tint your lip
      With a burnt stick's tip
And you turn into such a man!
      Just the two spots that span
Half the bill of the young male swan.

Dearest, three months ago
When the mesmerizer Snow
       With his hand's first sweep
       Put the earth to sleep:
'T was a time when the heart could show
       All—how was earth to know,
'Neath the mute hand's to-and-fro?

Dearest, three months ago
When we loved each other so,
       Lived and loved the same
       Till an evening came
When a shaft from the devil's bow
       Pierced to our ingle-glow,
And the friends were friend and foe!

Not from the heart beneath—
'T was a bubble born of breath,
       Neither sneer nor vaunt,
       Nor reproach nor taunt.
See a word, how it severeth!
       Oh, power of life and death
In the tongue, as the Preacher saith!

Woman, and will you cast
For a word, quite off at last
       Me, your own, your You,—
       Since, as truth is true,
I was You all the happy past—
       Me do you leave aghast
With the memories We amassed?

Love, if you knew the light
That your soul casts in my sight,
       How I look to you
       For the pure and true,

And the beauteous and the right,—
    Bear with a moment's spite
When a mere mote threats the white!

What of a hasty word?
Is the fleshly heart not stirred
    By a worm's pin-prick
    Where its roots are quick?
See the eye, by a fly's-foot blurred—
    Ear, when a straw is heard
Scratch the brain's coat of curd!

Foul be the world or fair
More or less, how can I care?
    'T is the world the same
    For my praise or blame,
And endurance is easy there.
    Wrong in the one thing rare—
Oh, it is hard to bear!

Here's the spring back or close,
When the almond-blossom blows;
    We shall have the word
    In a minor third,
There is none but the cuckoo knows:
    Heaps of the guelder-rose!
I must bear with it, I suppose.

Could but November come,
Were the noisy birds struck dumb
    At the warning slash
    Of his driver's-lash—
I would laugh like the valiant Thumb
    Facing the castle glum
And the giant's fee-faw-fum!

Then, were the world well stripped
Of the gear wherein equipped
     We can stand apart,
     Heart dispense with heart
In the sun, with the flowers unnipped,
     Oh, the world's hangings ripped,
We were both in a bare-walled crypt!

Each in the crypt would cry
"But one freezes here! and why?
     When a heart, as chill,
     At my own would thrill
Back to life, and its fires out-fly?
     Heart, shall we live or die?
The rest, . . . settle by and by!"

So, she'd efface the score,
And forgive me as before.
     It is twelve o'clock:
     I shall hear her knock
In the worst of a storm's uproar,
     I shall pull her through the door,
I shall have her for evermore!

EVELYN HOPE

Beautiful Evelyn Hope is dead!
  Sit and watch by her side an hour.
That is her book-shelf, this her bed;
  She plucked that piece of geranium-flower,
Beginning to die too, in the glass;
  Little has yet been changed, I think:
The shutters are shut, no light may pass
  Save two long rays through the hinge's chink.

Sixteen years old when she died!
    Perhaps she had scarcely heard my name;
It was not her time to love; beside,
    Her life had many a hope and aim,
Duties enough and little cares,
    And now was quiet, now astir,
Till God's hand beckoned unawares,—
    And the sweet white brow is all of her.

Is it too late then, Evelyn Hope?
    What, your soul was pure and true,
The good stars met in your horoscope,
    Made you of spirit, fire and dew—
And, just because I was thrice as old
    And our paths in the world diverged so wide,
Each was naught to each, must I be told?
    We were fellow mortals, naught beside?

No, indeed! for God above
    Is great to grant, as mighty to make,
And creates the love to reward the love:
    I claim you still, for my own love's sake!
Delayed it may be for more lives yet,
    Through worlds I shall traverse, not a few:
Much is to learn, much to forget
    Ere the time be come for taking you.

But the time will come,—at last it will,
    When, Evelyn Hope, what meant (I shall say)
In the lower earth, in the years long still,
    That body and soul so pure and gay?
Why your hair was amber, I shall divine,
    And your mouth of your own geranium's red—
And what you would do with me, in fine,
    In the new life come in the old one's stead.

I have lived (I shall say) so much since then,
   Given up myself so many times,
Gained me the gains of various men,
   Ransacked the ages, spoiled the climes;
Yet one thing, one, in my soul's full scope,
   Either I missed or itself missed me:
And I want and find you, Evelyn Hope!
   What is the issue? let us see!

I loved you, Evelyn, all the while!
   My heart seemed full as it could hold;
There was place and to spare for the frank young smile,
   And the red young mouth, and the hair's young gold.
So, hush,—I will give you this leaf to keep:
   See, I shut it inside the sweet cold hand!
There, that is our secret: go to sleep!
   You will wake, and remember, and understand.

UP AT A VILLA—DOWN IN THE CITY

(AS DISTINGUISHED BY AN ITALIAN PERSON OF QUALITY)

HAD I but plenty of money, money enough and to spare,
The house for me, no doubt, were a house in the city-
   square;
Ah, such a life, such a life, as one leads at the window
   there!

Something to see, by Bacchus, something to hear, at
   least!
There, the whole day long, one's life is a perfect feast;
While up at a villa one lives, I maintain it, no more
   than a beast.

Well now, look at our villa! stuck like the horn of a bull
Just on a mountain-edge as bare as the creature's skull,

Save a mere shag of a bush with hardly a leaf to pull!
—I scratch my own, sometimes, to see if the hair's turned
    wool.

But the city, oh the city—the square with the houses!
    Why?
They are stone-faced, white as a curd, there's something
    to take the eye!
Houses in four straight lines, not a single front awry;
You watch who crosses and gossips, who saunters, who
    hurries by;
Green blinds, as a matter of course, to draw when the
    sun gets high;
And the shops with fanciful signs which are painted
    properly.

What of a villa? Though winter be over in March by
    rights,
'Tis May perhaps ere the snow shall have withered well
    off the heights:
You've the brown ploughed land before, where the oxen
    steam and wheeze,
And the hills over-smoked behind by the faint gray
    olive-trees.

Is it better in May, I ask you? You've summer all at
    once;
In a day he leaps complete with a few strong April suns.
'Mid the sharp short emerald wheat, scarce risen three
    fingers well,
The wild tulip, at end of its tube, blows out its great red
    bell
Like a thin clear bubble of blood, for the children to
    pick and sell.

Is it ever hot in the square? There's a fountain to spout
    and splash!

In the shade it sings and springs; in the shine such foam-
bows flash
On the horses with curling fish-tails, that prance and
paddle and pash
Round the lady atop in her conch—fifty gazers do not
abash,
Though all that she wears is some weeds round her
waist in a sort of sash.

All the year long at the villa, nothing to see though you
linger,
Except yon cypress that points like death's lean lifted
forefinger.
Some think fireflies pretty, when they mix i' the corn and
mingle,
Or thrid the stinking hemp till the stalks of it seem
a-tingle.
Late August or early September, the stunning cicala is
shrill,
And the bees keep their tiresome whine round the
resinous firs on the hill.
Enough of the seasons,—I spare you the months of the
fever and chill.

Ere you open your eyes in the city, the blessed church-
bells begin:
No sooner the bells leave off than the diligence rattles in:
You get the pick of the news, and it costs you never
a pin.
By and by there's the travelling doctor gives pills, lets
blood, draws teeth;
Or the Pulcinello-trumpet breaks up the market beneath.
At the post-office such a scene-picture—the new play,
piping hot!
And a notice how, only this morning, three liberal thieves
were shot.

Above it, behold the Archbishop's most fatherly of re-
    bukes,
And beneath, with his crown and his lion, some little new
    law of the Duke's!
Or a sonnet with flowery marge, to the Reverend Don
    So-and-so,
Who is Dante, Boccaccio, Petrarca, Saint Jerome, and
    Cicero,
"And moreover," (the sonnet goes rhyming,) "the skirts
    of Saint Paul has reached,
Having preached us those six Lent-lectures more unctuous
    than ever he preached."
Noon strikes,—here sweeps the procession! our Lady
    borne smiling and smart
With a pink gauze gown all spangles, and seven swords
    stuck in her heart!
Bang-whang-whang goes the drum, *tootle-te-tootle* the
    fife;
No keeping one's haunches still: it's the greatest pleasure
    in life.

But bless you, it's dear—it's dear! fowls, wine, at double
    the rate.
They have clapped a new tax upon salt, and what oil
    pays passing the gate
It's a horror to think of. And so, the villa for me, not
    the city!
Beggars can scarcely be choosers: but still—ah, the pity,
    the pity!
Look, two and two go the priests, then the monks with
    cowls and sandals,
And the penitents dressed in white shirts, a-holding the
    yellow candles;
One, he carries a flag up straight, and another a cross
    with handles,

And the Duke's guard brings up the rear, for the better
    prevention of scandals:
Bang-whang-whang goes the drum, *tootle-te-tootle* the
    fife.
Oh, a day in the city-square, there is no such pleasure
    in life!

A WOMAN'S LAST WORD

LET'S contend no more, Love,
    Strive nor weep:
All be as before, Love,
    —Only sleep!

What so wild as words are?
    I and thou
In debate, as birds are,
    Hawk on bough!

See the creature stalking
    While we speak!
Hush and hide the talking,
    Cheek on cheek!

What so false as truth is,
    False to thee?
Where the serpent's tooth is
    Shun the tree—

Where the apple reddens
    Never pry—
Lest we lose our Edens,
    Eve and I.

Be a god and hold me
    With a charm!

Be a man and fold me
  With thine arm!

Teach me, only teach, Love!
  As I ought
I will speak thy speech, Love,
  Think thy thought—

Meet, if thou require it,
  Both demands,
Laying flesh and spirit
  In thy hands.

That shall be tomorrow,
  Not tonight:
I must bury sorrow
  Out of sight:

—Must a little weep, Love,
  (Foolish me!)
And so fall asleep, Love,
  Loved by thee.

FRA LIPPO LIPPI

I AM poor brother Lippo, by your leave!
You need not clap your torches to my face.
Zooks, what's to blame? you think you see a monk!
What, 't is past midnight, and you go the rounds,
And here you catch me at an alley's end
Where sportive ladies leave their doors ajar?
The Carmine's my cloister: hunt it up,
Do,—harry out, if you must show your zeal,
Whatever rat, there, haps on his wrong hole,
And nip each softling of a wee white mouse,
Weke, weke, that's crept to keep him company!

Aha, you know your betters! Then, you'll take
Your hand away that's fiddling on my throat,
And please to know me likewise. Who am I?
Why, one, sir, who is lodging with a friend
Three streets off—he's a certain . . . how d' ye call?
Master—a . . . Cosimo of the Medici,
I' the house that caps the corner. Boh! you were best!
Remember and tell me, the day you're hanged,
How you affected such a gullet's-gripe!
But you, sir, it concerns you that your knaves
Pick up a manner nor discredit you:
Zooks, are we pilchards, that they sweep the streets
And count fair prize what comes into their net?
He's Judas to a tittle, that man is!
Just such a face! Why, sir, you make amends.
Lord, I'm not angry! Bid your hangdogs go
Drink out this quarter-florin to the health
Of the munificent House that harbors me
(And many more beside, lads! more beside!)
And all's come square again. I'd like his face—
His, elbowing on his comrade in the door
With the pike and lantern,—for the slave that holds
John Baptist's head a-dangle by the hair
With one hand ("Look you, now," as who should say)
And his weapon in the other, yet unwiped!
It's not your chance to have a bit of chalk,
A wood-coal or the like? or you should see!
Yes, I'm the painter, since you style me so.
What, brother Lippo's doings, up and down,
You know them and they take you? like enough!
I saw the proper twinkle in your eye—
'Tell you, I liked your looks at very first.
Let's sit and set things straight now, hip to haunch.
Here's spring come, and the nights one makes up bands
To roam the town and sing out carnival,
And I've been three weeks shut within my mew,

A-painting for the great man, saints and saints
And saints again. I could not paint all night—
Ouf! I leaned out of window for fresh air.
There came a hurry of feet and little feet,
A sweep of lute-strings, laughs, and whifts of song,—
Flower o' the broom,
Take away love, and our earth is a tomb!
Flower o' the quince,
I let Lisa go, and what good in life since?
Flower o' the thyme—and so on. Round they went.
Scarce had they turned the corner when a titter
Like the skipping of rabbits by moonlight,—three slim
      shapes,
And a face that looked up . . . zooks, sir, flesh and blood,
That's all I'm made of! Into shreds it went,
Curtain and counterpane and coverlet,
All the bed-furniture—a dozen knots,
There was a ladder! Down I let myself,
Hands and feet, scrambling somehow, and so dropped,
And after them. I came up with the fun
Hard by Saint Laurence, hail fellow, well met,—
Flower o' the rose,
If I've been merry, what matter who knows?
And so as I was stealing back again
To get to bed and have a bit of sleep
Ere I rise up tomorrow and go work
On Jerome knocking at his poor old breast
With his great round stone to subdue the flesh,
You snap me of the sudden. Ah, I see!
Though your eye twinkles still, you shake your head—
Mine's shaved—a monk, you say—the sting's in that!
If Master Cosimo announced himself,
Mum's the word naturally; but a monk!
Come, what am I a beast for? tell us, now!
I was a baby when my mother died
And father died and left me in the street.

I starved there, God knows how, a year or two
On fig-skins, melon-parings, rinds and shucks,
Refuse and rubbish. One fine frosty day,
My stomach being empty as your hat,
The wind doubled me up and down I went.
Old Aunt Lapaccia trussed me with one hand,
(Its fellow was a stinger as I knew)
And so along the wall, over the bridge,
By the straight cut to the convent. Six words there,
While I stood munching my first bread that month:
"So, boy, you're minded," quoth the good fat father,
Wiping his own mouth, 't was refection-time,—
"To quit this very miserable world?
Will you renounce" . . . "the mouthful of bread?"
        thought I;
By no means! Brief, they made a monk of me;
I did renounce the world, its pride and greed,
Palace, farm, villa, shop, and banking-house,
Trash, such as these poor devils of Medici
Have given their hearts to—all at eight years old.
Well, sir, I found in time, you may be sure,
'T was not for nothing—the good bellyful,
The warm serge and the rope that goes all round,
And day-long blessed idleness beside!
"Let's see what the urchin's fit for"—that came next.
Not overmuch their way, I must confess.
Such a to-do! They tried me with their books;
Lord, they'd have taught me Latin in pure waste!
Flower o' the clove,
All the Latin I construe is "amo," I love!
But, mind you, when a boy starves in the streets
Eight years together, as my fortune was,
Watching folk's faces to know who will fling
The bit of half-stripped grape-bunch he desires,
And who will curse or kick him for his pains,—
Which gentleman processional and fine,

Holding a candle to the Sacrament,
Will wink and let him lift a plate and catch
The droppings of the wax to sell again,
Or holla for the Eight and have him whipped,—
How say I?—nay, which dog bites, which lets drop
His bone from the heap of offal in the street,—
Why, soul and sense of him grow sharp alike,
He learns the look of things, and none the less
For admonition from the hunger-pinch.
I had a store of such remarks, be sure,
Which, after I found leisure, turned to use.
I drew men's faces on my copy-books,
Scrawled them within the antiphonary's marge,
Joined legs and arms to the long music-notes,
Found eyes and nose and chin for A's and B's,
And made a string of pictures of the world
Betwixt the ins and outs of verb and noun,
On the wall, the bench, the door. The monks looked
        black.
"Nay," quoth the Prior, "turn him out, d' ye say?
In no wise. Lose a crow and catch a lark.
What if at last we get our man of parts,
We Carmelites, like those Camaldolese
And Preaching Friars, to do our church up fine
And put the front on it that ought to be!"
And hereupon he bade me daub away.
Thank you! my head being crammed, the walls a blank,
Never was such prompt disemburdening.
First, every sort of monk, the black and white,
I drew them, fat and lean: then, folk at church,
From good old gossips waiting to confess
Their cribs of barrel-droppings, candle-ends,—
To the breathless fellow at the altar-foot,
Fresh from his murder, safe and sitting there
With the little children round him in a row
Of admiration, half for his beard and half

For that white anger of his victim's son
Shaking a fist at him with one fierce arm,
Signing himself with the other because of Christ
(Whose sad face on the cross sees only this
After the passion of a thousand years)
Till some poor girl, her apron o'er her head,
(Which the intense eyes looked through) came at eve
On tiptoe, said a word, dropped in a loaf,
Her pair of earrings and a bunch of flowers
(The brute took growling), prayed, and so was gone.
I painted all, then cried " 'T is ask and have;
Choose, for more's ready!"—laid the ladder flat,
And showed my covered bit of cloister-wall.
The monks closed in a circle and praised loud
Till checked, taught what to see and not to see,
Being simple bodies,—"That's the very man!
Look at the boy who stoops to pat the dog!
That woman's like the Prior's niece who comes
To care about his asthma: it's the life!"
But there my triumph's straw-fire flared and funked;
Their betters took their turn to see and say:
The Prior and the learned pulled a face
And stopped all that in no time. "How? what's here?
Quite from the mark of painting, bless us all!
Faces, arms, legs, and bodies like the true
As much as pea and pea! it's devil's-game!
Your business is not to catch men with show,
With homage to the perishable clay,
But lift them over it, ignore it all,
Make them forget there's such a thing as flesh.
Your business is to paint the souls of men—
Man's soul, and it's a fire, smoke . . . no, it's not . . .
It's vapor done up like a new-born babe—
(In that shape when you die it leaves your mouth)
It's . . . well, what matters talking, it's the soul!
Give us no more of body than shows soul!

Here's Giotto, with his Saint a-praising God,
That sets us praising,—why not stop with him?
Why put all thoughts of praise out of our head
With wonder at lines, colors, and what not?
Paint the soul, never mind the legs and arms!
Rub all out, try at it a second time.
Oh, that white smallish female with the breasts,
She's just my niece . . . Herodias, I would say,—
Who went and danced and got men's heads cut off!
Have it all out!"   Now, is this sense, I ask?
A fine way to paint soul, by painting body
So ill, the eye can't stop there, must go further
And can't fare worse!   Thus, yellow does for white
When what you put for yellow's simply black,
And any sort of meaning looks intense
When all beside itself means and looks naught.
Why can't a painter lift each foot in turn,
Left foot and right foot, go a double step,
Make his flesh liker and his soul more like,
Both in their order?   Take the prettiest face,
The Prior's niece . . . patron-saint—is it so pretty
You can't discover if it means hope, fear,
Sorrow or joy? won't beauty go with these?
Suppose I've made her eyes all right and blue,
Can't I take breath and try to add life's flash,
And then add soul and heighten them three-fold?
Or say there's beauty with no soul at all-
(I never saw it—put the case the same—)
If you get simple beauty and naught else,
You get about the best thing God invents:
That's somewhat: and you'll find the soul you have
    missed,
Within yourself, when you return him thanks.
"Rub all out!"   Well, well, there's my life, in short,
And so the thing has gone on ever since.
I'm grown a man no doubt, I've broken bounds:

You should not take a fellow eight years old
And make him swear to never kiss the girls.
I'm my own master, paint now as I please—
Having a friend, you see, in the Corner-house!
Lord, it's fast holding by the rings in front—
Those great rings serve more purposes than just
To plant a flag in, or tie up a horse!
And yet the old schooling sticks, the old grave eyes
Are peeping o'er my shoulder as I work,
The heads shake still—"It's art's decline, my son!
You're not of the true painters, great and old;
Brother Angelico's the man, you'll find;
Brother Lorenzo stands his single peer:
Fag on at flesh, you'll never make the third!"
Flower o' the pine,
You keep your mistr . . . manners, and I'll stick to mine!
I'm not the third, then: bless us, they must know!
Don't you think they're the likeliest to know,
They with their Latin? So, I swallow my rage,
Clench my teeth, suck my lips in tight, and paint
To please them—sometimes do and sometimes don't;
For, doing most, there's pretty sure to come
A turn, some warm eve finds me at my saints—
A laugh, a cry, the business of the world—
(Flower o' the peach,
Death for us all, and his own life for each!)
And my whole soul revolves, the cup runs over,
The world and life's too big to pass for a dream,
And I do these wild things in sheer despite,
And play the fooleries you catch me at,
In pure rage! The old mill-horse, out at grass
After hard years, throws up his stiff heels so,
Although the miller does not preach to him
The only good of grass is to make chaff.
What would men have? Do they like grass or no—
May they or mayn't they? all I want's the thing

Settled forever one way. As it is,
You tell too many lies and hurt yourself:
You don't like what you only like too much,
You do like what, if given you at your word,
You find abundantly detestable.
For me, I think I speak as I was taught;
I always see the garden and God there
A-making man's wife: and, my lesson learned,
The value and significance of flesh,
I can't unlearn ten minutes afterwards.

You understand me: I'm a beast, I know.
But see, now—why, I see as certainly
As that the morning-star's about to shine,
What will hap some day. We've a youngster here
Comes to our convent, studies what I do,
Slouches and stares and lets no atom drop:
His name is Guidi—he'll not mind the monks—
They call him Hulking Tom, he lets them talk—
He picks my practice up—he'll paint apace,
I hope so—though I never live so long,
I know what's sure to follow. You be judge!
You speak no Latin more than I, belike;
However, you're my man, you've seen the world
—The beauty and the wonder and the power,
The shapes of things, their colors, lights and shades,
Changes, surprises,—and God made it all!
—For what? Do you feel thankful, ay or no,
For this fair town's face, yonder river's line,
The mountain round it and the sky above,
Much more the figures of man, woman, child,
These are the frame to? What's it all about?
To be passed over, despised? or dwelt upon,
Wondered at? oh, this last of course!—you say.
But why not do as well as say,—paint these
Just as they are, careless what comes of it?

God's works—paint any one, and count it crime
To let a truth slip. Don't object, "His works
Are here already; nature is complete:
Suppose you reproduce her— (which you can't)
There's no advantage! you must beat her, then."
For, don't you mark? we're made so that we love
First when we see them painted, things we have passed
Perhaps a hundred times nor cared to see;
And so they are better, painted—better to us,
Which is the same thing. Art was given for that;
God uses us to help each other so,
Lending our minds out. Have you noticed, now,
Your cullion's hanging face? A bit of chalk,
And trust me but you should, though! How much more,
If I drew higher things with the same truth!
That were to take the Prior's pulpit-place,
Interpret God to all of you! Oh, oh,
It makes me mad to see what men shall do
And we in our graves! This world's no blot for us,
Nor blank; it means intensely, and means good:
To find its meaning is my meat and drink.
"Ay, but you don't so instigate to prayer!"
Strikes in the Prior: "when your meaning's plain
It does not say to folk—remember matins,
Or, mind you fast next Friday!" Why, for this
What need of art at all? A skull and bones,
Two bits of stick nailed crosswise, or, what's best,
A bell to chime the hour with, does as well.
I painted a Saint Laurence six months since
At Prato, splashed the fresco in fine style:
"How looks my painting, now the scaffold's down?"
I ask a brother: "Hugely," he returns—
"Already not one phiz of your three slaves
Who turn the Deacon off his toasted side,
But's scratched and prodded to our heart's content,
The pious people have so eased their own

With coming to say prayers there in a rage:
We get on fast to see the bricks beneath.
Expect another job this time next year,
For pity and religion grow i' the crowd—
Your painting serves its purpose!"   Hang the fools!

   —That is—you'll not mistake an idle word
Spoke in a huff by a poor monk, God wot,
Tasting the air this spicy night which turns
The unaccustomed head like Chianti wine!
Oh, the church knows! don't misreport me, now!
It's natural a poor monk out of bounds
Should have his apt word to excuse himself:
And hearken how I plot to make amends.
I have bethought me: I shall paint a piece
. . . There's for you!   Give me six months, then go, see
Something in Sant' Ambrogio's!   Bless the nuns!
They want a cast o' my office.   I shall paint
God in the midst, Madonna and her babe,
Ringed by a bowery, flowery angel-brood,
Lilies and vestments and white faces, sweet
As puff on puff of grated orris-root
When ladies crowd to Church at midsummer.
And then i' the front, of course a saint or two—
Saint John, because he saves the Florentines,
Saint Ambrose, who puts down in black and white
The convent's friends and gives them a long day,
And Job, I must have him there past mistake,
The man of Uz (and Us without the z,
Painters who need his patience).   Well, all these
Secured at their devotion, up shall come
Out of a corner when you least expect,
As one by a dark stair into a great light,
Music and talking, who but Lippo!   I!—
Mazed, motionless, and moonstruck—I'm the man!
Back I shrink—what is this I see and hear?

I, caught up with my monk's-things by mistake,
My old serge gown and rope that goes all round,
I, in this presence, this pure company!
Where's a hole, where's a corner for escape?
Then steps a sweet angelic slip of a thing
Forward, puts out a soft palm—"Not so fast!"
—Addresses the celestial presence, "nay—
He made you and devised you, after all,
Though he's none of you!   Could Saint John there draw—
His camel-hair make up a painting-brush?
We come to brother Lippo for all that,
Iste perfecit opus!"   So, all smile—
I shuffle sideways with my blushing face
Under the cover of a hundred wings
Thrown like a spread of kirtles when you're gay
And play hot cockles, all the doors being shut,
Till, wholly unexpected, in there pops
The hothead husband!   Thus I scuttle off
To some safe bench behind, not letting go
The palm of her, the little lily thing
That spoke the good word for me in the nick,
Like the Prior's niece . . . Saint Lucy, I would say.
And so all's saved for me, and for the church
A pretty picture gained.   Go, six months hence!
Your hand, sir, and good-by: no lights, no lights!
The street's hushed, and I know my own way back,
Don't fear me! There's the gray beginning. Zooks!

A TOCCATA OF GALUPPI'S

OH Galuppi, Baldassare, this is very sad to find!
I can hardly misconceive you; it would prove me deaf
      and blind;
But although I take your meaning, 't is with such a
      heavy mind!

Here you come with your old music, and here's all the
    good it brings.
What, they lived once thus at Venice where the merchants
    were the kings,
Where St. Mark's is, where the Doges used to wed the
    sea with rings?

Ay, because the sea's the street there; and 't is arched
    by . . . what you call
. . . Shylock's bridge with houses on it, where they kept
    the carnival:
I was never out of England—it's as if I saw it all.

Did young people take their pleasure when the sea was
    warm in May?
Balls and masks begun at midnight, burning ever to
    mid-day,
When they made up fresh adventures for the morrow,
    do you say?

Was a lady such a lady, cheeks so round and lips so red,—
On her neck the small face buoyant, like a bellflower
    on its bed,
O'er the breast's superb abundance where a man might
    base his head?

Well, and it was graceful of them—they'd break talk off
    and afford
—She, to bite her mask's black velvet—he, to finger on
    his sword,
While you sat and played Toccatas, stately at the
    clavichord?

What? Those lesser thirds so plaintive, sixths diminished,
    sigh on sigh,

Told them something? Those suspensions, those solu-
 tions—"Must we die?"
Those commiserating sevenths—"Life might last! we can
 but try!"

"Were you happy?"—"Yes."—"And are you still as
 happy?"—"Yes. And you?"
—"Then, more kisses!"—"Did *I* stop them, when a million
 seemed so few?"
Hark, the dominant's persistence till it must be answered
 to!

So, an octave struck the answer. Oh, they praised you,
 I dare say!
"Brave Galuppi! that was music! good alike at grave
 and gay!
I can always leave off talking when I hear a master play!"

Then they left you for their pleasure: till in due time,
 one by one,
Some with lives that came to nothing, some with deeds
 as well undone,
Death stepped tacitly and took them where they never
 see the sun.

But when I sit down to reason, think to take my stand
 nor swerve,
While I triumph o'er a secret wrung from nature's close
 reserve,
In you come with your cold music till I creep through
 every nerve.

Yes, you, like a ghostly cricket, creaking where a house
 was burned:
"Dust and ashes, dead and done with, Venice spent what
 Venice earned.

The soul, doubtless, is immortal—where a soul can be
    discerned.

"Yours for instance: you know physics, something of
    geology,
Mathematics are your pastime; souls shall rise in their
    degree;
Butterflies may dread extinction,—you'll not die, it can-
    not be!

"As for Venice and her people, merely born to bloom
    and drop,
Here on earth they bore their fruitage, mirth and folly
    were the crop:
What of soul was left, I wonder, when the kissing had
    to stop?

"Dust and ashes!" So you creak it, and I want the heart
    to scold.
Dear dead women, with such hair, too—what's become of
    all the gold
Used to hang and brush their bosoms? I feel chilly and
    grown old.

BY THE FIRESIDE

How well I know what I mean to do
    When the long dark autumn evenings come;
And where, my soul, is thy pleasant hue?
    With the music of all thy voices, dumb
In life's November too!

I shall be found by the fire, suppose,
    O'er a great wise book as beseemeth age,
While the shutters flap as the cross-wind blows,

And I turn the page, and I turn the page,
Not verse now, only prose!

Till the young ones whisper, finger on lip,
    "There he is at it, deep in Greek:
Now then, or never, out we slip
    To cut from the hazels by the creek
A mainmast for our ship!"

I shall be at it indeed, my friends!
    Greek puts already on either side
Such a branch-work forth as soon extends
    To a vista opening far and wide,
And I pass out where it ends.

The outside-frame, like your hazel-trees—
    But the inside-archway widens fast,
And a rarer sort succeeds to these,
    And we slope to Italy at last
And youth, by green degrees.

I follow wherever I am led,
    Knowing so well the leader's hand:
Oh woman-country, wooed not wed,
    Loved all the more by earth's male-lands,
Laid to their hearts instead!

Look at the ruined chapel again
    Half-way up in the Alpine gorge!
Is that a tower, I point you plain,
    Or is it a mill, or an iron forge
Breaks solitude in vain?

A turn, and we stand in the heart of things;
    The woods are round us, heaped and dim;
From slab to slab how it slips and springs,

The thread of water single and slim,
Through the ravage some torrent brings!

Does it feed the little lake below?
    That speck of white just on its marge
Is Pella; see, in the evening-glow,
    How sharp the silver spear-heads charge
When Alp meets heaven in snow!

On our other side is the straight-up rock;
    And a path is kept 'twixt the gorge and it
By boulder-stones where lichens mock
    The marks on a moth, and small ferns fit
Their teeth to the polished block.

Oh the sense of the yellow mountain-flowers,
    And thorny balls, each three in one,
The chestnuts throw on our path in showers!
    For the drop of the woodland fruit's begun,
These early November hours,

That crimson the creeper's leaf across
    Like a splash of blood, intense, abrupt,
O'er a shield else gold from rim to boss,
    And lay it for show on the fairy-cupped
Elf-needled mat of moss,

By the rose-flesh mushrooms, undivulged
    Last evening—nay, in today's first dew
Yon sudden coral nipple bulged,
    Where a freaked fawn-colored flaky crew
Of toad-stools peep indulged.

And yonder, at foot of the fronting ridge
    That takes the turn to a range beyond,
Is the chapel reached by the one-arched bridge

Where the water is stopped in a stagnant pond
Danced over by the midge.

The chapel and bridge are of stone alike,
　Blackish-gray and mostly wet;
Cut hemp-stalks steep in the narrow dyke.
　See here again, how the lichens fret
And the roots of the ivy strike!

Poor little place, where its one priest comes
　On a festa-day, if he comes at all,
To the dozen folk from their scattered homes,
　Gathered within that precinct small
By the dozen ways one roams—

To drop from the charcoal-burners' huts,
　Or climb from the hemp-dressers' low shed,
Leave the grange where the woodman stores his nuts,
　Or the wattled cote where the fowlers spread
Their gear on the rock's bare juts.

It has some pretension too, this front,
　With its bit of fresco half-moon-wise
Set over the porch, Art's early wont:
　'T is John in the Desert, I surmise,
But has borne the weather's brunt—

Not from the fault of the builder, though,
　For a pent-house properly projects
Where three carved beams make a certain show,
　Dating—good thought of our architect's—
'Five, six, nine, he lets you know.

And all day long a bird sings there,
　And a stray sheep drinks at the pond at times;
The place is silent and aware;

It has had its scenes, its joys and crimes,
But that is its own affair.

My perfect wife, my Leonor,
    Oh heart, my own, oh eyes, mine too,
Whom else could I dare look backward for,
    With whom beside should I dare pursue
The path gray heads abhor?

For it leads to a crag's sheer edge with them;
    Youth, flowery all the way, there stops—
Not they; age threatens and they contemn,
    Till they reach the gulf wherein youth drops,
One inch from life's safe hem!

With me, youth led . . . I will speak now,
    No longer watch you as you sit
Reading by fire-light, that great brow
    And the spirit-small hand propping it,
Mutely, my heart knows how—

When, if I think but deep enough,
    You are wont to answer, prompt as rhyme;
And you, too, find without rebuff
    Response your soul seeks many a time
Piercing its fine flesh-stuff.

My own, confirm me! If I tread
    This path back, is it not in pride
To think how little I dreamed it led
    To an age so blest that, by its side,
Youth seems the waste instead?

My own, see where the years conduct!
    At first, 't was something our two souls
Should mix as mists do; each is sucked

In each now: on, the new stream rolls,
Whatever rocks obstruct.

Think, when our one soul understands
    The great Word which makes all things new,
When earth breaks up and heaven expands,
    How will the change strike me and you
In the house not made with hands?

Oh, I must feel your brain prompt mine,
    Your heart anticipate my heart,
You must be just before, in fine,
    See and make me see, for your part,
New depths of the divine!

But who could have expected this
    When we two drew together first
Just for the obvious human bliss,
    To satisfy life's daily thirst
With a thing men seldom miss?

Come back with me to the first of all,
    Let us lean and love it over again,
Let us now forget and now recall,
    Break the rosary in a pearly rain
And gather what we let fall!

What did I say?—that a small bird sings
    All day long, save when a brown pair
Of hawks from the wood float with wide wings
    Strained to a bell: 'gainst noon-day glare
You count the streaks and rings.

But at afternoon or almost eve
    'T is better; then the silence grows
To that degree, you half believe

It must get rid of what it knows,
Its bosom does so heave.

Hither we walked then, side by side,
　Arm in arm and cheek to cheek,
And still I questioned or replied,
　While my heart, convulsed to really speak
Lay choking in its pride.

Silent the crumbling bridge we cross,
　And pity and praise the chapel sweet,
And care about the fresco's loss,
　And wish for our souls a like retreat,
And wonder at the moss.

Stoop and kneel on the settle under,
　Look through the window's grated square:
Nothing to see!　For fear of plunder,
　The cross is down and the altar bare,
As if thieves don't fear thunder.

We stoop and look in through the grate,
　See the little porch and rustic door,
Read duly the dead builder's date;
　Then cross the bridge that we crossed before,
Take the path again—but wait!

Oh moment, one and infinite!
　The water slips o'er stock and stone;
The West is tender, hardly bright:
　How gray at once is the evening grown—
One star, its chrysolite!

We two stood there with never a third,
　But each by each, as each knew well:
The sights we saw and the sounds we heard,

The lights and the shades made up a spell
Till the trouble grew and stirred.

Oh, the little more, and how much it is!
    And the little less, and what worlds away!
How a sound shall quicken content to bliss,
    Or a breath suspend the blood's best play,
And life be a proof of this!

Had she willed it, still had stood the screen
    So slight, so sure, 'twixt my love and her:
I could fix her face with a guard between,
    And find her soul as when friends confer,
Friends—lovers that might have been.

For my heart had a touch of the woodland-time,
    Wanting to sleep now over its best.
Shake the whole tree in the summer-prime,
    But bring to the last leaf no such test!
"Hold the last fast!" runs the rhyme.

For a chance to make your little much,
    To gain a lover and lose a friend,
Venture the tree and a myriad such,
    When nothing you mar but the year can mend:
But a last leaf—fear to touch!

Yet should it unfasten itself and fall
    Eddying down till it find your face
At some slight wind—best chance of all!
    Be your heart henceforth its dwelling-place
You trembled to forestall!

Worth how well, those dark gray eyes,
    That hair so dark and dear, how worth

That a man should strive and agonize,
    And taste a veriest hell on earth
For the hope of such a prize!

You might have turned and tried a man,
    Set him a space to weary and wear,
And prove which suited more your plan,
    His best of hope or his worst despair,
Yet end as he began.

But you spared me this, like the heart you are,
    And filled my empty heart at a word.
If two lives join, there is oft a scar,
    They are one and one, with a shadowy third;
One near one is too far.

A moment after, and hands unseen
    Were hanging the night around us fast;
But we knew that a bar was broken between
    Life and life: we were mixed at last
In spite of the mortal screen.

The forests had done it; there they stood;
    We caught for a moment the powers at play:
They had mingled us so, for once and good,
    Their work was done—we might go or stay,
They relapsed to their ancient mood.

How the world is made for each of us!
    How all we perceive and know in it
Tends to some moment's product thus,
    When a soul declares itself—to wit,
By its fruit, the thing it does!

Be hate that fruit or love that fruit,
    It forwards the general deed of man,

And each of the Many helps to recruit
    The life of the race by a general plan;
Each living his own, to boot.

I am named and known by that moment's feat;
    There took my station and degree;
So grew my own small life complete,
    As nature obtained her best of me—
One born to love you, sweet!

And to watch you sink by the fireside now
    Back again, as you mutely sit
Musing by fire-light, that great brow
    And the spirit-small hand propping it,
Yonder, my heart knows how!

So, earth has gained by one man the more,
    And the gain of earth must be heaven's gain too;
And the whole is well worth thinking o'er
    When autumn comes: which I mean to do
One day, as I said before.

ANY WIFE TO ANY HUSBAND

My love, this is the bitterest, that thou—
Who art all truth, and who dost love me now
    As thine eyes say, as thy voice breaks to say—
Shouldst love so truly, and couldst love me still
A whole long life through, had but love its will,
    Would death that leads me from thee brook delay.

I have but to be by thee, and thy hand
Will never let mine go, nor heart withstand
    The beating of my heart to reach its place.
When shall I look for thee and feel thee gone?

When cry for the old comfort and find none?
   Never, I know!　Thy soul is in thy face.

Oh, I should fade—'t is willed so!　Might I save,
Gladly I would, whatever beauty gave
   Joy to thy sense, for that was precious too.
It is not to be granted.　But the soul
Whence the love comes, all ravage leaves that whole;
   Vainly the flesh fades; soul makes all things new.

It would not be because my eye grew dim
Thou couldst not find the love there, thanks to Him
   Who never is dishonored in the spark
He gave us from his fire of fires, and bade
Remember whence it sprang, nor be afraid
   While that burns on, though all the rest grow dark.

So, how thou wouldst be perfect, white and clean
Outside as inside, soul and soul's demesne
   Alike, this body given to show it by!
Oh, three-parts through the worst of life's abyss,
What plaudits from the next world after this,
   Couldst thou repeat a stroke and gain the sky!

And is it not the bitterer to think
That disengage our hands and thou wilt sink
   Although thy love was love in very deed?
I know that nature!　Pass a festive day,
Thou dost not throw its relic-flower away
   Nor bid its music's loitering echo speed.

Thou let'st the stranger's glove lie where it fell;
If old things remain old things all is well,
   For thou art grateful as becomes man best:
And hadst thou only heard me play one tune,

Or viewed me from a window, not so soon
　With thee would such things fade as with the rest.

I seem to see!   We meet and part; 't is brief;
The book I opened keeps a folded leaf,
　The very chair I sat on, breaks the rank;
That is a portrait of me on the wall—
Three lines, my face comes at so slight a call:
　And for all this, one little hour to thank!

But now, because the hour through years was fixed,
Because our inmost beings met and mixed,
　Because thou once hast loved me—wilt thou dare
Say to thy soul and Who may list beside,
"Therefore she is immortally my bride;
　Chance cannot change my love, nor time impair.

"So, what if in the dusk of life that's left,
I, a tired traveller of my sun bereft,
　Look from my path when, mimicking the same,
The fire-fly glimpses past me, come and gone?
—Where was it till the sunset?   Where anon
　It will be at the sunrise!   What's to blame?"

Is it so helpful to thee?   Canst thou take
The mimic up, nor, for the true thing's sake,
　Put gently by such efforts at a beam?
Is the remainder of the way so long,
Thou need'st the little solace, thou the strong?
　Watch out thy watch, let weak ones doze and dream!

Ah, but the fresher faces!   "Is it true,"
Thou 'lt ask, "some eyes are beautiful and new?
　Some hair,—how can one choose but grasp such wealth?
And if a man would press his lips to lips

Fresh as the wilding hedge-rose-cup there slips
　　The dewdrop out of, must it be by stealth?

"It cannot change the love still kept for Her,
More than if such a picture I prefer
　　Passing a day with, to a room's bare side:
The painted form takes nothing she possessed,
Yet, while the Titian's Venus lies at rest,
　　A man looks. Once more, what is there to chide?"

So must I see, from where I sit and watch,
My own self sell myself, my hand attach
　　Its warrant to the very thefts from me—
Thy singleness of soul that made me proud,
Thy purity of heart I loved aloud,
　　Thy man's-truth I was bold to bid God see!

Love so, then, if thou wilt! Give all thou canst
Away to the new faces—disentranced,
　　(Say it and think it) obdurate no more:
Re-issue looks and words from the old mint,
Pass them afresh, no matter whose the print
　　Image and superscription once they bore!

Re-coin thyself and give it them to spend,—
It all comes to the same thing at the end,
　　Since mine thou wast, mine art and mine shalt be,
Faithful or faithless, sealing up the sum
Or lavish of my treasure, thou must come
　　Back to the heart's place here I keep for thee!

Only, why should it be with stain at all?
Why must I, 'twixt the leaves of coronal,
　　Put any kiss of pardon on thy brow?
Why need the other women know so much,

And talk together, "Such the look and such
   The smile he used to love with, then as now!"

Might I die last and show thee! Should I find
Such hardship in the few years left behind,
   If free to take and light my lamp, and go
Into thy tomb, and shut the door and sit,
Seeing thy face on those four sides of it
   The better that they are so blank, I know!

Why, time was what I wanted, to turn o'er
Within my mind each look, get more and more
   By heart each word, too much to learn at first:
And join thee all the fitter for the pause
'Neath the low doorway's lintel. That were cause
   For lingering, though thou calledst, if I durst!

And yet thou art the nobler of us two:
What dare I dream of, that thou canst not do,
   Outstripping my ten small steps with one stride?
I'll say then, here's a trial and a task—
Is it to bear?—if easy, I'll not ask:
   Though love fail, I can trust on in thy pride.

Pride?—when those eyes forestall the life behind
The death I have to go through!—when I find,
   Now that I want thy help most, all of thee!
What did I fear? Thy love shall hold me fast
Until the little minute's sleep is past
   And I wake saved.—And yet it will not be!

MY STAR

   ALL that I know
     Of a certain star
   Is, it can throw

(Like the angled spar)
Now a dart of red,
Now a dart of blue;
Till my friends have said
They would fain see, too,
My star that dartles the red and the blue!
Then it stops like a bird; like a flower, hangs furled:
They must solace themselves with the Saturn above it.
What matter to me if their star is a world?
Mine has opened its soul to me; therefore I love it.

Threatening Tyrant —

INSTANS TYRANNUS

I

OF the million or two, more or less,
I rule and possess,
One man, for some cause undefined,
Was least to my mind.

II

I struck him, he grovelled of course—
For, what was his force?
I pinned him to earth with my weight
And persistence of hate:
And he lay, would not moan, would not curse,
As his lot might be worse.

III

"Were the object less mean, would he stand
At the swing of my hand!
For obscurity helps him and blots
The hole where he squats."
So, I set my five wits on the stretch
To inveigle the wretch.
All in vain! Gold and jewels I threw,

Still he couched there perdue;
I tempted his blood and his flesh,
Hid in roses my mesh,
Choicest cates and the flagon's best spilth:
Still he kept to his filth.

IV

Had he kith now or kin, were access
To his heart, did I press:
Just a son or a mother to seize!
No such booty as these.
Were it simply a friend to pursue
'Mid my million or two,
Who could pay me in person or pelf
What he owes me himself!
No: I could not but smile through my chafe:
For the fellow lay safe
As his mates do, the midge and the nit,
—Through minuteness, to wit.

V

Then a humor more great took its place
At the thought of his face,
The droop, the low cares of the mouth,
The trouble uncouth
'Twixt the brows, all that air one is fain
To put out of its pain.
And, "no!" I admonished myself,
"Is one mocked by an elf,
Is one baffled by toad or by rat?
The gravamen's in that!
How the lion, who crouches to suit
His back to my foot,
Would admire that I stand in debate!
But the small turns the great
If it vexes you,—that is the thing!

Toad or rat vex the king?
Though I waste half my realm to unearth
Toad or rat, 't is well worth!"

VI

So, I soberly laid my last plan
To extinguish the man.
Round his creep-hole, with never a break,
Ran my fires for his sake;
Over-head, did my thunder combine
With my underground mine:
Till I looked from my labor content
To enjoy the event.

VII

When sudden . . . how think ye, the end?
Did I say "without friend"?
Say rather, from marge to blue marge
The whole sky grew his targe
With the sun's self for visible boss,
While an Arm ran across
Which the earth heaved beneath like a breast
Where the wretch was safe prest!
Do you see? Just my vengeance complete,
The man sprang to his feet,
Stood erect, caught at God's skirts, and prayed!
—So, I was afraid!

"CHILDE ROLAND TO THE DARK TOWER CAME"

(See Edgar's song in *Lear*.)

My first thought was, he lied in every word,
That hoary cripple, with malicious eye
Askance to watch the working of his lie
On mine, and mouth scarce able to afford

Suppression of the glee, that pursed and scored
   Its edge, at one more victim gained thereby.

What else should he be set for, with his staff?
   What, save to waylay with his lies, ensnare
   All travellers who might find him posted there,
And ask the road? I guessed what skull-like laugh
Would break, what crutch 'gin write my epitaph
   For pastime in the dusty thoroughfare,

If at his counsel I should turn aside
   Into that ominous tract which, all agree,
   Hides the Dark Tower. Yet acquiescingly
I did turn as he pointed: neither pride
Nor hope rekindling at the end descried,
   So much as gladness that some end might be.

For, what with my whole world-wide wandering,
   What with my search drawn out through years, my
       hope
   Dwindled into a ghost not fit to cope
With that obstreperous joy success would bring,—
I hardly tried now to rebuke the spring
   My heart made, finding failure in its scope.

As when a sick man very near to death
   Seems dead indeed, and feels begin and end
   The tears, and takes the farewell of each friend,
And hears one bid the other go, draw breath
Freelier outside, ("since all is o'er," he saith,
   "And the blow fallen no grieving can amend;")

While some discuss if near the other graves
   Be room enough for this, and when a day
   Suits best for carrying the corpse away,
With care about the banners, scarves and staves:

And still the man hears all, and only craves
   He may not shame such tender love and stay.

Thus, I had so long suffered in this quest,
   Heard failure prophesied so oft, been writ
   So many times among "The Band"—to wit,
The knights who to the Dark Tower's search addressed
Their steps—that just to fail as they, seemed best,
   And all the doubt was now—should I be fit?

So, quiet as despair, I turned from him,
   That hateful cripple, out of his highway
   Into the path he pointed. All the day
Had been a dreary one at best, and dim
Was settling to its close, yet shot one grim
   Red leer to see the plain catch its estray.

For mark! no sooner was I fairly found
   Pledged to the plain, after a pace or two,
   Than, pausing to throw backward a last view
O'er the safe road, 't was gone; gray plain all round:
Nothing but plain to the horizon's bound.
   I might go on; naught else remained to do.

So, on I went. I think I never saw
   Such starved ignoble nature; nothing throve:
   For flowers—as well expect a cedar grove!
But cockle, spurge, according to their law
Might propagate their kind, with none to awe,
   You'd think: a burr had been a treasure trove.

No! penury, inertness and grimace,
   In some strange sort, were the land's portion. "See
   Or shut your eyes," said Nature peevishly,
"It nothing skills: I cannot help my case:

'T is the Last Judgment's fire must cure this place,
  Calcine its clods and set my prisoners free."

If there pushed any ragged thistle-stalk
  Above its mates, the head was chopped; the bents
  Were jealous else.   What made those holes and rents
In the dock's harsh swarth leaves, bruised as to balk
All hope of greenness? 't is a brute must walk
  Pashing their life out, with a brute's intents.

As for the grass, it grew as scant as hair
  In leprosy; thin dry blades pricked the mud
  Which underneath looked kneaded up with blood.
One stiff blind horse, his every bone a-stare,
Stood stupefied, however he came there:
  Thrust out past service from the devil's stud!

Alive? he might be dead for aught I know,
  With that red gaunt and colloped neck a-strain,
  And shut eyes underneath the rusty mane;
Seldom went such grotesqueness with such woe;
I never saw a brute I hated so;
  He must be wicked to deserve such pain.

I shut my eyes and turned them on my heart.
  As a man calls for wine before he fights,
  I asked one draught of earlier, happier sights,
Ere fitly I could hope to play my part.
Think first, fight afterwards—the soldier's art:
  One taste of the old time sets all to rights.

Not it! I fancied Cuthbert's reddening face
  Beneath its garniture of curly gold,
  Dear fellow, till I almost felt him fold
An arm in mine to fix me to the place,

That way he used. Alas, one night's disgrace!
  Out went my heart's new fire and left it cold.

Giles then, the soul of honor—there he stands
  Frank as ten years ago when knighted first.
  What honest man should dare (he said) he durst.
Good—but the scene shifts—faugh! what hangman hands
Pin to his breast a parchment? His own bands
  Read it. Poor traitor, spit upon and curst!

Better this present than a past like that;
  Back therefore to my darkening path again!
  No sound, no sight as far as eye could strain.
Will the night send a howlet or a bat?
I asked: when something on the dismal flat
  Came to arrest my thoughts and change their train.

A sudden little river crossed my path
  As unexpected as a serpent comes.
  No sluggish tide congenial to the glooms;
This, as it frothed by, might have been a bath
For the fiend's glowing hoof—to see the wrath
  Of its black eddy bespate with flakes and spumes.

So petty yet so spiteful! All along,
  Low scrubby alders kneeled down over it;
  Drenched willows flung them headlong in a fit
Of mute despair, a suicidal throng:
The river which had done them all the wrong,
  Whate'er that was, rolled by, deterred no whit.

Which, while I forded,—good saints, how I feared
  To set my foot upon a dead man's cheek,
  Each step, or feel the spear I thrust to seek
For hollows, tangled in his hair or beard!

—It may have been a water-rat I speared,
  But, ugh! it sounded like a baby's shriek.

Glad was I when I reached the other bank.
  Now for a better country. Vain presage!
  Who were the strugglers, what war did they wage,
Whose savage trample thus could pad the dank
Soil to a plash? Toads in a poisoned tank,
  Or wild cats in a red-hot iron cage—

The fight must so have seemed in that fell cirque.
  What penned them there, with all the plain to choose?
  No footprint leading to that horrid mews,
None out of it. Mad brewage set to work
Their brains, no doubt, like galley-slaves the Turk
  Pits for his pastime, Christians against Jews.

And more than that—a furlong on—why, there!
  What bad use was that engine for, that wheel,
  Or brake, not wheel—that harrow fit to reel
Men's bodies out like silk? with all the air
Of Tophet's tool, on earth left unaware,
  Or brought to sharpen its rusty teeth of steel.

Then came a bit of stubbed ground, once a wood,
  Next a marsh, it would seem, and now mere earth
  Desperate and done with; (so a fool finds mirth,
Makes a thing and then mars it, till his mood
Changes and off he goes!) within a rood—
  Bog, clay and rubble, sand and stark black dearth.

Now blotches rankling, colored gay and grim,
  Now patches where some leanness of the soil's
  Broke into moss or substances like boils;
Then came some palsied oak, a cleft in him

Like a distorted mouth that splits its rim
   Gaping at death, and dies while it recoils.

And just as far as ever from the end!
   Naught in the distance but the evening, naught
   To point my footstep further! At the thought,
A great black bird, Apollyon's bosom-friend,
Sailed past, nor beat his wide wing dragon-penned
   That brushed my cap—perchance the guide I sought.

For, looking up, aware I somehow grew,
   'Spite of the dusk, the plain had given place
   All round to mountains—with such name to grace
Mere ugly heights and heaps now stolen in view.
How thus they had surprised me,—solve it, you!
   How to get from them was no clearer case.

Yet half I seemed to recognize some trick
   Of mischief happened to me, God knows when—
   In a bad dream perhaps. Here ended, then,
Progress this way. When, in the very nick
Of giving up, one time more, came a click
   As when a trap shuts—you're inside the den!

Burningly it came on me all at once,
   This was the place! those two hills on the right,
   Crouched like two bulls locked horn in horn in fight;
While to the left, a tall scalped mountain . . . Dunce,
Dotard, a-dozing at the very nonce,
   After a life spent training for the sight!

What in the midst lay but the Tower itself?
   The round squat turret, blind as the fool's heart,
   Built of brown stone, without a counterpart
In the whole world. The tempest's mocking elf

Points to the shipman thus the unseen shelf
   He strikes on, only when the timbers start.

Not see? because of night perhaps?—why, day
   Came back again for that! before it left,
   The dying sunset kindled through a cleft:
The hills, like giants at a hunting, lay,
Chin upon hand, to see the game at bay,—
   "Now stab and end the creature—to the heft!"

Not hear? when noise was everywhere! it tolled
   Increasing like a bell. Names in my ears,
   Of all the lost adventurers my peers,—
How such a one was strong, and such was bold,
And such was fortunate, yet each of old
   Lost, lost! one moment knelled the woe of years.

There they stood, ranged along the hillsides, met
   To view the last of me, a living frame
   For one more picture! in a sheet of flame
I saw them and I knew them all. And yet
Dauntless the slug-horn to my lips I set,
   And blew. *Childe Roland to the Dark Tower came.*

RESPECTABILITY

DEAR, had the world in its caprice
   Deigned to proclaim "I know you both,
   Have recognized your plighted troth,
Am sponsor for you: live in peace!"—
How many precious months and years
   Of youth had passed, that speed so fast,
   Before we found it out at last,
The world, and what it fears!

How much of priceless life were spent
 With men that every virtue decks,
 And women models of their sex,
Society's true ornament,—
Ere we dared wander, nights like this,
 Through wind and rain, and watch the Seine,
 And feel the Boulevard break again
To warmth and light and bliss!

I know! the world proscribes not love;
 Allows my finger to caress
 Your lips' contour and downiness,
Provided it supply a glove.
The world's good word!—the Institute!
 Guizot receives Montalembert!
 Eh? Down the court three lampions flare:
Put forward your best foot!

A LIGHT WOMAN

So far as our story approaches the end,
 Which do you pity the most of us three?—
My friend, or the mistress of my friend
 With her wanton eyes, or me?

My friend was already too good to lose,
 And seemed in the way of improvement yet,
When she crossed his path with her hunting-noose,
 And over him drew her net.

When I saw him tangled in her toils,
 A shame, said I, if she adds just him
To her nine-and-ninety other spoils,
 The hundredth for a whim!

And before my friend be wholly hers,
   How easy to prove to him, I said,
An eagle's the game her pride prefers,
   Though she snaps at a wren instead!

So, I gave her eyes my own eyes to take,
   My hand sought hers as in earnest need,
And round she turned for my noble sake,
   And gave me herself indeed.

The eagle am I, with my fame in the world,
   The wren is he, with his maiden face.
—You look away and your lip is curled?
   Patience, a moment's space!

For see, my friend goes shaking and white;
   He eyes me as the basilisk:
I have turned, it appears, his day to night,
   Eclipsing his sun's disk.

And I did it, he thinks, as a very thief:
   "Though I love her—that, he comprehends—
One should master one's passions, (love, in chief)
   And be loyal to one's friends!"

And she,—she lies in my hand as tame
   As a pear late basking over a wall;
Just a touch to try and off it came;
   'T is mine,—can I let it fall?

With no mind to eat it, that's the worst!
   Were it thrown in the road, would the case assist?
'T was quenching a dozen blue-flies' thirst
   When I gave its stalk a twist.

And I,—what I seem to my friend, you see:
   What I soon shall seem to his love, you guess:

What I seem to myself, do you ask of me?
  No hero, I confess.

'T is an awkward thing to play with souls,
  And matter enough to save one's own:
Yet think of my friend, and the burning coals
  He played with for bits of stone!

One likes to show the truth for the truth;
  That the woman was light is very true:
But suppose she says,—Never mind that youth!
  What wrong have I done to you?

Well, anyhow, here the story stays,
  So far at least as I understand;
And, Robert Browning, you writer of plays,
  Here's a subject made to your hand!

THE STATUE AND THE BUST

THERE's a palace in Florence, the world knows well,
And a statue watches it from the square,
And this story of both do our townsmen tell.

Ages ago, a lady there,
At the farthest window facing the East
Asked, "Who rides by with the royal air?"

The bridesmaids' prattle around her ceased;
She leaned forth, one on either hand;
They saw how the blush of the bride increased—

They felt by its beats her heart expand—
As one at each ear and both in a breath
Whispered, "The Great-Duke Ferdinand."

That selfsame instant, underneath,
The Duke rode past in his idle way,
Empty and fine like a swordless sheath.

Gay he rode, with a friend as gay,
Till he threw his head back—"Who is she?"
—"A bride the Riccardi brings home today."

Hair in heaps lay heavily
Over a pale brow spirit-pure—
Carved like the heart of the coal-black tree,

Crisped like a war-steed's encolure—
And vainly sought to dissemble her eyes
Of the blackest black our eyes endure,

And lo, a blade for a knight's emprise
Filled the fine empty sheath of a man,—
The Duke grew straightway brave and wise.

He looked at her, as a lover can;
She looked at him, as one who awakes:
The past was a sleep, and her life began.

Now, love so ordered for both their sakes,
A feast was held that selfsame night
In the pile which the mighty shadow makes.

(For Via Larga is three-parts light,
But the palace overshadows one,
Because of a crime, which may God requite!

To Florence and God the wrong was done,
Through the first republic's murder there
By Cosimo and his cursed son.)

The Duke (with the statue's face in the square)
Turned in the midst of his multitude
At the bright approach of the bridal pair.

Face to face the lovers stood
A single minute and no more,
While the bridegroom bent as a man subdued—

Bowed till his bonnet brushed the floor—
For the Duke on the lady a kiss conferred,
As the courtly custom was of yore.

In a minute can lovers exchange a word?
If a word did pass, which I do not think,
Only one out of a thousand heard.

That was the bridegroom. At day's brink
He and his bride were alone at last
In a bedchamber by a taper's blink.

Calmly he said that her lot was cast,
That the door she had passed was shut on her
Till the final catafalk repassed.

The world meanwhile, its noise and stir,
Through a certain window facing the East
She could watch like a convent's chronicler.

Since passing the door might lead to a feast,
And a feast might lead to so much beside,
He, of many evils, chose the least.

"Freely I choose too," said the bride—
"Your window and its world suffice,"
Replied the tongue, while the heart replied—

"If I spend the night with that devil twice,
May his window serve as my loop of hell
Whence a damned soul looks on paradise!

"I fly to the Duke who loves me well,
Sit by his side and laugh at sorrow
Ere I count another ave-bell.

" 'Tis only the coat of a page to borrow,
And tie my hair in a horse-boy's trim.
And I save my soul—but not tomorrow"—

(She checked herself and her eye grew dim)
"My father tarries to bless my state:
I must keep it one day more for him.

"Is one day more so long to wait?
Moreover the Duke rides past, I know;
We shall see each other, sure as fate."

She turned on her side and slept.   Just so!
So we resolve on a thing and sleep:
So did the lady, ages ago.

That night the Duke said, "Dear or cheap
As the cost of this cup of bliss may prove
To body or soul, I will drain it deep."

And on the morrow, bold with love,
He beckoned the bridegroom (close on call,
As his duty bade, by the Duke's alcove)

And smiled " 'Twas a very funeral,
Your lady will think, this feast of ours,—
A shame to efface, whate'er befall!

"What if we break from the Arno bowers,
And try if Petraja, cool and green,
Cure last night's fault with this morning's flowers?"

The bridegroom, not a thought to be seen
On his steady brow and quiet mouth,
Said, "Too much favor for me so mean!

"But, alas! my lady leaves the South;
Each wind that comes from the Apennine
Is a menace to her tender youth:

"Nor a way exists, the wise opine,
If she quits her palace twice this year,
To avert the flower of life's decline."

Quoth the Duke, "A sage and a kindly fear.
Moreover Petraja is cold this spring:
Be our feast tonight as usual here!"

And then to himself—"Which night shall bring
Thy bride to her lover's embraces, fool—
Or I am the fool, and thou art the king!

"Yet my passion must wait a night, nor cool—
For tonight the Envoy arrives from France
Whose heart I unlock with thyself, my tool.

"I need thee still and might miss perchance.
Today is not wholly lost, beside,
With its hope of my lady's countenance:

"For I ride—what should I do but ride?
And passing her palace, if I list,
May glance at its window—well betide!"

So said, so done: nor the lady missed
One ray that broke from the ardent brow,
Nor a curl of the lips where the spirit kissed.

Be sure that each renewed the vow,
No morrow's sun should arise and set
And leave them then as it left them now.

But next day passed, and next day yet,
With still fresh cause to wait one day more
Ere each leaped over the parapet.

And still, as love's brief morning wore,
With a gentle start, half smile, half sigh,
They found love not as it seemed before.

They thought it would work infallibly,
But not in despite of heaven and earth:
The rose would blow when the storm passed by.

Meantime they could profit in winter's dearth
By store of fruits that supplant the rose:
The world and its ways have a certain worth:

And to press a point while these oppose
Were simple policy; better wait:
We lose no friends and we gain no foes.

Meantime, worse fates than a lover's fate,
Who daily may ride and pass and look
Where his lady watches behind the grate!

And she—she watched the square like a book
Holding one picture and only one,
Which daily to find she undertook:

When the picture was reached the book was done,
And she turned from the picture at night to scheme
Of tearing it out for herself next sun.

So weeks grew months, years; gleam by gleam
The glory dropped from their youth and love,
And both perceived they had dreamed a dream;

Which hovered as dreams do, still above:
But who can take a dream for a truth?
Oh, hide our eyes from the next remove!

One day as the lady saw her youth
Depart, and the silver thread that streaked
Her hair, and, worn by the serpent's tooth,

The brow so puckered, the chin so peaked,—
And wondered who the woman was,
Hollow-eyed and haggard-cheeked,

Fronting her silent in the glass—
"Summon here," she suddenly said,
"Before the rest of my old self pass,

"Him, the Carver, a hand to aid,
Who fashions the clay no love will change,
And fixes a beauty never to fade.

"Let Robbia's craft so apt and strange
Arrest the remains of young and fair,
And rivet them while the seasons range.

"Make me a face on the window there,
Waiting as ever, mute the while,
My love to pass below in the square!

"And let me think that it may beguile
Dreary days which the dead must spend
Down in their darkness under the aisle,

"To say, 'What matters it at the end?
I did no more while my heart was warm
Than does that image, my pale-faced friend.'

"Where is the use of the lip's red charm,
The heaven of hair, the pride of the brow,
And the blood that blues the inside arm—

"Unless we turn, as the soul knows how,
The earthly gift to an end divine?
A lady of clay is as good, I trow."

But long ere Robbia's cornice, fine,
With flowers and fruits which leaves enlace,
Was set where now is the empty shrine—

(And, leaning out of a bright blue space,
As a ghost might lean from a chink of sky,
The passionate pale lady's face—

Eying ever, with earnest eye
And quick-turned neck at its breathless stretch,
Some one who ever is passing by—)

The Duke had sighed like the simplest wretch
In Florence, "Youth—my dream escapes!
Will its record stay?" And he bade them fetch

Some subtle moulder of brazen shapes—
"Can the soul, the will, die out of a man
Ere his body find the grave that gapes?

"John of Douay shall effect my plan,
Set me on horseback here aloft,
Alive, as the crafty sculptor can,

"In the very square I have crossed so oft:
That men may admire, when future suns
Shall touch the eyes to a purpose soft,

"While the mouth and the brow stay brave in bronze—
Admire and say, 'When he was alive
How he would take his pleasure once!'

"And it shall go hard but I contrive
To listen the while, and laugh in my tomb
At idleness which aspires to strive."

———————————

So! While these wait the trump of doom,
How do their spirits pass, I wonder,
Nights and days in the narrow room?

Still, I suppose, they sit and ponder
What a gift life was, ages ago,
Six steps out of the chapel yonder.

Only they see not God, I know,
Nor all that chivalry of his,
The soldier-saints who, row on row,

Burn upward each to his point of bliss—
Since, the end of life being manifest,
He had burned his way through the world to this.

I hear you reproach, "But delay was best,
For their end was a crime."—Oh, a crime will do
As well, I reply, to serve for a test,

As a virtue golden through and through,
Sufficient to vindicate itself
And prove its worth at a moment's view!

Must a game be played for the sake of pelf?
Where a button goes, 'twere an epigram
To offer the stamp of the very Guelph.

The true has no value beyond the sham:
As well the counter as coin, I submit,
When your table's a hat, and your prize, a dram.

Stake your counter as boldly every whit,
Venture as warily, use the same skill,
Do your best, whether winning or losing it,

If you choose to play!—is my principle.
Let a man contend to the uttermost
For his life's set prize, be it what it will!

The counter our lovers staked was lost
As surely as if it were lawful coin:
And the sin I impute to each frustrate ghost

Is—the unlit lamp and the ungirt loin,
Though the end in sight was a vice, I say.
You of the virtue (we issue join)
How strive you?   *De te, fabula!*

LOVE IN A LIFE

Room after room,
I hunt the house through
We inhabit together.

Heart, fear nothing, for, heart, thou shalt find her—
Next time, herself!—not the trouble behind her
Left in the curtain, the couch's perfume!
As she brushed it, the cornice-wreath blossomed anew:
Yon looking-glass gleamed at the wave of her feather.

Yet the day wears,
And door succeeds door;
I try the fresh fortune—
Range the wide house from the wing to the centre.
Still the same chance! she goes out as I enter.
Spend my whole day in the quest,—who cares?
But 'tis twilight, you see,—with such suites to explore,
Such closets to search, such alcoves to importune!

LIFE IN A LOVE

ESCAPE me?
Never—
Beloved!
While I am I, and you are you,
    So long as the world contains us both,
    Me the loving and you the loth,
While the one eludes, must the other pursue.
My life is a fault at last, I fear:
    It seems too much like a fate, indeed!
    Though I do my best I shall scarce succeed.
But what if I fail of my purpose here?
It is but to keep the nerves at strain,
    To dry one's eyes and laugh at a fall,
And baffled, get up and begin again,—
    So the chase takes up one's life, that's all.
While, look but once from your farthest bound
    At me so deep in the dust and dark,
No sooner the old hope goes to ground

Than a new one, straight to the selfsame mark,
    I shape me—
    Ever
    Removed!

HOW IT STRIKES A CONTEMPORARY

I ONLY knew one poet in my life:
And this, or something like it, was his way.

   You saw go up and down Valladolid,
A man of mark, to know next time you saw.
His very serviceable suit of black
Was courtly once and conscientious still,
And many might have worn it, though none did:
The cloak, that somewhat shone and showed the
    threads,
Had purpose, and the ruff, significance.
He walked and tapped the pavement with his cane,
Scenting the world, looking it full in face,
An old dog, bald and blindish, at his heels.
They turned up, now, the alley by the church,
That leads nowhither; now, they breathed themselves
On the main promenade just at the wrong time:
You'd come upon his scrutinizing hat,
Making a peaked shade blacker than itself
Against the single window spared some house
Intact yet with its mouldered Moorish work,—
Or else surprise the ferrel of his stick
Trying the mortar's temper 'tween the chinks
Of some new shop a-building, French and fine.
He stood and watched the cobbler at his trade,
The man who slices lemons into drink,
The coffee-roaster's brazier, and the boys
That volunteer to help him turn its winch.
He glanced o'er books on stalls with half an eye,

And fly-leaf ballads on the vender's string,
And broad-edge bold-print posters by the wall.
He took such cognizance of men and things,
If any beat a horse, you felt he saw;
If any cursed a woman, he took note;
Yet stared at nobody,—you stared at him,
And found, less to your pleasure than surprise,
He seemed to know you and expect as much.
So, next time that a neighbor's tongue was loosed,
It marked the shameful and notorious fact,
We had among us, not so much a spy,
As a recording chief-inquisitor,
The town's true master if the town but knew!
We merely kept a governor for form,
While this man walked about and took account
Of all thought, said and acted, then went home,
And wrote it fully to our Lord the King
Who has an itch to know things, he knows why,
And reads them in his bedroom of a night.
Oh, you might smile! there wanted not a touch,
A tang of . . . well, it was not wholly ease
As back into your mind the man's look came.
Stricken in years a little,—such a brow
His eyes had to live under!—clear as flint
On either side the formidable nose
Curved, cut and colored like an eagle's claw.
Had he to do with A's surprising fate?
When altogether old B disappeared
And young C got his mistress,—was't our friend,
His letter to the King, that did it all?

What paid the bloodless man for so much pains?
Our Lord the King has favorites manifold,
And shifts his ministry some once a month;
Our city gets new governors at whiles,—
But never word or sign, that I could hear,

Notified to this man about the streets
The King's approval of those letters conned
The last thing duly at the dead of night.
Did the man love his office? Frowned our Lord,
Exhorting when none heard—"Beseech me not!
Too far above my people,—beneath me!
I set the watch,—how should the people know?
Forget them, keep me all the more in mind!"
Was some such understanding 'twixt the two?

I found no truth in one report at least—
That if you tracked him to his home, down lanes
Beyond the Jewry, and as clean to pace,
You found he ate his supper in a room
Blazing with lights, four Titians on the wall,
And twenty naked girls to change his plate!
Poor man, he lived another kind of life
In that new stuccoed third house by the bridge
Fresh-painted, rather smart than otherwise!
The whole street might o'erlook him as he sat
Leg crossing leg, one foot on the dog's back,
Playing a decent cribbage with his maid
(Jacynth, you're sure her name was) o'er the cheese
And fruit, three red halves of starved winter-pears,
Or treat of radishes in April. Nine,
Ten, struck the church clock, straight to bed went he.

My father, like the man of sense he was,
Would point him out to me a dozen times;
" 'St—'St," he'd whisper, "the Corregidor!"
I had been used to think that personage
Was one with lacquered breeches, lustrous belt,
And feathers like a forest in his hat,
Who blew a trumpet and proclaimed the news,
Announced the bull-fights, gave each church its turn,
And memorized the miracle in vogue!

He had a great observance from us boys;
We were in error; that was not the man.

   I'd like now, yet had haply been afraid,
To have just looked, when this man came to die,
And seen who lined the clean gay garret-sides
And stood about the neat low truckle-bed,
With the heavenly manner of relieving guard.
Here had been, mark, the general-in-chief,
Through a whole campaign of the world's life and
     death,
Doing the King's work all the dim day long,
In his old coat and up to knees in mud,
Smoked like a herring, dining on a crust,—
And, now the day was won, relieved at once!
No further show or need for that old coat,
You are sure, for one thing! Bless us, all the while
How sprucely we are dressed out, you and I!
A second, and the angels alter that.
Well, I could never write a verse,—could you?
Let's to the Prado and make the most of time.

THE LAST RIDE TOGETHER

   I SAID—Then, dearest, since 'tis so,
Since now at length my fate I know,
Since nothing all my love avails,
Since all, my life seemed meant for, fails,
   Since this was written and needs must be—
My whole heart rises up to bless
Your name in pride and thankfulness!
Take back the hope you gave,—I claim
Only a memory of the same,
—And this beside, if you will not blame,
   Your leave for one more last ride with me.

My mistress bent that brow of hers;
Those deep dark eyes where pride demurs
When pity would be softening through,
Fixed me a breathing-while or two
    With life or death in the balance: right!
The blood replenished me again;
My last thought was at least not vain:
I and my mistress, side by side
Shall be together, breathe and ride,
So, one day more am I deified.
    Who knows but the world may end tonight?

Hush! if you saw some western cloud
All billowy-bosomed, over-bowed
· By many benedictions—sun's
And moon's and evening-star's at once—
    And so, you, looking and loving best,
Conscious grew, your passion drew
Cloud, sunset, moonrise, star-shine too,
Down on you, near and yet more near,
· Till flesh must fade for heaven was here!—
Thus leant she and lingered—joy and fear!
    Thus lay she a moment on my breast.

Then we began to ride. My soul
Smoothed itself out, a long-cramped scroll
Freshening and fluttering in the wind.
Past hopes already lay behind.
    What need to strive with a life awry?
Had I said that, had I done this,
So might I gain, so might I miss.
Might she have loved me? just as well
She might have hated, who can tell!
Where had I been now if the worst befell?
    And here we are riding, she and I.

Fail I alone, in words and deeds?
Why, all men strive, and who succeeds?
We rode; it seemed my spirit flew,
Saw other regions, cities new,
    As the world rushed by on either side.
I thought,—All labor, yet no less
Bear up beneath their unsuccess.
Look at the end of work, contrast
The petty done, the undone vast,
This present of theirs with the hopeful past!
    I hoped she would love me; here we ride.

What hand and brain went ever paired?
What heart alike conceived and dared?
What act proved all its thought had been?
What will but felt the fleshly screen?
    We ride and I see her bosom heave.
There's many a crown for who can reach.
Ten lines, a statesman's life in each!
The flag stuck on a heap of bones,
A soldier's doing! what atones?
They scratch his name on the Abbey-stones.
    My riding is better, by their leave.

What does it all mean, poet? Well,
Your brains beat into rhythm, you tell
What we felt only; you expressed
You hold things beautiful the best,
    And place them in rhyme so, side by side.
'T is something, nay 't is much: but then,
Have you yourself what's best for men?
Are you—poor, sick, old ere your time—
Nearer one whit your own sublime
Than we who never have turned a rhyme?
    Sing, riding's a joy! For me, I ride.

And you, great sculptor—so, you gave
A score of years to Art, her slave,
And that's your Venus, whence we turn
To yonder girl that fords the burn!
    You acquiesce, and shall I repine?
What, man of music, you grown gray
With notes and nothing else to say,
Is this your sole praise from a friend,
"Greatly his opera's strains intend,
But in music we know how fashions end!"
    I gave my youth; but we ride, in fine.

Who knows what's fit for us?   Had fate
Proposed bliss here should sublimate
My being—had I signed the bond—
Still one must lead some life beyond,
    Have a bliss to die with, dim-descried.
This foot once planted on the goal,
This glory-garland round my soul,
Could I descry such?   Try and test!
I sink back shuddering from the quest.
Earth being so good, would heaven seem best?
    Now, heaven and she are beyond this ride.

And yet—she has not spoke so long!
What if heaven be that, fair and strong
At life's best, with our eyes upturned
Whither life's flower is first discerned,
    We, fixed so, ever should so abide?
What if we still ride on, we two,
With life forever old yet new,
Changed not in kind but in degree,
The instant made eternity,—
And heaven just prove that I and she
    Ride, ride together, forever ride?

MASTER HUGUES OF SAXE-GOTHA

Hist, but a word, fair and soft!
　　Forth and be judged, Master Hugues!
Answer the question I've put you so oft:
　　What do you mean by your mountainous fugues?
See, we're alone in the loft,—

I, the poor organist here,
　　Hugues, the composer of note,
Dead though, and done with, this many a year:
　　Let's have a colloquy, something to quote,
Make the world prick up its ear!

See, the church empties apace:
　　Fast they extinguish the lights.
Hallo there, sacristan!　Five minutes' grace!
　　Here's a crank pedal wants setting to rights,
Balks one of holding the base.

See, our huge house of the sounds,
　　Hushing its hundreds at once
Bids the last loiterer back to his bounds!
　　—O you may challenge them, not a response
Get the church-saints on their rounds!

(Saints go their rounds, who shall doubt?
　　—March, with the moon to admire,
Up nave, down chancel, turn transept about,
　　Supervise all betwixt pavement and spire,
Put rats and mice to the rout—

Aloys and Jurien and Just—
　　Order things back to their place,
Have a sharp eye lest the candlesticks rust,

Rub the church-plate, darn the sacrament-lace,
Clear the desk-velvet of dust.)

Here's your book, younger folks shelve!
   Played I not off-hand and runningly,
Just now, your masterpiece, hard number twelve?
   Here's what should strike, could one handle it
      cunningly:
Help the axe, give it a helve!

Page after page as I played,
   Every bar's rest where one wipes
Sweat from one's brow, I looked up and surveyed,
   O'er my three claviers, yon forest of pipes
Whence you still peeped in the shade.

Sure you were wishful to speak?
   You, with brow ruled like a score,
Yes, and eyes buried in pits on each cheek,
   Like two great breves, as they wrote them of yore,
Each side that bar, your straight beak!

Sure you said—"Good, the mere notes!
   Still, couldst thou take my intent,
Know what procured me our Company's votes—
   A master were lauded and sciolists shent,
Parted the sheep from the goats!"

Well then, speak up, never flinch!
   Quick, ere my candle's a snuff
—Burnt, do you see? to its uttermost inch—
   I believe in you, but that's not enough:
Give my conviction a clinch!

First you deliver your phrase
   —Nothing propound, that I see,
Fit in itself for much blame or much praise—

Answered no less, where no answer needs be;
Off start the Two on their ways.

Straight must a Third interpose,
    Volunteer needlessly help;
In strikes a Fourth, a Fifth thrusts in his nose,
    So the cry's open, the kennel's a-yelp,
Argument's hot to the close.

One dissertates, he is candid;
    Two must discept,—has distinguished;
Three helps the couple, if ever yet man did;
        Four protests; Five makes a dart at the thing
            wished:
Back to One, goes the case bandied.

One says his say with a difference;
    More of expounding, explaining!
All now is wrangle, abuse and vociferance;
    Now there's a truce, all's subdued, self-restraining:
Five, though, stands out all the stiffer hence.

One is incisive, corrosive;
    Two retorts, nettled, curt, crepitant;
Three makes rejoinder, expansive, explosive;
    Four overbears them all, strident and strepitant:
Five . . . O Danaides, O Sieve!

Now, they ply axes and crowbars;
    Now, they prick pins at a tissue
Fine as a skein of the casuist Escobar's
    Worked on the bone of a lie. To what issue?
Where is our gain at the Two-bars?

Est fuga, volvitur rota.
    On we drift: where looms the dim port?

One, Two, Three, Four, Five, contribute their quota;
   Something is gained, if one caught but the import—
Show it us, Hugues of Saxe-Gotha!

What with affirming, denying,
   Holding, risposting, subjoining,
All's like . . . it's like . . . for an instance I'm try-
      ing . . .
   There! See our roof, its gilt moulding and
      groining
Under those spider-webs lying!

So your fugue broadens and thickens,
   Greatens and deepens and lengthens,
Till we exclaim—"But where's music, the dickens?
   Blot ye the gold, while your spider-web strengthens
—Blacked to the stoutest of tickens?"

I for man's effort am zealous:
   Prove me such censure unfounded!
Seems it surprising a lover grows jealous—
   Hopes 't was for something, his organ-pipes
      sounded,
Tiring three boys at the bellows?

Is it your moral of Life?
   Such a web, simple and subtle,
Weave we on earth here in impotent strife,
   Backward and forward each throwing his shuttle,
Death ending all with a knife?

Over our heads truth and nature—
   Still our life's zigzags and dodges,
Ins and outs, weaving a new legislature—
   God's gold just shining its last where that lodges,
Palled beneath man's usurpature.

So we o'ershroud stars and roses,
   Cherub and trophy and garland;
Nothings grow something which quietly closes
   Heaven's earnest eye: not a glimpse of the far land
Gets through our comments and glozes.

Ah, but traditions, inventions,
   (Say we and make up a visage)
So many men with such various intentions,
   Down the past ages, must know more than this age!
Leave we the web its dimensions!

Who thinks Hugues wrote for the deaf,
   Proved a mere mountain in labor?
Better submit; try again; what's the clef?
   'Faith, 't is no trifle for pipe and for tabor—
Four flats, the minor in F.

Friend, your fugue taxes the finger:
   Learning it once, who would lose it?
Yet all the while a misgiving will linger,
   Truth's golden o'er us although we refuse it—
Nature, through cobwebs we string her.

Hugues! I advise *mea pœnâ*
   (Counterpoint glares like a Gorgon)
Bid One, Two, Three, Four, Five, clear the arena!
   Say the word, straight I unstop the full organ,
Blare out the *mode Palestrina*.

While in the roof, if I'm right there,
   . . . Lo you, the wick in the socket!
Hallo, you sacristan, show us a light there!
   Down it dips, gone like a rocket.
What, you want, do you, to come unawares,
Sweeping the church up for first morning-prayers,

And find a poor devil has ended his cares
At the foot of your rotten-runged rat-riddled stairs?
  Do I carry the moon in my pocket?

BISHOP BLOUGRAM'S APOLOGY

  No more wine? then we'll push back chairs and talk.
A final glass for me, though: cool, i' faith!
We ought to have our Abbey back, you see.
It's different, preaching in basilicas,
And doing duty in some masterpiece
Like this of brother Pugin's, bless his heart!
I doubt if they're half baked, those chalk rosettes,
Ciphers and stucco-twiddlings everywhere;
It's just like breathing in a lime-kiln: eh?
These hot long ceremonies of our church
Cost us a little—oh, they pay the price,
You take me—amply pay it!   Now, we'll talk.

  So, you despise me, Mr. Gigadibs.
No deprecation,—nay, I beg you, sir!
Beside 't is our engagement; don't you know,
I promised, if you'd watch a dinner out,
We'd see truth dawn together?—truth that peeps
Over the glasses' edge when dinner's done,
And body gets its sop and holds its noise
And leaves soul free a little.   Now's the time:
Truth's break of day!   You do despise me then.
And if I say, "despise me,"—never fear!
I know you do not in a certain sense—
Not in my arm-chair, for example: here,
I well imagine you respect my place
 (Status, entourage, worldly circumstance)
Quite to its value—very much indeed:
—Are up to the protesting eyes of you

In pride at being seated here for once—
You'll turn it to such capital account!
When somebody, through years and years to come,
Hints of the bishop,—names me—that's enough:
"Blougram? I knew him"— (into it you slide)
"Dined with him once, a Corpus Christi Day,
All alone, we two; he's a clever man:
And after dinner,—why, the wine you know,—
Oh, there was wine, and good!—what with the wine . . .
'Faith, we began upon all sorts of talk!
He's no bad fellow, Blougram; he had seen
Something of mine he relished, some review:
He's quite above their humbug in his heart,
Half-said as much, indeed—the thing's his trade.
I warrant, Blougram's skeptical at times:
How otherwise? I liked him, I confess!"
Che che, my dear sir, as we say at Rome,
Don't you protest now! It's fair give and take;
You have had your turn and spoken your home-truths:
The hand's mine now, and here you follow suit.

    Thus much conceded, still the first fact stays—
You do despise me; your ideal of life
Is not the bishop's; you would not be I.
You would like better to be Goethe, now,
Or Buonaparte, or, bless me, lower still,
Count D'Orsay,—so you did what you preferred,
Spoke as you thought, and, as you cannot help,
Believed or disbelieved, no matter what,
So long as on that point, whate'er it was,
You loosed your mind, were whole and sole yourself.
—That, my ideal never can include,
Upon that element of truth and worth
Never be based! for say they make me Pope—
(They can't—suppose it for our argument!)
Why, there I'm at my tether's end, I've reached

My height, and not a height which pleases you:
An unbelieving Pope won't do, you say.
It's like those eerie stories nurses tell,
Of how some actor on a stage played Death,
With pasteboard crown, sham orb and tinselled dart,
And called himself the monarch of the world;
Then, going in the tire-room afterward,
Because the play was done, to shift himself,
Got touched upon the sleeve familiarly,
The moment he had shut the closet door,
By Death himself. Thus God might touch a Pope
At unawares, ask what his baubles mean,
And whose part he presumed to play just now.
Best be yourself, imperial, plain and true!

So, drawing comfortable breath again,
You weigh and find, whatever more or less
I boast of my ideal realized
Is nothing in the balance when opposed
To your ideal, your grand simple life,
Of which you will not realize one jot.
I am much, you are nothing; you would be all,
I would be merely much: you beat me there.

No, friend, you do not beat me: hearken why!
The common problem, yours, mine, every one's,
Is—not to fancy what were fair in life
Provided it could be,—but, finding first
What may be, then find how to make it fair
Up to our means: a very different thing!
No abstract intellectual plan of life
Quite irrespective of life's plainest laws,
But one, a man, who is man and nothing more,
May lead within a world which (by your leave)
Is Rome or London, not Fool's-paradise.
Embellish Rome, idealize away,

Make paradise of London if you can,
You're welcome, nay, you're wise.

                              A simile!
  We mortals cross the ocean of this world
Each in his average cabin of a life;
The best's not big, the worst yields elbow-room.
Now for our six months' voyage—how prepare?
You come on shipboard with a landsman's list
Of things he calls convenient: so they are!
An India screen is pretty furniture,
A piano-forte is a fine resource,
All Balzac's novels occupy one shelf,
The new edition fifty volumes long;
And little Greek books, with the funny type
They get up well at Leipsic, fill the next:
Go on! slabbed marble, what a bath it makes!
And Parma's pride, the Jerome, let us add!
'T were pleasant could Correggio's fleeting glow
Hang full in face of one where'er one roams,
Since he more than the others brings with him
Italy's self,—the marvellous Modenese!—
Yet was not on your list before, perhaps.
—Alas, friend, here's the agent . . . is't the name?
The captain, or whoever's master here—
You see him screw his face up; what's his cry
Ere you set foot on shipboard? "Six feet square!"
If you won't understand what six feet mean,
Compute and purchase stores accordingly—
And if, in pique because he overhauls
Your Jerome, piano, bath, you come on board
Bare—why, you cut a figure at the first
While sympathetic landsmen see you off;
Not afterward, when long ere half seas over,
You peep up from your utterly naked boards
Into some snug and well-appointed berth,

Like mine for instance (try the cooler jug—
Put back the other, but don't jog the ice!)
And mortified you mutter, "Well and good;
He sits enjoying his sea-furniture;
'T is stout and proper, and there's store of it:
Though I've the better notion, all agree,
Of fitting rooms up. Hang the carpenter,
Neat ship-shape fixings and contrivances—
I would have brought my Jerome, frame and all!"
And meantime you bring nothing: never mind—
You've proved your artist-nature: what you don't
You might bring, so despise me, as I say.

Now come, let's backward to the starting-place.
See my way: we're two college friends, suppose.
Prepare together for our voyage, then;
Each note and check the other in his work,—
Here's mine, a bishop's outfit; criticize!
What's wrong? why won't you be a bishop too?

Why first, you don't believe, you don't and can't,
(Not statedly, that is, and fixedly
And absolutely and exclusively)
In any revelation called divine.
No dogmas nail your faith; and what remains
But say so, like the honest man you are?
First, therefore, overhaul theology!
Nay, I too, not a fool, you please to think,
Must find believing every whit as hard:
And if I do not frankly say as much,
The ugly consequence is clear enough.

Now wait, my friend: well, I do not believe—
If you'll accept no faith that is not fixed,
Absolute and exclusive, as you say.
You're wrong—I mean to prove it in due time.
Meanwhile, I know where difficulties lie

I could not, cannot solve, nor ever shall,
So give up hope accordingly to solve—
(To you, and over the wine).   Our dogmas then
With both of us, though in unlike degree,
Missing full credence—overboard with them!
I mean to meet you on your own premise:
Good, there go mine in company with yours!

And now what are we? unbelievers both,
Calm and complete, determinately fixed
Today, tomorrow, and forever, pray?
You'll guarantee me that?   Not so, I think!
In no wise! all we've gained is, that belief,
As unbelief before, shakes us by fits,
Confounds us like its predecessor.   Where's
The gain? how can we guard our unbelief,
Make it bear fruit to us?—the problem here.
Just when we are safest, there's a sunset-touch,
A fancy from a flower-bell, some one's death,
A chorus-ending from Euripides,—
And that's enough for fifty hopes and fears
As old and new at once as nature's self,
To rap and knock and enter in our soul,
Take hands and dance there, a fantastic ring,
Round the ancient idol, on his base again,—
The grand Perhaps!   We look on helplessly.
There the old misgivings, crooked questions are—
This good God,—what he could do, if he would,
Would, if he could—then must have done long since:
If so, when, where, and how? some way must be,—
Once feel about, and soon or late you hit
Some sense, in which it might be, after all.
Why not, "The Way, the Truth, the Life?"

                                        —That way
Over the mountain, which who stands upon

Is apt to doubt if it be meant for a road;
While, if he views it from the waste itself,
Up goes the line there, plain from base to brow,
Not vague, mistakable! what's a break or two
Seen from the unbroken desert either side?
And then (to bring in fresh philosophy)
What if the breaks themselves should prove at last
The most consummate of contrivances
To train a man's eye, teach him what is faith?
And so we stumble at truth's very test!
All we have gained then by our unbelief
Is a life of doubt diversified by faith,
For one of faith diversified by doubt:
We called the chess-board white,—we call it black.

"Well," you rejoin, "the end's no worse, at least;
We've reason for both colors on the board:
Why not confess then, where I drop the faith
And you the doubt, that I'm as right as you?"

Because, friend, in the next place, this being so,
And both things even,—faith and unbelief
Left to a man's choice,—we'll proceed a step,
Returning to our image, which I like.

A man's choice, yes—but a cabin-passenger's—
The man made for the special life o' the world—
Do you forget him?   I remember though!
Consult our ship's conditions and you find
One and but one choice suitable to all;
The choice, that you unluckily prefer,
Turning things topsy-turvy—they or it
Going to the ground.   Belief or unbelief
Bears upon life, determines its whole course,
Begins at its beginning.   See the world
Such as it is,—you made it not, nor I;

I mean to take it as it is,—and you,
Not so you'll take it,—though you get naught else.
I know the special kind of life I like,
What suits the most my idiosyncrasy,
Brings out the best of me and bears me fruit
In power, peace, pleasantness, and length of days.
I find that positive belief does this
For me, and unbelief, no whit of this.
—For you, it does, however?—that, we'll try!
'T is clear, I cannot lead my life, at least,
Induce the world to let me peaceably,
Without declaring at the outset, "Friends,
I absolutely and peremptorily
Believe!"—I say, faith is my waking life:
One sleeps, indeed, and dreams at intervals,
We know, but waking's the main point with us,
And my provision's for life's waking part.
Accordingly, I use heart, head, and hand
All day, I build, scheme, study, and make friends;
And when night overtakes me, down I lie,
Sleep, dream a little, and get done with it,
The sooner the better, to begin afresh.
What's midnight doubt before the dayspring's faith?
You, the philosopher, that disbelieve,
That recognize the night, give dreams their weight—
To be consistent you should keep your bed,
Abstain from healthy acts that prove you man,
For fear you drowse perhaps at unawares!
And certainly at night you'll sleep and dream,
Live through the day and bustle as you please.
And so you live to sleep as I to wake,
To unbelieve as I to still believe?
Well, and the common sense o' the world calls you
Bed-ridden,—and its good things come to me.
Its estimation, which is half the fight,
That's the first-cabin comfort I secure:

The next . . . but you perceive with half an eye!
Come, come, it's best believing, if we may;
You can't but own that!

                    Next, concede again,
If once we choose belief, on all accounts
We can't be too decisive in our faith,
Conclusive and exclusive in its terms,
To suit the world which gives us the good things.
In every man's career are certain points
Whereon he dares not be indifferent;
The world detects him clearly, if he dare,
As baffled at the game, and losing life.
He may care little or he may care much
For riches, honor, pleasure, work, repose.
Since various theories of life and life's
Success are extant which might easily
Comport with either estimate of these:
And whoso chooses wealth or poverty,
Labor or quiet, is not judged a fool
Because his fellow would choose otherwise:
We let him choose upon his own account
So long as he's consistent with his choice.
But certain points, left wholly to himself,
When once a man has arbitrated on,
We say he must succeed there or go hang.
Thus, he should wed the woman he loves most
Or needs most, whatsoe'er the love or need—
For he can't wed twice. Then, he must avouch,
Or follow, at the least, sufficiently,
The form of faith his conscience holds the best,
Whate'er the process of conviction was:
For nothing can compensate his mistake
On such a point, the man himself being judge:
He cannot wed twice, nor twice lose his soul.

Well now, there's one great form of Christian faith
I happened to be born in—which to teach
Was given me as I grew up, on all hands,
As best and readiest means of living by;
The same on examination being proved
The most pronounced moreover, fixed, precise,
And absolute form of faith in the whole world—
Accordingly, most potent of all forms
For working on the world. Observe, my friend!
Such as you know me, I am free to say,
In these hard latter days which hamper one,
Myself—by no immoderate exercise
Of intellect and learning, but the tact
To let external forces work for me,
—Bid the street's stones be bread and they are bread;
Bid Peter's creed, or rather, Hildebrand's,
Exalt me o'er my fellows in the world
And make my life an ease and joy and pride;
It does so,—which for me's a great point gained,
Who have a soul and body that exact
A comfortable care in many ways.
There's power in me and will to dominate
Which I must exercise, they hurt me else:
In many ways I need mankind's respect,
Obedience, and the love that's born of fear:
While at the same time, there's a taste I have,
A toy of soul, a titillating thing,
Refuses to digest these dainties crude.
The naked life is gross till clothed upon:
I must take what men offer, with a grace
As though I would not, could I help it, take!
An uniform I wear though over-rich—
Something imposed on me, no choice of mine;
No fancy-dress worn for pure fancy's sake
And despicable therefore! now folk kneel
And kiss my hand—of course the Church's hand.

Thus I am made, thus life is best for me,
And thus that it should be I have procured;
And thus it could not be another way,
I venture to imagine.

                              You'll reply,
So far my choice, no doubt, is a success;
But were I made of better elements,
With nobler instincts, purer tastes, like you,
I hardly would account the thing success
Though it did all for me I say.

                              But, friend,
We speak of what is; not of what might be,
And how 't were better if 't were otherwise.
I am the man you see here plain enough:
Grant I'm a beast, why, beasts must lead beasts' lives!
Suppose I own at once to tail and claws;
The tailless man exceeds me: but being tailed
I'll lash out lion fashion, and leave apes
To dock their stump and dress their haunches up.
My business is not to remake myself,
But make the absolute best of what God made.
Or—our first simile—though you prove me doomed
To a viler berth still, to the steerage-hole,
The sheep-pen or the pig-sty, I should strive
To make what use of each were possible;
And as this cabin gets upholstery,
That hutch should rustle with sufficient straw.

But, friend, I don't acknowledge quite so fast
I fail of all your manhood's lofty tastes
Enumerated so complacently,
On the mere ground that you forsooth can find
In this particular life I choose to lead
No fit provision for them. Can you not?

Say you, my fault is I address myself
To grosser estimators than should judge?
And that's no way of holding up the soul,
Which, nobler, needs men's praise perhaps, yet knows
One wise man's verdict outweighs all the fools'—
Would like the two, but, forced to choose, takes that.
I pine among my million imbeciles
 (You think) aware some dozen men of sense
Eye me and know me, whether I believe
In the last winking Virgin, as I vow,
And am a fool, or disbelieve in her
And am a knave,—approve in neither case,
Withhold their voices though I look their way:
Like Verdi when, at his worst opera's end
 (The thing they gave at Florence,—what's its name?)
While the mad houseful's plaudits near outbang
His orchestra of salt-box, tongs, and bones,
He looks through all the roaring and the wreaths
Where sits Rossini patient in his stall.

   Nay, friend, I meet you with an answer here—
That even your prime men who appraise their kind
Are men still, catch a wheel within a wheel,
See more in a truth than the truth's simple self,
Confuse themselves. You see lads walk the street
Sixty the minute; what's to note in that?
You see one lad o'erstride a chimney-stack;
Him you must watch—he's sure to fall, yet stands!
Our interest's on the dangerous edge of things.
The honest thief, the tender murderer,
The superstitious atheist, demirep
That loves and saves her soul in new French books—
We watch while these in equilibrium keep
The giddy line midway: one step aside,
They're classed and done with. I, then, keep the line
Before your sages,—just the men to shrink

From the gross weights, coarse scales, and labels broad
You offer their refinement. Fool or knave?
Why needs a bishop be a fool or knave
When there's a thousand diamond weights between?
So, I enlist them. Your picked twelve, you'll find,
Profess themselves indignant, scandalized
At thus being held unable to explain
How a superior man who disbelieves
May not believe as well: that's Schelling's way!
It's through my coming in the tail of time,
Nicking the minute with a happy tact.
Had I been born three hundred years ago
They'd say, "What's strange?   Blougram of course
    believes;"
And, seventy years since, "disbelieves of course."
But now, "He may believe; and yet, and yet
How can he?" All eyes turn with interest.
Whereas, step off the line on either side—
You, for example, clever to a fault,
The rough and ready man who write apace,
Read somewhat seldomer, think perhaps even less—
You disbelieve! Who wonders and who cares?
Lord So-and-So—his coat bedropped with wax,
All Peter's chains about his waist, his back
Brave with the needlework of Noodledom—
Believes! Again, who wonders and who cares?
But I, the man of sense and learning too,
The able to think yet act, the this, the that,
I, to believe at this late time of day!
Enough; you see, I need not fear contempt.

    —Except it's yours! Admire me as these may,
You don't. But whom at least do you admire?
Present your own perfection, your ideal,
Your pattern man for a minute—oh, make haste!
Is it Napoleon you would have us grow?

Concede the means; allow his head and hand,
(A large concession, clever as you are)
Good! In our common primal element
Of unbelief (we can't believe, you know—
We're still at that admission, recollect!)
Where do you find—apart from, towering o'er
The secondary temporary aims
Which satisfy the gross taste you despise—
Where do you find his star?—his crazy trust
God knows through what or in what? it's alive
And shines and leads him, and that's all we want.
Have we aught in our sober night shall point
Such ends as his were, and direct the means
Of working out our purpose straight as his,
Nor bring a moment's trouble on success
With after-care to justify the same?
—Be a Napoleon, and yet disbelieve—
Why, the man's mad, friend, take his light away!
What's the vague good o' the world, for which you dare
With comfort to yourself blow millions up?
We neither of us see it! we do see
The blown-up millions—spatter of their brains
And writhing of their bowels and so forth,
In that bewildering entanglement
Of horrible eventualities
Past calculation to the end of time!
Can I mistake for some clear word of God
(Which were my ample warrant for it all)
His puff of hazy instinct, idle talk,
"The State, that's I," quack-nonsense about crowns,
And (when one beats the man to his last hold)
A vague idea of setting things to rights,
Policing people efficaciously,
More to their profit, most of all to his own;
The whole to end that dismallest of ends
By an Austrian marriage, cant to us the Church,

And resurrection of the old régime?
Would I, who hope to live a dozen years,
Fight Austerlitz for reasons such and such?
No: for, concede me but the merest chance
Doubt may be wrong—there's judgment, life to come!
With just that chance, I dare not. Doubt proves right?
This present life is all?—you offer me
Its dozen noisy years, without a chance
That wedding an archduchess, wearing lace,
And getting called by divers new-coined names,
Will drive off ugly thoughts and let me dine,
Sleep, read, and chat in quiet as I like!
Therefore I will not.

                    Take another case;
Fit up the cabin yet another way.
What say you to the poets? shall we write
Hamlet, Othello—make the world our own,
Without a risk to run of either sort?
I can't!—to put the strongest reason first.
"But try," you urge, "the trying shall suffice;
The aim, if reached or not, makes great the life:
Try to be Shakespeare, leave the rest to fate!"
Spare my self-knowledge—there's no fooling me!
If I prefer remaining my poor self,
I say so not in self-dispraise but praise.
If I'm a Shakespeare, let the well alone;
Why should I try to be what now I am?
If I'm no Shakespeare, as too probable,—
His power and consciousness and self-delight
And all we want in common, shall I find—
Trying forever? while on points of taste
Wherewith, to speak it humbly, he and I
Are dowered alike—I'll ask you, I or he,
Which in our two lives realizes most?
Much, he imagined—somewhat, I possess.

He had the imagination; stick to that!
Let him say, "In the face of my soul's works
Your world is worthless and I touch it not
Lest I should wrong them"—I'll withdraw my plea.
But does he say so? look upon his life!
Himself, who only can, gives judgment there.
He leaves his towers and gorgeous palaces
To build the trimmest house in Stratford town;
Saves money, spends it, owns the worth of things,
Giulio Romano's pictures, Dowland's lute;
Enjoys a show, respects the puppets, too,
And none more, had he seen its entry once,
Than "Pandulph, of fair Milan cardinal."
Why then should I who play that personage,
The very Pandulph Shakespeare's fancy made,
Be told that had the poet chanced to start
From where I stand now (some degree like mine
Being just the goal he ran his race to reach)
He would have run the whole race back, forsooth,
And left being Pandulph, to begin write plays?
Ah, the earth's best can be but the earth's best!
Did Shakespeare live, he could but sit at home
And get himself in dreams the Vatican,
Greek busts, Venetian paintings, Roman walls,
And English books, none equal to his own,
Which I read, bound in gold (he never did).
—Terni's fall, Naples' bay, and Gothard's top—
Eh, friend? I could not fancy one of these;
But, as I pour this claret, there they are:
I've gained them—crossed Saint Gothard last July
With ten mules to the carriage and a bed
Slung inside; is my hap the worse for that?
We want the same things, Shakespeare and myself,
And what I want, I have: he, gifted more,
Could fancy he too had them when he liked,
But not so thoroughly that, if fate allowed,

He would not have them also in my sense.
We play one game; I send the ball aloft
No less adroitly that of fifty strokes
Scarce five go o'er the wall so wide and high
Which sends them back to me: I wish and get.
He struck balls higher and with better skill,
But at a poor fence level with his head,
And hit—his Stratford house, a coat of arms,
Successful dealings in his grain and wool,—
While I receive heaven's incense in my nose
And style myself the cousin of Queen Bess.
Ask him, if this life's all, who wins the game?

Believe—and our whole argument breaks up.
Enthusiasm's the best thing, I repeat;
Only, we can't command it; fire and life
Are all, dead matter's nothing, we agree:
And be it a mad dream or God's very breath,
The fact's the same,—belief's fire, once in us,
Makes of all else mere stuff to show itself:
We penetrate our life with such a glow
As fire lends wood and iron—this turns steel,
That burns to ash—all's one, fire proves its power
For good or ill, since men call flare success.
But paint a fire, it will not therefore burn.
Light one in me, I'll find it food enough!
Why, to be Luther—that's a life to lead,
Incomparably better than my own.
He comes, reclaims God's earth for God, he says,
Sets up God's rule again by simple means,
Reopens a shut book, and all is done.
He flared out in the flaring of mankind;
Such Luther's luck was: how shall such be mine?
If he succeeded, nothing's left to do:
And if he did not altogether—well,
Strauss is the next advance. All Strauss should be

I might be also. But to what result?
He looks upon no future: Luther did.
What can I gain on the denying side?
Ice makes no conflagration. State the facts,
Read the text right, emancipate the world—
The emancipated world enjoys itself
With scarce a thank-you: Blougram told it first
It could not owe a farthing,—not to him
More than Saint Paul! 't would press its pay, you think?
Then add there's still that plaguy hundredth chance
Strauss may be wrong. And so a risk is run—
For what gain? not for Luther's, who secured
A real heaven in his heart throughout his life,
Supposing death a little altered things.

   "Ay, but since really you lack faith," you cry,
"You run the same risk really on all sides,
In cool indifference as bold unbelief.
As well be Strauss as swing 'twixt Paul and him.
It's not worth having, such imperfect faith,
No more available to do faith's work
Than unbelief like mine. Whole faith, or none!"

   Softly, my friend! I must dispute that point.
Once own the use of faith, I'll find you faith.
We're back on Christian ground. You call for faith:
I show you doubt, to prove that faith exists.
The more of doubt, the stronger faith, I say,
If faith o'ercomes doubt. How I know it does?
By life and man's free will, God gave for that
To mold life as we choose it, shows our choice:
That's our one act, the previous work's his own.
You criticise the soul? it reared this tree—
This broad life and whatever fruit it bears!
What matter though I doubt at every pore,
Head-doubts, heart-doubts, doubts at my fingers' ends,

Doubts in the trivial work of every day,
Doubts at the very bases of my soul
In the grand moments when she probes herself—
If finally I have a life to show,
The thing I did, brought out in evidence
Against the thing done to me underground
By hell and all its brood, for aught I know?
I say, whence sprang this? shows it faith or doubt?
All's doubt in me; where's break of faith in this?
It is the idea, the feeling and the love,
God means mankind should strive for and show forth
Whatever be the process to that end,—
And not historic knowledge, logic sound,
And metaphysical acumen, sure!
"What think ye of Christ," friend? when all's done and
        said,
Like you this Christianity or not?
It may be false, but will you wish it true?
Has it your vote to be so if it can?
Trust you an instinct silenced long ago
That will break silence and enjoin you love
What mortified philosophy is hoarse,
And all in vain, with bidding you despise?
If you desire faith—then you've faith enough:
What else seeks God—nay, what else seek ourselves?
You form a notion of me, we'll suppose,
On hearsay; it's a favorable one:
"But still" (you add), "there was no such good man,
Because of contradiction in the facts.
One proves, for instance, he was born in Rome,
This Blougram; yet throughout the tales of him
I see he figures as an Englishman."
Well, the two things are reconcilable.
But would I rather you discovered that,
Subjoining—"Still, what matter though they be?
Blougram concerns me naught, born here or there."

Pure faith indeed—you know not what you ask!
Naked belief in God the Omnipotent,
Omniscient, Omnipresent, sears too much
The sense of conscious creatures to be borne.
It were the seeing him, no flesh shall dare.
Some think, Creation's meant to show him forth:
I say it's meant to hide him all it can,
And that's what all the blessed evil's for.
Its use in Time is to environ us,
Our breath, our drop of dew, with shield enough
Against that sight till we can bear its stress.
Under a vertical sun, the exposed brain
And lidless eye and disemprisoned heart
Less certainly would wither up at once
Than mind, confronted with the truth of him.
But time and earth case-harden us to live;
The feeblest sense is trusted most; the child
Feels God a moment, ichors o'er the place,
Plays on and grows to be a man like us.
With me, faith means perpetual unbelief
Kept quiet like the snake 'neath Michael's foot
Who stands calm just because he feels it writhe.
Or, if that's too ambitious,—here's my box—
I need the excitation of a pinch
Threatening the torpor of the inside-nose
Nigh on the imminent sneeze that never comes.
"Leave it in peace," advise the simple folk:
Make it aware of peace by itching-fits,
Say I—let doubt occasion still more faith!

You'll say, once all believed, man, woman, child,
In that dear middle-age these noodles praise.
How you'd exult if I could put you back
Six hundred years, blot out cosmogony,
Geology, ethnology, what not,
(Greek endings, each the little passing-bell

That signifies some faith's about to die),
And set you square with Genesis again,—
When such a traveller told you his last news,
He saw the ark a-top of Ararat
But did not climb there since 't was getting dusk
And robber-bands infest the mountain's foot!
How should you feel, I ask, in such an age,
How act? As other people felt and did;
With soul more blank than this decanter's knob,
Believe—and yet lie, kill, rob, fornicate,
Full in belief's face, like the beast you'd be!

No, when the fight begins within himself,
A man's worth something. God stoops o'er his head,
Satan looks up between his feet—both tug—
He's left, himself, i' the middle: the soul wakes
And grows. Prolong that battle through his life!
Never leave growing till the life to come!
Here, we've got callous to the Virgin's winks
That used to puzzle people wholesomely:
Men have outgrown the shame of being fools.
What are the laws of nature, not to bend
If the Church bid them?—brother Newman asks.
Up with the Immaculate Conception, then—
On to the rack with faith!—is my advice.
Will not that hurry us upon our knees,
Knocking our breasts, "It can't be—yet it shall!
Who am I, the worm, to argue with my Pope?
Low things confound the high things!" and so forth.
That's better than acquitting God with grace
As some folk do. He's tried—no case is proved,
Philosophy is lenient—he may go!

You'll say, the old system's not so obsolete
But men believe still: ay, but who and where?
King Bomba's lazzaroni foster yet

The sacred flame, so Antonelli writes;
But even of these, what ragamuffin-saint
Believes God watches him continually,
As he believes in fire that it will burn,
Or rain that it will drench him? Break fire's law,
Sin against rain, although the penalty
Be just a singe or soaking? "No," he smiles;
"Those laws are laws that can enforce themselves."

    The sum of all is—yes, my doubt is great,
My faith's still greater, then my faith's enough.
I have read much, thought much, experienced much,
Yet would die rather than avow my fear
The Naples' liquefaction may be false,
When set to happen by the palace-clock
According to the clouds or dinner-time.
I hear you recommend, I might at least
Eliminate, decrassify my faith
Since I adopt it; keeping what I must
And leaving what I can—such points as this.
I won't—that is, I can't throw one away.
Supposing there's no truth in what I hold
About the need of trial to man's faith,
Still, when you bid me purify the same,
To such a process I discern no end.
Clearing off one excrescence to see two,
There's ever a next in size, now grown as big,
That meets the knife: I cut and cut again!
First cut the Liquefaction, what comes last
But Fichte's clever cut at God himself?
Experimentalize on sacred things!
I trust nor hand nor eye nor heart nor brain
To stop betimes: they all get drunk alike.
The first step, I am master not to take.

You'd find the cutting-process to your taste
As much as leaving growths of lies unpruned,
Nor see more danger in it,—you retort.
Your taste's worth mine; but my taste proves more wise
When we consider that the steadfast hold
On the extreme end of the chain of faith
Gives all the advantage, makes the difference
With the rough purblind mass we seek to rule:
We are their lords, or they are free of us,
Just as we tighten or relax our hold.
So, other matters equal, we'll revert
To the first problem—which, if solved my way
And thrown into the balance, turns the scale—
How we may lead a comfortable life,
How suit our luggage to the cabin's size.

Of course you are remarking all this time
How narrowly and grossly I view life,
Respect the creature-comforts, care to rule
The masses, and regard complacently
"The cabin," in our old phrase. Well, I do.
I act for, talk for, live for this world now,
As this world prizes action, life and talk:
No prejudice to what next world may prove,
Whose new laws and requirements, my best pledge
To observe then, is that I observe these now,
Shall do hereafter what I do meanwhile.
Let us concede (gratuitously though)
Next life relieves the soul of body, yields
Pure spiritual enjoyment: well, my friend,
Why lose this life i' the meantime, since its use
May be to make the next life more intense?

Do you know, I have often had a dream
(Work it up in your next month's article)
Of man's poor spirit in its progress, still

Losing true life forever and a day
Through ever trying to be and ever being—
In the evolution of successive spheres—
Before its actual sphere and place of life,
Halfway into the next, which having reached,
It shoots with corresponding foolery
Halfway into the next still, on and off!
As when a traveller, bound from North to South,
Scouts fur in Russia: what's its use in France?
In France spurns flannel: where's its need in Spain?
In Spain drops cloth, too cumbrous for Algiers!
Linen goes next, and last the skin itself,
A superfluity at Timbuctoo.
When, through his journey, was the fool at ease?
I'm at ease now, friend; worldly in this world,
I take and like its way of life; I think
My brothers, who administer the means,
Live better for my comfort—that's good too;
And God, if he pronounce upon such life,
Approves my service, which is better still.
If he keep silence,—why, for you or me
Or that brute beast pulled-up in today's "Times,"
What odds is't, save to ourselves, what life we lead?

You meet me at this issue: you declare,—
All special-pleading done with—truth is truth,
And justifies itself by undreamed ways.
You don't fear but it's better, if we doubt,
To say so, act up to our truth perceived
However feebly. Do then,—act away!
'Tis there I'm on the watch for you. How one acts
Is, both of us agree, our chief concern:
And how you'll act is what I fain would see
If, like the candid person you appear,
You dare to make the most of your life's scheme
As I of mine, live up to its full law

Since there's no higher law that counterchecks.
Put natural religion to the test
You've just demolished the revealed with—quick,
Down to the root of all that checks your will,
All prohibition to lie, kill and thieve,
Or even to be an atheistic priest!
Suppose a pricking to incontinence—
Philosophers deduce you chastity
Or shame, from just the fact that at the first
Whoso embraced a woman in the field,
Threw club down and forewent his brains beside,
So, stood a ready victim in the reach
Of any brother savage, club in hand;
Hence saw the use of going out of sight
In wood or cave to prosecute his loves:
I read this in a French book t'other day.
Does law so analyzed coerce you much?
Oh, men spin clouds of fuzz where matters end,
But you who reach where the first thread begins,
You'll soon cut that!—which means you can, but won't,
Through certain instincts, blind, unreasoned-out,
You dare not set aside, you can't tell why,
But there they are, and so you let them rule.
Then, friend, you seem as much a slave as I,
A liar, conscious coward and hypocrite,
Without the good the slave expects to get,
In case he has a master after all!
You own your instincts? why, what else do I,
Who want, am made for, and must have a God
Ere I can be aught, do aught?—no mere name
Want, but the true thing with what proves its truth,
To wit, a relation from that thing to me,
Touching from head to foot—which touch I feel,
And with it take the rest, this life of ours!
I live my life here; yours you dare not live.

—Not as I state it, who (you please subjoin)
Disfigure such a life and call it names,
While, to your mind, remains another way
For simple men: knowledge and power have rights,
But ignorance and weakness have rights too.
There needs no crucial effort to find truth
If here or there or anywhere about:
We ought to turn each side, try hard and see,
And if we can't, be glad we've earned at least
The right, by one laborious proof the more,
To graze in peace earth's pleasant pasturage.
Men are not angels, neither are they brutes:
Something we may see, all we cannot see.
What need of lying? I say, I see all,
And swear to each detail the most minute
In what I think a Pan's face—you, mere cloud:
I swear I hear him speak and see him wink,
For fear, if once I drop the emphasis,
Mankind may doubt there's any cloud at all.
You take the simple life—ready to see,
Willing to see (for no cloud's worth a face)—
And leaving quiet what no strength can move,
And which, who bids you move? who has the right?
I bid you; but you are God's sheep, not mine:
"Pastor est tui Dominus." You find
In this the pleasant pasture of our life
Much you may eat without the least offence,
Much you don't eat because your maw objects,
Much you would eat but that your fellow-flock
Open great eyes at you and even butt,
And thereupon you like your mates so well
You cannot please yourself, offending them;
Though when they seem exorbitantly sheep,
You weigh your pleasure with their butts and bleats
And strike the balance. Sometimes certain fears
Restrain you, real checks since you find them so;

Sometimes you please yourself and nothing checks:
And thus you graze through life with not one lie,
And like it best.

                But do you, in truth's name?
If so, you beat—which means you are not I—
Who needs must make earth mine and feed my fill
Not simply unbutted at, unbickered with,
But motioned to the velvet of the sward
By those obsequious wethers' very selves.
Look at me, sir; my age is double yours:
At yours, I knew beforehand, so enjoyed,
What now I should be—as, permit the word,
I pretty well imagine your whole range
And stretch of tether twenty years to come.
We both have minds and bodies much alike.
In truth's name, don't you want my bishopric,
My daily bread, my influence, and my state?
You're young. I'm old; you must be old one day;
Will you find then, as I do hour by hour,
Women their lovers kneel to, who cut curls
From your fat lap-dog's ear to grace a brooch—
Dukes, who petition just to kiss your ring—
With much beside you know or may conceive?
Suppose we die tonight: well, here am I,
Such were my gains, life bore this fruit to me,
While writing all the same my articles
On music, poetry, the fictile vase
Found at Albano, chess, Anacreon's Greek.
But you—the highest honor in your life,
The thing you'll crown yourself with, all your days,
Is—dining here and drinking this last glass
I pour you out in sign of amity
Before we part forever. Of your power
And social influence, worldly worth in short,
Judge what's my estimation by the fact,

I do not condescend to enjoin, beseech,
Hint secrecy on one of all these words!
You're shrewd and know that should you publish one
The world would brand the lie—my enemies first,
Who'd sneer—"the bishop's an arch-hypocrite
And knave perhaps, but not so frank a fool."
Whereas I should not dare for both my ears
Breathe one such syllable, smile one such smile,
Before the chaplain who reflects myself—
My shade's so much more potent than your flesh.
What's your reward, self-abnegating friend?
Stood you confessed of those exceptional
And privileged great natures that dwarf mine—
A zealot with a mad ideal in reach,
A poet just about to print his ode,
A statesman with a scheme to stop this war,
An artist whose religion is his art—
I should have nothing to object: such men
Carry the fire, all things grow warm to them,
Their drugget's worth my purple, they beat me.
But you,—you're just as little those as I—
You, Gigadibs, who, thirty years of age,
Write stately for Blackwood's Magazine,
Believe you see two points in Hamlet's soul
Unseized by the Germans yet—which view you'll print—
Meantime the best you have to show being still
That lively lightsome article we took
Almost for the true Dickens,—what's its name?
"The Slum and Cellar, or Whitechapel life
Limned after dark!" it made me laugh, I know,
And pleased a month, and brought you in ten pounds.
—Success I recognize and compliment,
And therefore give you, if you choose, three words
(The card and pencil-scratch is quite enough)
Which whether here, in Dublin or New York,
Will get you, prompt as at my eyebrow's wink,

Such terms as never you aspired to get
In all our own reviews and some not ours.
Go write your lively sketches! be the first
"Blougram, or The Eccentric Confidence"—
Or better simply say, "The Outward-bound."
Why, men as soon would throw it in my teeth
As copy and quote the infamy chalked broad
About me on the church-door opposite.
You will not wait for that experience though,
I fancy, howsoever you decide,
To discontinue—not detesting, not
Defaming, but at least—despising me!

Over his wine so smiled and talked his hour
Sylvester Blougram, styled *in partibus*
Episcopus, nec non— (the deuce knows what
It's changed to by our novel hierarchy)
With Gigadibs the literary man,
Who played with spoons, explored his plate's design,
And ranged the olive-stones about its edge,
While the great bishop rolled him out a mind
Long crumpled, till creased consciousness lay smooth.

For Blougram, he believed, say, half he spoke.
The other portion, as he shaped it thus
For argumentatory purposes,
He felt his foe was foolish to dispute.
Some arbitrary accidental thoughts
That crossed his mind, amusing because new,
He chose to represent as fixtures there,
Invariable convictions (such they seemed
Beside his interlocutor's loose cards
Flung daily down, and not the same way twice),
While certain hell-deep instincts, man's weak tongue
Is never bold to utter in their truth

Because styled hell-deep ('t is an old mistake
To place hell at the bottom of the earth),
He ignored these,—not having in readiness
Their nomenclature and philosophy:
He said true things, but called them by wrong names.
"On the whole," he thought, "I justify myself
On every point where cavillers like this
Oppugn my life: he tries one kind of fence,
I close, he's worsted, that's enough for him.
He's on the ground: if ground should break away
I take my stand on, there's a firmer yet
Beneath it, both of us may sink and reach.
His ground was over mine and broke the first:
So, let him sit with me this many a year!"

He did not sit five minutes.   Just a week
Sufficed his sudden healthy vehemence.
Something had struck him in the "Outward-bound"
Another way than Blougram's purpose was:
And having bought, not cabin-furniture
But settler's-implements   (enough for three)
And started for Australia—there, I hope,
By this time he has tested his first plough,
And studied his last chapter of Saint John.

MEMORABILIA

Ah, did you once see Shelley plain,
    And did he stop and speak to you,
And did you speak to him again?
    How strange it seems and new!

But you were living before that,
    And also you are living after;
And the memory I started at—
    My starting moves your laughter!

I crossed a moor, with a name of its own
     And a certain use in the world no doubt,
Yet a hand's-breadth of it shines alone
     'Mid the blank miles round about:

For there I picked up on the heather,
     And there I put inside my breast
A moulted feather, an eagle-feather!
     Well, I forget the rest.

ANDREA DEL SARTO

(CALLED "THE FAULTLESS PAINTER")

BUT do not let us quarrel any more,
No, my Lucrezia; bear with me for once:
Sit down and all shall happen as you wish.
You turn your face, but does it bring your heart?
I'll work then for your friend's friend, never fear,
Treat his own subject after his own way,
Fix his own time, accept too his own price,
And shut the money into this small hand
When next it takes mine.   Will it? tenderly?
Oh, I'll content him,—but tomorrow, Love!
I often am much wearier than you think,
This evening more than usual, and it seems
As if—forgive now—should you let me sit
Here by the window with your hand in mine
And look a half-hour forth on Fiesole,
Both of one mind, as married people use,
Quietly, quietly the evening through,
I might get up tomorrow to my work
Cheerful and fresh as ever.   Let us try.
Tomorrow, how you shall be glad for this!
Your soft hand is a woman of itself,
And mine the man's bared breast she curls inside.

Don't count the time lost, neither; you must serve
For each of the five pictures we require:
It saves a model. So! keep looking so—
My serpentining beauty, rounds on rounds!
—How could you ever prick those perfect ears,
Even to put the pearl there! oh, so sweet—
My face, my moon, my everybody's moon,
Which everybody looks on and calls his,
And, I suppose, is looked on by in turn,
While she looks—no one's: very dear, no less.
You smile? why, there's my picture ready made,
There's what we painters call our harmony!
A common grayness silvers everything,—
All in a twilight, you and I alike
—You, at the point of your first pride in me
(That's gone you know),—but I, at every point;
My youth, my hope, my art, being all toned down
To yonder sober pleasant Fiesole.
There's the bell clinking from the chapel-top;
That length of convent-wall across the way
Holds the trees safer, huddled more inside;
The last monk leaves the garden; days decrease,
And autumn grows, autumn in everything.
Eh? the whole seems to fall into a shape
As if I saw alike my work and self
And all that I was born to be and do,
A twilight-piece. Love, we are in God's hand.
How strange now looks the life he makes us lead;
So free we seem, so fettered fast we are!
I feel he laid the fetter: let it lie!
This chamber for example—turn your head—
All that's behind us! You don't understand
Nor care to understand about my art,
But you can hear at least when people speak:
And that cartoon, the second from the door
—It is the thing, Love! so such thing should be—

Behold Madonna!—I am bold to say.
I can do with my pencil what I know,
What I see, what at bottom of my heart
I wish for, if I ever wish so deep—
Do easily, too—when I say, perfectly,
I do not boast, perhaps: yourself are judge,
Who listened to the Legate's talk last week,
And just as much they used to say in France.
At any rate 't is easy, all of it!
No sketches first, no studies, that's long past:
I do what many dream of all their lives,
—Dream? strive to do, and agonize to do,
And fail in doing. I could count twenty such
On twice your fingers, and not leave this town,
Who strive—you don't know how the others strive
To paint a little thing like that you smeared
Carelessly passing with your robes afloat,—
Yet do much less, so much less, Someone says,
(I know his name, no matter)—so much less!
Well, less is more, Lucrezia: I am judged.
There burns a truer light of God in them,
In their vexed beating stuffed and stopped-up brain,
Heart, or whate'er else, than goes on to prompt
This low-pulsed forthright craftsman's hand of mine.
Their works drop groundward, but themselves, I
    know,
Reach many a time a heaven that's shut to me,
Enter and take their place there sure enough,
Though they come back and cannot tell the world.
My works are nearer heaven, but I sit here.
The sudden blood of these men! at a word—
Praise them, it boïls, or blame them, it boils too.
I, painting from myself and to myself,
Know what I do, am unmoved by men's blame
Or their praise either. Somebody remarks
Morello's outline there is wrongly traced,

His hue mistaken; what of that? or else,
Rightly traced and well ordered; what of that?
Speak as they please, what does the mountain care?
Ah, but a man's reach should exceed his grasp,
Or what's a heaven for?   All is silver-gray
Placid and perfect with my art: the worse!
I know both what I want and what might gain,
And yet how profitless to know, to sigh
"Had I been two, another and myself,
Our head would have o'erlooked the world!"   No
        doubt.
Yonder's a work now, of that famous youth
The Urbinate who died five years ago.
 ('T is copied, George Vasari sent it me.)
Well, I can fancy how he did it all,
Pouring his soul, with kings and popes to see,
Reaching, that heaven might so replenish him,
Above and through his art—for it gives way;
That arm is wrongly put—and there again—
A fault to pardon in the drawing's lines,
Its body, so to speak: its soul is right,
He means right—that, a child may understand.
Still, what an arm! and I could alter it:
But all the play, the insight and the stretch—
Out of me, out of me!   And wherefore out?
Had you enjoined them on me, given me soul,
We might have risen to Rafael, I and you!
Nay, Love, you did give all I asked, I think—
More than I merit, yes, by many times.
But had you—oh, with the same perfect brow,
And perfect eyes, and more than perfect mouth,
And the low voice my soul hears, as a bird
The fowler's pipe, and follows to the snare—
Had you, with these the same, but brought a mind!
Some women do so.   Had the mouth there urged
"God and the glory! never care for gain.

The present by the future, what is that? *Anglo*
Live for fame, side by side with Agnolo!
Rafael is waiting: up to God, all three!"
I might have done it for you. So it seems:
Perhaps not. All is as God overrules.
Beside, incentives come from the soul's self;
The rest avail not. Why do I need you?
What wife had Rafael, or has Agnolo?
In this world, who can do a thing, will not;
And who would do it, cannot, I perceive:
Yet the will's somewhat—somewhat, too, the power—
And thus we half-men struggle. At the end,
God, I conclude, compensates, punishes.
'T is safer for me, if the award be strict,
That I am something underrated here,
Poor this long while, despised, to speak the truth.
I dared not, do you know, leave home all day,
For fear of chancing on the Paris lords.
The best is when they pass and look aside;
But they speak sometimes; I must bear it all.
Well may they speak! That Francis, that first time,
And that long festal year at Fontainebleau!
I surely then could sometimes leave the ground,
Put on the glory, Rafael's daily wear,
In that humane great monarch's golden look,—
One finger in his beard or twisted curl
Over his mouth's good mark that made the smile,
One arm about my shoulder, round my neck,
The jingle of his gold chain in my ear,
I painting proudly with his breath on me,
All his court round him, seeing with his eyes,
Such frank French eyes, and such a fire of souls
Profuse, my hand kept plying by those hearts,—
And, best of all, this, this, this face beyond,
This in the background, waiting on my work,
To crown the issue with a last reward!

A good time, was it not, my kingly days?
And had you not grown restless . . . but I know—
'T is done and past; 't was right, my instinct said;
Too live the life grew, golden and not gray,
And I'm the weak-eyed bat no sun should tempt
Out of the grange whose four walls make his world.
How could it end in any other way?
You called me, and I came home to your heart.
The triumph was—to reach and stay there; since
I reached it ere the triumph, what is lost?
Let my hands frame your face in your hair's gold,
You beautiful Lucrezia that are mine!
"Rafael did this, Andrea painted that;
The Roman's is the better when you pray,
But still the other's Virgin was his wife"—
Men will excuse me. I am glad to judge
Both pictures in your presence; clearer grows
My better fortune, I resolve to think.
For, do you know, Lucrezia, as God lives,
Said one day Agnolo, his very self,
To Rafael . . . I have known it all these years . . .
(When the young man was flaming out his thoughts
Upon a palace-wall for Rome to see,
Too lifted up in heart because of it)
"Friend, there's a certain sorry little scrub
Goes up and down our Florence, none cares how,
Who, were he set to plan and execute
As you are, pricked on by your popes and kings,
Would bring the sweat into that brow of yours!"
To Rafael's!—And indeed the arm is wrong.
I hardly dare . . . yet, only you to see,
Give the chalk here—quick, thus the line should go!
Ay, but the soul! he's Rafael! rub it out!
Still, all I care for, if he spoke the truth,
(What he? why, who but Michel Agnolo?
Do you forget already words like those?)

If really there was such a chance, so lost,—
Is, whether you're—not grateful—but more pleased.
Well, let me think so. And you smile indeed!
This hour has been an hour! Another smile?
If you would sit thus by me every night
I should work better, do you comprehend?
I mean that I should earn more, give you more.
See, it is settled dusk now; there's a star;
Morello's gone, the watch-lights show the wall,
The cue-owls speak the name we call them by.
Come from the window, love,—come in, at last,
Inside the melancholy little house
We built to be so gay with. God is just.
King Francis may forgive me: oft at nights
When I look up from painting, eyes tired out,
The walls become illumined, brick from brick
Distinct, instead of mortar, fierce bright gold,
That gold of his I did cement them with!
Let us but love each other. Must you go?
That Cousin here again? he waits outside?
Must see you—you, and not with me? Those loans?
More gaming debts to pay? you smiled for that?
Well, let smiles buy me! have you more to spend?
While hand and eye and something of a heart
Are left me, work's my ware, and what's it worth?
I'll pay my fancy. Only let me sit
The gray remainder of the evening out,
Idle, you call it, and muse perfectly
How I could paint, were I but back in France,
One picture, just one more—the Virgin's face,
Not yours this time! I want you at my side
To hear them—that is, Michel Agnolo—
Judge all I do and tell you of its worth.
Will you? Tomorrow, satisfy your friend.
I take the subjects for his corridor,
Finish the portrait out of hand—there, there,

And throw him in another thing or two
If he demurs; the whole should prove enough
To pay for this same Cousin's freak. Beside,
What's better and what's all I care about,
Get you the thirteen scudi for the ruff!
Love, does that please you? Ah, but what does he,
The Cousin! what does he to please you more?

   I am grown peaceful as old age tonight.
I regret little, I would change still less.
Since there my past life lies, why alter it?
The very wrong to Francis!—it is true
I took his coin, was tempted and complied,
And built this house and sinned, and all is said.
My father and my mother died of want.
Well, had I riches of my own? you see
How one gets rich! Let each one bear his lot.
They were born poor, lived poor, and poor they died:
And I have labored somewhat in my time
And not been paid profusely. Some good son
Paint my two hundred pictures—let him try!
No doubt, there's something strikes a balance. Yes,
You loved me quite enough, it seems tonight.
This must suffice me here. What would one have?
In heaven, perhaps, new chances, one more chance—
Four great walls in the New Jerusalem,
Meted on each side by the angel's reed,
For Leonard, Rafael, Agnolo and me
To cover—the three first without a wife,
While I have mine! So—still they overcome
Because there's still Lucrezia,—as I choose.

   Again the Cousin's whistle! Go, my Love.

BEFORE

Let them fight it out, friend! things have gone too far.
God must judge the couple: leave them as they are
—Whichever one's the guiltless, to his glory,
And whichever one the guilt's with, to my story!

Why, you would not bid men, sunk in such a slough,
Strike no arm out further, stick and stink as now,
Leaving right and wrong to settle the embroilment,
Heaven with snaky hell, in torture and entoilment?

Who's the culprit of them? How must he conceive
God—the queen he caps to, laughing in his sleeve,
" 'T is but decent to profess one's self beneath her:
Still, one must not be too much in earnest, either!"

Better sin the whole sin, sure that God observes;
Then go live his life out! Life will try his nerves,
When the sky, which noticed all, makes no disclosure,
And the earth keeps up her terrible composure.

Let him pace at pleasure, past the walls of rose,
Pluck their fruits when grape-trees graze him as he goes!
For he 'gins to guess the purpose of the garden,
With the sly mute thing, beside there, for a warden.

What's the leopard-dog-thing, constant at his side,
A leer and lie in every eye of its obsequious hide?
When will come an end to all the mock obeisance,
And the price appear that pays for the misfeasance?

So much for the culprit. Who's the martyred man?
Let him bear one stroke more, for be sure he can!
He that strove thus evil's lump with good to leaven,
Let him give his blood at last and get his heaven!

All or nothing, stake it!   Trusts he God or no?
Thus far and no farther? farther? be it so!
Now, enough of your chicane of prudent pauses,
Sage provisos, sub-intents and saving-clauses!

Ah, "forgive" you bid him?   While God's champion
        lives,
Wrong shall be resisted: dead, why, he forgives.
But you must not end my friend ere you begin him;
Evil stands not crowned on earth, while breath is in him.

Once more—Will the wronger, at this last of all,
Dare to say, "I did wrong," rising in his fall?
No?—Let go, then!   Both the fighters to their places!
While I count three, step you back as many paces!

AFTER

TAKE the cloak from his face, and at first
    Let the corpse do its worst!

How he lies in his rights of a man!
    Death has done all death can.
And, absorbed in the new life he leads,
    He recks not, he heeds
Nor his wrong nor my vengeance; both strike
    On his senses alike,
And are lost in the solemn and strange
    Surprise of the change.

Ha, what avails death to erase
    His offence, my disgrace?
I would we were boys as of old
    In the field, by the fold:

His outrage, God's patience, man's scorn
  Were so easily borne!

I stand here now, he lies in his place:
  Cover the face!

IN THREE DAYS

So, I shall see her in three days
And just one night, but nights are short,
Then two long hours, and that is morn.
See how I come, unchanged, unworn!
Feel, where my life broke off from thine,
How fresh the splinters keep and fine,—
Only a touch and we combine!

Too long, this time of year, the days!
But nights, at least the nights are short.
As night shows where her one moon is,
A hand's-breadth of pure light and bliss,
So life's night gives my lady birth
And my eyes hold her!   What is worth
The rest of heaven, the rest of earth?

O loaded curls, release your store
Of warmth and scent, as once before
The tingling hair did, lights and darks
Outbreaking into fairy sparks,
When under curl and curl I pried
After the warmth and scent inside,
Through lights and darks how manifold—
The dark inspired, the light controlled!
As early Art embrowns the gold.

What great fear, should one say, "Three days
That change the world might change as well

Your fortune; and if joy delays,
Be happy that no worse befell!"
What small fear, if another says,
"Three days and one short night beside
May throw no shadow on your ways;
But years must teem with change untried,
With chance not easily defied,
With an end somewhere undescried."
No fear!—or if a fear be born
This minute, it dies out in scorn.
Fear? I shall see her in three days
And one night, now the nights are short,
Then just two hours, and that is morn.

IN A YEAR

Never any more,
    While I live,
Need I hope to see his face
    As before.
Once his love grown chill,
    Mine may strive:
Bitterly we re-embrace,
    Single still.

Was it something said,
    Something done,
Vexed him? Was it touch of hand,
    Turn of head?
Strange! that very way
    Love begun:
I as little understand
    Love's decay.

When I sewed or drew,
    I recall

How he looked as if I sung,
  —Sweetly too.
If I spoke a word,
  First of all
Up his cheek the color sprung,
  Then he heard.

Sitting by my side,
  At my feet,
So he breathed but air I breathed,
  Satisfied!
I, too, at love's brim
  Touched the sweet:
I would die if death bequeathed
  Sweet to him.

"Speak, I love thee best!"
  He exclaimed:
"Let thy love my own foretell!"
  I confessed:
"Clasp my heart on thine
  Now unblamed,
Since upon thy soul as well
  Hangeth mine!"

Was it wrong to own,
  Being truth?
Why should all the giving prove
  His alone?
I had wealth and ease,
  Beauty, youth:
Since my lover gave me love,
  I gave these.

That was all I meant,
  —To be just,

And the passion I had raised,
   To content.
Since he chose to change
   Gold for dust,
If I gave him what he praised
   Was it strange?

Would he loved me yet,
   On and on,
While I found some way undreamed
   —Paid my debt!
Gave more life and more,
   Till, all gone,
He should smile "She never seemed
   Mine before.

"What, she felt the while,
   Must I think?
Love's so different with us men!"
   He should smile:
"Dying for my sake—
   White and pink!
Can't we touch these bubbles then
   But they break?"

Dear, the pang is brief,
   Do thy part,
Have thy pleasure! How perplexed
   Grows belief!
Well, this cold clay clod
   Was man's heart:
Crumble it, and what comes next?
   Is it God?

OLD PICTURES IN FLORENCE

THE morn when first it thunders in March,
　The eel in the pond gives a leap, they say:
As I leaned and looked over the aloed arch
　Of the villa-gate this warm March day,
No flash snapped, no dumb thunder rolled
　In the valley beneath where, white and wide
And washed by the morning water-gold,
　Florence lay out on the mountain-side.

River and bridge and street and square
　Lay mine, as much at my beck and call,
Through the live translucent bath of air,
　As the sights in a magic crystal ball.
And of all I saw and of all I praised,
　The most to praise and the best to see,
Was the startling bell-tower Giotto raised:
　But why did it more than startle me?

Giotto, how, with that soul of yours,
　Could you play me false who loved you so?
Some slights if a certain heart endures
　Yet it feels, I would have your fellows know!
I' faith, I perceive not why I should care
　To break a silence that suits them best,
But the thing grows somewhat hard to bear
　When I find a Giotto join the rest.

On the arch where olives overhead
　Print the blue sky with twig and leaf,
(That sharp-curled leaf which they never shed)
　'Twixt the aloes, I used to lean in chief,
And mark through the winter afternoons,
　By a gift God grants me now and then,

In the mild decline of those suns like moons,
 Who walked in Florence, besides her men.

They might chirp and chaffer, come and go
 For pleasure or profit, her men alive—
My business was hardly with them, I trow,
 But with empty cells of the human hive;
—With the chapter-room, the cloister-porch,
 The church's apsis, aisle or nave,
Its crypt, one fingers along with a torch,
 Its face set full for the sun to shave.

Wherever a fresco peels and drops,
 Wherever an outline weakens and wanes
Till the latest life in the painting stops,
 Stands One whom each fainter pulse-tick pains:
One, wishful each scrap should clutch the brick,
 Each tinge not wholly escape the plaster,
—A lion who dies of an ass's kick,
 The wronged great soul of an ancient Master.

For oh, this world and the wrong it does!
 They are safe in heaven with their backs to it,
The Michaels and Rafaels, you hum and buzz
 Round the works of, you of the little wit!
Do their eyes contract to the earth's old scope,
 Now that they see God face to face,
And have all attained to be poets, I hope?
 'Tis their holiday now, in any case.

Much they reck of your praise and you!
 But the wronged great souls—can they be quit
Of a world where their work is all to do,
 Where you style them, you of the little wit,
Old Master This and Early the Other,
 Not dreaming that Old and New are fellows:

A younger succeeds to an elder brother,
  Da Vincis derive in good time from Dellos.

And here where your praise might yield returns,
  And a handsome word or two give help,
Here, after your kind, the mastiff girns
  And the puppy pack of poodles yelp.
What, not a word for Stefano there,
  Of brow once prominent and starry,
Called Nature's Ape, and the world's despair
  For his peerless painting? (See Vasari.)

There stands the Master. Study, my friends,
  What a man's work comes to! So he plans it,
Performs it, perfects it, makes amends
  For the toiling and moiling, and then, *sic transit!*
Happier the thrifty blind-folk labor,
  With upturned eye while the hand is busy,
Not sidling a glance at the coin of their neighbor!
  'Tis looking downward that makes one dizzy.

"If you knew their work you would deal your dole."
  May I take upon me to instruct you?
When Greek Art ran and reached the goal,
  Thus much had the world to boast *in fructu*—
The Truth of Man, as by God first spoken,
  Which the actual generations garble,
Was re-uttered, and Soul (which Limbs betoken)
  And Limbs (Soul informs) made new in marble.

So you saw yourself as you wished you were,
  As you might have been, as you cannot be;
Earth here, rebuked by Olympus there:
  And grew content in your poor degree
With your little power, by those statues' godhead,
  And your little scope, by their eyes' full sway,

And your little grace, by their grace embodied,
  And your little date, by their forms that stay.

You would fain be kinglier, say, than I am?
  Even so, you will not sit like Theseus.
You would prove a model? The Son of Priam
  Has yet the advantage in arms' and knees' use.
You're wroth—can you slay your snake like Apollo?
  You're grieved—still Niobe's the grander!
You live—there's the Racers' frieze to follow:
  You die—there's the dying Alexander.

So, testing your weakness by their strength,
  Your meagre charms by their rounded beauty,
Measured by Art in your breadth and length,
  You learned—to submit is a mortal's duty.
—When I say "you" 'tis the common soul,
  The collective, I mean: the race of Man
That receives life in parts to live in a whole,
  And grow here according to God's clear plan.

Growth came when, looking your last on them all,
  You turned your eyes inwardly one fine day
And cried with a start—What if we so small
  Be greater and grander the while than they?
Are they perfect of lineament, perfect of stature?
  In both, of such lower types are we
Precisely because of our wider nature;
  For time, theirs—ours, for eternity.

Today's brief passion limits their range;
  It seethes with the morrow for us and more.
They are perfect—how else? they shall never change:
  We are faulty—why not? we have time in store.
The Artificer's hand is not arrested
  With us; we are rough-hewn, nowise polished:

They stand for our copy, and, once invested
   With all they can teach, we shall see them
     abolished.

'Tis a life-long toil till our lump be leaven—
   The better! What's come to perfection perishes.
Things learned on earth, we shall practise in heaven:
   Works done least rapidly, Art most cherishes.
Thyself shalt afford the example, Giotto!
   Thy one work, not to decrease or diminish,
Done at a stroke, was just (was it not?) "O!"
   Thy great Campanile is still to finish.

Is it true that we are now, and shall be hereafter,
   But what and where depend on life's minute?
Hails heavenly cheer or infernal laughter
   Our first step out of the gulf or in it?
Shall Man, such step within his endeavor,
   Man's face, have no more play and action
Than joy which is crystallized forever,
   Or grief, an eternal petrifaction?

On which I conclude, that the early painters,
   To cries of "Greek Art and what more wish
     you?"—
Replied, "To become now self-acquainters,
   And paint man, man, whatever the issue!
Make new hopes shine through the flesh they fray,
   New fears aggrandize the rags and tatters:
To bring the invisible full into play!
   Let the visible go to the dogs—what matters?"

Give these, I exhort you, their guerdon and glory
   For daring so much, before they well did it.
The first of the new, in our race's story,
   Beats the last of the old; 'tis no idle quiddit.

The worthies began a revolution,
  Which if on earth you intend to acknowledge,
Why, honor them now! (ends my allocution)
    Nor confer your degree when the folk leave
    college.

There's a fancy some lean to and others hate—
  That, when this life is ended, begins
New work for the soul in another state,
  Where it strives and gets weary, loses and wins:
Where the strong and the weak, this world's con-
    geries,
  Repeat in large what they practised in small,
Through life after life in unlimited series;
  Only the scale's to be changed, that's all.

Yet I hardly know. When a soul has seen
  By the means of Evil that Good is best,
And, through earth and its noise, what is heaven's
    serene,—
  When our faith in the same has stood the test—
Why, the child grown man, you burn the rod,
  The uses of labor are surely done;
There remaineth a rest for the people of God:
  And I have had troubles enough, for one.

But at any rate I have loved the season
  Of Art's spring-birth so dim and dewy;
My sculptor is Nicolo the Pisan,
  My painter—who but Cimabue?
Nor ever was man of them all indeed,
  From these to Ghiberti and Ghirlandajo,
Could say that he missed my critic-meed.
  So, now to my special grievance—heigh-ho!

Their ghosts still stand, as I said before,
  Watching each fresco flaked and rasped,

Blocked up, knocked out, or whitewashed o'er:
 —No getting again what the church has grasped!
The works on the wall must take their chance;
 "Works never conceded to England's thick clime!"
(I hope they prefer their inheritance
 Of a bucketful of Italian quick-lime.)

When they go at length, with such a shaking
 Of heads o'er the old delusion, sadly
Each master his way through the black streets taking,
 Where many a lost work breathes though badly—
Why don't they bethink them of who has merited?
 Why not reveal, while their pictures dree
Such doom, how a captive might be out-ferreted?
 Why is it they never remember me?

Not that I expect the great Bigordi,
 Nor Sandro to hear me, chivalric, bellicose;
Nor the wronged Lippino; and not a word I
 Say of a scrap of Fra Angelico's:
But are you too fine, Taddeo Gaddi,
 To grant me a taste of your intonaco,
Some Jerome that seeks the heaven with a sad eye?
 Not a churlish saint, Lorenzo Monaco?

Could not the ghost with the close red cap,
 My Pollajolo, the twice a craftsman,
Save me a sample, give me the hap
 Of a muscular Christ that shows the draughtsman?
No Virgin by him the somewhat petty,
 Of finical touch and tempera crumbly—
Could not Alesso Baldovinetti
 Contribute so much, I ask him humbly?

Margheritone of Arezzo,
 With the grave-clothes garb and swaddling barret,

(Why purse up mouth and beak in a pet so,
    You bald old saturnine poll-clawed parrot?)
Not a poor glimmering Crucifixion,
    Where in the foreground kneels the donor?
If such remain, as is my conviction,
    The hoarding it does you but little honor.

They pass; for them the panels may thrill,
    The tempera grow alive and tinglish;
Their pictures are left to the mercies still
    Of dealers and stealers, Jews and the English,
Who, seeing mere money's worth in their prize,
    Will sell it to somebody calm as Zeno
At naked High Art, and in ecstasies
    Before some clay-cold vile Carlino!

No matter for these! But Giotto, you,
    Have you allowed, as the town-tongues babble it,—
Oh, never! it shall not be counted true—
    That a certain precious little tablet
Which Buonarroti eyed like a lover—
    Was buried so long in oblivion's womb
And, left for another than I to discover,
    Turns up at last! and to whom?—to whom?

I, that have haunted the dim San Spirito,
    (Or was it rather the Ognissanti?)
Patient on altar-step planting a weary toe!
    Nay, I shall have it yet! *Detur amanti!*
My Koh-i-noor—or (if that's a platitude)
    Jewel of Giamschid, the Persian Sofi's eye;
So, in anticipative gratitude,
    What if I take up my hope and prophesy?

When the hour grows ripe, and a certain dotard
    Is pitched, no parcel that needs invoicing,

To the worse side of the Mont St. Gothard,
   We shall begin by way of rejoicing;
None of that shooting the sky (blank cartridge),
   Nor a civic guard, all plumes and lacquer,
Hunting Radetzky's soul like a partridge
   Over Morello with squib and cracker.

This time we'll shoot better game and bag 'em hot—
   No mere display at the stone of Dante,
But a kind of sober Witanagemot
   (Ex: "Casa Guidi," *quod videas ante*)
Shall ponder, once Freedom restored to Florence,
   How Art may return that departed with her.
Go, hated house, go each trace of the Loraine's,
   And bring us the days of Orgagna hither!

How we shall prologuize, how we shall perorate,
   Utter fit things upon art and history,
Feel truth at blood-heat and falsehood at zero rate,
   Make of the want of the age no mystery;
Contrast the fructuous and sterile eras,
   Show—monarchy ever its uncouth cub licks
Out of the bear's shape into Chimæra's,
   While Pure Art's birth is still the republic's.

Then one shall propose in a speech (curt Tuscan,
   Expurgate and sober, with scarcely an *"issimo,"*)
To end now our half-told tale of Cambuscan,
   And turn the bell-tower's *alt* to *altissimo:*
And fine as the beak of a young beccaccia
   The Campanile, the Duomo's fit ally,
Shall soar up in gold full fifty braccia,
   Completing Florence, as Florence Italy.

Shall I be alive that morning the scaffold
   Is broken away, and the long-pent fire,

Like the golden hope of the world, unbaffled
    Springs from its sleep, and up goes the spire
While "God and the People" plain for its motto,
    Thence the new tricolor flaps at the sky?
At least to foresee that glory of Giotto
    And Florence together, the first am I!

"DE GUSTIBUS—"

YOUR ghost will walk, you lover of trees,
    (If our loves remain)
      In an English lane,
By a cornfield-side a-flutter with poppies.
Hark, those two in the hazel coppice—
A boy and a girl, if the good fates please,
    Making love, say,—
      The happier they!
Draw yourself up from the light of the moon,
And let them pass, as they will too soon,
    With the beanflowers' boon,
    And the blackbird's tune,
    And May, and June!

What I love best in all the world
Is a castle, precipice-encurled,
In a gash of the wind-grieved Apennine.
Or look for me, old fellow of mine,
 (If I get my head from out the mouth
O' the grave, and loose my spirit's bands,
And come again to the land of lands)—
In a sea-side house to the farther South,
Where the baked cicala dies of drouth,
And one sharp tree—'tis a cypress—stands
By the many hundred years red-rusted,
Rough iron-spiked, ripe fruit-o'ercrusted,

My sentinel to guard the sands
To the water's edge. For, what expands
Before the house, but the great opaque
Blue breadth of sea without a break?
While, in the house, forever crumbles
Some fragment of the frescoed walls,
From blisters where a scorpion sprawls.
A girl bare-footed brings, and tumbles
Down on the pavement, green-flesh melons,
And says there's news today—the king
Was shot at, touched in the liver-wing,
Goes with his Bourbon arm in a sling:
—She hopes they have not caught the felons.
Italy, my Italy!
Queen Mary's saying serves for me—
    (When fortune's malice
    Lost her, Calais)
Open my heart and you will see
Graved inside of it, "Italy."
Such lovers old are I and she;
So it always was, so shall ever be!

WOMEN AND ROSES

I

I DREAM of a red-rose tree.
And which of its roses three
Is the dearest rose to me?

II

Round and round, like a dance of snow
In a dazzling drift, as its guardians, go
Floating the women faded for ages,
Sculptured in stone, on the poet's pages.
Then follow women fresh and gay,

Living and loving and loved today,
Last, in the rear, flee the multitude of maidens,
Beauties yet unborn. And all, to one cadence,
They circle their rose on my rose tree.

III

Dear rose, thy term is reached,
Thy leaf hangs loose and bleached:
Bees pass it unimpeached.

IV

Stay then, stoop, since I cannot climb,
You, great shapes of the antique time!
How shall I fix you, fire you, freeze you,
Break my heart at your feet to please you?
Oh, to possess and be possessed!
Hearts that beat 'neath each pallid breast!
Once but of love, the poesy, the passion,
Drink but once and die!—In vain, the same
    fashion,
They circle their rose on my rose tree.

V

Dear rose, thy joy's undimmed,
Thy cup is ruby-rimmed,
Thy cup's heart nectar-brimmed.

VI

Deep, as drops from a statue's plinth
The bee sucked in by the hyacinth,
So will I bury me while burning,
Quench like him at a plunge my yearning,
Eyes in your eyes, lips on your lips!
Fold me fast where the cincture slips,
Prison all my soul in eternities of pleasure,

Girdle me for once! But no—the old measure,
They circle their rose on my rose tree.

VII

Dear rose without a thorn,
Thy bud's the babe unborn:
First streak of a new morn.

VIII

Wings, lend wings for the cold, the clear!
What is far conquers what is near.
Roses will bloom nor want beholders,
Sprung from the dust where our flesh moulders,
What shall arrive with the cycle's change?
A novel grace and a beauty strange.
I will make an Eve, be the artist that began her,
Shaped her to his mind!—Alas! in like manner
They circle their rose on my rose tree.

PROTUS

Among these latter busts we count by scores,
Half-emperors and quarter-emperors,
Each with his bay-leaf fillet, loose-thonged vest,
Loric and low-browed Gorgon on the breast,—
One loves a baby face, with violets there,
Violets instead of laurel in the hair,
As those were all the little locks could bear.

Now read here. "Protus ends a period
Of empery beginning with a god;
Born in the porphyry chamber at Byzant,
Queens by his cradle, proud and ministrant:
And if he quickened breath there, 'twould like fire
Pantingly through the dim vast realm transpire.

A fame that he was missing spread afar:
The world, from its four corners, rose in war,
Till he was borne out on a balcony
To pacify the world when it should see.
The captains ranged before him, one, his hand
Made baby points at, gained the chief command.
And day by day more beautiful he grew
In shape, all said, in feature and in hue,
While young Greek sculptors, gazing on the child,
Became with old Greek sculpture reconciled.
Already sages labored to condense
In easy tomes a life's experience:
And artists took grave counsel to impart
In one breath and one hand-sweep, all their art—
To make his graces prompt as blossoming
Of plentifully-watered palms in spring:
Since well beseems it, whoso mounts the throne,
For beauty, knowledge, strength, should stand alone,
And mortals love the letters of his name."

—Stop! Have you turned two pages? Still the same
New reign, same date. The scribe goes on to say
How that same year, on such a month and day,
"John the Pannonian, groundedly believed
A blacksmith's bastard, whose hard hand reprieved
The Empire from its fate the year before,—
Came, had a mind to take the crown, and wore
The same for six years (during which the Huns
Kept off their fingers from us), till his sons
Put something in his liquor"—and so forth.
Then a new reign. Stay—"Take at its just worth"
(Subjoins an annotator) "what I give
As hearsay. Some think, John let Protus live
And slip away. 'Tis said, he reached man's age
At some blind northern court; made, first a page,
Then tutor to the children; last, of use

About the hunting-stables. I deduce
He wrote the little tract 'On worming dogs,'
Whereof the name in sundry catalogues
Is extant yet. A Protus of the race
Is rumored to have died a monk in Thrace,—
And if the same, he reached senility."
Here's John the Smith's rough-hammered head.
    Great eye,
Gross jaw and griped lips do what granite can
To give you the crown-grasper. What a man!

CLEON

"As certain also of your own poets have said"—

CLEON the poet (from the sprinkled isles,
Lily on lily, that o'erlace the sea,
And laugh their pride when the light wave lisps
    "Greece")—
To Protus in his Tyranny: much health!

    They give thy letter to me, even now:
I read and seem as if I heard thee speak.
The master of thy galley still unlades
Gift after gift; they block my court at last
And pile themselves along its portico
Royal with sunset, like a thought of thee:
And one white she-slave from the group dispersed
Of black and white slaves (like the chequer-work
Pavement, at once my nation's work and gift,
Now covered with this settle-down of doves),
One lyric woman, in her crocus vest
Woven of sea-wools, with her two white hands
Commends to me the strainer and the cup
Thy lip hath bettered ere it blesses mine.

Well-counselled, king, in thy munificence!
For so shall men remark, in such an act
Of love for him whose song gives life its joy,
Thy recognition of the use of life;
Nor call thy spirit barely adequate
To help on life in straight ways, broad enough
For vulgar souls, by ruling and the rest.
Thou, in the daily building of thy tower,—
Whether in fierce and sudden spasms of toil,
Or through dim lulls of unapparent growth,
Or when the general work 'mid good acclaim
Climbed with the eye to cheer the architect,—
Didst ne'er engage in work for mere work's sake—
Hadst ever in thy heart the luring hope
Of some eventual rest a-top of it,
Whence, all the tumult of the building hushed,
Thou first of men mightst look out to the East:
The vulgar saw thy tower, thou sawest the sun.
For this, I promise on thy festival
To pour libation, looking o'er the sea,
Making this slave narrate thy fortunes, speak
Thy great words, and describe thy royal face—
Wishing thee wholly where Zeus lives the most
Within the eventual element of calm.

Thy letter's first requirement meets me here.
It is as thou hast heard: in one short life
I, Cleon, have effected all those things
Thou wonderingly dost enumerate.
That epos on thy hundred plates of gold
Is mine,—and also mine the little chant,
So sure to rise from every fishing-bark
When, lights at prow, the seamen haul their net.
The image of the sun-god on the phare,
Men turn from the sun's self to see, is mine;
The Pœcile, o'er-storied its whole length,

As thou didst hear, with painting, is mine too.
I know the true proportions of a man
And woman also, not observed before;
And I have written three books on the soul,
Proving absurd all written hitherto,
And putting us to ignorance again.
For music,—why, I have combined the moods,
Inventing one. In brief, all arts are mine;
Thus much the people know and recognize,
Throughout our seventeen islands. Marvel not.
We of these latter days, with greater mind
Than our forerunners, since more composite,
Look not so great, beside their simple way,
To a judge who only sees one way at once,
One mind-point and no other at a time,—
Compares the small part of a man of us
With some whole man of the heroic age,
Great in his way—not ours, nor meant for ours.
And ours is greater, had we skill to know:
For, what we call this life of men on earth,
This sequence of the soul's achievements here
Being, as I find much reason to conceive,
Intended to be viewed eventually
As a great whole, not analyzed to parts,
But each part having reference to all,—
How shall a certain part, pronounced complete,
Endure effacement by another part?
Was the thing done?—then, what's to do again?
See, in the chequered pavement opposite,
Suppose the artist made a perfect rhomb,
And next a lozenge, then a trapezoid—
He did not overlay them, superimpose
The new upon the old and blot it out,
But laid them on a level in his work,
Making at last a picture; there it lies.
So, first the perfect separate forms were made,

The portions of mankind; and after, so,
Occurred the combination of the same.
For where had been a progress, otherwise?
Mankind, made up of all the single men,—
In such a synthesis the labor ends.
Now mark me! those divine men of old time
Have reached, thou sayest well, each at one point
The outside verge that rounds our faculty;
And where they reached, who can do more than
    reach?
It takes but little water just to touch
At some one point the inside of a sphere,
And, as we turn the sphere, touch all the rest
In due succession: but the finer air
Which not so palpably nor obviously,
Though no less universally, can touch
The whole circumference of that emptied sphere
Fills it more fully than the water did;
Holds thrice the weight of water in itself
Resolved into a subtler element.
And yet the vulgar call the sphere first full
Up to the visible height—and after, void;
Not knowing air's more hidden properties.
And thus our soul, misknown, cries out to Zeus
To vindicate his purpose in our life:
Why stay we on the earth unless to grow?
Long since, I imaged, wrote the fiction out,
That he or other god descended here
And, once for all, showed simultaneously
What, in its nature, never can be shown,
Piecemeal or in succession;—showed, I say,
The worth both absolute and relative
Of all his children from the birth of time,
His instruments for all appointed work.
I now go on to image,—might we hear
The judgment which should give the due to each,

Show where the labor lay and where the ease,
And prove Zeus' self, the latent everywhere!
This is a dream:—but no dream, let us hope,
That years and days, the summers and the springs,
Follow each other with unwaning powers.
The grapes which dye thy wine are richer far,
Through culture, than the wild wealth of the rock;
The suave plum than the savage-tasted drupe;
The pastured honey-bee drops choicer sweet;
The flowers turn double, and the leaves turn flowers;
That young and tender crescent-moon, thy slave,
Sleeping above her robe as buoyed by clouds,
Refines upon the women of my youth.
What, and the soul alone deteriorates?
I have not chanted verse like Homer, no—
Nor swept string like Terpander, no—nor carved
And painted men like Phidias and his friend:
I am not great as they are, point by point.
But I have entered into sympathy
With these four, running these into one soul,
Who, separate, ignored each other's art.
Say, is it nothing that I know them all?
The wild flower was the larger; I have dashed
Rose-blood upon its petals, pricked its cup's
Honey with wine, and driven its seed to fruit,
And show a better flower if not so large:
I stand myself. Refer this to the gods
Whose gift alone it is! which, shall I dare
 (All pride apart) upon the absurd pretext
That such a gift by chance lay in my hand,
Discourse of lightly or depreciate?
It might have fallen to another's hand: what then?
I pass too surely: let at least truth stay!

   And next, of what thou followest on to ask.
This being with me as I declare, O king,

My works, in all these varicolored kinds,
So done by me, accepted so by men—
Thou askest, if (my soul thus in men's hearts)
I must not be accounted to attain
The very crown and proper end of life?
Inquiring thence how, now life closeth up,
I face death with success in my right hand:
Whether I fear death less than dost thyself
The fortunate of men? "For" (writest thou)
"Thou leavest much behind, while I leave naught.
Thy life stays in the poems men shall sing,
The pictures men shall study; while my life,
Complete and whole now in its power and joy,
Dies altogether with my brain and arm,
Is lost indeed; since, what survives myself?
The brazen statue to o'erlook my grave,
Set on the promontory which I named.
And that—some supple courtier of my heir
Shall use its robed and sceptred arm, perhaps,
To fix the rope to, which best drags it down.
I go then: triumph thou, who dost not go!"

Nay, thou art worthy of hearing my whole mind.
Is this apparent, when thou turn'st to muse
Upon the scheme of earth and man in chief,
That admiration grows as knowledge grows?
That imperfection means perfection hid,
Reserved in part, to grace the after-time?
If, in the morning of philosophy,
Ere aught had been recorded, nay perceived,
Thou, with the light now in thee, couldst have
    looked
On all earth's tenantry, from worm to bird,
Ere man, her last, appeared upon the stage—
Thou wouldst have seen them perfect, and deduced
The perfectness of others yet unseen.

Conceding which,—had Zeus then questioned thee,
"Shall I go on a step, improve on this,
Do more for visible creatures than is done?"
Thou wouldst have answered, "Ay, by making each
Grow conscious in himself—by that alone.
All's perfect else: the shell sucks fast the rock,
The fish strikes through the sea, the snake both
        swims
And slides, forth range the beasts, the birds take
        flight,
Till life's mechanics can no further go—
And all this joy in natural life is put
Like fire from off thy finger into each,
So exquisitely perfect is the same.
But 't is pure fire, and they mere matter are;
It has them, not they it: and so I choose
For man, thy last premeditated work
 (If I might add a glory to the scheme),
That a third thing should stand apart from both,
A quality arise within his soul,
Which, intro-active, made to supervise
And feel the force it has, may view itself,
And so be happy." (Man might live at first
The animal life: but is there nothing more?
In due time, let him critically learn
How he lives; and, the more he gets to know
Of his own life's adaptabilities,
The more joy-giving will his life become.
Thus man, who hath this quality, is best.)

    But thou, king, hadst more reasonably said:
"Let progress end at once,—man make no step
Beyond the natural man, the better beast,
Using his senses, not the sense of sense."
In man there's failure, only since he left
The lower and inconscious forms of life.

We called it an advance, the rendering plain
Man's spirit might grow conscious of man's life,
And, by new lore so added to the old,
Take each step higher over the brute's head.
This grew the only life, the pleasure-house,
Watch-tower and treasure-fortress of the soul,
Which whole surrounding flats of natural life
Seemed only fit to yield subsistence to;
A tower that crowns a country. But alas,
The soul now climbs it just to perish there!
For thence we have discovered ('t is no dream—
We know this, which we had not else perceived)
That there's a world of capability
For joy, spread round about us, meant for us,
Inviting us; and still the soul craves all,
And still the flesh replies, "Take no jot more
Than ere thou clombst the tower to look abroad!
Nay, so much less as that fatigue has brought
Deduction to it." We struggle, fain to enlarge
Our bounded physical recipiency,
Increase our power, supply fresh oil to life,
Repair the waste of age and sickness: no,
It skills not! life's inadequate to joy,
As the soul sees joy, tempting life to take.
They praise a fountain in my garden here
Wherein a Naiad sends the water-bow
Thin from her tube; she smiles to see it rise.
What if I told her, it is just a thread
From that great river which the hills shut up,
And mock her with my leave to take the same?
The artificer has given her one small tube
Past power to widen or exchange—what boots
To know she might spout oceans if she could?
She cannot lift beyond her first thin thread:
And so a man can use but a man's joy
While he sees God's. Is it for Zeus to boast,

"See, man, how happy I live, and despair—
That I may be still happier—for thy use!"
If this were so, we could not thank our lord,
As hearts beat on to doing; 't is not so—
Malice it is not. Is it carelessness?
Still, no. If care—where is the sign? I ask,
And get no answer, and agree in sum,
O king, with thy profound discouragement,
Who seest the wider but to sigh the more.
Most progress is most failure: thou sayest well.

The last point now:—thou dost except a case—
Holding joy not impossible to one
With artist-gifts—to such a man as I
Who leave behind me living works indeed;
For, such a poem, such a painting lives.
What? dost thou verily trip upon a word,
Confound the accurate view of what joy is
(Caught somewhat clearer by my eyes than thine)
With feeling joy? confound the knowing how
And showing how to live (my faculty)
With actually living?—Otherwise
Where is the artist's vantage o'er the king?
Because in my great epos I display
How divers men young, strong, fair, wise, can act—
Is this as though I acted? if I paint,
Carve the young Phœbus, am I therefore young?
Methinks I'm older that I bowed myself
The many years of pain that taught me art!
Indeed, to know is something, and to prove
How all this beauty might be enjoyed, is more:
But, knowing naught, to enjoy is something too.
Yon rower, with the moulded muscles there,
Lowering the sail, is nearer it than I.
I can write love-odes: thy fair slave's an ode.
I get to sing of love, when grown too gray

For being beloved: she turns to that young man,
The muscles all a-ripple on his back.
I know the joy of kingship: well, thou art king!

   "But," sayest thou— (and I marvel, I repeat,
To find thee trip on such a mere word) "what
Thou writest, paintest, stays; that does not die:
Sappho survives, because we sing her songs,
And Æschylus, because we read his plays!"
Why, if they live still, let them come and take
Thy slave in my despite, drink from thy cup,
Speak in my place. Thou diest while I survive?
Say rather that my fate is deadlier still,
In this, that every day my sense of joy
Grows more acute, my soul (intensified
By power and insight) more enlarged, more keen;
While every day my hairs fall more and more,
My hand shakes, and the heavy years increase—
The horror quickening still from year to year,
The consummation coming past escape,
When I shall know most, and yet least enjoy—
When all my works wherein I prove my worth,
Being present still to mock me in men's mouths,
Alive still, in the praise of such as thou,
I, I the feeling, thinking, acting man,
The man who loved his life so over-much,
Sleep in my urn. It is so horrible,
I dare at times imagine to my need
Some future state revealed to us by Zeus,
Unlimited in capability
For joy, as this is in desire for joy,
—To seek which, the joy-hunger forces us:
That, stung by straitness of our life, made strait
On purpose to make prized the life at large—
Freed by the throbbing impulse we call death,
We burst there as the worm into the fly,

Who, while a worm still, wants his wings. But no!
Zeus has not yet revealed it; and alas,
He must have done so, were it possible!

Live long and happy, and in that thought die:
Glad for what was! Farewell. And for the rest,
I cannot tell thy messenger aright
Where to deliver what he bears of thine
To one called Paulus; we have heard his fame
Indeed, if Christus be not one with him—
I know not, nor am troubled much to know.
Thou canst not think a mere barbarian Jew,
As Paulus proves to be, one circumcised,
Hath access to a secret shut from us?
Thou wrongest our philosophy, O king,
In stooping to inquire of such an one,
As if his answer could impose at all!
He writeth, doth he? well, and he may write.
Oh, the Jew findeth scholars! certain slaves
Who touched on this same isle, preached him and
       Christ;
And (as I gathered from a bystander)
Their doctrine could be held by no sane man.

POPULARITY

Stand still, true poet that you are!
    I know you; let me try and draw you.
Some night you'll fail us: when afar
    You rise, remember one man saw you,
Knew you, and named a star!

My star, God's glow-worm! Why extend
    That loving hand of his which leads you,
Yet locks you safe from end to end

Of this dark world, unless he needs you,
Just saves your light to spend?

His clenched hand shall unclose at last,
    I know, and let out all the beauty:
My poet holds the future fast,
    Accepts the coming ages' duty,
Their present for this past.

That day, the earth's feast-master's brow
    Shall clear, to God the chalice raising;
"Others give best at first, but thou
    Forever set'st our table praising,
Keep'st the good wine till now!"

Meantime, I'll draw you as you stand,
    With few or none to watch and wonder:
I'll say—a fisher, on the sand
    By Tyre the old, with ocean-plunder,
A netful, brought to land.

Who has not heard how Tyrian shells
    Enclosed the blue, that dye of dyes
Whereof one drop worked miracles,
    And colored like Astarte's eyes
Raw silk the merchant sells?

And each bystander of them all
    Could criticise, and quote tradition
How depths of blue sublimed some pall
    —To get which, pricked a king's ambition;
Worth sceptre, crown and ball.

Yet there's the dye, in that rough mesh,
    The sea has only just o'er-whispered!
Live whelks, each lip's beard dripping fresh,

As if they still the water's lisp heard
Through foam the rock-weeds thresh.

Enough to furnish Solomon
  Such hangings for his cedar-house,
That, when gold-robed he took the throne
  In that abyss of blue, the Spouse
Might swear his presence shone

Most like the centre-spike of gold
  Which burns deep in the bluebell's womb
What time, with ardors manifold,
  The bee goes singing to her groom,
Drunken and overbold.

Mere conchs! not fit for warp or woof!
  Till cunning come to pound and squeeze
And clarify,—refine to proof
  The liquor filtered by degrees,
While the world stands aloof.

And there's the extract, flasked and fine,
  And priced and salable at last!
And Hobbs, Nobbs, Stokes, and Nokes combine
  To paint the future from the past,
Put blue into their line.

Hobbs hints blue,—straight he turtle eats:
  Nobbs prints blue,—claret crowns his cup:
Nokes outdares Stokes in azure feats,—
  Both gorge. Who fished the murex up?
What porridge had John Keats?

TWO IN THE CAMPAGNA

I WONDER do you feel today
  As I have felt since, hand in hand,

We sat down on the grass, to stray
　　In spirit better through the land,
This morn of Rome and May?

For me, I touched a thought, I know.
　　Has tantalized me many times,
(Like turns of thread the spiders throw
　　Mocking across our path) for rhymes
To catch at and let go.

Possible a spiritual unity between them.

Help me to hold it! First it left
　　The yellowing fennel, run to seed
There, branching from the brickwork's cleft,
　　Some old tomb's ruin: yonder weed
Took up the floating weft,

Where one small orange cup amassed
　　Five beetles,—blind and green they grope
Among the honey-meal: and last,
　　Everywhere on the grassy slope
I traced it. Hold it fast!

The champaign with its endless fleece
　　Of feathery grasses everywhere!
Silence and passion, joy and peace,
　　An everlasting wash of air—
Rome's ghost since her decease.

Such life here, through such lengths of hours,
　　Such miracles performed in play,
Such primal naked forms of flowers,
　　Such letting nature have her way
While heaven looks from its towers!

How say you? Let us, O my dove,
　　Let us be unashamed of soul,

As earth lies bare to heaven above!
   How is it under our control
To love or not to love?

I would that you were all to me,
   You that are just so much, no more.
Nor yours nor mine, nor slave nor free!
   Where does the fault lie? What the core
O' the wound, since wound must be?

I would I could adopt your will,
   See with your eyes, and set my heart
Beating by yours, and drink my fill
   At your soul's springs,—your part my part
In life, for good and ill.

No. I yearn upward, touch you close,
   Then stand away. I kiss your cheek,
Catch your soul's warmth,—I pluck the rose
   And love it more than tongue can speak—
Then the good minute goes.

Already how am I so far
   Out of that minute? Must I go
Still like the thistle-ball, no bar,
   Onward, whenever light winds blow,
Fixed by no friendly star?

Just when I seemed about to learn!
   Where is the thread now? Off again!
The old trick! Only I discern—
   Infinite passion, and the pain
Of finite hearts that yearn.

A GRAMMARIAN'S FUNERAL

SHORTLY AFTER THE REVIVAL OF LEARNING IN EUROPE

LET us begin and carry up this corpse,
　　Singing together.
Leave we the common crofts, the vulgar thorpes
　　Each in its tether
Sleeping safe on the bosom of the plain,
　　Cared-for till cock-crow:
Look out if yonder be not day again
　　Rimming the rock-row!
That's the appropriate country; there, man's thought,
　　Rarer, intenser,
Self-gathered for an outbreak, as it ought,
　　Chafes in the censer.
Leave we the unlettered plain its herd and crop;
　　Seek we sepulture
On a tall mountain, cited to the top,
　　Crowded with culture!
All the peaks soar, but one the rest excels;
　　Clouds overcome it;
No! yonder sparkle is the citadel's
　　Circling its summit.
Thither our path lies; wind we up the heights;
　　Wait ye the warning?
Our low life was the level's and the night's;
　　He's for the morning.
Step to a tune, square chests, erect each head,
　　'Ware the beholders!
This is our master, famous, calm and dead,
　　Borne on our shoulders.

Sleep, crop and herd! sleep, darkling thrope and croft,
　　Safe from the weather!
He, whom we convoy to his grave aloft,
　　Singing together,

He was a man born with thy face and throat,
    Lyric Apollo!
Long he lived nameless: how should Spring take note
    Winter would follow?
Till lo, the little touch, and youth was gone!
    Cramped and diminished,
Moaned he, "New measures, other feet anon!
    My dance is finished"?
No, that's the world's way: (keep the mountain-side,
    Make for the city!)
He knew the signal, and stepped on with pride
    Over men's pity;
Left play for work, and grappled with the world
    Bent on escaping:
"What's in the scroll," quoth he, "thou keepest furled?
    Show me their shaping,
Theirs who most studied man, the bard and sage,—
    Give!"—So, he gowned him,
Straight got by heart that book to its last page:
    Learned, we found him.
Yea, but we found him bald too, eyes like lead,
    Accents uncertain:
"Time to taste life," another would have said,
    "Up with the curtain!"
This man said rather, "Actual life comes next?
    Patience a moment!
Grant I have mastered learning's crabbed text,
    Still there's the comment.
Let me know all! Prate not of most or least,
    Painful or easy!
Even to the crumbs I'd fain eat up the feast,
    Ay, nor feel queasy."
Oh, such a life as he resolved to live,
    When he had learned it,
When he had gathered all books had to give!
    Sooner, he spurned it.

Image the whole, then execute the parts—
    Fancy the fabric
Quite, ere you build, ere steel strike fire from quartz,
    Ere mortar dab brick!

(Here's the town-gate reached: there's the market-place
    Gaping before us.)
Yea, this in him was the peculiar grace
    (Hearten our chorus!)
That before living he'd learn how to live—
    No end to learning:
Earn the means first—God surely will contrive
    Use for our earning.
Others mistrust and say, "But time escapes:
    Live now or never!"
He said, "What's time? Leave Now for dogs and apes!
    Man has Forever."
Back to his book then: deeper drooped his head:
    Calculus racked him:
Leaden before, his eyes grew dross of lead:
    Tussis attacked him.
"Now, master, take a little rest!"—not he!
    (Caution redoubled,
Step two abreast, the way winds narrowly!)
    Not a whit troubled,
Back to his studies, fresher than at first,
    Fierce as a dragon
He (soul-hydroptic with a sacred thirst)
    Sucked at the flagon.
Oh, if we draw a circle premature,
    Heedless of far gain,
Greedy for quick returns of profit, sure
    Bad is our bargain!
Was it not great? did not he throw on God,
    (He loves the burthen)—
God's task to make the heavenly period

Perfect the earthen?
Did not he magnify the mind, show clear
    Just what it all meant?
He would not discount life, as fools do here,
    Paid by instalment.
He ventured neck or nothing—heaven's success
    Found, or earth's failure:
"Wilt thou trust death or not?" He answered "Yes!
    Hence with life's pale lure!"
That low man seeks a little thing to do,
    Sees it and does it:
This high man, with a great thing to pursue,
    Dies ere he knows it.
That low man goes on adding one to one,
    His hundred's soon hit:
This high man, aiming at a million,
    Misses an unit.
That, has the world here—should he need the next,
    Let the world mind him!
This, throws himself on God, and unperplexed
    Seeking shall find him.
So, with the throttling hands of death at strife,
    Ground he at grammar;
Still, through the rattle, parts of speech were rife:
    While he could stammer
He settled *Hoti's* business—let it be!—
    Properly based *Oun*—
Gave us the doctrine of the enclitic *De*,
    Dead from the waist down.
Well, here's the platform, here's the proper place:
    Hail to your purlieus,
All ye highfliers of the feathered race,
    Swallows and curlews!
Here's the top-peak; the multitude below
    Live, for they can, there:
This man decided not to Live but Know—

[handwritten marginal note:] Br. there's better to attack something big & fail than to take a little thing & do it.

Bury this man there?
Here—here's his place, where meteors shoot, clouds
  form,
  Lightnings are loosened,
Stars come and go! Let joy break with the storm,
  Peace let the dew send!
Lofty designs must close in like effects:
  Loftily lying,
Leave him—still loftier than the world suspects,
  Living and dying.

MISCONCEPTIONS

This is a spray the Bird clung to,
  Making it blossom with pleasure,
Ere the high tree-top she sprung to,
  Fit for her nest and her treasure.
  Oh, what a hope beyond measure
Was the poor spray's, which the flying feet hung to,—
So to be singled out, built in, and sung to!

This is a heart the Queen leant on,
  Thrilled in a minute erratic,
Ere the true bosom she bent on,
  Meet for love's regal dalmatic.
  Oh, what a fancy ecstatic
Was the poor heart's, ere the wanderer went on—
Love to be saved for it, proffered to, spent on!

ONE WORD MORE

TO E. B. B.

London, September, 1855

I

There they are, my fifty men and women
Naming me the fifty poems finished!

Take them, Love, the book and me together;
Where the heart lies, let the brain lie also.

II

Rafael made a century of sonnets,
Made and wrote them in a certain volume
Dinted with the silver-pointed pencil
Else he only used to draw Madonnas:
These, the world might view—but one, the volume.
Who that one, you ask? Your heart instructs you.
Did she live and love it all her lifetime?
Did she drop, his lady of the sonnets,
Die, and let it drop beside her pillow
Where it lay in place of Rafael's glory,
Rafael's cheek so duteous and so loving—
Cheek, the world was wont to hail a painter's,
Rafael's cheek, her love had turned a poet's?

III

You and I would rather read that volume,
(Taken to his beating bosom by it)
Lean and list the bosom-beats of Rafael,
Would we not? than wonder at Madonnas—
Her, San Sisto names, and Her, Foligno,
Her, that visits Florence in a vision,
Her, that's left with lilies in the Louvre—
Seen by us and all the world in circle.

IV

You and I will never read that volume.
Guido Reni, like his own eye's apple
Guarded long the treasure-book and loved it.
Guido Reni dying, all Bologna
Cried, and the world cried too, "Ours, the treasure!"
Suddenly, as rare things will, it vanished.

V

Dante once prepared to paint an angel:
Whom to please?   You whisper "Beatrice."
While he mused and traced it and retraced it,
(Peradventure with a pen corroded
Still by drops of that hot ink he dipped for,
When, his left-hand i' the hair o' the wicked,
Back he held the brow and pricked its stigma,
Bit into the live man's flesh for parchment,
Loosed him, laughed to see the writing rankle,
Let the wretch go festering through Florence)—
Dante, who loved well because he hated,
Hated wickedness that hinders loving,
Dante standing, studying his angel,—
In there broke the folk of his Inferno.
Says he—"Certain people of importance"
(Such he gave his daily dreadful line to)
"Entered and would seize, forsooth, the poet."
Says the poet—"Then I stopped my painting."

VI

You and I would rather see that angel,
Painted by the tenderness of Dante
Would we not?—than read a fresh Inferno.

VII

You and I will never see that picture.
While he mused on love and Beatrice,
While he softened o'er his outlined angel,
In they broke, those "people of importance:"
We and Bice bear the loss forever.

VIII

What of Rafael's sonnets, Dante's picture?
This: no artist lives and loves, that longs not

Once, and only once, and for one only,
(Ah, the prize!) to find his love a language
Fit and fair and simple and sufficient—
Using nature that's an art to others,
Not, this one time, art that's turned his nature.
Ay, of all the artists living, loving,
None but would forego his proper dowry,—
Does he paint? he fain would write a poem,—
Does he write? he fain would paint a picture,
Put to proof art alien to the artist's,
Once, and only once, and for one only,
So to be the man and leave the artist,
Gain the man's joy, miss the artist's sorrow.

IX

Wherefore? Heaven's gift takes earth's abatement!
He who smites the rock and spreads the water,
Bidding drink and live a crowd beneath him,
Even he, the minute makes immortal,
Proves, perchance, but mortal in the minute,
Desecrates, belike, the deed in doing.
While he smites, how can he but remember,
So he smote before, in such a peril,
When they stood and mocked—"Shall smiting help
    us?"
When they drank and sneered—"A stroke is easy!"
When they wiped their mouths and went their
    journey,
Throwing him for thanks—"But drought was
    pleasant."
Thus old memories mar the actual triumph;
Thus the doing savors of disrelish;
Thus achievement lacks a gracious somewhat;
O'er-importuned brows becloud the mandate,
Carelessness or consciousness—the gesture.
For he bears an ancient wrong about him,

Sees and knows again those phalanxed faces,
Hears, yet one time more, the 'customed prelude—
"How shouldst thou, of all men, smite, and save us?"
Guesses what is like to prove the sequel—
"Egypt's flesh-pots—nay, the drought was better."

X

Oh, the crowd must have emphatic warrant!
Theirs, the Sinai-forehead's cloven brilliance,
Right-arm's rod-sweep, tongue's imperial fiat.
Never dares the man put off the prophet.

XI

Did he love one face from out the thousands,
(Were she Jethro's daughter, white and wifely,
Were she but the Æthiopian bondslave,)
He would envy yon dumb patient camel,
Keeping a reserve of scanty water
Meant to save his own life in the desert;
Ready in the desert to deliver
(Kneeling down to let his breast be opened)
Hoard and life together for his mistress.

XII

I shall never, in the years remaining,
Paint you pictures, no, nor carve you statues,
Make you music that should all-express me;
So it seems: I stand on my attainment.
This of verse alone, one life allows me;
Verse and nothing else have I to give you.
Other heights in other lives, God willing:
All the gifts from all the heights, your own, Love!

XIII

Yet a semblance of resource avails us—
Shade so finely touched, love's sense must seize it.

Take these lines, look lovingly and nearly,
Lines I write the first time and the last time.
He who works in fresco, steals a hair-brush,
Curbs the liberal hand, subservient proudly,
Cramps his spirit, crowds its all in little,
Makes a strange art of an art familiar,
Fills his lady's missal-marge with flowerets.
He who blows through bronze, may breathe through
    silver,
Fitly serenade a slumbrous princess.
He who writes, may write for once as I do.

XIV

Love, you saw me gather men and women,
Live or dead or fashioned by my fancy,
Enter each and all, and use their service,
Speak from every mouth,—the speech, a poem.
Hardly shall I tell my joys and sorrows,
Hopes and fears, belief and disbelieving:
I am mine and yours—the rest be all men's,
Karshish, Cleon, Norbert, and the fifty.
Let me speak this once in my true person,
Not as Lippo, Roland, or Andrea,
Though the fruit of speech be just this sentence:
Pray you, look on these my men and women,
Take and keep my fifty poems finished;
Where my heart lies, let my brain lie also!
Poor the speech; be how I speak, for all things.

XV

Not but that you know me! Lo, the moon's self!
Here in London, yonder late in Florence,
Still we find her face, the thrice-transfigured.
Curving on a sky imbrued with color,
Drifted over Fiesole by twilight,
Came she, our new crescent of a hair's-breadth.

Full she flared it, lamping Samminiato,
Rounder 'twixt the cypresses and rounder,
Perfect till the nightingales applauded.
Now, a piece of her old self, impoverished,
Hard to greet, she traverses the house-roofs,
Hurries with unhandsome thrift of silver,
Goes dispiritedly, glad to finish.

XVI

What, there's nothing in the moon noteworthy?
Nay: for if that moon could love a mortal,
Use, to charm him (so to fit a fancy),
All her magic ('tis the old sweet mythos),
She would turn a new side to her mortal,
Side unseen of herdsman, huntsman, steersman—
Blank to Zoroaster on his terrace,
Blind to Galileo on his turret,
Dumb to Homer, dumb to Keats—him, even!
Think, the wonder of the moonstruck mortal—
When she turns round, comes again in heaven,
Opens out anew for worse or better!
Proves she like some portent of an iceberg
Swimming full upon the ship it founders,
Hungry with huge teeth of splintered crystals?
Proves she as the paved work of a sapphire
Seen by Moses when he climbed the mountain?
Moses, Aaron, Nadab and Abihu
Climbed and saw the very God, the Highest,
Stand upon the paved work of a sapphire.
Like the bodied heaven in his clearness
Shone the stone, the sapphire of that paved work,
When they ate and drank and saw God also!

XVII

What were seen? None knows, none ever shall know.
Only this is sure—the sight were other,

Not the moon's same side, born late in Florence,
Dying now impoverished here in London.
God be thanked, the meanest of his creatures
Boasts two soul-sides, one to face the world with,
One to show a woman when he loves her!

XVIII

This I say of me, but think of you, Love!
This to you—yourself my moon of poets!   " The Star ".
Ah, but that's the world's side, there's the wonder,
Thus they see you, praise you, think they know you!
There, in turn I stand with them and praise you—
Out of my own self, I dare to phrase it.
But the best is when I glide from out them,
Cross a step or two of dubious twilight,
Come out on the other side, the novel
Silent silver lights and darks undreamed of,
Where I hush and bless myself with silence.

XIX

Oh, their Rafael of the dear Madonnas,
Oh, their Dante of the dread Inferno,
Wrote one song—and in my brain I sing it,
Drew one angel—borne, see, on my bosom!

                                        R. B.

MAY AND DEATH

I wish that when you died last May,
    Charles, there had died along with you
Three parts of spring's delightful things;
    Ay, and, for me, the fourth part too.

A foolish thought, and worse, perhaps!
    There must be many a pair of friends

Who, arm in arm, deserve the warm
  Moon-births and the long evening-ends.

So, for their sake, be May still May!
  Let their new time, as mine of old,
Do all it did for me: I bid
  Sweet sights and sounds throng manifold.

Only, one little sight, one plant,
  Woods have in May, that starts up green
Save a sole streak which, so to speak,
  Is spring's blood, spilt its leaves between,—

That, they might spare; a certain wood
  Might miss the plant; their loss were small:
But I,—whene'er the leaf grows there,
  Its drop comes from my heart, that's all.

THE WORST OF IT

WOULD it were I had been false, not you!
  I that am nothing, not you that are all:
I, never the worse for a touch or two
  On my speckled hide; not you, the pride
Of the day, my swan, that a first fleck's fall
  On her wonder of white must unswan, undo!

I had dipped in life's struggle and, out again,
  Bore specks of it here, there, easy to see,
When I found my swan and the cure was plain;
  The dull turned bright as I caught your white
On my bosom: you saved me—saved in vain
  If you ruined yourself, and all through me!

Yes, all through the speckled beast that I am,
  Who taught you to stoop; you gave me yourself,

And bound your soul by the vows that damn:
  Since on better thought you break, as you ought,
Vows—words, no angel set down, some elf
  Mistook,—for an oath, an epigram!

Yes, might I judge you, here were my heart,
  And a hundred its like, to treat as you pleased!
I choose to be yours, for my proper part,
  Yours, leave or take, or mar me or make;
If I acquiesce, why should you be teased
  With the conscience-prick and the memory-smart?

But what will God say? Oh, my sweet,
  Think, and be sorry you did this thing!
Though earth were unworthy to feel your feet,
  There's a heaven above may deserve your love:
Should you forfeit heaven for a snapt gold ring
  And a promise broke, were it just or meet?

And I to have tempted you! I, who tried
  Your soul, no doubt, till it sank! Unwise,
I loved, and was lowly, loved and aspired,
  Loved, grieving or glad, till I made you mad,
And you meant to have hated and despised—
  Whereas, you deceived me nor inquired!

She, ruined? How? No heaven for her?
  Crowns to give, and none for the brow
That looked like marble and smelt like myrrh?
  Shall the robe be worn, and the palm-branch borne,
And she go graceless, she graced now
  Beyond all saints, as themselves aver?

Hardly! That must be understood!
  The earth is your place of penance, then;
And what will it prove? I desire your good,

But, plot as I may, I can find no way
How a blow should fall, such as falls on men,
    Nor prove too much for your womanhood.

It will come, I suspect, at the end of life,
    When you walk alone, and review the past;
And I, who so long shall have done with strife,
    And journeyed my stage and earned my wage
And retired as was right,—I am called at last
    When the devil stabs you, to lend the knife.

He stabs for the minute of trivial wrong,
    Nor the other hours are able to save,
The happy, that lasted my whole life long:
    For a promise broke, not for first words spoke,
The true, the only, that turn my grave
    To a blaze of joy and a crash of song.

Witness beforehand!   Off I trip
    On a safe path gay through the flowers you flung:
My very name made great by your lip,
    And my heart aglow with the good I know
Of a perfect year when we both were young,
    And I tasted the angels' fellowship.

And witness, moreover . . . Ah, but wait!
    I spy the loop whence an arrow shoots!
It may be for yourself, when you meditate,
    That you grieve—for slain ruth, murdered truth:
"Though falsehood escape in the end, what boots?
    How truth would have triumphed!"—you sigh too late.

Ay, who would have triumphed like you, I say!
    Well, it is lost now; well, you must bear,
Abide and grow fit for a better day:
    You should hardly grudge, could I be your judge!

But hush!   For you, can be no despair:
   There's amends: 'tis a secret: hope and pray!

For I was true at least—oh, true enough!
   And, Dear, truth is not as good as it seems!
Commend me to conscience!   Idle stuff!
   Much help is in mine, as I mope and pine,
And skulk through day, and scowl in my dreams
   At my swan's obtaining the crow's rebuff.

Men tell me of truth now—"False!" I cry:
   Of beauty—"A mask, friend!   Look beneath!"
We take our own method, the devil and I,
   With pleasant and fair and wise and rare:
And the best we wish to what lives, is—death;
   Which even in wishing, perhaps we lie!

Far better commit a fault and have done—
   As you, Dear!—forever; and choose the pure,
And look where the healing waters run,
   And strive and strain to be good again,
And a place in the other world ensure,
   All glass and gold, with God for its sun.

Misery!   What shall I say or do?
   I cannot advise, or, at least, persuade:
Most like, you are glad you deceived me—rue
   No whit of the wrong: you endured too long,
Have done no evil and want no aid,
   Will live the old life out and chance the new.

And your sentence is written all the same,
   And I can do nothing,—pray, perhaps:
But somehow the world pursues its game,—
   If I pray, if I curse,—for better or worse;

And my faith is torn to a thousand scraps,
   And my heart feels ice while my words breathe flame.

Dear, I look from my hiding-place.
   Are you still so fair? Have you still the eyes?
Be happy! Add but the other grace,
   Be good! Why want what the angels vaunt?
I knew you once: but in Paradise,
   If we meet, I will pass nor turn my face.

TOO LATE

HERE was I with my arm and heart
   And brain, all yours for a word, a want
Put into a look—just a look, your part,—
   While mine, to repay it . . . vainest vaunt
Were the woman, that's dead, alive to hear,
   Had her lover, that's lost, love's proof to show!
But I cannot show it; you cannot speak
   From the churchyard neither, miles removed,
Though I feel by a pulse within my cheek,
   Which stabs and stops, that the woman I loved
Needs help in her grave and finds none near,
   Wants warmth from the heart which sends it—so!

Did I speak once angrily, all the drear days
   You lived, you woman I loved so well,
Who married the other? Blame or praise,
   Where was the use then? Time would tell,
And the end declare what man for you,
   What woman for me, was the choice of God.
But, Edith dead! no doubting more!
   I used to sit and look at my life
As it rippled and ran till, right before,
   A great stone stopped it: oh, the strife

Of waves at the stone some devil threw
  In my life's midcurrent, thwarting God!

But either I thought, "They may churn and chide
  Awhile, my waves which came for their joy
And found this horrible stone full-tide:
  Yet I see just a thread escape, deploy
Through the evening-country, silent and safe,
  And it suffers no more till it finds the sea."
Or else I would think, "Perhaps some night
  When new things happen, a meteor-ball
May slip through the sky in a line of light,
  And earth breathe hard, and landmarks fall,
And my waves no longer champ nor chafe,
  Since a stone will have rolled from its place: let be!"

But, dead! All's done with: wait who may,
  Watch and wear and wonder who will.
Oh, my whole life that ends today!
  Oh, my soul's sentence, sounding still,
"The woman is dead that was none of his;
  And the man that was none of hers may go!"
There's only the past left: worry that!
  Wreak, like a bull, on the empty coat,
Rage, its late wearer is laughing at!
  Tear the collar to rags, having missed his throat;
Strike stupidly on—"This, this and this,
  Where I would that a bosom received the blow!"

I ought to have done more: once my speech,
  And once your answer, and there, the end,
And Edith was henceforth out of reach!
  Why, men do more to deserve a friend,
Be rid of a foe, get rich, grow wise,
  Nor, folding their arms, stare fate in the face.
Why, better even have burst like a thief

And borne you away to a rock for us two,
In a moment's horror, bright, bloody and brief,
    Then changed to myself again—"I slew
Myself in that moment; a ruffian lies
    Somewhere: your slave, see, born in his place!"

What did the other do? You be judge!
    Look at us, Edith! Here are we both!
Give him his six whole years: I grudge
    None of the life with you, nay, loathe
Myself that I grudged his start in advance
    Of me who could overtake and pass.
But, as if he loved you! No, not he,
    Nor any one else in the world, 'tis plain:
Who ever heard that another, free
    As I, young, prosperous, sound and sane,
Poured life out, proffered it—"Half a glance
    Of those eyes of yours and I drop the glass!"

Handsome, were you? 'Tis more than they held,
    More than they said; I was 'ware and watched:
I was the scapegrace, this rat belled
    The cat, this fool got his whiskers scratched:
The others? No head that was turned, no heart
    Broken, my lady, assure yourself!
Each soon made his mind up; so and so
    Married a dancer, such and such
Stole his friend's wife, stagnated slow,
    Or maundered, unable to do as much,
And muttered of peace where he had no part:
    While, hid in the closet, laid on the shelf,—

On the whole, you were let alone, I think!
    So, you looked to the other, who acquiesced;
My rival, the proud man,—prize your pink
    Of poets! A poet he was! I've guessed:
He rhymed you his rubbish nobody read,

Loved you and doved you—did not I laugh!
There was a prize!　But we both were tried.
　　Oh, heart of mine, marked broad with her mark,
Tekel, found wanting, set aside,
　　Scorned!　See, I bleed these tears in the dark
Till comfort come and the last be bled:
　　He?　He is tagging your epitaph.

If it would only come over again!
　　—Time to be patient with me, and probe
This heart till you punctured the proper vein,
　　Just to learn what blood is: twitch the robe
From that blank lay-figure your fancy draped,
　　Prick the leathern heart till the—verses spirt!
And late it was easy; late, you walked
　　Where a friend might meet you; Edith's name
Arose to one's lip if one laughed or talked;
　　If I heard good news, you heard the same;
When I woke, I knew that your breath escaped;
　　I could bide my time, keep alive, alert.

And alive I shall keep and long, you will see!
　　I knew a man, was kicked like a dog
From gutter to cesspool; what cared he
　　So long as he picked from the filth his prog?
He saw youth, beauty and genius die,
　　And jollily lived to his hundredth year.
But I will live otherwise: none of such life!
　　At once I begin as I mean to end.
Go on with the world, get gold in its strife,
　　Give your spouse the slip and betray your friend!
There are two who decline, a woman and I,
　　And enjoy our death in the darkness here.

I liked that way you had with your curls
　　Wound to a ball in a net behind:

Your cheek was chaste as a Quaker-girl's,
　　And your mouth—there was never, to my mind,
Such a funny mouth, for it would not shut;
　　And the dented chin too—what a chin!
There were certain ways when you spoke, some words
　　That you know you never could pronounce:
You were thin, however; like a bird's
　　Your hand seemed—some would say, the pounce
Of a scaly-footed hawk—all but!
　　The world was right when it called you thin.

But I turn my back on the world: I take
　　Your hand, and kneel, and lay to my lips.
Bid me live, Edith! Let me slake
　　Thirst at your presence! Fear no slips:
'Tis your slave shall pay, while his soul endures,
　　Full due, love's whole debt, *summum jus.*
My queen shall have high observance, planned
　　Courtship made perfect, no least line
Crossed without warrant. There you stand,
　　Warm too, and white too: would this wine
Had washed all over that body of yours.
　　Ere I drank it, and you down with it, thus!

ABT VOGLER

(AFTER HE HAS BEEN EXTEMPORIZING UPON THE MUSICAL INSTRUMENT OF HIS INVENTION)

WOULD that the structure brave, the manifold music I
　　build,
　　Bidding my organ obey, calling its keys to their work,
Claiming each slave of the sound, at a touch, as when
　　Solomon willed
　　Armies of angels that soar, legions of demons that lurk,
Man, brute, reptile, fly,—alien of end and of aim,

Adverse, each from the other heaven-high, hell-deep
    removed,—
Should rush into sight at once as he named the ineffable
    Name,
    And pile him a palace straight, to pleasure the princess
      he loved!

Would it might tarry like his, the beautiful building of
    mine,
    This which my keys in a crowd pressed and importuned
      to raise!
Ah, one and all, how they helped, would dispart now and
    now combine,
    Zealous to hasten the work, heighten their master his
      praise!
And one would bury his brow with a blind plunge down
    to hell,
    Burrow awhile and build, broad on the roots of things,
Then up again swim into sight, having based me my
    palace well,
    Founded it, fearless of flame, flat on the nether springs.

And another would mount and march, like the excellent
    minion he was,
    Ay, another and yet another, one crowd but with many
      a crest,
Raising my rampired walls of gold as transparent as glass,
    Eager to do and die, yield each his place to the rest:
For higher still and higher (as a runner tips with fire,
    When a great illumination surprises a festal night—
Outlined round and round Rome's dome from space to
    spire)
    Up, the pinnacled glory reached, and the pride of my
      soul was in sight.

In sight? Not half! for it seemed, it was certain, to match
    man's birth,

Nature in turn conceived, obeying an impulse as I;
And the emulous heaven yearned down, made effort to
reach the earth,
As the earth had done her best, in my passion, to scale
the sky:
Novel splendors burst forth, grew familiar and dwelt
with mine,
Not a point nor peak but found and fixed its wandering
star;
Meteor-moons, balls of blaze: and they did not pale nor
pine,
For earth had attained to heaven, there was no more
near nor far.

Nay more; for there wanted not who walked in the glare
and glow,
Presences plain in the place; or, fresh from the Proto-
plast,
Furnished for ages to come, when a kindlier wind should
blow,
Lured now to begin and live, in a house to their liking
at last;
Or else the wonderful Dead who have passed through the
body and gone,
But were back once more to breathe in an old world
worth their new:
What never had been, was now; what was, as it shall be
anon;
And what is,—shall I say, matched both? for I was made
perfect too.

All through my keys that gave their sounds to a wish of
my soul,
All through my soul that praised as its wish flowed
visibly forth,

All through music and me! For think, had I painted the
   whole,
   Why, there it had stood, to see, nor the process so
   wonder-worth:
Had I written the same, made verse—still, effect proceeds
   from cause,
   Ye know why the forms are fair, ye hear how the tale
   is told;
It is all triumphant art, but art in obedience to laws,
   Painter and poet are proud in the artist-list enrolled:—

But here is the finger of God, a flash of the will that can,
   Existent behind all laws, that made them and, lo, they
   are!
And I know not if, save in this, such gift be allowed to
   man,
   That out of three sounds he frame, not a fourth sound,
   but a star.
Consider it well: each tone of our scale in itself is naught:
   It is everywhere in the world—loud, soft, and all is
   said:
Give it to me to use! I mix it with two in my thought:
   And there! Ye have heard and seen: consider and bow
   the head!

Well, it is gone at last, the palace of music I reared;
   Gone! and the good tears start, the praises that come
   too slow;
For one is assured at first, one scarce can say that he
   feared,
   That he even gave it a thought, the gone thing was
   to go.
Never to be again! But many more of the kind
   As good, nay, better perchance: is this your comfort
   to me?
To me, who must be saved because I cling with my mind

To the same, same self, same love, same God: ay, what
   was, shall be.

Therefore to whom turn I but to thee, the ineffable
      Name?
   Builder and maker, thou, of houses not made with
      hands!
What, have fear of change from thee who art ever the
      same?
   Doubt that thy power can fill the heart that thy power
      expands?
There shall never be one lost good!   What was, shall live
      as before;
   The evil is null, is naught, is silence implying sound;
What was good shall be good, with, for evil, so much
      good more;
   On the earth the broken arcs; in the heaven a perfect
      round.

All we have willed or hoped or dreamed of good shall
      exist;
   Not its semblance, but itself; no beauty, nor good, nor
      power
Whose voice has gone forth, but each survives for the
      melodist
   When eternity affirms the conception of an hour.
The high that proved too high, the heroic for earth too
      hard,
   The passion that left the ground to lose itself in the
      sky,
Are music sent up to God by the lover and the bard;
   Enough that he heard it once: we shall hear it by
      and by.

And what is our failure here but a triumph's evidence

For the fulness of the days? Have we withered or
    agonized?
Why else was the pause prolonged but that singing might
    issue thence?
  Why rushed the discords in, but that harmony should
    be prized? *Evil makes us appreciate good*
Sorrow is hard to bear, and doubt is slow to clear,
  Each sufferer says his say, his scheme of the weal and
    woe:
But God has a few of us whom he whispers in the ear;
  The rest may reason and welcome: 'tis we musicians
    know.

Well, it is earth with me; silence resumes her reign:
  I will be patient and proud, and soberly acquiesce.
Give me the keys. I feel for the common chord again,
  Sliding by semitones till I sink to the minor,—yes,
And I blunt it into a ninth, and I stand on alien ground,
  Surveying awhile the heights I rolled from into the
    deep;
Which, hark, I have dared and done, for my resting-place
    is found,
  The C Major of this life: so, now I will try to sleep.
Common ground.

RABBI BEN EZRA

Grow old along with me!
The best is yet to be,
The last of life, for which the first was made:
Our times are in His hand
Who saith, "A whole I planned,
Youth shows but half; trust God: see all, nor be afraid.

Not that, amassing flowers,
Youth sighed "Which rose make ours,

Which lily leave and then as best recall?"
Not that, admiring stars,
It yearned "Nor Jove, nor Mars;
Mine be some figured flame which blends, transcends
   them all!"

Not for such hopes and fears
Annulling youth's brief years,
Do I remonstrate: folly wide the mark!
Rather I prize the doubt
Low kinds exist without,
Finished and finite clods, untroubled by a spark.

Poor vaunt of life indeed,
Were man but formed to feed
On joy, to solely seek and find and feast:
Such feasting ended, then
As sure an end to men;
Irks care the crop-full bird? Frets doubt the maw-
   crammed beast?

Rejoice we are allied
To that which doth provide
And not partake, effect and not receive!
A spark disturbs our clod;
Nearer we hold of God
Who gives, than of His tribes that take, I must believe.

Then, welcome each rebuff
That turns earth's smoothness rough,
Each sting that bids nor sit nor stand but go!
Be our joys three-parts pain!
Strive, and hold cheap the strain;
Learn, nor account the pang; dare, never grudge the throe!

For thence,—a paradox
Which comforts while it mocks,—

Shall life succeed in that it seems to fail:
What I aspired to be,
And was not, comforts me:
A brute I might have been, but would not sink i' the scale.

What is he but a brute
Whose flesh has soul to suit,
Whose spirit works lest arms and legs want play?
To man, propose this test—
Thy body at its best,
How far can that project thy soul on its lone way?

Yet gifts should prove their use:
I own the Past profuse
Of power each side, perfection every turn:
Eyes, ears took in their dole,
Brain treasured up the whole;
Should not the heart beat once "How good to live and
    learn"?

Not once beat "Praise be thine!
I see the whole design,
I, who saw power, see now love perfect too:
Perfect I call Thy plan:
Thanks that I was a man!
Maker, remake, complete,—I trust what Thou shalt do!"

For pleasant is this flesh;
Our soul, in its rose-mesh
Pulled ever to the earth, still yearns for rest:
Would we some prize might hold
To match those manifold
Possessions of the brute,—gain most, as we did best!

Let us not always say,
"Spite of this flesh today
I strove, made head, gained ground upon the whole!"

As the bird wings and sings,
Let us cry "All good things
Are ours, nor soul helps flesh more, now, than flesh
    helps soul!"

Therefore I summon age
To grant youth's heritage,
Life's struggle having so far reached its term:
Thence shall I pass, approved
A man, for aye removed
From the developed brute; a god though in the germ.

And I shall thereupon
Take rest, ere I be gone
Once more on my adventure brave and new:
Fearless and unperplexed,
When I wage battle next,
What weapons to select, what armor to indue.

Youth ended, I shall try
My gain or loss thereby;
Leave the fire ashes, what survives is gold:
And I shall weigh the same,
Give life its praise or blame:
Young, all lay in dispute; I shall know, being old.

For note, when evening shuts,
A certain moment cuts
The deed off, calls the glory from the gray:
A whisper from the west
Shoots—"Add this to the rest,
Take it and try its worth: here dies another day."

So, still within this life,
Though lifted o'er its strife,
Let me discern, compare, pronounce at last,

"This rage was right i' the main,
That acquiescence vain:
The Future I may face now I have proved the Past."

For more is not reserved
To man, with soul just nerved
To act tomorrow what he learns today:
Here, work enough to watch
The Master work, and catch
Hints of the proper craft, tricks of the tool's true play.

As it was better, youth
Should strive, through acts uncouth,
Toward making, than repose on aught found made:
So, better, age, exempt
From strife, should know, than tempt
Further. Thou waitedest age: wait death nor be afraid!

Enough now, if the Right
And Good and Infinite
Be named here, as thou callest thy hand thine own,
With knowledge absolute,
Subject to no dispute
From fools that crowded youth, nor let thee feel alone.

Be there, for once and all,
Severed great minds from small,
Announced to each his station in the Past!
Was I, the world arraigned,
Were they, my soul disdained,
Right? Let age speak the truth and give us peace at last!

Now, who shall arbitrate?
Ten men love what I hate,
Shun what I follow, slight what I receive;
Ten, who in ears and eyes

Match me: we all surmise,
They this thing, and I that: whom shall my soul believe?

Not on the vulgar mass
Called "work," must sentence pass,
Things done, that took the eye and had the price;
O'er which, from level stand,
The low world laid its hand,
Found straightway to its mind, could value in a trice:

But all, the world's coarse thumb
And finger failed to plumb,
So passed in making up the main account;
All instincts immature,
All purposes unsure,
That weighed not as his work, yet swelled the man's
    amount:

Thoughts hardly to be packed
Into a narrow act,
Fancies that broke through language and escaped;
All I could never be,
All, men ignored in me,
This, I was worth to God, whose wheel the pitcher shaped.

Ay, note that Potter's wheel,
That metaphor! and feel
Why time spins fast, why passive lies our clay,—
Thou, to whom fools propound,
When the wine makes its round,
"Since life fleets, all is change; the Past gone, seize today!"

Fool! All that is, at all,
Lasts ever, past recall;
Earth changes, but thy soul and God stand sure:
What entered into thee,

That was, is, and shall be:
Time's wheel runs back or stops: Potter and clay endure.

He fixed thee 'mid this dance
Of plastic circumstance,
This Present, thou, forsooth, would fain arrest:
Machinery just meant
To give thy soul its bent,
Try thee and turn thee forth, sufficiently impressed.

What though the earlier grooves,
Which ran the laughing loves
Around thy base, no longer pause and press?
What though, about thy rim,
Skull-things in order grim
Grow out, in graver mood, obey the sterner stress?

Look not thou down but up!
To uses of a cup,
The festal board, lamp's flash and trumpet's peal,
The new wine's foaming flow,
The Master's lips aglow!
Thou, heaven's consummate cup, what needst
      thou with earth's wheel?

But I need, now as then,
Thee, God, who mouldest men;
And since, not even while the whirl was worst,
Did I—to the wheel of life
With shapes and colors rife,
Bound dizzily—mistake my end, to slake Thy thirst:

So, take and use Thy work:
Amend what flaws may lurk,
What strain o' the stuff, what warpings past the aim!

My times be in Thy hand!
Perfect the cup as planned!
Let age approve of youth, and death complete the same!

CALIBAN UPON SETEBOS;

OR, NATURAL THEOLOGY IN THE ISLAND

"Thou thoughtest that I was altogether such an one as thyself."

['WILL sprawl, now that the heat of day is best,
Flat on his belly in the pit's much mire,
With elbows wide, fists clenched to prop his chin.
And, while he kicks both feet in the cool slush,
And feels about his spine small eft-things course,
Run in and out each arm, and make him laugh:
And while above his head a pompion-plant,
Coating the cave-top as a brow its eye,
Creeps down to touch and tickle hair and beard,
And now a flower drops with a bee inside,
And now a fruit to snap at, catch and crunch,—
He looks o'er yon sea which sunbeams cross
And recross till they weave a spider-web,
(Meshes of fire, some great fish breaks at times,)
And talks to his own self, howe'er he please,
Touching that other, whom his dam called God.
Because to talk about Him, vexes—ha,
Could He but know! and time to vex is now,
When talk is safer than in winter-time.
Moreover Prosper and Miranda sleep
In confidence he drudges at their task,
And it is good to cheat the pair, and gibe,
Letting the rank tongue blossom into speech.]

Setebos, Setebos, and Setebos!
'Thinketh, He dwelleth i' the cold o' the moon.

'Thinketh He made it, with the sun to match,
But not the stars; the stars came otherwise;
Only made clouds, winds, meteors, such as that:
Also this isle, what lives and grows thereon,
And snaky sea which rounds and ends the same.

'Thinketh, it came of being ill at ease:
He hated that He cannot change His cold,
Nor cure its ache. ' 'Hath spied an icy fish
That longed to 'scape the rock-stream where she
    lived,
And thaw herself within the lukewarm brine
O' the lazy sea her stream thrusts far amid,
A crystal spike 'twixt two warm walls of wave;
Only, she ever sickened, found repulse
At the other kind of water, not her life,
(Green-dense and dim-delicious, bred o' the sun,)
Flounced back from bliss she was not born to breathe,
And in her old bounds buried her despair,
Hating and loving warmth alike: so He.

'Thinketh, He made thereat the sun, this isle,
Trees and the fowls here, beast and creeping thing.
Yon otter, sleek-wet, black, lithe as a leech;
Yon auk, one fire-eye in a ball of foam,
That floats and feeds; a certain badger brown
He hath watched hunt with that slant white-wedge
    eye
By moonlight; and the pie with the long tongue
That pricks deep into oakwarts for a worm,
And says a plain word when she finds her prize,
But will not eat the ants; the ants themselves
That build a wall of seeds and settled stalks
About their hole—He made all these and more,
Made all we see, and us, in spite: how else?
He could not, Himself, make a second self

To be His mate; as well have made Himself:
He would not make what He mislikes or slights,
An eyesore to Him, or not worth His pains:
But did, in envy, listlessness or sport,
Make what Himself would fain, in a manner, be—
Weaker in most points, stronger in a few,
Worthy, and yet mere playthings all the while,
Things He admires and mocks too,—that is it.
Because, so brave, so better though they be,
It nothing skills if He begin to plague.
Look now, I melt a gourd-fruit into mash,
Add honeycomb and pods, I have perceived,
Which bite like finches when they bill and kiss,—
Then, when froth rises bladdery, drink up all,
Quick, quick, till maggots scamper through my brain;
Last, throw me on my back i' the seeded thyme,
And wanton, wishing I were born a bird.
Put case, unable to be what I wish,
I yet could make a live bird out of clay:
Would not I take clay, pinch my Caliban
Able to fly?—for, there, see, he hath wings,
And great comb like the hoopoe's to admire,
And there, a sting to do his foes offence,
There, and I will that he begin to live,
Fly to yon rock-top, nip me off the horns
Of grigs high up that make the merry din,
Saucy through their veined wings, and mind me not.
In which feat, if his leg snapped, brittle clay,
And he lay stupid-like,—why, I should laugh;
And if he, spying me, should fall to weep,
Beseech me to be good, repair his wrong,
Bid his poor leg smart less or grow again,—
Well, as the chance were, this might take or else
Not take my fancy: I might hear his cry,
And give the mankin three sound legs for one,
Or pluck the other off, leave him like an egg,

And lessoned he was mine and merely clay.
Were this no pleasure, lying in the thyme,
Drinking the mash, with brain become alive,
Making and marring clay at will?   So He.

'Thinketh, such shows nor right nor wrong in Him,
Nor kind, nor cruel: He is strong and Lord.
'Am strong myself compared to yonder crabs
That march now from the mountain to the sea;
'Let twenty pass, and stone the twenty-first,
Loving not, hating not, just choosing so.
'Say, the first straggler that boasts purple spots
Shall join the file, one pincer twisted off;
'Say, this bruised fellow shall receive a worm,
And two worms he whose nippers end in red;
As it likes me each time, I do: so He.

Well then, 'supposeth He is good i' the main,
Placable if His mind and ways were guessed,
But rougher than His handiwork, be sure!
Oh, He hath made things worthier than Himself,
And envieth that, so helped, such things do more
Than He who made them!   What consoles but this?
That they, unless through Him, do naught at all,
And must submit: what other use in things?
'Hath cut a pipe of pithless elder-joint
That, blown through, gives exact the scream o' the jay
When from her wing you twitch the feathers blue:
Sound this, and little birds that hate the jay
Flock within stone's throw, glad their foe is hurt:
Put case such pipe could prattle and boast forsooth,
"I catch the birds, I am the crafty thing,
I make the cry my maker cannot make
With his great round mouth; he must blow through
     mine!"
Would not I smash it with my foot?   So He.

But wherefore rough, why cold and ill at ease?
Aha, that is a question! Ask, for that,
What knows,—the something over Setebos
That made Him, or He, may be, found and fought,
Worsted, drove off and did to nothing, perchance.
There may be something quiet o'er His head,
Out of His reach, that feels nor joy nor grief,
Since both derive from weakness in some way.
I joy because the quails come; would not joy
Could I bring quails here when I have a mind:
This Quiet, all it hath a mind to, doth.
'Esteemeth stars the outposts of its couch,
But never spends much thought nor care that way.
It may look up, work up,—the worse for those
It works on! 'Careth but for Setebos
The many-handed as a cuttle-fish,
Who, making Himself feared through what He does,
Looks up, first, and perceives he cannot soar
To what is quiet and hath happy life;
Next looks down here, and out of very spite
Makes this a bauble-world to ape yon real,
These good things to match those as hips do grapes.
'Tis solace making baubles, ay, and sport.
Himself peeped late, eyed Prosper at his books
Careless and lofty, lord now of the isle:
Vexed, 'stitched a book of broad leaves, arrow-
    shaped,
Wrote thereon, he knows what, prodigious words;
Has peeled a wand and called it by a name;
Weareth at whiles for an enchanter's robe
The eyed skin of a supple oncelot;
And hath an ounce sleeker than youngling mole,
A four-legged serpent he makes cower and couch,
Now snarl, now hold its breath and mind his eye,
And saith she is Miranda and my wife:
'Keeps for his Ariel a tall pouch-bill crane

He bids go wade for fish and straight disgorge;
Also a sea-beast, lumpish, which he snared,
Blinded the eyes of, and brought somewhat tame,
And split its toe-webs, and now pens the drudge
In a hole o' the rock and calls him Caliban;
A bitter heart that bides its time and bites.
'Plays thus at being Prosper in a way,
Taketh his mirth with make-believes: so He.

His dam held that the Quiet made all things
Which Setebos vexed only: 'holds not so.
Who made them weak, meant weakness He might
     vex.
Had He meant other, while His hand was in,
Why not make horny eyes no thorn could prick,
Or plate my scalp with bone against the snow,
Or overscale my flesh 'neath joint and joint,
Like an orc's armor? Ay,—so spoil His sport!
He is the One now: only He doth all.

'Saith, He may like, perchance, what profits Him.
Ay, himself loves what does him good; but why?
'Gets good no otherwise. This blinded beast
Loves whoso places flesh-meat on his nose,
But, had he eyes, would want no help, but hate
Or love, just as it liked him: He hath eyes.
Also it pleaseth Setebos to work,
Use all His hands, and exercise much craft,
By no means for the love of what is worked.
'Tasteth, himself, no finer good i' the world
When all goes right, in this safe summer-time,
And he wants little, hungers, aches not much,
Than trying what to do with wit and strength.
'Falls to make something: 'piled yon pile of turfs,
And squared and stuck there squares of soft white
     chalk,

And, with a fish-tooth, scratched a moon on each,
And set up endwise certain spikes of tree,
And crowned the whole with a sloth's skull a-top,
Found dead i' the woods, too hard for one to kill.
No use at all i' the work, for work's sole sake;
'Shall some day knock it down again: so He.

'Saith He is terrible: watch His feats in proof!
One hurricane will spoil six good months' hope.
He hath a spite against me, that I know,
Just as He favors Prosper, who knows why?
So it is, all the same, as well I find.
'Wove wattles half the winter, fenced them firm
With stone and stake to stop she-tortoises
Crawling to lay their eggs here: well, one wave,
Feeling the foot of Him upon its neck,
Gaped as a snake does, lolled out its large tongue,
And licked the whole labor flat: so much for spite.

'Saw a ball flame down late (yonder it lies)
Where, half an hour before, I slept i' the shade:
Often they scatter sparkles: there is force!
'Dug up a newt He may have envied once
And turned to stone, shut up inside a stone.
Please Him and hinder this?—What Prosper does?
Aha, if He would tell me how! Not He!
There is the sport: discover how or die!
All need not die, for of the things o' the isle
Some flee afar, some dive, some run up trees;
Those at His mercy,—why, they please Him most
When . . . when . . . well, never try the same way
       twice!
Repeat what act has pleased, He may grow wroth.
You must not know His ways, and play Him off,
Sure of the issue. 'Doth the like himself:
'Spareth a squirrel that it nothing fears

But steals the nut from underneath my thumb,
And when I threat, bites stoutly in defence:
'Spareth an urchin that contrariwise,
Curls up into a ball, pretending death
For fright at my approach: the two ways please.
But what would move my choler more than this,
That either creature counted on its life
Tomorrow and next day and all days to come,
Saying, forsooth, in the inmost of its heart,
"Because he did so yesterday with me,
And otherwise with such another brute,
So must he do henceforth and always."—Ay?
Would teach the reasoning couple what "must"
        means!
'Doth as he likes, or wherefore Lord? So He.
'Conceiveth all things will continue thus,
And we shall have to live in fear of Him
So long as He lives, keeps His strength: no change,
If He have done His best, make no new world
To please Him more, so leave off watching this,—
If He surprise not even the Quiet's self
Some strange day,—or, suppose, grow into it
As grubs grow butterflies: else, here we are,
And there is He, and nowhere help at all.

'Believeth with the life, the pain shall stop.
His dam held different, that after death
He both plagued enemies and feasted friends:
Idly! He doth His worst in this our life,
Giving just respite lest we die through pain,
Saving last pain for worst,—with which, an end.
Meanwhile, the best way to escape His ire
Is, not to seem too happy. 'Sees, himself,
Yonder two flies, with purple films and pink,
Bask on the pompion-bell above: kills both.
'Sees two black painful beetles roll their ball

On head and tail as if to save their lives:
Moves them the stick away they strive to clear.

Even so, 'would have Him misconceive, suppose
This Caliban strives hard and ails no less,
And always, above all else, envies Him;
Wherefore he mainly dances on dark nights,
Moans in the sun, gets under holes to laugh,
And never speaks his mind save housed as now:
Outside, 'groans, curses. If He caught me here,
O'erheard this speech, and asked "What chucklest
          at?"
'Would, to appease Him, cut a finger off,
Or of my three kid yearlings burn the best,
Or let the toothsome apples rot on tree,
Or push my tame beast for the orc to taste:
While myself lit a fire, and made a song
And sung it, *"What I hate, be consecrate*
To celebrate Thee and Thy state, no mate
For Thee; what see for envy in poor me?"
Hoping the while, since evils sometimes mend,
Warts rub away and sores are cured with slime,
That some strange day, will either the Quiet catch
And conquer Setebos, or likelier He
Decrepit may doze, doze, as good as die.

[What, what? A curtain o'er the world at once!
Crickets stop hissing; not a bird—or, yes,
There scuds His raven that has told Him all!
It was fool's play, this prattling! Ha! The wind
Shoulders the pillared dust, death's house o' the
          move,
And fast invading fires begin! White blaze—
A tree's head snaps—and there, there, there, there,
          there,

His thunder follows! Fool to gibe at Him!
Lo! 'Lieth flat and loveth Setebos!
'Maketh his teeth meet through his upper lip,
Will let those quails fly, will not eat this month
One little mess of whelks, so he may 'scape!]

CONFESSIONS

WHAT is he buzzing in my ears?
    "Now that I come to die,
Do I view the world as a vale of tears?"
    Ah, reverend sir, not I!

What I viewed there once, what I view again
    Where the physic bottles stand
On the table's edge,—is a suburb lane,
    With a wall to my bedside hand.

That lane sloped, much as the bottles do,
    From a house you could descry
O'er the garden-wall; is the curtain blue
    Or green to a healthy eye?

To mine, it serves for the old June weather
    Blue above lane and wall;
And that farthest bottle labelled "Ether"
    Is the house o'ertopping all.

At a terrace, somewhere near the stopper,
    There watched for me, one June,
A girl: I know, sir, it's improper,
    My poor mind's out of tune.

Only, there was a way . . . you crept
   Close by the side, to dodge
Eyes in the house, two eyes except:
   They styled their house "The Lodge."

What right had a lounger up their lane?
   But, by creeping very close,
With the good wall's help,—their eyes might
     strain
   And stretch themselves to Oes,

Yet never catch her and me together,
   As she left the attic, there,
By the rim of the bottle labelled "Ether,"
   And stole from stair to stair,

And stood by the rose-wreathed gate. Alas,
   We loved, sir—used to meet:
How sad and bad and mad it was—
   But then, how it was sweet!

One of most unusual of Br. love poem

PROSPICE

FEAR death?—to feel the fog in my throat,
   The mist in my face,
When the snows begin, and the blasts denote
   I am nearing the place,
The power of the night, the press of the storm,
   The post of the foe;
Where he stands, the Arch Fear in a visible form,
   Yet the strong man must go:
For the journey is done and the summit attained,
   And the barriers fall,
Though a battle's to fight ere the guerdon be gained,
   The reward of it all.

I was ever a fighter, so—one fight more,
   The best and the last!
I would hate that death bandaged my eyes, and forbore,
   And bade me creep past.
No! let me taste the whole of it, fare like my peers
   The heroes of old,
Bear the brunt, in a minute pay glad life's arrears
   Of pain, darkness and cold.
For sudden the worst turns the best to the brave,
   The black minute's at end,
And the elements' rage, the fiend-voices that rave,
   Shall dwindle, shall blend,
Shall change, shall become first a peace out of pain,
   Then a light, then thy breast,
O thou soul of my soul! I shall clasp thee again,
   And with God be the rest!

YOUTH AND ART

It once might have been, once only:
   We lodged in a street together,
You, a sparrow on the housetop lonely,
   I, a lone she-bird of his feather.

Your trade was with sticks and clay,
   You thumbed, thrust, patted and polished,
Then laughed "They will see some day
   Smith made, and Gibson demolished."

My business was song, song, song;
   I chirped, cheeped, trilled and twittered,
"Kate Brown's on the boards ere long,
   And Grisi's existence embittered!"

I earned no more by a warble
　　Than you by a sketch in plaster;
You wanted a piece of marble,
　　I needed a music-master.

We studied hard in our styles,
　　Chipped each at a crust like Hindoos,
For air, looked out on the tiles,
　　For fun, watched each other's windows.

You lounged, like a boy of the South,
　　Cap and blouse—nay, a bit of beard too;
Or you got it, rubbing your mouth
　　With fingers the clay adhered to.

And I—soon managed to find
　　Weak points in the flower-fence facing,
Was forced to put up a blind
　　And be safe in my corset-lacing.

No harm! It was not my fault
　　If you never turned your eye's tail up
As I shook upon E *in alt.,*
　　Or ran the chromatic scale up:

For spring bade the sparrows pair,
　　And the boys and girls gave guesses,
And stalls in our street looked rare
　　With bulrush and watercresses.

Why did not you pinch a flower
　　In a pellet of clay and fling it?
Why did not I put a power
　　Of thanks in a look, or sing it?

I did look, sharp as a lynx,
   (And yet the memory rankles,)
When models arrived, some minx
   Tripped up-stairs, she and her ankles.

But I think I gave you as good!
   "That foreign fellow,—who can know
How she pays, in a playful mood,
   For his tuning her that piano?"

Could you say so, and never say,
   "Suppose we join hands and fortunes,
And I fetch her from over the way,
   Her, piano, and long tunes and short tunes"?

No, no: you would not be rash,
   Nor I rasher and something over:
You've to settle yet Gibson's hash,
   And Grisi yet lives in clover.

But you meet the Prince at the Board,
   I'm queen myself at *bals-paré,*
I've married a rich old lord,
   And you're dubbed knight and an R. A.

Each life unfulfilled, you see;
   It hangs still, patchy and scrappy:
We have not sighed deep, laughed free,
   Starved, feasted, despaired,—been happy.

And nobody calls you a dunce,
   And people suppose me clever:
This could but have happened once,
   And we missed it, lost it forever.

APPARENT FAILURE

"We shall soon lose a celebrated building."
Paris Newspaper

No, for I'll save it!   Seven years since,
　I passed through Paris, stopped a day
To see the baptism of your Prince;
　Saw, made my bow, and went my way:
Walking the heat and headache off,
　I took the Seine-side, you surmise,
Thought of the Congress, Gortschakoff,
　Cavour's appeal and Buol's replies,
So sauntered till—what met my eyes?

Only the Doric little Morgue!
　The dead-house where you show your drowned:
Petrarch's Vaucluse makes proud the Sorgue,
　Your Morgue has made the Seine renowned.
One pays one's debt in such a case;
　I plucked up heart and entered,—stalked,
Keeping a tolerable face
　Compared with some whose cheeks were chalked:
Let them!   No Briton's to be balked!

First came the silent gazers; next,
　A screen of glass, we're thankful for;
Last, the sight's self, the sermon's text,
　The three men who did most abhor
Their life in Paris yesterday,
　So killed themselves: and now, enthroned
Each on his copper couch, they lay
　Fronting me, waiting to be owned.
I thought, and think, their sin's atoned.

Poor men, God made, and all for that!
  The reverence struck me; o'er each head
Religiously was hung its hat,
  Each coat dripped by the owner's bed,
Sacred from touch: each had his berth,
  His bounds, his proper place of rest,
Who last night tenanted on earth
  Some arch, where twelve such slept abreast,—
Unless the plain asphalt seemed best.

How did it happen, my poor boy?
  You wanted to be Buonaparte
And have the Tuileries for toy,
  And could not, so it broke your heart?
You, old one by his side, I judge,
  Were, red as blood, a socialist,
A leveller! Does the Empire grudge
  You've gained what no Republic missed?
Be quiet, and unclench your fist!

And this—why, he was red in vain,
Or black,—poor fellow that is blue!
What fancy was it, turned your brain?
  Oh, women were the prize for you!
Money gets women, cards and dice
  Get money, and ill-luck gets just
The copper couch and one clear nice
  Cool squirt of water o'er your bust,
The right thing to extinguish lust!

It's wiser being good than bad;
  It's safer being meek than fierce:
It's fitter being sane than mad.
  My own hope is, a sun will pierce
The thickest cloud earth ever stretched;
  That, after Last, returns the First,

Though a wide compass round be fetched;
That what began best, can't end worst,
Nor what God blessed once, prove accurst.

THE RING AND THE BOOK

EDITOR'S NOTE

The Story of the Roman Murder Case, 1698

PIETRO and Violante Comparini, a comfortable middle class couple of Rome, enjoyed the reversionary interest of funds, which, unless they had an heir, would go out of the family after their decease. In order to ensure the retaining of this property, Violante deceived her simple, honest husband by presenting him (although she was fifty years of age) with a daughter, whom she had secured from a woman of low birth. A dozen years later, "Count" Guido Franceschini, an improverished noble-man of Arezzo, looked about for a wife with money enough to rehabilitate his fortunes. He was informed of the daughter in the Comparini family, Pompilia, who was reputed to be the heir of considerable wealth. Al-though she was known to be only thirteen years old, while Guido was thirty-six (Browning represents him as older), he did not hesitate to send his brother, the Abate Paolo, to negotiate a marriage for him. Violante, the supposed mother, was flattered by his addresses, and wished to marry Pompilia to the nobleman, believing that the latter had wealth as well as gentility. But Pietro objected, probably because he knew more than she did about the Franceschini family of Arezzo. It was necessary, then, for Violante to deceive her husband a second time. She conspired with Abate Paolo and

Guido to the end that the marriage was secretly performed in Rome, on Sunday, September 6, 1693. When
he learned of it, Pietro was forced to make the best of
a bad matter. Pompilia returned to her father's home
for the time being.

In December, 1693, however, Pompilia and the Comparini went to Arezzo, to live in the "ghost-haunted
palace" of Guido. This arrangement was not a happy
one. It was made necessary by the fact that Pietro had
been obliged to put nearly everything he had into a
marriage settlement. Guido had expected that the
Comparini were richer than they proved to be; the
supposed parents of Pompilia soon discovered that they
also had been deceived—that Guido's estate was heavily
burdened with debts. A sordid story of irritation and
persecution followed and resulted in the return of the
impoverished Comparini to Rome in April, 1694. Some
of the citizens of Arezzo believed the fault lay with the
Comparini; others thought the Franceschini were to
blame.

Immediately after her return to Rome, Violante confessed to a priest her deception regarding the parentage
of Pompilia. She had nothing to lose now by this confession; Guido had much to lose. During the summer of
1694, Pietro sufficiently recovered from the shock of the
revelation to prosecute a suit to recover the dowry.
Guido, further aggrieved by this development, began to
make plans to destroy the character of his wife so that
he might divorce her legally and retain the marriage
settlement. To this end, he allowed her to be systemat-
ically persecuted by the members of his family, and he
abused her himself until she was really in fear of her
life. After she had appealed without success to the

Bishop and the Governor of Arezzo, she turned to a young priest, Caponsacchi, an intimate of Canon Conti, her cousin-by-marriage. Caponsacchi believed her in danger, and therefore agreed somewhat reluctantly to take her to Rome, so that she could join her parents. It appeared later that Guido had plotted to drive her into the arms of this same gallant priest. His plot thus far succeeded.

Pompilia's flight was hastened by her discovery that she was to have a child, and had, therefore, more than her own life to consider. Caponsacchi and Pompilia set out on their secret journey by night, on April 29, 1697, and reached Castelnuovo, fifteen miles from Rome, on the evening of the next day. There they were obliged to halt for a few hours because of Pompilia's weakness and weariness. Guido overtook them, on the morning of May 1, and had them arrested. They were taken to Rome and lodged in prison on the criminal charge of adulterous elopement. Guido produced love letters, which he offered as a proof of the adultery of his wife, but these were shown to be forgeries, and were thrown out by the Court. They proved only that Guido had schemed to drive his wife into dishonorable flight, so that he might legally be rid of her. The trial dragged on through the summer, the authorities looking with some good-natured indulgence upon what appeared to them no more than the rather harmless indiscretions of a young priest and a more youthful wife. Finally, on September 24, Caponsacchi was "relegated" for three years to Civita Vecchia—a light sentence, designed presumably to put him temporarily out of reach of temptation. Pompilia was sent to the convent known as the Scalette, until October 12, when she was allowed to go to the home of the Comparini, there to be regarded as still under the authority of the police. All this had given little satisfaction to Guido, who withdrew to Arezzo and began to plot more extreme measures.

On December 18, 1697, Pompilia's son, Gaetano, was born. He was—since the Comparini feared Guido's vengeance—removed secretly to a place of safety. That the family were justified in these fears was proved when, on the evening of January 2, 1698, Guido and four bravos appeared at the door of the Comparini home, gained admittance by the trick of using Caponsacchi's name, and brutally murdered with daggers Violante, Pietro, and Pompilia. The last, although grievously wounded by twenty-two dagger thrusts, lived until January 6. She was given religious consolation during this time by Fra Celestino Angelo, a bare-footed Augustinian priest, who attested afterward that she had declared she never in point of chastity had offended her husband. It was from the warm attestation of Fra Celestino, particularly, that Browning gained most of his faith in the innocence and saintlike character of Pompilia.

In the meantime, on January 3, Guido and his associates had been captured and imprisoned. Almost at once, that is, soon after the affidavit of Fra Celestino, on January 19, the second trial began—the trial of Guido and his hirelings for murder. It is this second trial that furnished the framework and the most dramatic elements of *The Ring and the Book*. In the so-called *Old Yellow Book*, Browning found all the documents of the trial—a record of the court procedure for the seven weeks between the arrest of Guido and the execution. These documents, it should be noted, constituted the actual trial. The opposing lawyers submitted their pleas in writing to the Court, along with the depositions, affidavits, etc., used to bolster their cases. The judges handed down their decision on February 18, but a stay of sentence was granted. On February 21, the Pope overruled the delay and the execution was set for the following day, when the "four" were hung, while Guido, because of higher social rank, was beheaded.

Such are the bare facts of the tragic story which Browning read in the *Old Yellow Book* and in the pamphlet—a story in which all the principals except Caponsacchi were violently removed from the stage. The poet saw that through it all Pompilia was the one person without blame, and the one who was the chief sufferer. He also saw what he stated eloquently in the last part (see address to the British public), that art was the one way possible of speaking the truth about the innocence of Pompilia or the noble unselfishness of Caponsacchi.

Nine times Browning tells the story—from the varied points of view of the citizens of Rome who sympathized with Guido ("Half-Rome"), those who took the wife's part ("Other Half-Rome"), and those who were idly curious but cared for neither Guido nor Pompilia ("Tertium Quid"); he tells it from the lips of Guido, speaking in his own defense, from those of Caponsacchi in accusation of Guido and in defence of Pompilia, and from those of Pompilia herself; he tells it finally in the arguments of Guido's counsel, in those of the public prosecutor, and in the noble language of the Pope. Several excerpts from *The Ring and the Book* are included here to show at its highest development Browning's faculty for putting himself into the minds of different characters—his "passionate psychology." No finer contrasts can be found than those revealed here between the self-justifying shrewdness and suavity of Guido, the simple purity of Pompilia, and the reckless unselfishness and noble indignation of Caponsacchi. Those who have time and inclination to read the whole work will find a convenient cheap edition in the Scribner's Modern Student's Library. The documents of the *Old Yellow Book* are available, in translation, in the Everyman's Library, No. 503. This edition contains also a translation of the so-called "secondary source" of Browning (a pamphlet containing a version of the story, which he used); and, in addition, a translation of a pamphlet which was discovered about 1900, and was first published in the *Monthly Review* of that year. This second pamphlet, which was unknown to Browning, contains a very interesting version of the tragic story. It is to be found, also, in appendix B of the Griffin-Minchin *Life*.

[THE FINDING OF THE YELLOW BOOK]

(*From* Book I)

Do you see this square old yellow Book, I toss
I' the air, and catch again, and twirl about
By the crumpled vellum covers,—pure crude fact
Secreted from man's life when hearts beat hard,
And brains, high-blooded, ticked two centuries since?
Examine it yourselves! I found this book,
Gave a *lira* for it, eightpence English just,
(Mark the predestination!) when a Hand,
Always above my shoulder, pushed me once,
One day still fierce 'mid many a day struck calm,
Across a Square in Florence, crammed with booths,
Buzzing and blaze, noontide and market-time,
Toward Baccio's marble,—ay, the basement-ledge

O' the pedestal where sits and menaces
John of the Black Bands with the upright spear,
'Twixt palace and church,—Riccardi where they lived,
His race, and San Lorenzo where they lie.
This book,—precisely on that palace-step
Which, meant for lounging knaves o' the Medici,
Now serves re-venders to display their ware,—
'Mongst odds and ends of ravage, picture-frames
White through the worn gilt, mirror-sconces chipped,
Bronze angel-heads once knobs attached to chests
(Handled when ancient dames chose forth brocade),
Modern chalk drawings, studies from the nude,
Samples of stone, jet, breccia, porphyry
Polished and rough, sundry amazing busts
In baked earth (broken, Providence be praised!)
A wreck of tapestry, proudly-purposed web
When reds and blues were indeed red and blue,
Now offered as a mat to save bare feet
(Since carpets constitute a cruel cost)
Treading the chill scagliola bedward; then
A pile of brown-etched prints, two *crazie* each,
Stopped by a conch a-top from fluttering forth
—Sowing the Square with works of one and the same
Master, the imaginative Sienese
Great in the scenic backgrounds— (name and fame
None of you know, nor does he fare the worse:)
From these ... Oh, with a Lionard going cheap
If it should prove, as promised, that Joconde
Whereof a copy contents the Louvre!—these
I picked this book from. Five compeers in flank
Stood left and right of it as tempting more—
A dogs-eared Spicilegium, the fond tale
O' the Frail One of the Flower, by young Dumas,
Vulgarized Horace for the use of schools,
The Life, Death, Miracles of Saint Somebody,
Saint Somebody Else, his Miracles, Death, and Life,—

With this, one glance at the lettered back of which,
And "Stall!" cried I: a *lira* made it mine.

Here it is, this I toss and take again;
Small-quarto size, part print, part manuscript:
A book in shape but, really, pure crude fact
Secreted from man's life when hearts beat hard,
And brains, high-blooded, ticked two centuries since.
Give it me back! The thing's restorative
I' the touch and sight.

       That memorable day,
(June was the month, Lorenzo named the Square),
I leaned a little and overlooked my prize
By the low railing round the fountain-source
Close to the statue, where a step descends:
While clinked the cans of copper, as stooped and rose
Thick-ankled girls who brimmed them, and made
 place
For marketmen glad to pitch basket down,
Dip a broad melon-leaf that holds the wet,
And whisk their faded fresh. And on I read
Presently, though my path grew perilous
Between the outspread straw-work, piles of plait
Soon to be flapping, each o'er two black eyes
And swathe of Tuscan hair, on festas fine:
Through fire-irons, tribes of tongs, shovels in sheaves,
Skeleton bedsteads, wardrobe-drawers agape,
Rows of tall slim brass lamps with dangling gear,—
And worse, cast clothes a-sweetening in the sun:
None of them took my eye from off my prize.
Still read I on, from written title-page
To written index, on, through street and street,
At the Strozzi, at the Pillar, at the Bridge;
Till, by the time I stood at home again
In Casa Guidi by Felice Church,

Under the doorway where the black begins
With the first stone-slab of the staircase cold,
I had mastered the contents, knew the whole truth
Gathered together, bound up in this book,
Print three-fifths, written supplement the rest.
"*Romana Homicidiorum*"—nay,
Better translate—"A Roman murder-case:
Position of the entire criminal cause
Of Guido Franceschini, nobleman,
With certain Four the cutthroats in his pay,
Tried, all five, and found guilty and put to death
By heading or hanging as befitted ranks,
At Rome on February Twenty Two,
Since our salvation Sixteen Ninety Eight:
Wherein it is disputed if, and when,
Husbands may kill adulterous wives, yet 'scape
The customary forfeit."

              Word for word,
So ran the title-page: murder, or else
Legitimate punishment of the other crime,
Accounted murder by mistake,—just that
And no more, in a Latin cramp enough
When the law had her eloquence to launch,
But interfilleted with Italian streaks
When testimony stooped to mother-tongue,—
That, was this old square yellow book about.

[THE CONTENTS OF THE YELLOW BOOK]

(*From* Book I)

              Enough of me!
The Book! I turn its medicinable leaves
In London now till, as in Florence erst,
A spirit laughs and leaps through every limb,
And lights my eye, and lifts me by the hair,

Letting me have my will again with these
—How title I the dead alive once more?

Count Guido Franceschini the Aretine,
Descended of an ancient house, though poor,
A beak-nosed bushy-bearded black-haired lord,
Lean, pallid, low of stature yet robust,
Fifty years old,—having four years ago
Married Pompilia Comparini, young,
Good, beautiful, at Rome, where she was born,
And brought her to Arezzo, where they lived
Unhappy lives, whatever curse the cause,—
This husband, taking four accomplices,
Followed this wife to Rome, where she was fled
From their Arezzo to find peace again,
In convoy, eight months earlier, of a priest,
Aretine also, of still nobler birth,
Giuseppe Caponsacchi,—caught her there
Quiet in a villa on a Christmas night,
With only Pietro and Violante by,
Both her putative parents; killed the three,
Aged they, seventy each, and she, seventeen,
And, two weeks since, the mother of his babe
First-born and heir to what the style was worth
O' the Guido who determined, dared and did
This deed just as he purposed point by point.
Then, bent upon escape, but hotly pressed,
And captured with his co-mates that same night,
He, brought to trial, stood on this defence—
Injury to his honor caused the act;
And since his wife was false, (as manifest
By flight from home in such companionship,)
Death, punishment deserved of the false wife
And faithless parents who abetted her
I' the flight aforesaid, wronged nor God nor man.
"Nor false she, nor yet faithless they," replied

The accuser; "cloaked and masked this murder glooms;
True was Pompilia, loyal too the pair;
Out of the man's own heart a monster curled,
Which—crime coiled with connivancy at crime—
His victim's breast, he tells you, hatched and reared;
Uncoil we and stretch stark the worm of hell!"
A month the trial swayed this way and that
Ere judgment settled down on Guido's guilt;
Then was the Pope, that good Twelfth Innocent,
Appealed to: who well weighed what went before,
Affirmed the guilt and gave the guilty doom.

Let this old woe step on the stage again!
Act itself o'er anew for men to judge,
Not by the very sense and sight indeed—
(Which take at best imperfect cognizance,
Since, how heart moves brain, and how both move hand,
What mortal ever in entirety saw?)
—No dose of purer truth than man digests,
But truth with falsehood, milk that feeds him now,
Not strong meat he may get to bear some day—
To wit, by voices we call evidence,
Uproar in the echo, live fact deadened down,
Talked over, bruited abroad, whispered away,
Yet helping us to all we seem to hear:
For how else know we save by worth of word?

Here are the voices presently shall sound
In due succession. First, the world's outcry
Around the rush and ripple of any fact
Fallen stonewise, plumb on the smooth face of things;
The world's guess, as it crowds the bank o' the pool,
At what were figure and substance, by their splash:
Then, by vibrations in the general mind,
At depth of deed already out of reach.
This threefold murder of the day before,—

Say, Half-Rome's feel after the vanished truth;
Honest enough, as the way is: all the same,
Harboring in the centre of its sense
A hidden germ of failure, shy but sure,
To neutralize that honesty and leave
That feel for truth at fault, as the way is too.
Some prepossession such as starts amiss,
By but a hair's breadth at the shoulder-blade,
The arm o' the feeler, dip he ne'er so bold;
So leads arm waveringly, lets fall wide
O' the mark its finger, sent to find and fix
Truth at the bottom, that deceptive speck.
With this Half-Rome,—the source of swerving, call
Over-belief in Guido's right and wrong
Rather than in Pompilia's wrong and right:
Who shall say how, who shall say why? 'Tis there—
The instinctive theorizing whence a fact
Looks to the eye as the eye likes the look.
Gossip in a public place, a sample-speech.
Some worthy, with his previous hint to find
A husband's side the safer, and no whit
Aware he is not Æacus the while,—
How such an one supposes and states fact
To whosoever of a multitude
Will listen, and perhaps prolong thereby
The not-unpleasant flutter at the breast,
Born of a certain spectacle shut in
By the church Lorenzo opposite. So, they lounge
Midway the mouth o' the street, on Corso side,
'Twixt palace Fiano and palace Ruspoli,
Linger and listen; keeping clear o' the crowd,
Yet wishful one could lend that crowd one's eyes,
(So universal is its plague of squint)
And make hearts beat our time that flutter false:
—All for the truth's sake, mere truth, nothing else!
How Half-Rome found for Guido much excuse.

Next, from Rome's other half, the opposite feel
For truth with a like swerve, like unsuccess,—
Or if success, by no skill but more luck,
This time, through siding rather with the wife
Because a fancy-fit inclined that way,
Than with the husband. One wears drab, one pink;
Who wears pink, ask him "Which shall win the race,
Of coupled runners like as egg and egg?"
"—Why, if I must choose, he with the pink scarf."
Doubtless for some such reason choice fell here.
A piece of public talk to correspond
At the next stage of the story; just a day
Let pass and new day brings the proper change.
Another sample-speech i' the market-place
O' the Barberini by the Capucins;
Where the old Triton, at his fountain-sport,
Bernini's creature plated to the paps,
Puffs up steel sleet which breaks to diamond dust,
A spray of sparkles snorted from his conch,
High over the caritellas, out o' the way
O' the motley merchandising multitude.
Our murder has been done three days ago,
The frost is over and gone, the south wind laughs,
And, to the very tiles of each red roof
A-smoke i' the sunshine, Rome lies gold and glad:
So, listen how, to the other half of Rome,
Pompilia seemed a saint and martyr both!

Then, yet another day let come and go,
With pause prelusive still of novelty,
Hear a fresh speaker!—neither this nor that
Half-Rome aforesaid; something bred of both:
One and one breed the inevitable three.
Such is the personage harangues you next;
The elaborated product, *tertium quid:*
Rome's first commotion in subsidence gives

The curd o' the cream, flower o' the wheat, as it were,
And finer sense o' the city. Is this plain?
You get a reasoned statement of the case,
Eventual verdict of the curious few
Who care to sift a business to the bran
Nor coarsely bolt it like the simpler sort.
Here, after ignorance, instruction speaks;
Here, clarity of candor, history's soul,
The critical mind, in short: no gossip-guess.
What the superior social section thinks,
In person of some man of quality
Who—breathing musk from lace-work and brocade,
His solitaire amid the flow of frill,
Powdered peruke on nose, and bag at back,
And cane dependent from the ruffled wrist—
Harangues in silvery and selectest phrase
'Neath waxlight in a glorified saloon
Where mirrors multiply the girandole:
Courting the approbation of no mob,
But Eminence This and All-Illustrious That
Who take snuff softly, range in well-bred ring,
Card-table-quitters for observance' sake,
Around the argument, the rational word—
Still, spite its weight and worth, a sample-speech.
How Quality dissertated on the case.

So much for Rome and rumor; smoke comes first:
Once let smoke rise untroubled, we descry
Clearlier what tongues of flame may spire and spit
To eye and ear, each with appropriate tinge
According to its food, or pure or foul.
The actors, no mere rumors of the act,
Intervene. First you hear Count Guido's voice,
In a small chamber that adjoins the court,
Where Governor and Judges, summoned thence,
Tommati, Venturini and the rest,

Find the accused ripe for declaring truth.
Soft-cushioned sits he; yet shifts seat, shirks touch,
As, with a twitchy brow and wincing lip
And cheek that changes to all kinds of white,
He proffers his defence, in tones subdued
Near to mock-mildness now, so mournful seems
The obtuser sense truth fails to satisfy;
Now, moved, from pathos at the wrong endured,
To passion; for the natural man is roused
At fools who first do wrong, then pour the blame
Of their wrong-doing, Satan-like, on Job.
Also his tongue at times is hard to curb;
Incisive, nigh satiric bites the phrase,
Rough-raw, yet somehow claiming privilege
—It is so hard for shrewdness to admit
Folly means no harm when she calls black white!
—Eruption momentary at the most,
Modified forthwith by a fall o' the fire,
Sage acquiescence; for the world's the world,
And, what it errs in, Judges rectify:
He feels he has a fist, then folds his arms
Crosswise and makes his mind up to be meek.
And never once does he detach his eye
From those ranged there to slay him or to save,
But does his best man's-service for himself,
Despite,—what twitches brow and makes lip wince,—
His limbs' late taste of what was called the Cord,
Or Vigil-torture more facetiously.
Even so; they were wont to tease the truth
Out of loth witness (toying, trifling time)
By torture: 'twas a trick, a vice of the age,
Here, there and everywhere, what would you have?
Religion used to tell Humanity
She gave him warrant or denied him course.
And since the course was much to his own mind,
Of pinching flesh and pulling bone from bone

To unhusk truth a-hiding in its hulls,
Nor whisper of a warning stopped the way,
He, in their joint behalf, the burly slave,
Bestirred him, mauled and maimed all recusants,
While, prim in place, Religion overlooked;
And so had done till doomsday, never a sign
Nor sound of interference from her mouth,
But that at last the burly slave wiped brow,
Let eye give notice as if soul were there,
Muttered " 'Tis a vile trick, foolish more than vile,
Should have been counted sin; I make it so:
At any rate no more of it for me—
Nay, for I break the torture-engine thus!"
Then did Religion start up, stare amain,
Look round for help and see none, smile and say
"What, broken is the rack? Well done of thee!
Did I forget to abrogate its use?
Be the mistake in common with us both!
—One more fault our blind age shall answer for,
Down in my book denounced though it must be
Somewhere. Henceforth find truth by milder means!"
Ah but, Religion, did we wait for thee
To ope the book, that serves to sit upon,
And pick such place out, we should wait indeed!
That is all history: and what is not now,
Was then, defendants found it to their cost.
How Guido, after being tortured, spoke.

Also hear Caponsacchi who comes next,
Man and priest—could you comprehend the coil!—
In days when that was rife which now is rare.
How, mingling each its multifarious wires,
Now heaven, now earth, now heaven and earth at once,
Had plucked at and perplexed their puppet here,
Played off the young frank personable priest;
Sworn fast and tonsured plain heaven's celibate,

And yet earth's clear-accepted servitor,
A courtly spiritual Cupid, squire of dames
By law of love and mandate of the mode.
The Church's own, or why parade her seal,
Wherefore that chrism and consecrative work?
Yet verily the world's, or why go badged
A prince of sonneteers and lutanists,
Show color of each vanity in vogue
Borne with decorum due on blameless breast?
All that is changed now, as he tells the court
How he had played the part excepted at;
Tells it, moreover, now the second time:
Since, for his cause of scandal, his own share
I' the flight from home and husband of the wife,
He has been censured, punished in a sort
By relegation,—exile, we should say,
To a short distance for a little time,—
Whence he is summoned on a sudden now,
Informed that she, he thought to save, is lost,
And, in a breath, bidden re-tell his tale,
Since the first telling somehow missed effect,
And then advise in the matter. There stands he,
While the same grim black-panelled chamber blinks
As though rubbed shiny with the sins of Rome
Told the same oak for ages—wave-washed wall
Against which sets a sea of wickedness.
There, where you yesterday heard Guido speak,
Speaks Caponsacchi; and there face him too
Tommati, Venturini and the 'rest
Who, eight months earlier, scarce repressed the smile,
Forewent the wink; waived recognition so
Of peccadillos incident to youth,
Especially youth high-born; for youth means love,
Vows can't change nature, priests are only men,
And love likes stratagem and subterfuge:
Which age, that once was youth, should recognize,

May blame, but needs not press too hard upon.
Here sit the old Judges then, but with no grace
Of reverend carriage, magisterial port.
For why? The accused of eight months since,—the
    same
Who cut the conscious figure of a fool,
Changed countenance, dropped bashful gaze to
    ground,
While hesitating for an answer then,—
Now is grown judge himself, terrifies now
This, now the other culprit called a judge,
Whose turn it is to stammer and look strange,
As he speaks rapidly, angrily, speech that smites:
And they keep silence, bear blow after blow,
Because the seeming-solitary man,
Speaking for God, may have an audience too,
Invisible, no discreet judge provokes.
How the priest Caponsacchi said his say.

Then a soul sighs its lowest and its last
After the loud ones,—so much breath remains
Unused by the four-days'-dying; for she lived
Thus long, miraculously long, 'twas thought,
Just that Pompilia might defend herself.
How, while the hireling and the alien stoop,
Comfort, yet question,—since the time is brief,
And folk, allowably inquisitive,
Encircle the low pallet where she lies
In the good house that helps the poor to die,—
Pompilia tells the story of her life.
For friend and lover,—leech and man of law
Do service; busy helpful ministrants
As varied in their calling as their mind,
Temper and age: and yet from all of these,
About the white bed under the arched roof,
Is somehow, as it were, evolved a one,—

Small separate sympathies combined and large,
Nothings that were, grown something very much:
As if the bystanders gave each his straw,
All he had, though a trifle in itself,
Which, plaited all together, made a Cross
Fit to die looking on and praying with,
Just as well as if ivory or gold.
So, to the common kindliness she speaks,
There being scarce more privacy at the last
For mind than body: but she is used to bear,
And only unused to the brotherly look.
How she endeavored to explain her life.

Then, since a Trial ensued, a touch o' the same
To sober us, flustered with frothy talk,
And teach our common sense its helplessness.
For why deal simply with divining-rod,
Scrape where we fancy secret sources flow,
And ignore law, the recognized machine,
Elaborate display of pipe and wheel
Framed to unchoke, pump up and pour apace
Truth till a flowery foam shall wash the world?
The patent truth-extracting process,—ha?
Let us make that grave mystery turn one wheel,
Give you a single grind of law at least!
One orator, of two on either side,
Shall teach us the puissance of the tongue
—That is, o' the pen which simulated tongue
On paper and saved all except the sound
Which never was. Law's speech beside law's thought?
That were too stunning, too immense an odds:
That point of vantage law lets nobly pass.
One lawyer shall admit us to behold
The manner of the making out a case,
First fashion of a speech; the chick in egg,
The masterpiece law's bosom incubates.

How Don Giacinto of the Arcangeli,
Called Procurator of the Poor at Rome,
Now advocate for Guido and his mates,—
The jolly learned man of middle age,
Cheek and jowl all in laps with fat and law,
Mirthful as mighty, yet, as great hearts use,
Despite the name and fame that tempt our flesh
Constant to that devotion of the hearth,
Still captive in those dear domestic ties!—
How he,—having a cause to triumph with,
All kind of interests to keep intact,
More than one efficacious personage
To tranquillize, conciliate and secure,
And above all, public anxiety
To quiet, show its Guido in good hands,—
Also, as if such burdens were too light,
A certain family-feast to claim his care,
The birthday-banquet for the only son—
Paternity at smiling strife with law—
How he brings both to buckle in one bond;
And, thick at throat, with waterish under-eye,
Turns to his task and settles in his seat
And puts his utmost means in practice now:
Wheezes out law-phrase, whiffles Latin forth,
And, just as though roast lamb would never be,
Makes logic levigate the big crime small:
Rubs palm on palm, rakes foot with itchy foot,
Conceives and inchoates the argument,
Sprinkling each flower appropriate to the time,
—Ovidian quip or Ciceronian crank,
A-bubble in the larynx while he laughs,
As he had fritters deep down frying there.
How he turns, twists, and tries the oily thing
Shall be—first speech for Guido 'gainst the Fisc.
Then with a skip as it were from heel to head,
Leaving yourselves fill up the middle bulk

O' the Trial, reconstruct its shape august,
From such exordium clap we to the close;
Give you, if we dare wing to such a height,
The absolute glory in some full-grown speech
On the other side, some finished butterfly,
Some breathing diamond-flake with leaf-gold fans,
That takes the air, no trace of worm it was,
Or cabbage-bed it had production from.
Giovambattista o' the Bottini, Fisc,
Pompilia's patron by the chance of the hour,
Tomorrow her persecutor,—composite, he,
As becomes who must meet such various calls—
Odds of age joined in him with ends of youth.
A man of ready smile and facile tear,
Improvised hopes, despairs at nod and beck,
And language—ah, the gift of eloquence!
Language that goes, goes, easy as a glove,
O'er good and evil, smoothens both to one.
Rashness helps caution with him, fires the straw,
In free enthusiastic careless fit,
On the first proper pinnacle of rock
Which offers, as reward for all that zeal,
To lure some bark to founder and bring gain:
While calm sits Caution, rapt with heavenward eye,
A true confessor's gaze, amid the glare
Beaconing to the breaker, death and hell.
"Well done, thou good and faithful!" she approves:
"Hadst thou let slip a fagot to the beach,
The crew might surely spy thy precipice
And save their boat; the simple and the slow
Might so, forsooth, forestall the wrecker's fee!
Let the next crew be wise and hail in time!"
Just so compounded is the outside man,
Blue juvenile pure eye and pippin cheek,
And brow all prematurely soiled and seamed
With sudden age, bright devastated hair.

Ah, but you miss the very tones o' the voice,
The scrannel pipe that screams in heights of head,
As, in his modest studio, all alone,
The tall wight stands a-tiptoe, strives and strains,
Both eyes shut, like the cockerel that would crow,
Tries to his own self amorously o'er
What never will be uttered else than so—
Since to the four walls, Forum and Mars' Hill,
Speaks out the poesy which, penned, turns prose.
Clavecinist debarred his instrument,
He yet thrums—shirking neither turn nor trill,
With desperate finger on dumb table-edge—
The sovereign rondo, shall conclude his *Suite,*
Charm an imaginary audience there,
From old Corelli to young Haendel, both
I' the flesh at Rome, ere he perforce go print
The cold black score, mere music for the mind—
The last speech against Guido and his gang,
With special end to prove Pompilia pure.
How the Fisc vindicates Pompilia's fame.

Then comes the all but end, the ultimate
Judgment save yours. Pope Innocent the Twelfth,
Simple, sagacious, mild yet resolute,
With prudence, probity and—what beside
From the other world he feels impress at times,
Having attained to fourscore years and six,—
How, when the court found Guido and the rest
Guilty, but law supplied a subterfuge
And passed the final sentence to the Pope,
He, bringing his intelligence to bear
This last time on what ball behoves him drop
In the urn, or white or black, does drop a black,
Send five souls more to just precede his own,
Stand him in stead and witness, if need were,
How he is wont to do God's work on earth.

The manner of his sitting out the dim
Droop of a sombre February day
In the plain closet where he does such work,
With, from all Peter's treasury, one stool,
One table and one lathen crucifix.
There sits the Pope, his thoughts for company;
Grave but not sad,—nay, something like a cheer
Leaves the lips free to be benevolent,
Which, all day long, did duty firm and fast.
A cherishing there is of foot and knee,
A chafing loose-skinned large-veined hand with hand,—
What steward but knows when stewardship earns its
    wage,
May levy praise, anticipate the lord?
He reads, notes, lays the papers down at last,
Muses, then takes a turn about the room;
Unclasps a huge tome in an antique guise,
Primitive print and tongue half obsolete,
That stands him in diurnal stead; opes page,
Finds place where falls the passage to be conned
According to an order long in use:
And, as he comes upon the evening's chance,
Starts somewhat, solemnizes straight his smile,
Then reads aloud that portion first to last,
And at the end lets flow his own thoughts forth
Likewise aloud, for respite and relief,
Till by the dreary relics of the west
Wan through the half-moon window, all his light,
He bows the head while the lips move in prayer,
Writes some three brief lines, signs and seals the same,
Tinkles a hand-bell, bids the obsequious Sir
Who puts foot presently o' the closet-sill
He watched outside of, bear as superscribed
That mandate to the Governor forthwith:
Then heaves abroad his cares in one good sigh,
Traverses corridor with no arm's help,

And so to sup as a clear conscience should.
The manner of the judgment of the Pope.

Then must speak Guido yet a second time,
Satan's old saw being apt here—skin for skin,
All a man hath that will he give for life.
While life was graspable and gainable,
And bird-like buzzed her wings round Guido's brow,
Not much truth stiffened out the web of words
He wove to catch her: when away she flew
And death came, death's breath rivelled up the lies,
Left bare the metal thread, the fibre fine
Of truth, i' the spinning: the true words shone last.
How Guido, to another purpose quite,
Speaks and despairs, the last night of his life,
In that New Prison by Castle Angelo
At the bridge-foot: the same man, another voice.
On a stone bench in a close fetid cell,
Where the hot vapor of an agony,
Struck into drops on the cold wall, runs down—
Horrible worms made out of sweat and tears—
There crouch, wellnigh to the knees in dungeon-straw,
Lit by the sole lamp suffered for their sake,
Two awe-struck figures, this a Cardinal,
That an Abate, both of old styled friends
O' the thing part man, part monster in the midst,
So changed is Franceschini's gentle blood.
The tiger-cat screams now, that whined before,
That pried and tried and trod so gingerly,
Till in its silkiness the trap-teeth joined;
Then you know how the bristling fury foams.
They listen, this wrapped in his folds of red,
While his feet fumble for the filth below;
The other, as beseems a stouter heart,
Working his best with beads and cross to ban
The enemy that comes in like a flood

Spite of the standard set up, verily
And in no trope at all, against him there:
For at the prison-gate, just a few steps
Outside, already, in the doubtful dawn,
Thither, from this side and from that, slow sweep
And settle down in silence solidly,
Crow-wise, the frightful Brotherhood of Death.
Black-hatted and black-hooded huddle they,
Black rosaries a-dangling from each waist;
So take they their grim station at the door,
Torches lit, skull-and-crossbones-banner spread,
And that gigantic Christ with open arms,
Grounded. Nor lacks there aught but that the group
Break forth, intone the lamentable psalm,
"Out of the deeps, Lord, have I cried to thee!"—
When inside, from the true profound, a sign
Shall bear intelligence that the foe is foiled,
Count Guido Franceschini has confessed,
And is absolved and reconciled with God.
Then they, intoning, may begin their march,
Make by the longest way for the People's Square,
Carry the criminal to his crime's award:
A mob to cleave, a scaffolding to reach,
Two gallows and Mannaia crowning all.

[DEDICATION TO ELIZABETH BARRETT BROWNING]

(*From* Book I)

O lyric Love, half angel and half bird,
And all a wonder and a wild desire,—
Boldest of hearts that ever braved the sun,
Took sanctuary within the holier blue,
And sang a kindred soul out to his face,—
Yet human at the red-ripe of the heart—
When the first summons from the darkling earth

Reached thee amid thy chambers, blanched their blue,
And bared them of the glory—to drop down,
To toil for man, to suffer or to die,—
This is the same voice: can thy soul know change?
Hail then, and hearken from the realms of help!
Never may I commence my song, my due
To God who best taught song by gift of thee,
Except with bent head and beseeching hand—
That still, despite the distance and the dark,
What was, again may be; some interchange
Of grace, some splendor once thy very thought,
Some benediction anciently thy smile:
—Never conclude, but raising hand and head
Thither where eyes, that cannot reach, yet yearn
For all hope, all sustainment, all reward,
Their utmost up and on,—so blessing back
In those thy realms of help, that heaven thy home,
Some whiteness which, I judge, thy face makes proud,
Some wanness where, I think, thy foot may fall!

[CAPONSACCHI'S REPLY TO THE JUDGES]

(*From* Book VI)

Answer you, Sirs? Do I understand aright?
Have patience! In this sudden smoke from hell,—
So things disguise themselves,—I cannot see
My own hand held thus broad before my face
And know it again. Answer you? Then that means
Tell over twice what I, the first time, told
Six months ago: 'twas here, I do believe,
Fronting you same three in this very room,
I stood and told you: yet now no one laughs,
Who then . . . nay, dear my lords, but laugh you did,
As good as laugh, what in a judge we style
Laughter—no levity, nothing indecorous, lords!

Only,—I think I apprehend the mood:
There was the blameless shrug, permissible smirk,
The pen's pretence at play with the pursed mouth,
The titter stifled in the hollow palm
Which rubbed the eyebrow and caressed the nose,
When I first told my tale: they meant, you know,
"The sly one, all this we are bound believe!
Well, he can say no other than what he says.
We have been young, too,—come, there's greater guilt!
Let him but decently disembroil himself,
Scramble from out the scrape nor move the mud,—
We solid ones may risk a finger-stretch!"
And now you sit as grave, stare as aghast
As if I were a phantom: now 'tis—"Friend,
Collect yourself!"—no laughing matter more—
"Counsel the Court in this extremity,
Tell us again!"—tell that, for telling which,
I got the jocular piece of punishment,
Was sent to lounge a little in the place
Whence now of a sudden here you summon me
To take the intelligence from just—your lips!
You, Judge Tommati, who then tittered most,—
That she I helped eight months since to escape
Her husband, was retaken by the same,
Three days ago, if I have seized your sense,—
(I being disallowed to interfere,
Meddle or make in a matter none of mine,
For you and law were guardians quite enough
O' the innocent, without a pert priest's help)—
And that he has butchered her accordingly,
As she foretold and as myself believed,—
And, so foretelling and believing so,
We were punished, both of us, the merry way:
Therefore, tell once again the tale! For what?
Pompilia is only dying while I speak!
Why does the mirth hang fire and miss the smile?

My masters, there's an old book, you should con
For strange adventures, applicable yet,
'Tis stuffed with. Do you know that there was once
This thing: a multitude of worthy folk
Took recreation, watched a certain group
Of soldiery intent upon a game,—
How first they wrangled, but soon fell to play,
Threw dice,—the best diversion in the world.
A word in your ear,—they are now casting lots,
Ay, with that gesture quaint and cry uncouth,
For the coat of One murdered an hour ago!
I am a priest,—talk of what I have learned.
Pompilia is bleeding out her life belike,
Gasping away the latest breath of all,
This minute, while I talk—not while you laugh.

Yet, being sobered now, what is it you ask
By way of explanation? There's the fact!
It seems to fill the universe with sight
And sound,—from the four corners of this earth
Tells itself over, to my sense at least.
But you may want it lower set i' the scale,—
Too vast, too close it clangs in the ear, perhaps;
You'd stand back just to comprehend it more.
Well then, let me, the hollow rock, condense
The voice o' the sea and wind, interpret you
The mystery of this murder. God above!
It is too paltry, such a transference
O' the storm's roar to the cranny of the stone!

This deed, you saw begin—why does its end
Surprise you? Why should the event enforce
The lesson, we ourselves learned, she and I,
From the first o' the fact, and taught you, all in vain?
This Guido from whose throat you took my grasp,
Was this man to be favored, now, or feared,

Let do his will, or have his will restrained,
In the relation with Pompilia?—say!
Did any other man need interpose
—Oh, though first comer, though as strange at the work
As fribble must be, coxcomb, fool that's near
To knave as, say, a priest who fears the world—
Was he bound brave the peril, save the doomed,
Or go on, sing his snatch and pluck his flower,
Keep the straight path and let the victim die?
I held so; you decided otherwise,
Saw no such peril, therefore no such need
To stop song, loosen flower, and leave path. Law,
Law was aware and watching, would suffice,
Wanted no priest's intrusion, palpably
Pretence, too manifest a subterfuge!
Whereupon I, priest, coxcomb, fribble and fool,
Ensconced me in my corner, thus rebuked,
A kind of culprit, over-zealous hound
Kicked for his pains to kennel; I gave place
To you, and let the law reign paramount:
I left Pompilia to your watch and ward,
And now you point me—there and thus she lies!

Men, for the last time, what do you want with me?
Is it,—you acknowledge, as it were, a use,
A profit in employing me?—at length
I may conceivably help the august law?
I am free to break the blow, next hawk that swoops
On next dove, nor miss much of good repute?
Or what if this your summons, after all,
Be but the form of mere release, no more,
Which turns the key and lets the captive go?
I have paid enough in person at Civita,
Am free,—what more need I concern me with?
Thank you! I am rehabilitated then,
A very reputable priest. But she—

The glory of life, the beauty of the world,
The splendor of heaven, ... well, Sirs, does no one move?
Do I speak ambiguously? The glory, I say,
And the beauty, I say, and splendor, still say I,
Who, priest and trained to live my whole life long
On beauty and splendor, solely at their source,
God,—have thus recognized my food in her,
You tell me, that's fast dying while we talk,
Pompilia! How does lenity to me
Remit one death-bed pang to her? Come, smile!
The proper wink at the hot-headed youth
Who lets his soul show, through transparent words,
The mundane love that's sin and scandal too!
You are all struck acquiescent now, it seems:
It seems the oldest, gravest signor here,
Even the redoubtable Tommati, sits
Chopfallen,—understands how law might take
Service like mine, of brain and heart and hand,
In good part. Better late than never, law!
You understand of a sudden, gospel too
Has a claim here, may possibly pronounce
Consistent with my priesthood, worthy Christ,
That I endeavored to save Pompilia?
                                        Then,
You were wrong, you see: that's well to see, though late:
That's all we may expect of man, this side
The grave: his good is—knowing he is bad:
Thus will it be with us when the books ope
And we stand at the bar on judgment-day.
Well then, I have a mind to speak, see cause
To relume the quenched flax by this dreadful light,
Burn my soul out in showing you the truth.
I heard, last time I stood here to be judged,
What is priest's-duty,—labor to pluck tares
And weed the corn of Molinism; let me
Make you hear, this time, how, in such a case,

Man, be he in the priesthood or at plough,
Mindful of Christ or marching step by step
With . . . what's his style, the other potentate
Who bids have courage and keep honor safe,
Nor let minuter admonition tease?—
How he is bound, better or worse, to act.
Earth will not end through this misjudgment, no!
For you and the others like you sure to come,
Fresh work is sure to follow,—wickedness
That wants withstanding. Many a man of blood,
Many a man of guile will clamor yet,
Bid you redress his grievance,—as he clutched
The prey, forsooth a stranger stepped between,
And there's the good gripe in pure waste! My part
Is done; i' the doing it, I pass away
Out of the world. I want no more with earth.
Let me, in heaven's name, use the very snuff
O' the taper in one last spark shall show truth
For a moment, show Pompilia who was true!
Not for her sake, but yours: if she is dead,
Oh, Sirs, she can be loved by none of you
Most or least priestly! Saints, to do us good,
Must be in heaven, I seem to understand:
We never find them saints before, at least.
Be her first prayer then presently for you—
She has done the good to me . . .
                                        What is all this?
There, I was born, have lived, shall die, a fool!
This is a foolish outset:—might with cause
Give color to the very lie o' the man,
The murderer,—make as if I loved his wife
In the way he called love. He is the fool there!
Why, had there been in me the touch of taint,
I had picked up so much of knaves'-policy
As hide it, keep one hand pressed on the place
Suspected of a spot would damn us both.

Or no, not her!—not even if any of you
Dares think that I, i' the face of death, her death
That's in my eyes and ears and brain and heart,
Lie,—if he does, let him!   I mean to say,
So he stop there, stay thought from smirching her
The snow-white soul that angels fear to take
Untenderly.   But, all the same, I know
I too am taintless, and I bare my breast.
You can't think, men as you are, all of you,
But that, to hear thus suddenly such an end
Of such a wonderful white soul, that comes
Of a man and murderer calling the white black,
Must shake me, trouble and disadvantage. Sirs,
Only seventeen!

[CAPONSACCHI'S STORY OF THE FLIGHT]
(*From* Book VI)

I know not how the night passed: morning broke,
Presently came my servant. "Sir, this eve—
Do you forget?"   I started. "How forget?
What is it you know?" "With due submission, Sir,
This being last Monday in the month but one,
And a vigil, since tomorrow is Saint George,
And feast-day, and moreover day for copes,
And Canon Conti now away a month,
And Canon Crispi sour because, forsooth,
You let him sulk in stall and bear the brunt
Of the octave . . . Well, Sir, 'tis important!"

                                        "True!

Hearken, I have to start for Rome this night.
No word, lest Crispi overboil and burst!
Provide me with a laic dress!   Throw dust
I' the Canon's eye, stop his tongue's scandal so!
See there's a sword in case of accident."
I knew the knave, the knave knew me.

                And thus
Through each familiar hindrance of the day
Did I make steadily for its hour and end,—
Felt time's old barrier-growth of right and fit
Give way through all its twines, and let me go.
Use and wont recognized the excepted man,
Let speed the special service,—and I sped
Till, at the dead between midnight and morn,
There was I at the goal, before the gate,
With a tune in the ears, low leading up to loud,
A light in the eyes, faint that would soon be flare,
Ever some spiritual witness new and new
In faster frequence, crowding solitude
To watch the way o' the warfare,—till, at last,
When the ecstatic minute must bring birth,
Began a whiteness in the distance, waxed
Whiter and whiter, near grew and more near,
Till it was she: there did Pompilia come:
The white I saw shine through her was her soul's,
Certainly, for the body was one black,
Black from head down to foot. She did not speak,
Glided into the carriage,—so a cloud
Gathers the moon up. "By San Spirito,
To Rome, as if the road burned underneath!
Reach Rome, then hold my head in pledge, I pay
The run and the risk to heart's content!" Just that,
I said,—then, in another tick of time,
Sprang, was beside her, she and I alone.
So it began, our flight through dusk to clear,
Through day and night and day again to night
Once more, and to last dreadful dawn of all.
Sirs, how should I lie quiet in my grave
Unless you suffer me wring, drop by drop,
My brain dry, make a riddance of the drench
Of minutes with a memory in each,
Recorded motion, breath or look of hers,

Which poured forth would present you one pure
　glass,
Mirror you plain—as God's sea, glassed in gold,
His saints—the perfect soul Pompilia? Men,
You must know that a man gets drunk with truth
Stagnant inside him! Oh, they've killed her, Sirs!
Can I be calm?
　　　　　　Calmly! Each incident
Proves, I maintain, that action of the flight
For the true thing it was. The first faint scratch
O' the stone will test its nature, teach its worth
To idiots who name Parian—coprolite.
After all, I shall give no glare—at best
Only display you certain scattered lights
Lamping the rush and roll of the abyss:
Nothing but here and there a fire-point pricks
Wavelet from wavelet: well!
　　　　　　　　For the first hour
We both were silent in the night, I know:
Sometimes I did not see nor understand.
Blackness engulfed me,—partial stupor, say—
Then I would break way, breathe through the surprise,
And be aware again, and see who sat
In the dark vest with the white face and hands.
I said to myself—"I have caught it, I conceive
The mind o' the mystery: 'tis the way they wake
And wait, two martyrs somewhere in a tomb
Each by each as their blessing was to die;
Some signal they are promised and expect,—
When to arise before the trumpet scares:
So, through the whole course of the world they wait
The last day, but so fearless and so safe!
No otherwise, in safety and not fear,
I lie, because she lies too by my side."
You know this is not love, Sirs,—it is faith,
The feeling that there's God, he reigns and rules

Out of this low world: that is all; no harm!
At times she drew a soft sigh—music seemed
Always to hover just above her lips,
Not settle,—break a silence music too.

In the determined morning, I first found
Her head erect, her face turned full to me,
Her soul intent on mine through two wide eyes.
I answered them. "You are saved hitherto.
We have passed Perugia,—gone round by the wood,
Not through, I seem to think,—and opposite
I know Assisi; this is holy ground."
Then she resumed. "How long since we both left
Arezzo?"—"Years—and certain hours beside."
It was at . . . ah, but I forget the names!
'Tis a mere post-house and a hovel or two;
I left the carriage and got bread and wine
And brought it her.—"Does it detain to eat?"
"—They stay perforce, change horses,—therefore eat!
We lose no minute: we arrive, be sure!"
This was—I know not where—there's a great hill
Close over, and the stream has lost its bridge,
One fords it. She began—"I have heard say
Of some sick body that my mother knew,
'Twas no good sign when in a limb diseased
All the pain suddenly departs,—as if
The guardian angel discontinued pain
Because the hope of cure was gone at last:
The limb will not again exert itself,
It needs be pained no longer: so with me,
—My soul whence all the pain is past at once:
All pain must be to work some good in the end.
True, this I feel now, this may be that good,
Pain was because of,—otherwise, I fear!"

She said,—a long while later in the day,
When I had let the silence be,—abrupt—

"Have you a mother?"   "She died, I was born."
"A sister then?"   "No sister."   "Who was it—
What woman were you used to serve this way,
Be kind to, till I called you and you came?"
I did not like that word.   Soon afterward—
"Tell me, are men unhappy, in some kind
Of mere unhappiness at being men,
As women suffer, being womanish?
Have you, now, some unhappiness, I mean,
Born of what may be man's strength overmuch,
To match the undue susceptibility,
The sense at every pore when hate is close?
It hurts us if a baby hides its face
Or child strikes at us punily, calls names
Or makes a mouth,—much more if stranger men
Laugh or frown,—just as that were much to bear!
Yet rocks split,—and the blow-ball does no more,
Quivers to feathery nothing at a touch;
And strength may have its drawback, weakness 'scapes."

Once she asked, "What is it that made you smile,
At the great gate with the eagles and the snakes,
Where the company entered, 'tis a long time since?"
"—Forgive—I think you would not understand:
Ah, but you ask me,—therefore, it was this.
That was a certain bishop's villa-gate,
I knew it by the eagles,—and at once
Remember this same bishop was just he
People of old were wont to bid me please
If I would catch preferment: so, I smiled
Because an impulse came to me, a whim—
What if I prayed the prelate leave to speak,
Began upon him in his presence-hall
—'What, still at work so gray and obsolete?
Still rocheted and mitred more or less?
Don't you feel all that out of fashion now?
I find out when the day of things is done!' "

At eve we heard the *angelus:* she turned—
"I told you I can neither read nor write.
My life stopped with the play-time; I will learn,
If I begin to live again: but you—
Who are a priest—wherefore do you not read
The service at this hour? Read Gabriel's song,
The lesson, and then read the little prayer
To Raphael, proper for us travellers!"
I did not like that, neither, but I read.

When we stopped at Foligno it was dark.
The people of the post came out with lights:
The driver said, "This time tomorrow, may
Saints only help, relays continue good,
Nor robbers hinder, we arrive at Rome.
I urged,—"Why tax your strength a second night?
Trust me, alight here and take brief repose!
We are out of harm's reach, past pursuit: go sleep
If but an hour! I keep watch, guard the while
Here in the doorway." But her whole face changed,
The misery grew again about her mouth,
The eyes burned up from faintness, like the fawn's
Tired to death in the thicket, when she feels
The probing spear o' the huntsman. "Oh, no stay!"
She cried, in the fawn's cry, "On to Rome, on, on—
Unless 'tis you who fear,—which cannot be!"

We did go on all night; but at its close
She was troubled, restless, moaned low, talked at whiles
To herself, her brow on quiver with the dream:
Once, wide awake, she menaced, at arms' length
Waved away something—"Never again with you!
My soul is mine, my body is my soul's:
You and I are divided ever more
In soul and body: get you gone!" Then I—

"Why, in my whole life I have never prayed!
Oh, if the God, that only can, would help!
Am I his priest with power to cast out fiends?
Let God arise and all his enemies
Be scattered!" By morn, there was peace, no sigh
Out of the deep sleep.

                When she woke at last,
I answered the first look—"Scarce twelve hours more,
Then, Rome! There probably was no pursuit,
There cannot now be peril: bear up brave!
Just some twelve hours to press through to the prize:
Then, no more of the terrible journey!" "Then,
No more, o' the journey: if it might but last!
Always, my life long, thus to journey still!
It is the interruption that I dread,-
With no dread, ever to be here and thus!
Never to see a face nor hear a voice!
Yours is no voice; you speak when you are dumb;
Nor face, I see it in the dark. I want
No face nor voice that change and grow unkind."
That I liked, that was the best thing she said.

In the broad day, I dared entreat, "Descend!"
I told a woman, at the garden-gate
By the post-house, white and pleasant in the sun,
"It is my sister,—talk with her apart!
She is married and unhappy, you perceive;
I take her home because her head is hurt;
Comfort her as you women understand!"
So, there I left them by the garden-wall,
Paced the road, then bade put the horses to,
Came back, and there she sat: close to her knee,
A black-eyed child still held the bowl of milk,
Wondered to see how little she could drink,

And in her arms the woman's infant lay.
She smiled at me, "How much good this has done!
This is a whole night's rest and how much more!
I can proceed now, though I wish to stay.
How do you call that tree with the thick top
That holds in all its leafy green and gold
The sun now like an immense egg of fire?"
(It was a million-leaved mimosa.)   "Take
The babe away from me and let me go!"
And in the carriage, "Still a day, my friend!
And perhaps half a night, the woman fears.
I pray it finish since it cannot last.
There may be more misfortune at the close,
And where will you be?   God suffice me then!"
And presently—for there was a roadside-shrine—
"When I was taken first to my own church
Lorenzo in Lucina, being a girl,
And bid confess my faults, I interposed
'But teach me what fault to confess and know!'
So, the priest said—'You should bethink yourself:
Each human being needs must have done wrong!'
Now, be you candid and no priest but friend—
Were I surprised and killed here on the spot,
A runaway from husband and his home,
Do you account it were in sin I died?
My husband used to seem to harm me, not . . .
Not on pretence he punished sin of mine,
Nor for sin's sake and lust of cruelty,
But as I heard him bid a farming-man
At the villa take a lamb once to the wood
And there ill-treat it, meaning that the wolf
Should hear its cries, and so come, quick be caught,
Enticed to the trap: he practised thus with me
That so, whatever were his gain thereby,
Others than I might become prey and spoil.
Had it been only between our two selves,—

His pleasure and my pain,—why, pleasure him
By dying, nor such need to make a coil!
But this was worth an effort, that my pain
Should not become a snare, prove pain threefold
To other people—strangers—or unborn—
How should I know? I sought release from that—
I think, or else from,—dare I say, some cause
Such as is put into a tree, which turns
Away from the north wind with what nest it holds,—
The woman said that trees so turn: now, friend,
Tell me, because I cannot trust myself!
You are a man: what have I done amiss?"
You must conceive my answer,—I forget—
Taken up wholly with the thought, perhaps,
This time she might have said,—might, did not say—
"You are a priest."   She said, "my friend."

                                        Day wore,
We passed the places, somehow the calm went,
Again the restless eyes began to rove
In new fear of the foe mine could not see.
She wandered in her mind,—addressed me once
"Gaetano!"—that is not my name: whose name?
I grew alarmed, my head seemed turning too.
I quickened pace with promise now, now threat:
Bade drive and drive, nor any stopping more.
"Too deep i' the thick of the struggle, struggle through!
Then drench her in repose though death's self pour
The plenitude of quiet,—help us, God,
Whom the winds carry!"

                                   Suddenly I saw
The old tower, and the little white-walled clump
Of buildings and the cypress-tree or two,—
"Already Castelnuovo—Rome!" I cried,
"As good as Rome,—Rome is the next stage, think!
This is where travellers' hearts are wont to beat.

Say you are saved, sweet lady!" Up she woke.
The sky was fierce with color from the sun
Setting. She screamed out, "No, I must not die!
Take me no farther, I should die: stay here!
I have more life to save than mine!"

                                        She swooned.
We seemed safe: what was it foreboded so?
Out of the coach into the inn I bore
The motionless and breathless pure and pale
Pompilia,—bore her through a pitying group
And laid her on a couch, still calm and cured
By deep sleep of all woes at once. The host
Was urgent, "Let her stay an hour or two!
Leave her to us, all will be right by morn!"
Oh, my foreboding! But I could not choose.
I paced the passage, kept watch all night long.
I listened,—not one movement, not one sigh.
"Fear not: she sleeps so sound!" they said: but I
Feared, all the same, kept fearing more and more,
Found myself throb with fear from head to foot,
Filled with a sense of such impending woe,
That, at first pause of night, pretence of gray,
I made my mind up it was morn.—"Reach Rome,
Lest hell reach her! A dozen miles to make,
Another long breath, and we emerge!" I stood
I' the courtyard, roused the sleepy grooms. "Have out
Carriage and horse, give haste, take gold!" said I.
While they made ready in the doubtful morn,—
'Twas the last minute,—needs must I ascend
And break her sleep; I turned to go.

                                        And there
Faced me Count Guido, there posed the mean man
As master,—took the field, encamped his rights,
Challenged the world: there leered new triumph, there
Scowled the old malice in the visage bad
And black o' the scamp. Soon triumph suppled the
   tongue

A little, malice glued to his dry throat,
And he part howled, part hissed . . . oh, how he kept
Well out o' the way, at arm's length and to spare!—
"My salutation to your priestship!   What?
Matutinal, busy with book so soon
Of an April day that's damp as tears that now
Deluge Arezzo at its darling's flight?—
'Tis unfair, wrongs feminity at large,
To let a single dame monopolize
A heart the whole sex claims, should share alike:
Therefore I overtake you, Canon!   Come!
The lady,—could you leave her side so soon?
You have not yet experienced at her hands
My treatment, you lay down undrugged, I see!
Hence this alertness—hence no death-in-life
Like what held arms fast when she stole from mine.
To be sure, you took the solace and repose
That first night at Foligno!—news abound
O' the road by this time,—men regaled me much,
As past them I came halting after you,
Vulcan pursuing Mars, as poets sing,—
Still at the last here pant I, but arrive,
Vulcan—and not without my Cyclops too,
The Commissary and the unpoisoned arm
O' the Civil Force, should Mars turn mutineer.
Enough of fooling: capture the culprits, friend!
Here is the lover in the smart disguise
With the sword,—he is a priest, so mine lies still.
There upstairs hides my wife the runaway,
His leman: the two plotted, poisoned first,
Plundered me after, and eloped thus far
Where now you find them.   Do your duty quick!
Arrest and hold him!   That's done: now catch her!"
During this speech of that man,—well, I stood
Away, as he managed,—still, I stood as near
The throat of him,—with these two hands, my own,—
As now I stand near yours, Sir,—one quick spring,

One great good satisfying gripe, and lo!
There had he lain abolished with his lie,
Creation purged o' the miscreate, man redeemed,
A spittle wiped off from the face of God!
I, in some measure, seek a poor excuse
For what I left undone, in just this fact
That my first feeling at the speech I quote
Was—not of what a blasphemy was dared,
Not what a bag of venomed purulence
Was split and noisome,—but how splendidly
Mirthful, how ludicrous a lie was launched!
Would Molière's self wish more than hear such man
Call, claim such woman for his own, his wife,
Even though, in due amazement at the boast,
He had stammered, she moreover was divine?
She to be his,—were hardly less absurd
Than that he took her name into his mouth,
Licked, and then let it go again, the beast,
Signed with his slaver. Oh, she poisoned him,
Plundered him, and the rest! Well, what I wished
Was, that he would but go on, say once more
So to the world, and get his meed of men,
The fist's reply to the filth. And while I mused,
The minute, oh the misery, was gone!
On either idle hand of me there stood
Really an officer, nor laughed i' the least:
Nay, rendered justice to his reason, laid
Logic to heart, as 'twere submitted them
"Twice two makes four."

                          "And now, catch her!" he cried.
That sobered me. "Let myself lead the way—
Ere you arrest me, who am somebody,
Being, as you hear, a priest and privileged,—
To the lady's chamber! I presume you—men
Expert, instructed how to find out truth,
Familiar with the guise of guilt. Detect

Guilt on her face when it meets mine, then judge
Between us and the mad dog howling there!"
Up we all went together, in they broke
O' the chamber late my chapel. There she lay,
Composed as when I laid her, that last eve,
O' the couch, still breathless, motionless, sleep's self,
Wax-white, seraphic, saturate with the sun
O' the morning that now flooded from the front
And filled the window with a light like blood.
"Behold the poisoner, the adulteress,
—And feigning sleep too! Seize, bind!" Guido hissed.

She started up, stood erect, face to face
With the husband: back he fell, was buttressed there
By the window all aflame with morning-red,
He the black figure, the opprobrious blur
Against all peace and joy and light and life.
"Away from between me and hell!" she cried:
"Hell for me, no embracing any more!
I am God's, I love God, God—whose knees I clasp,
Whose utterly most just award I take,
But bear no more love-making devils: hence!"
I may have made an effort to reach her side
From where I stood i' the doorway,—anyhow
I found the arms, I wanted, pinioned fast,
Was powerless in the clutch to left and right
O' the rabble pouring in, rascality
Enlisted, rampant on the side of hearth,
Home and the husband,—pay in prospect too!
They heaped themselves upon me. "Ha!—and him
Also you outrage? Him, too, my sole friend,
Guardian and savior? That I balk you of,
Since—see how God can help at last and worst!"
She sprang at the sword that hung beside him, seized,
Drew, brandished it, the sunrise burned for joy
O' the blade, "Die," cried she, "devil, in God's name!"

Ah, but they all closed round her, twelve to one
—The unmanly men, no woman-mother made,
Spawned somehow! Dead-white and disarmed she lay.
No matter for the sword, her word sufficed
To spike the coward through and through: he shook,
Could only spit between the teeth—"You see?
You hear? Bear witness, then! Write down ... but no—
Carry these criminals to the prison-house,
For first thing! I begin my search meanwhile
After the stolen effects, gold, jewels, plate,
Money, and clothes, they robbed me of and fled,
With no few amorous pieces, verse and prose,
I have much reason to expect to find."

When I saw that—no more than the first mad speech,
Made out the speaker mad and a laughing-stock,
So neither did this next device explode
One listener's indignation,—that a scribe
Did sit down; set himself to write indeed,
While sundry knaves began to peer and pry
In corner and hole,—that Guido, wiping brow
And getting him a countenance, was fast
Losing his fear, beginning to strut free
O' the stage of his exploit, snuff here, sniff there,—
Then I took truth in, guessed sufficiently
The service for the moment. "What I say,
Slight at your peril! We are aliens here,
My adversary and I, called noble both;
I am the nobler, and a name men know.
I could refer our cause to our own court
In our own country, but prefer appeal
To the nearer jurisdiction. Being a priest,
Though in a secular garb,—for reasons good
I shall adduce in due time to my peers,—
I demand that the Church I serve, decide
Between us, right the slandered lady there.

A Tuscan noble, I might claim the Duke:
A priest, I rather choose the Church,—bid Rome
Cover the wronged with her inviolate shield."

There was no refusing this: they bore me off,
They bore her off, to separate cells o' the same
Ignoble prison, and, separate, thence to Rome.
Pompilia's face, then and thus, looked on me
The last time in this life: not one sight since,
Never another sight to be! And yet
I thought I had saved her. I appealed to Rome:
It seems I simply sent her to her death.
You tell me she is dying now, or dead;
I cannot bring myself to quite believe
This is a place you torture people in:
What if this your intelligence were just
A subtlety, and honest wile to work
On a man at unawares? 'Twere worthy you.
No, Sirs, I cannot have the lady dead!
That erect form, flashing brow, fulgurant eye,
That voice immortal (oh, that voice of hers!)
That vision in the blood-red daybreak—that
Leap to life of the pale electric sword
Angels go armed with,—that was not the last
O' the lady! Come, I see through it, you find—
Know the manœuvre! Also herself said
I had saved her: do you dare say she spoke false?
Let me see for myself if it be so!
Though she were dying, a Priest might be of use,
The more when he's a friend too,—she called me
Far beyond "friend." Come, let me see her—indeed
It is my duty, being a priest: I hope
I stand confessed, established, proved a priest?
My punishment had motive that, a priest
I, in a laic garb, a mundane mode,
Did what were harmlessly done otherwise.

I never touched her with my finger-tip
Except to carry her to the couch, that eve,
Against my heart, beneath my head, bowed low,
As we priests carry the paten: that is why
—To get leave and go see her of your grace—
I have told you this whole story over again.
Do I deserve grace? For I might lock lips,
Laugh at your jurisdiction: what have you
To do with me in the matter? I suppose
You hardly think I donned a bravo's dress
To have a hand in the new crime; on the old,
Judgment's delivered, penalty imposed,
I was chained fast at Civita hand and foot—
She had only you to trust to, you and Rome,
Rome and the Church, and no pert meddling priest
Two days ago, when Guido, with the right,
Hacked her to pieces. One might well be wroth;
I have been patient, done my best to help:
I come from Civita and punishment
As friend of the court—and for pure friendship's sake
Have told my tale to the end,—nay, not the end—
For, wait—I'll end—not leave you that excuse!

When we were parted,—shall I go on there?
I was presently brought to Rome—yes, here I stood
Opposite yonder very crucifix—
And there sat you and you, Sirs, quite the same.
I heard charge, and bore question, and told tale
Noted down in the book there,—turn and see
If, by one jot or tittle, I vary now!
I' the color the tale takes, there's change perhaps;
'Tis natural, since the sky is different,
Eclipse in the air now; still, the outline stays.
I showed you how it came to be my part
To save the lady. Then your clerk produced
Papers, a pack of stupid and impure

Banalities called letters about love—
Love, indeed,—I could teach who styled them so,
Better, I think, though priest and loveless both!
"—How was it that a wife, young, innocent,
And stranger to your person, wrote this page?"—
"—She wrote it when the Holy Father wrote
The bestiality that posts through Rome,
Put in his mouth by Pasquin." "Nor perhaps
Did you return these answers, verse and prose,
Signed, sealed, and sent the lady? There's your hand!"
"—This precious piece of verse, I really judge,
Is meant to copy my own character,
A clumsy mimic; and this other prose,
Not so much even; both rank forgery:
Verse, quotha? Bembo's verse! When Saint John wrote
The tract 'De Tribus,' I wrote this to match."
"—How came it, then, the documents were found
At the inn on your departure?"—"I opine,
Because there were no documents to find
In my presence,—you must hide before you find.
Who forged them hardly practised in my view;
Who found them waited till I turned my back."
"—And what of the clandestine visits paid,
Nocturnal passage in and out the house
With its lord absent? 'Tis alleged you climbed" . . .
"—Flew on a broomstick to the man i' the moon!
Who witnessed or will testify this trash?"
"—The trusty servant, Margherita's self,
Even she who brought you letters, you confess,
And, you confess, took letters in reply:
Forget not we have knowledge of the facts!"
"—Sirs, who have knowledge of the facts, defray
The expenditure of wit I waste in vain,
Trying to find out just one fact of all!
She who brought letters from who could not write,
And took back letters to who could not read,—

Who was that messenger, of your charity?"
"—Well, so far favors you the circumstance
That this same messenger . . . how shall we say? . . .
Sub imputatione meretricis
Laborat,—which makes accusation null:
We waive this woman's:—naught makes void the next.
Borsi, called Venerino, he who drove,
O' the first night when you fled away, at length
Deposes to your kissings in the coach,
—Frequent, frenetic" . . . "When deposed he so?"
"After some weeks of sharp imprisonment" . . .
"Granted by friend the Governor, I engage"—
"—For his participation in your flight!
At length his obduracy melting made
The avowal mentioned" . . . "Was dismissed forthwith
To liberty, poor knave, for recompense.
Sirs, give what credit to the lie you can!
For me, no word in my defence I speak,
And God shall argue for the lady!"

                                              So
Did I stand question, and make answer, still
With the same result of smiling disbelief,
Polite impossibility of faith
In such affected virtue in a priest;
But a showing fair play, an indulgence, even,
To one no worse than others after all—
Who had not brought disgrace to the order, played
Discreetly, ruffled gown nor ripped the cloth
In a bungling game at romps: I have told you, Sirs—
If I pretended simply to be pure
Honest and Christian in the case,—absurd!
As well go boast myself above the needs
O' the human nature, careless how meat smells,
Wine tastes,—a saint above the smack! But once
Abate my crest, own flaws i' the flesh, agree
To go with the herd, be hog no more nor less,

Why, hogs in common herd have common rights:
I must not be unduly borne upon,
Who just romanced a little, sowed wild oats,
But 'scaped without a scandal, flagrant fault.
My name helped to a mirthful circumstance:
"Joseph" would do well to amend his plea:
Undoubtedly—some toying with the wife,
But as for ruffian violence and rape,
Potiphar pressed too much on the other side!
The intrigue, the elopement, the disguise,—well
    charged!
The letters and verse looked hardly like the truth.
Your apprehension was—of guilt enough
To be compatible with innocence,
So, punished best a little and not too much.
Had I struck Guido Franceschini's face,
You had counselled me withdraw for my own sake,
Balk him of bravo-hiring. Friends came round,
Congratulated, "Nobody mistakes!
The pettiness o' the forfeiture defines
The peccadillo: Guido gets his share:
His wife is free of husband and hook-nose,
The mouldy viands and the mother-in-law.
To Civita with you and amuse the time,
Travesty us '*De Raptu Helenæ!*'
A funny figure must the husband cut
When the wife makes him skip,—too ticklish, eh?
Do it in Latin, not the Vulgar, then!
Scazons—we'll copy and send his Eminence.
Mind—one iambus in the final foot!
He'll rectify it, be your friend for life!"
Oh, Sirs, depend on me for much new light
Thrown on the justice and religion here
By this proceeding, much fresh food for thought!

And I was just set down to study these
In relegation, two short days ago,
Admiring how you read the rules, when, clap,
A thunder comes into my solitude—
I am caught up in a whirlwind and cast here,
Told of a sudden, in this room where so late
You dealt out law adroitly, that those scales,
I meekly bowed to, took my allotment from,
Guido has snatched at, broken in your hands,
Metes to himself the murder of his wife,
Full measure, pressed down, running over now!
Can I assist to an explanation?—Yes,
I rise in your esteem, sagacious Sirs,
Stand up a renderer of reasons, not
The officious priest would personate Saint George
For a mock Princess in undragoned days.
What, the blood startles you? What, after all
The priest who needs must carry sword on thigh
May find imperative use for it? Then, there was
A Princess, was a dragon belching flame,
And should have been a Saint George also? Then,
There might be worse schemes than to break the bonds
At Arezzo, lead her by the little hand,
Till she reached Rome, and let her try to live?
But you were law and gospel,—would one please
Stand back, allow your faculty elbow-room?
You blind guides who must needs lead eyes that see!
Fools, alike ignorant of man and God!
What was there here should have perplexed your wit
For a wink of the owl-eyes of you? How miss, then,
What's now forced on you by this flare of fact—
As if Saint Peter failed to recognize
Nero as no apostle, John or James,
Till some one burned a martyr, made a torch
O' the blood and fat to show his features by!
Could you fail read this cartulary aright

On head and front of Franceschini there,—
Large-lettered like hell's masterpiece of print,—
That he, from the beginning pricked at heart
By some lust, letch of hate against his wife,
Plotted to plague her into overt sin
And shame, would slay Pompilia body and soul,
And save his mean self—miserably caught
I' the quagmire of his own tricks, cheats and lies?
—That himself wrote those papers,—from himself
To himself,—which, i' the name of me and her,
His mistress-messenger gave her and me,
Touching us with such pustules of the soul
That she and I might take the taint, be shown
To the world and shuddered over, speckled so?
—That the agent put her sense into my words,
Made substitution of the thing she hoped,
For the thing she had and held, its opposite,
While the husband in the background bit his lips
At each fresh failure of his precious plot?
—That when at the last we did rush each on each,
By no chance but because God willed it so—
The spark of truth was struck from out our souls—
Made all of me, descried in the first glance,
Seem fair and honest and permissible love
O' the good and true—as the first glance told me
There was no duty patent in the world
Like daring try be good and true myself,
Leaving the shows of things to the Lord of Show
And Prince o' the Power of the Air. Our very flight,
Even to its most ambiguous circumstance,
Irrefragably proved how futile, false . . .
Why, men—men and not boys—boys and not babes—
Babes and not beasts—beasts and not stocks and stones!—
Had the liar's lie been true one pin-point speck,
Were I the accepted suitor, free o' the place,
Disposer of the time, to come at a call

And go at a wink as who should say me nay,—
What need of flight, what were the gain therefrom
But just damnation, failure or success?
Damnation pure and simple to her the wife
And me the priest—who bartered private bliss
For public reprobation, the safe shade
For the sunshine which men see to pelt me by:
What other advantage—we who led the days
And nights alone i' the house—was flight to find?
In our whole journey did we stop an hour,
Diverge a foot from strait road till we reached
Or would have reached—but for that fate of ours—
The father and mother, in the eye of Rome,
The eye of yourselves we made aware of us
At the first fall of misfortune? And indeed
You did so far give sanction to our flight,
Confirm its purpose, as lend helping hand,
Deliver up Pompilia not to him
She fled, but those the flight was ventured for.
Why then could you, who stopped short, not go on
One poor step more, and justify the means,
Having allowed the end?—not see and say,
"Here's the exceptional conduct that should claim
To be exceptionally judged on rules
Which, understood, make no exception here"—
Why play instead into the devil's hands
By dealing so ambiguously as gave
Guido the power to intervene like me,
Prove one exception more? I saved his wife
Against law: against law he slays her now:
Deal with him!

             I have done with being judged.
I stand here guiltless in thought, word and deed,
To the point that I apprise you,—in contempt
For all misapprehending ignorance

O' the human heart, much more the mind of Christ,—
That I assuredly did bow, was blessed
By the revelation of Pompilia. There!
Such is the final fact I fling you, Sirs,
To mouth and mumble and misinterpret: there!
"The priest's in love," have it the vulgar way!
Unpriest me, rend the rags o' the vestment, do—
Degrade deep, disenfranchise all you dare—
Remove me from the midst, no longer priest
And fit companion for the like of you—
Your gay Abati with the well-turned leg
And rose i' the hat-rim, Canons, cross at neck
And silk mask in the pocket of the gown,
Brisk Bishops with the world's musk still unbrushed
From the rochet; I'll no more of these good things:
There's a crack somewhere, something that's unsound
I' the rattle!

         For Pompilia—be advised,
Build churches, go pray! You will find me there,
I know, if you come,—and you will come, I know.
Why, there's a Judge weeping! Did not I say
You were good and true at bottom? You see the truth—
I am glad I helped you: she helped me just so.

But for Count Guido,—you must counsel there!
I bow my head, bend to the very dust,
Break myself up in shame of faultiness.
I had him one whole moment, as I said—
As I remember, as will never out
O' the thoughts of me,—I had him in arm's reach
There,—as you stand, Sir, now you cease to sit,—
I could have killed him ere he killed his wife,
And did not: he went off alive and well
And then effected this last feat—through me!
Me—not through you—dismiss that fear! 'Twas you

Hindered me staying here to save her,—not
From leaving you and going back to him
And doing service in Arezzo. Come,
Instruct me in procedure! I conceive—
In all due self-abasement might I speak—
How you will deal with Guido: oh, not death!
Death, if it let her life be: otherwise
Not death,—your lights will teach you clearer! I
Certainly have an instinct of my own
I' the matter: bear with me and weigh its worth!
Let us go away—leave Guido all alone
Back on the world again that knows him now!
I think he will be found (indulge so far!)
Not to die so much as slide out of life,
Pushed by the general horror and common hate
Low, lower,—left o' the very ledge of things,
I seem to see him catch convulsively
One by one at all honest forms of life,
At reason, order, decency and use—
To cramp him and get foothold by at least;
And still they disengage them from his clutch.
"What, you are he, then, had Pompilia once
And so forwent her? Take not up with us!"
And thus I see him slowly and surely edged
Off all the table-land whence life upsprings
Aspiring to be immortality,
As the snake, hatched on hill-top by mischance,
Despite his wriggling, slips, slides, slidders down
Hillside, lies low and prostrate on the smooth
Level of the outer place, lapsed in the vale:
So I lose Guido in the loneliness,
Silence and dusk, till at the doleful end,
At the horizontal line, creation's verge,
From what just is to absolute nothingness—
Whom is it, straining onward still, he meets?
What other man deep further in the fate,

Who, turning at the prize of a footfall
To flatter him and promise fellowship,
Discovers in the act a frightful face—
Judas, made monstrous by much solitude!
The two are at one now! Let them love their love
That bites and claws like hate, or hate their hate
That mops and mows and makes as it were love!
There, let them each tear each in devil's-fun,
Or fondle this the other while malice aches—
Both teach, both learn detestability!
Kiss him the kiss, Iscariot! Pay that back,
That smatch o' the slaver blistering on your lip,
By the better trick, the insult he spared Christ—
Lure him the lure o' the letters, Aretine!
Lick him o'er slimy-smooth with jelly-filth
O' the verse-and-prose pollution in love's guise!
The cockatrice is with the basilisk!
There let them grapple, denizens o' the dark,
Foes or friends, but indissolubly bound,
In their one spot out of the ken of God
Or care of man, forever and evermore!

Why, Sirs, what's this? Why, this is sorry and strange!
Futility, divagation: this from me
Bound to be rational, justify an act
Of sober man!—whereas, being moved so much,
I give you cause to doubt the lady's mind:
A pretty sarcasm for the world! I fear
You do her wit injustice,—all through me!
Like my fate all through,—ineffective help!
A poor rash advocate I prove myself.
You might be angry with good cause: but sure
At the advocate,—only at the undue zeal
That spoils the force of his own plea, I think?
My part was just to tell you how things stand,
State facts and not be flustered at their fume.

But then 'tis a priest speaks: as for love,—no!
If you let buzz a vulgar fly like that
About your brains, as if I loved, forsooth,
Indeed, Sirs, you do wrong!   We had no thought
Of such infatuation, she and I:
There are many points that prove it: do be just!
I told you,—at one little roadside-place
I spent a good half-hour, paced to and fro
The garden; just to leave her free awhile,
I plucked a handful of Spring herb and bloom:
I might have sat beside her on the bench
Where the children were: I wish the thing had been,
Indeed: the event could not be worse, you know:
One more half-hour of her saved! She's dead now, Sirs!
While I was running on at such a rate,
Friends should have plucked me by the sleeve: I went
Too much o' the trivial outside of her face
And the purity that shone there—plain to me,
Not to you, what more natural?   Nor am I
Infatuated,—oh, I saw, be sure!
Her brow had not the right line, leaned too much,
Painters would say; they like the straight-up Greek:
This seemed bent somewhat with an invisible crown
Of martyr and saint, not such as art approves.
And how the dark orbs dwelt deep underneath,
Looked out of such a sad sweet heaven on me!
The lips, compressed a little, came forward too,
Careful for a whole world of sin and pain.
That was the face, her husband makes his plea,
He sought just to disfigure,—no offence
Beyond that!   Sirs, let us be rational!
He needs must vindicate his honor,—ay,
Yet shirks, the coward, in a clown's disguise,
Away from the scene, endeavors to escape.
Now, had he done so, slain and left no trace
O' the slayer,—what were vindicated, pray?

You had found his wife disfigured or a corpse,
For what and by whom? It is too palpable!
Then, here's another point involving law:
I use this argument to show you meant
No calumny against us by that title
O' the sentence,—liars try to twist it so:
What penalty it bore, I had to pay
Till further proof should follow of innocence—
Probationis ob defectum,—proof?
How could you get proof without trying us?
You went through the preliminary form,
Stopped there, contrived this sentence to amuse
The adversary. If the title ran
For more than fault imputed and not proved,
That was a simple penman's error, else
A slip i' the phrase,—as when we say of you
"Charged with injustice"—which may either be
Or not be,—'tis a name that sticks meanwhile.
Another relevant matter: fool that I am!
Not what I wish true, yet a point friends urge:
It is not true,—yet, since friends think it helps,—
She only tried me when some others failed—
Began with Conti, whom I told you of,
And Guillichini, Guido's kinsfolk both,
And when abandoned by them, not before,
Turned to me. That's conclusive why she turned.
Much good they got by the happy cowardice!
Conti is dead, poisoned a month ago:
Does that much strike you as a sin? Not much,
After the present murder,—one mark more
On the Moor's skin,—what is black by blacker still?
Conti had come here and told truth. And so
With Guillichini; he's condemned of course
To the galleys, as a friend in this affair,
Tried and condemned for no one thing i' the world,
A fortnight since by who but the Governor?—

The just judge, who refused Pompilia help
At first blush, being her husband's friend, you know.
There are two tales to suit the separate courts,
Arezzo and Rome: he tells you here, we fled
Alone, unhelped,—lays stress on the main fault,
The spiritual sin, Rome looks to: but elsewhere
He likes best we should break in, steal, bear off,
Be fit to brand and pillory and flog—
That's the charge goes to the heart of the Governor:
If these unpriest me, you and I may yet
Converse, Vincenzo Marzi-Medici!
Oh, Sirs, there are worse men than you, I say!
More easily duped, I mean; this stupid lie,
Its liar never dared propound in Rome,
He gets Arezzo to receive,—nay more,
Gets Florence and the Duke to authorize!
This is their Rota's sentence, their Granduke
Signs and seals! Rome for me henceforward—Rome,
Where better men are,—most of all, that man
The Augustinian of the Hospital,
Who writes the letter,—he confessed, he says,
Many a dying person, never one
So sweet and true and pure and beautiful.
A good man! Will you make him Pope one day?
Not that he is not good too, this we have—
But old,—else he would have his word to speak,
His truth to teach the world: I thirst for truth,
But shall not drink it till I reach the source.

Sirs, I am quiet again. You see, we are
So very pitiable, she and I,
Who had conceivably been otherwise.
Forget distemperature and idle heat!
Apart from truth's sake, what's to move so much?
Pompilia will be presently with God;
I am, on earth, as good as out of it,

A relegated priest; when exile ends,
I mean to do my duty and live long.
She and I are mere strangers now: but priests
Should study passion; how else cure mankind,
Who come for help in passionate extremes?
I do but play with an imagined life
Of who, unfettered by a vow, unblessed
By the higher call,—since you will have it so,—
Leads it companioned by the woman there.
To live, and see her learn, and learn by her,
Out of the low obscure and petty world—
Or only see one purpose and one will
Evolve themselves i' the world, change wrong to right:
To have to do with nothing but the true,
The good, the eternal—and these, not alone
In the main current of the general life,
But small experiences of every day,
Concerns of the particular hearth and home:
To learn not only by a comet's rush
But a rose's birth,—not by the grandeur, God,—
But the comfort, Christ. All this, how far away!
Mere delectation, meet for a minute's dream!—
Just as a drudging student trims his lamp,
Opens his Plutarch, puts him in the place
Of Roman, Grecian; draws the patched gown close,
Dreams, "Thus should I fight, save or rule the world!"—
Then smilingly, contentedly, awakes
To the old solitary nothingness.
So I, from such communion, pass content . . .

O great, just, good God!   Miserable me!

[POMPILIA'S STORY OF HER LIFE]

(*From* Book VII)

I am just seventeen years and five months old,
And, if I lived one day more, three full weeks;
'Tis writ so in the church's register,
Lorenzo in Lucina, all my names
At length, so many names for one poor child,
—Francesca Camilla Vittoria Angela
Pompilia Comparini,—laughable!
Also 'tis writ that I was married there
Four years ago: and they will add, I hope,
When they insert my death, a word or two,—
Omitting all about the mode of death,—
This, in its place, this which one cares to know
That I had been a mother of a son
Exactly two weeks. It will be through grace
O' the Curate, not through any claim I have;
Because the boy was born at, so baptized
Close to, the Villa, in the proper church:
A pretty church, I say no word against,
Yet stranger-like,—while this Lorenzo seems
My own particular place, I always say.
I used to wonder, when I stood scarce high
As the bed here, what the marble lion meant,
With half his body rushing from the wall,
Eating the figure of a prostrate man—
(To the right, it is, of entry by the door)—
An ominous sign to one baptized like me,
Married, and to be buried there, I hope.
And they should add, to have my life complete,
He is a boy and Gaetan by name—
Gaetano, for a reason,—if the friar
Don Celestine will ask this grace for me
Of Curate Ottoboni: he it was

Baptized me: he remembers my whole life
As I do his gray hair.

                        All these few things
I know are true,—will you remember them?
Because time flies. The surgeon cared for me,
To count my wounds,—twenty-two dagger-wounds,
Five deadly, but I do not suffer much—
Or too much pain,—and am to die tonight.

Oh how good God is that my babe was born,
—Better than born, baptized and hid away
Before this happened, safe from being hurt!
That had been sin God could not well forgive:
He was too young to smile and save himself.
When they took, two days after he was born,
My babe away from me to be baptized
And hidden awhile, for fear his foe should find,—
The country-woman, used to nursing babes,
Said, "Why take on so? where is the great loss?
These next three weeks he will but sleep and feed,
Only begin to smile at the month's end;
He would not know you, if you kept him here,
Sooner than that; so, spend three merry weeks
Snug in the Villa, getting strong and stout,
And then I bring him back to be your own,
And both of you may steal to—we know where!"
The month—there wants of it two weeks this day!
Still, I half fancied when I heard the knock
At the Villa in the dusk, it might prove she—
Come to say, "Since he smiles before the time,
Why should I cheat you out of one good hour?
Back I have brought him; speak to him and judge!"
Now I shall never see him; what is worse,
When he grows up and gets to be my age,
He will seem hardly more than a great boy;

And if he asks, "What was my mother like?"
People may answer, "Like girls of seventeen"—
And how can he but think of this and that,
Lucias, Marias, Sofias, who titter or blush
When he regards them as such boys may do?
Therefore I wish some one will please to say
I looked already old though I was young;
Do I not . . . say, if you are by to speak . . .
Look nearer twenty? No more like, at least,
Girls who look arch or redden when boys laugh,
Than the poor Virgin that I used to know
At our street-corner in a lonely niche,—
The babe, that sat upon her knees, broke off,—
Thin white glazed clay, you pitied her the more:
She, not the gay ones, always got my rose.

How happy those are who know how to write!
Such could write what their son should read in time,
Had they a whole day to live out like me.
Also my name is not a common name,
"Pompilia," and may help to keep apart
A little the thing I am from what girls are.
But then how far away, how hard to find
Will anything about me have become,
Even if the boy bethink himself and ask!
No father that ever knew at all,
Nor ever had—no, never had, I say!
That is the truth,—nor any mother left,
Out of the little two weeks that she lived,
Fit for such memory as might assist:
As good too as no family, no name,
Not even poor old Pietro's name, nor hers,
Poor kind unwise Violante, since it seems
They must not be my parents any more.
That is why something put it in my head
To call the boy "Gaetano"—no old name

For sorrow's sake; I looked up to the sky
And took a new saint to begin anew.
One who has only been made saint—how long?
Twenty-five years: so, carefuller, perhaps,
To guard a namesake than those old saints grow,
Tired out by this time,—see my own five saints!

On second thoughts, I hope he will regard
The history of me as what some one dreamed,
And get to disbelieve it at the last:
Since to myself it dwindles fast to that,
Sheer dreaming and impossibility,—
Just in four days too! All the seventeen years,
Not once did a suspicion visit me
How very different a lot is mine
From any other woman's in the world.
The reason must be, 'twas by step and step
It got to grow so terrible and strange.
These strange woes stole on tiptoe, as it were,
Into my neighborhood and privacy,
Sat down where I sat, laid them where I lay;
And I was found familiarized with fear,
When friends broke in, held up a torch and cried,
"Why, you Pompilia in the cavern thus,
How comes that arm of yours about a wolf?
And the soft length,—lies in and out your feet
And laps you round the knee,—a snake it is!"
And so on.

                    Well, and they are right enough,
By the torch they hold up now: for first, observe,
I never had a father,—no, nor yet
A mother: my own boy can say at least,
"I had a mother whom I kept two weeks!"
Not I, who little used to doubt . . . I doubt
Good Pietro, kind Violante, gave me birth?

They loved me always as I love my babe
(—Nearly so, that is—quite so could not be—)
Did for me all I meant to do for him,
Till one surprising day, three years ago,
They both declared, at Rome, before some judge
In some court where the people flocked to hear,
That really I had never been their child,
Was a mere castaway, the careless crime
Of an unknown man, the crime and care too much
Of a woman known too well,—little to these,
Therefore, of whom I was the flesh and blood:
What then to Pietro and Violante, both
No more my relatives than you or you?
Nothing to them! You know what they declared.

So with my husband,—just such a surprise,
Such a mistake, in that relationship!
Every one says that husbands love their wives,
Guard them and guide them, give them happiness;
'Tis duty, law, pleasure, religion: well,
You see how much of this comes true in mine!
People indeed would fain have somehow proved
He was no husband: but he did not hear,
Or would not wait, and so has killed us all.
Then there is . . . only let me name one more!
There is the friend,—men will not ask about,
But tell untruths of, and give nicknames to,
And think my lover, most surprise of all!
Do only hear, it is the priest they mean,
Giuseppe Caponsacchi: a priest—love,
And love me! Well, yet people think he did.
I am married, he has taken priestly vows,
They know that, and yet go on, say, the same,
"Yes, how he loves you!" "That was love"—they say,
When anything is answered that they ask:
Or else "No wonder you love him"—they say.

Then they shake heads, pity much, scarcely blame—
As if we neither of us lacked excuse,
And anyhow are punished to the full,
And downright love atones for everything!
Nay, I heard read out in the public court
Before the judge, in presence of my friends,
Letters 'twas said the priest had sent to me,
And other letters sent him by myself,
We being lovers!

                    Listen what this is like!
When I was a mere child, my mother . . . that's
Violante, you must let me call her so,
Nor waste time, trying to unlearn the word, . . .
She brought a neighbor's child of my own age
To play with me of rainy afternoons:
And, since there hung a tapestry on the wall,
We two agreed to find each other out
Among the figures.   "Tisbe, that is you,
With half-moon on your hair-knot, spear in hand,
Flying, but no wings, only the great scarf
Blown to a bluish rainbow at your back:
Call off your hound and leave the stag alone!"
"—And there are you, Pompilia, such green leaves
Flourishing out of your five finger-ends,
And all the rest of you so brown and rough:
Why is it you are turned a sort of tree?"
You know the figures never were ourselves
Though we nicknamed them so.   Thus, all my life,—
As well what was, as what, like this, was not,—
Looks old, fantastic and impossible:
I touch a fairy thing that fades and fades.
—Even to my babe!   I thought, when he was born,
Something began for once that would not end,
Nor change into a laugh at me, but stay
Forevermore, eternally quite mine.

Well, so he is,—but yet they bore him off,
The third day, lest my husband should lay traps
And catch him, and by means of him catch me.
Since they have saved him so, it was well done:
Yet thence comes such confusion of what was
With what will be,—that late seems long ago,
And, what years should bring round, already come,
Till even he withdraws into a dream
As the rest do: I fancy him grown great,
Strong, stern, a tall young man who tutors me,
Frowns with the others, "Poor imprudent child!
Why did you venture out of the safe street?
Why go so far from help to that lone house?
Why open at the whisper and the knock?"

Six days ago when it was New Year's day,
We bent above the fire and talked of him,
What he should do when he was grown and great.
Violante, Pietro, each had given the arm
I leant on, to walk by, from couch to chair
And fireside,—laughed, as I lay safe at last,
"Pompilia's march from bed to board is made,
Pompilia back again and with a babe,
Shall one day lend his arm and help her walk!"
Then we all wished each other more New Years.
Pietro began to scheme—"Our cause is gained;
The law is stronger than a wicked man:
Let him henceforth go his way, leave us ours!
We will avoid the city, tempt no more
The greedy ones by feasting and parade,—
Live at the other villa, we know where,
Still farther off, and we can watch the babe
Grow fast in the good air; and wood is cheap
And wine sincere outside the city gate.
I still have two or three old friends will grope
Their way along the mere half-mile of road,
With staff and lantern on a moonless night

When one needs talk: they'll find me, never fear,
And I'll find them a flask of the old sort yet!"
Violante said, "You chatter like a crow:
Pompilia tires o' the tattle, and shall to bed:
Do not too much the first day,—somewhat more
Tomorrow, and, the next, begin the cape
And hood and coat! I have spun wool enough."
Oh what a happy friendly eve was that!

And, next day, about noon, out Pietro went—
He was so happy and would talk so much,
Until Violante pushed and laughed him forth
Sight-seeing in the cold,—"So much to see
I' the churches! Swathe your throat three times!" she
    cried,
"And, above all, beware the slippery ways,
And bring us all the news by supper-time!"
He came back late, laid by cloak, staff and hat,
Powdered so thick with snow it made us laugh,
Rolled a great log upon the ash o' the hearth,
And bade Violante treat us to a flask,
Because he had obeyed her faithfully,
Gone sight-see through the seven, and found no church
To his mind like San Giovanni—"There's the fold,
And all the sheep together, big as cats!
And such a shepherd, half the size of life,
Starts up and hears the angel"—when, at the door,
A tap: we started up: you know the rest.

Pietro at least had done no harm, I know;
Nor even Violante, so much harm as makes
Such revenge lawful. Certainly she erred—
Did wrong, how shall I dare say otherwise?—
In telling that first falsehood, buying me
From my poor faulty mother at a price,
To pass off upon Pietro as his child.
If one should take my babe, give him a name,

Say he was not Gaetano and my own,
But that some other woman made his mouth
And hands and feet,—how very false were that!
No good could come of that; and all harm did.
Yet if a stranger were to represent
"Needs must you either give your babe to me
And let me call him mine forevermore,
Or let your husband get him"—ah, my God,
That were a trial I refuse to face!
Well, just so here: it proved wrong but seemed right
To poor Violante—for there lay, she said,
My poor real dying mother in her rags,
Who put me from her with the life and all,
Poverty, pain, shame and disease at once,
To die the easier by what price I fetched—
Also (I hope) because I should be spared
Sorrow and sin,—why may not that have helped?
My father,—he was no one, any one,—
The worse, the likelier,—call him,—he who came,
Was wicked for his pleasure, went his way,
And left no trace to track by; there remained
Nothing but me, the unnecessary life,
To catch up or let fall,—and yet a thing
She could make happy, be made happy with,
This poor Violante,—who would frown thereat?

Well, God, you see! God plants us where we grow.
It is not that, because a bud is born
At a wild brier's end, full i' the wild beast's way,
We ought to pluck and put it out of reach
On the oak-tree top,—say, "There the bud belongs!"
She thought, moreover, real lies were lies told
For harm's sake; whereas this had good at heart,
Good for my mother, good for me, and good
For Pietro who was meant to love a babe,
And needed one to make his life of use,

Receive his house and land when he should die.
Wrong, wrong, and always wrong! how plainly
  wrong!
For see, this fault kept pricking, as faults do,
All the same at her heart: this falsehood hatched,
She could not let it go nor keep it fast.
She told me so,—the first time I was found
Locked in her arms once more after the pain,
When the nuns let me leave them and go home,
And both of us cried all the cares away,—
This it was set her on to make amends,
This brought about the marriage—simply this!
Do let me speak for her you blame so much!
When Paul, my husband's brother, found me out,
Heard there was wealth for who should marry me,
So, came and made a speech to ask my hand
For Guido,—she, instead of piercing straight
Through the pretence to the ignoble truth,
Fancied she saw God's very finger point,
Designate just the time for planting me
(The wild-brier slip she plucked to love and wear)
In soil where I could strike real root, and grow,
And get to be the thing I called myself:
For, wife and husband are one flesh, God says,
And I, whose parents seemed such and were none,
Should in a husband have a husband now,
Find nothing, this time, but was what it seemed,
—All truth and no confusion any more.
I know she meant all good to me, all pain
To herself,—since how could it be aught but pain
To give me up, so, from her very breast,
The wilding flower-tree-branch that, all those years,
She had got used to feel for and find fixed?
She meant well: has it been so ill i' the main?
That is but fair to ask: one cannot judge
Of what has been the ill or well of life,

The day that one is dying,—sorrows change,
Into not altogether sorrow-like;
I do see strangeness but scarce misery,
Now it is over, and no danger more.
My child is safe; there seems not so much pain.
It comes, most like, that I am just absolved,
Purged of the past, the foul in me, washed fair,—
One cannot both have and not have, you know,—
Being right now, I am happy and color things.
Yes, everybody that leaves life sees all
Softened and bettered: so with other sights:
To me at least was never evening yet
But seemed far beautifuller than its day,
For past is past.

            There was a fancy came,
When somewhere, in the journey with my friend,
We stepped into a hovel to get food;
And there began a yelp here, a bark there,—
Misunderstanding creatures that were wroth
And vexed themselves and us till we retired.
The hovel is life: no matter what dogs bit
Or cat scratched in the hovel I break from,
All outside is lone field, moon and such peace—
Flowing in, filling up as with a sea
Whereon comes Someone, walks fast on the white,
Jesus Christ's self, Don Celestine declares,
To meet me and calm all things back again.

Beside, up to my marriage, thirteen years
Were, each day, happy as the day was long:
This may have made the change too terrible.
I know that when Violante told me first
The cavalier—she meant to bring next morn,
Whom I must also let take, kiss my hand—
Would be at San Lorenzo the same eve

And marry me,—which over, we should go
Home both of us without him as before,
And, till she bade speak, I must hold my tongue,
Such being the correct way with girl-brides,
From whom one word would make a father blush,—
I know, I say, that when she told me this,
—Well, I no more saw sense in what she said
Than a lamb does in people clipping wool;
Only lay down and let myself be clipped.
And when next day the cavalier who came—
(Tisbe had told me that the slim young man
With wings at head, and wings at feet, and sword
Threatening a monster, in our tapestry,
Would eat a girl else,—was a cavalier)—
When he proved Guido Franceschini,—old
And nothing like so tall as I myself,
Hook-nosed and yellow in a bush of beard,
Much like a thing I saw on a boy's wrist,
He called an owl and used for catching birds,—
And when he took my hand and made a smile—
Why, the uncomfortableness of it all
Seemed hardly more important in the case
Than—when one gives you, say, a coin to spend—
Its newness or its oldness; if the piece
Weigh properly and buy you what you wish,
No matter whether you get grime or glare!
Men take the coin, return you grapes and figs.
Here, marriage was the coin, a dirty piece
Would purchase me the praise of those I loved:
About what else should I concern myself?

So, hardly knowing what a husband meant,
I supposed this or any man would serve,
No whit the worse for being so uncouth:
For I was ill once and a doctor came
With a great ugly hat, no plume thereto,

Black jerkin and black buckles and black sword,
And white sharp beard over the ruff in front,
And oh so lean, so sour-faced and austere!—
Who felt my pulse, made me put out my tongue,
Then oped a phial, dripped a drop or two
Of a black bitter something,—I was cured!
What mattered the fierce beard or the grim face?
It was the physic beautified the man,
Master Malpichi,—never met his match
In Rome, they said,—so ugly all the same!

However, I was hurried through a storm,
Next dark eve of December's deadest day—
How it rained!—through our street and the Lion's-mouth
And the bit of Corso,—cloaked round, covered close,
I was like something strange or contraband,—
Into blank San Lorenzo, up the aisle,
My mother keeping hold of me so tight,
I fancied we were come to see a corpse
Before the altar which she pulled me toward.
There we found waiting an unpleasant priest
Who proved the brother, not our parish friend,
But one with mischief-making mouth and eye,
Paul, whom I know since to my cost. And then
I heard the heavy church-door lock out help
Behind us: for the customary warmth,
Two tapers shivered on the altar. "Quick—
Lose no time!" cried the priest. And straightway down
From . . . what's behind the altar where he hid—
Hawk-nose and yellowness and bush and all,
Stepped Guido, caught my hand, and there was I
O' the chancel, and the priest had opened book,
Read here and there, made me say that and this,
And after, told me I was now a wife,
Honored indeed, since Christ thus weds the Church,
And therefore turned he water into wine,

To show I should obey my spouse like Christ.
Then the two slipped aside and talked apart,
And I, silent and scared, got down again
And joined my mother, who was weeping now.
Nobody seemed to mind us any more,
And both of us on tiptoe found our way
To the door which was unlocked by this, and wide.
When we were in the street, the rain had stopped,
All things looked better. At our own house-door,
Violante whispered, "No one syllable
To Pietro! Girl-brides never breathe a word!"
"—Well treated to a wetting, draggle-tails!"
Laughed Pietro as he opened—"Very near
You made me brave the gutter's roaring sea
To carry off from roost old dove and young,
Trussed up in church, the cote, by me, the kite!
What do these priests mean, praying folk to death
On stormy afternoons, with Christmas close
To wash our sins off nor require the rain?"
Violante gave my hand a timely squeeze,
Madonna saved me from immodest speech,
I kissed him and was quiet, being a bride.

When I saw nothing more, the next three weeks,
Of Guido—"Nor the Church sees Christ" thought I:
"Nothing is changed however, wine is wine
And water only water in our house.
Nor did I see that ugly doctor since
That cure of the illness: just as I was cured,
I am married,—neither scarecrow will return."

Three weeks, I chuckled—"How would Giulia stare,
And Tecla smile and Tisbe laugh outright,
Were it not impudent for brides to talk!"—
Until one morning, as I sat and sang
At the broidery-frame alone i' the chamber,—loud

Voices, two, three together, sobbings too,
And my name, "Guido," "Paolo," flung like stones
From each to the other! In I ran to see.
There stood the very Guido and the priest
With sly face,—formal but nowise afraid,—
While Pietro seemed all red and angry, scarce
Able to stutter out his wrath in words;
And this it was that made my mother sob,
As he reproached her—"You have murdered us,
Me and yourself and this our child beside!"
Then Guido interposed, "Murdered or not,
Be it enough your child is now my wife!
I claim and come to take her." Paul put in,
"Consider—kinsman, dare I term you so?—
What is the good of your sagacity
Except to counsel in a strait like this?
I guarantee the parties man and wife
Whether you like or loathe it, bless or ban.
May spilt milk be put back within the bowl—
The done thing, undone? You, it is, we look
For counsel to, you fitliest will advise!
Since milk, though spilt and spoilt, does marble good,
Better we down on knees and scrub the floor,
Than sigh, 'the waste would make a syllabub!'
Help us so turn disaster to account,
So predispose the groom, he needs shall grace
The bride with favor from the very first,
Not begin marriage an embittered man!"
He smiled,—the game so wholly in his hands!
While fast and faster sobbed Violante—"Ay,
All of us murdered, past averting now!
O my sin, O my secret!" and such like.

Then I began to half surmise the truth;
Something had happened, low, mean, underhand,
False, and my mother was to blame, and I

To pity, whom all spoke of, none addressed:
I was the chattel that had caused a crime.
I stood mute,—those who tangled must untie
The embroilment. Pietro cried, "Withdraw, my child!
She is not helpful to the sacrifice
At this stage,—do you want the victim by
While you discuss the value of her blood?
For her sake, I consent to hear you talk:
Go, child, and pray God help the innocent!"

I did go and was praying God, when came
Violante, with eyes swollen and red enough,
But movement on her mouth for make-believe
Matters were somehow getting right again.
She bade me sit down by her side and hear.
"You are too young and cannot understand,
Nor did your father understand at first.
I wished to benefit all three of us,
And when he failed to take my meaning,—why,
I tried to have my way at unaware—
Obtained him the advantage he refused.
As if I put before him wholesome food
Instead of broken victual,—he finds change
I' the viands, never cares to reason why,
But falls to blaming me, would fling the plate
From window, scandalize the neighborhood,
Even while he smacks his lips,—men's way, my child!
But either you have prayed him unperverse
Or I have talked him back into his wits:
And Paolo was a help in time of need,—
Guido, not much—my child, the way of men!
A priest is more a woman than a man,
And Paul did wonders to persuade. In short,
Yes, he was wrong, your father sees and says;
My scheme was worth attempting: and bears fruit,
Gives you a husband and a noble name,

A palace and no end of pleasant things.
What do you care about a handsome youth?
They are so volatile, and tease their wives!
This is the kind of man to keep the house.
We lose no daughter,—gain a son, that's all:
For 'tis arranged we never separate,
Nor miss, in our gray time of life, the tints
Of you that color eve to match with morn.
In good or ill, we share and share alike,
And cast our lots into a common lap,
And all three die together as we lived!
Only, at Arezzo,—that's a Tuscan town,
Not so large as this noisy Rome, no doubt,
But older far and finer much, say folk,—
In a great palace where you will be queen,
Know the Archbishop and the Governor,
And we see homage done you ere we die.
Therefore, be good and pardon!"—"Pardon what?
You know things, I am very ignorant:
All is right if you only will not cry!"

And so an end! Because a blank begins
From when, at the word, she kissed me hard and hot,
And took me back to where my father leaned
Opposite Guido—who stood eying him,
As eyes the butcher the cast panting ox
That feels his fate is come, nor struggles more,—
While Paul looked archly on, pricked brow at whiles
With the pen-point as to punish triumph there.—
And said, "Count Guido, take your lawful wife
Until death part you!"

                            All since is one blank,
Over and ended; a terrific dream.
It is the good of dreams—so soon they go!
Wake in a horror of heart-beats, you may—

Cry, "The dread thing will never from my thoughts!"
Still, a few daylight doses of plain life,
Cock-crow and sparrow-chirp, or bleat and bell
Of goats that trot by, tinkling, to be milked;
And when you rub your eyes awake and wide,
Where is the harm o' the horror?   Gone!   So here.
I know I wake,—but from what?   Blank, I say!
This is the note of evil: for good lasts.
Even when Don Celestine bade "Search and find!
For your soul's sake, remember what is past,
The better to forgive it,"—all in vain!
What was fast getting indistinct before,
Vanished outright.   By special grace perhaps,
Between that first calm and this last, four years
Vanish,—one quarter of my life, you know.
I am held up, amid the nothingness,
By one or two truths only—thence I hang,
And there I live,—the rest is death or dream,
All but those points of my support.   I think
Of what I saw at Rome once in the Square
O' the Spaniards, opposite the Spanish House:
There was a foreigner had trained a goat,
A shuddering white woman of a beast,
To climb up, stand straight on a pile of sticks
Put close, which gave the creature room enough:
When she was settled there, he, one by one,
Took away all the sticks, left just the four
Whereon the little hoofs did really rest,
There she kept firm, all underneath was air.
So, what I hold by, are my prayer to God,
My hope, that came in answer to the prayer,
Some hand would interpose and save me—hand
Which proved to be my friend's hand: and,—blest bliss,—
That fancy which began so faint at first,
That thrill of dawn's suffusion through my dark,
Which I perceive was promise of my child,

The light his unborn face sent long before,—
God's way of breaking the good news to flesh.
That is all left now of those four bad years.
Don Celestine urged, "But remember more!
Other men's faults may help me find your own.
I need the cruelty exposed, explained,
Or how can I advise you to forgive?"
He thought I could not properly forgive
Unless I ceased forgetting,—which is true:
For, bringing back reluctantly to mind
My husband's treatment of me,—by a light
That's later than my lifetime, I review
And comprehend much and imagine more,
And have but little to forgive at last.
For now,—be fair and say,—is it not true
He was ill-used and cheated of his hope
To get enriched by marriage? Marriage gave
Me and no money, broke the compact so:
He had a right to ask me on those terms,
As Pietro and Violante to declare
They would not give me: so the bargain stood:
They broke it, and he felt himself aggrieved,
Became unkind with me to punish them.
They said 'twas he began deception first,
Nor, in one point whereto he pledged himself,
Kept promise: what of that, suppose it were?
Echoes die off, scarcely reverberate
Forever,—why should ill keep echoing ill,
And never let our ears have done with noise?
Then my poor parents took the violent way
To thwart him,—he must needs retaliate,—wrong,
Wrong, and all wrong,—better say, all blind!
As I myself was, that is sure, who else
Had understood the mystery: for his wife
Was bound in some sort to help somehow there.
It seems as if I might have interposed,

Blunted the edge of their resentment so,
Since he vexed me because they first vexed him;
"I will entreat them to desist, submit,
Give him the money and be poor in peace,—
Certainly not go tell the world: perhaps
He will grow quiet with his gains."

                    Yes, say
Something to this effect and you do well!
But then you have to see first: I was blind.
That is the fruit of all such wormy ways,
The indirect, the unapproved of God:
You cannot find their author's end and aim,
Not even to substitute your good for bad,
Your straight for the irregular; you stand
Stupefied, profitless, as cow or sheep
That miss a man's mind; anger him just twice
By trial at repairing the first fault.
Thus, when he blamed me, "You are a coquette,
A lure-owl posturing to attract birds,
You look love-lures at theatre and church,
In walk, at window!"—that, I knew, was false:
But why he charged me falsely, whither sought
To drive me by such charge,—how could I know?
So, unaware, I only made things worse.
I tried to soothe him by abjuring walk,
Window, church, theatre, for good and all,
As if he had been in earnest: that, you know,
Was nothing like the object of his charge.
Yes, when I got my maid to supplicate
The priest, whose name she read when she would read
Those feigned false letters I was forced to hear
Though I could read no word of,—he should cease
Writing,—nay, if he minded prayer of mine,
Cease from so much as even pass the street
Whereon our house looked,—in my ignorance
I was just thwarting Guido's true intent;

Which was, to bring about a wicked change
Of sport to earnest, tempt a thoughtless man
To write indeed, and pass the house, and more,
Till both of us were taken in a crime.
He ought not to have wished me thus act lies,
Simulate folly: but—wrong or right, the wish—
I failed to apprehend its drift.   How plain
It follows,—if I fell into such fault,
He also may have overreached the mark,
Made mistake, by perversity of brain,
I' the whole sad strange plot, the grotesque intrigue
To make me and my friend unself ourselves,
Be other man and woman than we were!
Think it out, you who have the time! for me,—
I cannot say less; more I will not say.
Leave it to God to cover and undo!
Only, my dulness should not prove too much!
—Not prove that in a certain other point
Wherein my husband blamed me,—and you blame,
If I interpret smiles and shakes of head,—
I was dull too.   Oh, if I dared but speak!
Must I speak?   I am blamed that I forwent
A way to make my husband's favor come.
That is true: I was firm, withstood, refused . . .
—Women as you are, how can I find the words?

I felt there was just one thing Guido claimed
I had no right to give nor he to take;
We being in estrangement, soul from soul:
Till, when I sought help, the Archbishop smiled,
Inquiring into privacies of life,
—Said I was blamable—(he stands for God)
Nowise entitled to exemption there.
Then I obeyed,—as surely had obeyed
Were the injunction "Since your husband bids,
Swallow the burning coal he proffers you!"

But I did wrong, and he gave wrong advice
Though he were thrice Archbishop,—that, I know!—
Now I have got to die and see things clear.
Remember I was barely twelve years old—
A child at marriage: I was let alone
For weeks, I told you, lived my child-life still
Even at Arezzo, when I woke and found
First . . . but I need not think of that again—
Over and ended! Try and take the sense
Of what I signify, if it must be so.
After the first, my husband, for hate's sake,
Said one eve, when the simpler cruelty
Seemed somewhat dull at edge and fit to bear,
"We have been man and wife six months almost:
How long is this your comedy to last?
Go this night to my chamber, not your own!"
At which word, I did rush—most true the charge—
And gain the Archbishop's house—he stands for God—
And fall upon my knees and clasp his feet,
Praying him hinder what my estranged soul
Refused to bear, though patient of the rest:
"Place me within a convent," I implored—
"Let me henceforward lead the virgin life
You praise in her you bid me imitate!"
What did he answer? "Folly of ignorance!
Know, daughter, circumstances make or mar
Virginity,—'tis virtue or 'tis vice.
That which was glory in the Mother of God
Had been, for instance, damnable in Eve
Created to be mother of mankind.
Had Eve, in answer to her Maker's speech
'Be fruitful, multiply, replenish earth'—
Pouted 'But I choose rather to remain
Single'—why, she had spared herself forthwith
Further probation by the apple and snake,
Been pushed straight out of Paradise! For see—

If motherhood be qualified impure,
I catch you making God command Eve sin!
—A blasphemy so like these Molinists',
I must suspect you dip into their books."
Then he pursued " 'Twas in your covenant!"

No!   There my husband never used deceit.
He never did by speech nor act imply
"Because of our souls' yearning that we meet
And mix in soul through flesh, which yours and mine
Wear and impress, and make their visible selves,
—All which means, for the love of you and me,
Let us become one flesh, being one soul!"
He only stipulated for the wealth;
Honest so far.   But when he spoke as plain—
Dreadfully honest also—"Since our souls
Stand each from each, a whole world's width be-
        tween,
Give me the fleshly vesture I can reach
And rend and leave just fit for hell to burn!"—
Why, in God's name, for Guido's soul's own sake
Imperilled by polluting mine,—I say,
I did resist; would I had overcome!

My heart died out at the Archbishop's smile;
—It seemed so stale and worn a way o' the world,
As though 'twere nature frowning—"Here is Spring,
The sun shines as he shone at Adam's fall,
The earth requires that warmth reach everywhere:
What, must your patch of snow be saved forsooth
Because you rather fancy snow than flowers?"
Something in this style be began with me.
Last he said, savagely for a good man,
"This explains why you call your husband harsh,
Harsh to you, harsh to whom you love.   God's Bread!
The poor Count has to manage a mere child

Whose parents leave untaught the simplest things
Their duty was and privilege to teach,—
Goodwives' instruction, gossips' lore: they laugh
And leave the Count the task,—or leave it me!"
Then I resolved to tell a frightful thing.
"I am not ignorant,—know what I say,
Declaring this is sought for hate, not love.
Sir, you may hear things like almighty God.
I tell you that my housemate, yes—the priest
My husband's brother, Canon Girolamo—
Has taught me what depraved and misnamed love
Means, and what outward signs denote the sin,
For he solicits me and says he loves,
The idle young priest with naught else to do.
My husband sees this, knows this, and lets be.
Is it your counsel I bear this beside?"
"—More scandal, and against a priest this time!
What, 'tis the Canon now?"—less snappishly—
"Rise up, my child, for such a child you are,
The rod were too advanced a punishment!
Let's try the honeyed cake. A parable!
'Without a parable spake he not to them.'
There was a ripe round long black toothsome fruit,
Even a flower-fig, the prime boast of May;
And, to the tree, said . . . either the spirit o' the fig,
Or, if we bring in men, the gardener,
Archbishop of the orchard—had I time
To try o' the two which fits in best: indeed
It might be the Creator's self, but then
The tree should bear an apple, I suppose,—
Well, anyhow, one with authority said,
'Ripe fig, burst skin, regale the fig-pecker—
The bird whereof thou art a perquisite!'
'Nay,' with a flounce, replied the restif fig,
'I much prefer to keep my pulp myself:
He may go breakfastless and dinnerless,

Supperless of one crimson seed, for me!'
So, back she flopped into her bunch of leaves.
He flew off, left her,—did the natural lord,—
And lo, three hundred thousand bees and wasps
Found her out, feasted on her to the shuck:
Such gain the fig's that gave its bird no bite!
The moral,—fools elude their proper lot,
Tempt other fools, get ruined all alike.
Therefore go home, embrace your husband quick!
Which if his Canon brother chance to see,
He will the sooner back to book again."

So, home I did go; so, the worst befell:
So, I had proof the Archbishop was just man,
And hardly that, and certainly no more.
For, miserable consequence to me,
My husband's hatred waxed nor waned at all,
His brother's boldness grew effrontery soon,
And my last stay and comfort in myself
Was forced from me: henceforth I looked to God
Only, nor cared my desecrated soul
Should have fair walls, gay windows for the world.
God's glimmer, that came through the ruin-top,
Was witness why all lights were quenched inside:
Henceforth I asked God counsel, not mankind.

So, when I made the effort, freed myself,
They said—"No care to save appearance here!
How cynic,—when, how wanton, were enough!"
—Adding, it all came of my mother's life—
My own real mother, whom I never knew,
Who did wrong (if she needs must have done wrong)
Through being all her life, not my four years,
At mercy of the hateful: every beast
O' the field was wont to break that fountain fence,
Trample the silver into mud so murk

Heaven could not find itself reflected there.
Now they cry, "Out on her, who, plashy pool,
Bequeathed turbidity and bitterness
To the daughter-stream where Guido dipt and drank!"

Well, since she had to bear this brand—let me!
The rather do I understand her now,—
From my experience of what hate calls love,—
Much love might be in what their love called hate.
If she sold . . . what they call, sold . . . me, her
        child—
I shall believe she hoped in her poor heart
That I at least might try be good and pure,
Begin to live untempted, not go doomed
And done with ere once found in fault, as she.
Oh and, my mother, it all came to this?
Why should I trust those that speak ill of you,
When I mistrust who speaks even well of them?
Why, since all bound to do me good, did harm,
May not you, seeming as you harmed me most,
Have meant to do most good—and feed your child
From bramble-bush, whom not one orchard-tree
But drew bough back from, nor let one fruit fall?
This it was for you sacrificed your babe?
Gained just this, giving your heart's hope away
As I might give mine, loving it as you,
If . . . but that never could be asked of me!

There, enough! I have my support again,
Again the knowledge that my babe was, is,
Will be mine only. Him, by death, I give
Outright to God, without a further care,—
But not to any parent in the world,—
So to be safe: why is it we repine?
What guardianship were safer could we choose?
All human plans and projects come to naught:

My life, and what I know of other lives,
Prove that: no plan nor project! God shall care!

And now you are not tired? How patient then
All of you,—oh yes, patient this long while
Listening, and understanding, I am sure!
Four days ago, when I was sound and well
And like to live, no one would understand.
People were kind, but smiled, "And what of him,
Your friend, whose tonsure the rich dark-brown hides?
There, there!—your lover, do we dream he was?
A priest too—never were such naughtiness!
Still, he thinks many a long think, never fear,
After the shy pale lady,—lay so light
For a moment in his arms, the lucky one!"
And so on: wherefore should I blame you much?
So we are made, such difference in minds,
Such difference too in eyes that see the minds!
That man, you misinterpret and misprise—
The glory of his nature, I had thought,
Shot itself out in white light, blazed the truth
Through every atom of his act with me:
Yet where I point you, through the crystal shrine,
Purity in quintessence, one dew-drop,
You all descry a spider in the midst.
One says, "The head of it is plain to see,"
And one, "They are the feet by which I judge,"
All say, "Those films were spun by nothing else."

Then, I must lay my babe away with God,
Nor think of him again for gratitude.
Yes, my last breath shall wholly spend itself
In one attempt more to disperse the stain,
The mist from other breath fond mouths have made,
About a lustrous and pellucid soul:
So that, when I am gone but sorrow stays,

And people need assurance in their doubt
If God yet have a servant, man a friend,
The weak a savior, and the vile a foe,—
Let him be present, by the name invoked,
Giuseppe-Maria Caponsacchi!

                                    There,
Strength comes already with the utterance!
I will remember once more for his sake
The sorrow: for he lives and is belied.
Could he be here, how he would speak for me!

[POMPILIA'S TRIBUTE TO CAPONSACCHI—HER DEATH]

(*From* Book VII)

Ah! Friends, I thank and bless you every one!
No more now: I withdraw from earth and man
To my own soul, compose myself for God.

Well, and there is more! Yes, my end of breath
Shall bear away my soul in being true!
He is still here, not outside with the world,
Here, here, I have him in his rightful place!
'Tis now, when I am most upon the move,
I feel for what I verily find—again
The face, again the eyes, again, through all,
The heart and its immeasurable love
Of my one friend, my only, all my own,
Who put his breast between the spears and me.
Ever with Caponsacchi!   Otherwise
Here alone would be failure, loss to me—
How much more loss to him, with life debarred
From giving life, love locked from love's display,
The day-star stopped its task that makes night morn!
O lover of my life, O soldier-saint,

No work begun shall ever pause for death!
Love will be helpful to me more and more
I' the coming course, the new path I must tread—
My weak hand in thy strong hand, strong for that!
Tell him that if I seem without him now,
That's the world's insight! Oh, he understands!
He is at Civita—do I once doubt
The world again is holding us apart?
He had been here, displayed in my behalf
The broad brow that reverberates the truth,
And flashed the word God gave him, back to man!
I know where the free soul is flown! My fate
Will have been hard for even him to bear:
Let it confirm him in the trust of God,
Showing how holily he dared the deed!
And, for the rest,—say, from the deed, no touch
Of harm came, but all good, all happiness,
Not one faint fleck of failure! Why explain?
What I see, oh, he sees and how much more!
Tell him,—I know not wherefore the true word
Should fade and fall unuttered at the last—
It was the name of him I sprang to meet
When came the knock, the summons and the end.
"My great heart, my strong hand are back again!"
I would have sprung to these, beckoning across
Murder and hell gigantic and distinct
O' the threshold, posted to exclude me heaven:
He is ordained to call and I to come!
Do not the dead wear flowers when dressed for God?
Say,—I am all in flowers from head to foot!
Say,—not one flower of all he said and did,
Might seem to flit unnoticed, fade unknown,
But dropped a seed, has grown a balsam-tree
Whereof the blossoming perfumes the place
At this supreme of moments! He is a priest;
He cannot marry therefore, which is right:

I think he would not marry if he could.
Marriage on earth seems such a counterfeit,
Mere imitation of the inimitable:
In heaven we have the real and true and sure.
'Tis there they neither marry nor are given
In marriage but are as the angels: right,
Oh how right that is, how like Jesus Christ
To say that!   Marriage-making for the earth,
With gold so much,—birth, power, repute so much,
Or beauty, youth so much, in lack of these!
Be as the angels rather, who, apart,
Know themselves into one, are found at length
Married, but marry never, no, nor give
In marriage; they are man and wife at once
When the true time is: here we have to wait
Not so long neither!   Could we by a wish
Have what we will and get the future now,
Would we wish aught done undone in the past?
So, let him wait God's instant men call years;
Meantime hold hard by truth and his great soul,
Do out the duty!   Through such souls alone
God stooping shows sufficient of his light
For us i' the dark to rise by.   And I rise.

[THE POPE'S PRAISE OF POMPILIA AND CAPONSACCHI]

(*From* Book X)

                              First of the first,
Such I pronounce Pompilia, then as now
Perfect in whiteness: stoop thou down, my child,
Give one good moment to the poor old Pope
Heart-sick at having all his world to blame—
Let me look at thee in the flesh as erst,
Let me enjoy the old clean linen garb,
Not the new splendid vesture!   Armed and crowned,

Would Michael, yonder, be, nor crowned nor armed,
The less pre-eminent angel?   Everywhere
I see in the world the intellect of man,
That sword, the energy his subtle spear,
The knowledge which defends him like a shield—
Everywhere; but they make not up, I think,
The marvel of a soul like thine, earth's flower
She holds up to the softened gaze of God!
It was not given Pompilia to know much,
Speak much, to write a book, to move mankind,
Be memorized by who records my time.
Yet if in purity and patience, if
In faith held fast despite the plucking fiend,
Safe like the signet stone with the new name
That saints are known by,—if in right returned
For wrong, most pardon for worst injury,
If there be any virtue, any praise,—
Then will this woman child have proved—who knows?—
Just the one prize vouchsafed unworthy me,
Seven years a gardener of the untoward ground
I till,—this earth, my sweat and blood manure
All the long day that barrenly grows dusk:
At least one blossom makes me proud at eve
Born 'mid the briers of my enclosure!   Still
(Oh, here as elsewhere, nothingness of man!)
Those be the plants, imbedded yonder South
To mellow in the morning, those made fat
By the master's eye, that yield such timid leaf,
Uncertain bud, as product of his pains!
While—see how this mere chance-sown, cleft-nursed seed,
That sprang up by the wayside 'neath the foot
Of the enemy, this breaks all into blaze,
Spreads itself, one wide glory of desire
To incorporate the whole great sun it loves
From the inch-height whence it looks and longs!   My
    flower,

My rose, I gather for the breast of God,
This I praise most in thee, where all I praise,
That having been obedient to the end
According to the light allotted, law
Prescribed thy life, still tried, still standing test,—
Dutiful to the foolish parents first,
Submissive next to the bad husband,—nay,
Tolerant of those meaner miserable
That did his hests, eked out the dole of pain,—
Thou, patient thus, couldst rise from law to law,
The old to the new, promoted at one cry
O' the trump of God to the new service, not
To longer bear, but henceforth fight, be found
Sublime in new impatience with the foe!
Endure man and obey God: plant firm foot
On neck of man, tread man into the hell
Meet for him, and obey God all the more!
Oh child that didst despise thy life so much
When it seemed only thine to keep or lose,
How the fine ear felt fall the first low word
"Value life, and preserve life for My sake!"
Thou didst . . . how shall I say? . . . receive so long
The standing ordinance of God on earth,
What wonder if the novel claim had clashed
With old requirement, seemed to supersede
Too much the customary law?   But, brave,
Thou at first prompting of what I call God,
And fools call Nature, didst hear, comprehend,
Accept the obligation laid on thee,
Mother elect, to save the unborn child,
As brute and bird do, reptile and the fly,
Ay and, I nothing doubt, even tree, shrub, plant
And flower o' the field, all in a common pact
To worthily defend the trust of trusts,
Life from the Ever Living:—didst resist—
Anticipate the office that is mine—

And with his own sword stay the upraised arm,
The endeavor of the wicked, and defend
Him who—again in my default—was there
For visible providence: one less true than thou
To touch, i' the past, less practised in the right,
Approved less far in all docility
To all instruction,—how had such an one
Made scruple "Is this motion a decree?"
It was authentic to the experienced ear
O' the good and faithful servant. Go past me
And get thy praise,—and be not far to seek
Presently when I follow if I may!

And surely not so very much apart
Need I place thee, my warrior-priest,—in whom
What if I gain the other rose, the gold,
We grave to imitate God's miracle,
Greet monarchs with, good rose in its degree?
Irregular noble scapegrace—son the same!
Faulty—and peradventure ours the fault
Who still misteach, mislead, throw hook and line,
Thinking to land leviathan forsooth,
Tame the scaled neck, play with him as a bird,
And bind him for our maidens! Better bear
The King of Pride go wantoning awhile,
Unplagued by cord in nose and thorn in jaw,
Through deep to deep, followed by all that shine,
Churning the blackness hoary: He who made
The comely terror, He shall make the sword
To match that piece of netherstone his heart,
Ay, nor miss praise thereby; who else shut fire
I' the stone, to leap from mouth at sword's first stroke,
In lamps of love and faith, the chivalry
That dares the right and disregards alike
The yea and nay o' the world? Self-sacrifice,—
What if an idol took it? Ask the Church

Why she was wont to turn each Venus here,—
Poor Rome perversely lingered round, despite
Instruction, for the sake of purblind love,—
Into Madonna's shape, and waste no whit
Of aught so rare on earth as gratitude!
All this sweet savor was not ours but thine,
Nard of the rock, a natural wealth we name
Incense, and treasure up as food for saints,
When flung to us—whose function was to give
Not find the costly perfume. Do I smile?
Nay, Caponsacchi, much I find amiss,
Blameworthy, punishable in this freak
Of thine, this youth prolonged, though age was ripe,
This masquerade in sober day, with change
Of motley too,—now hypocrite's disguise,
Now fool's-costume: which lie was least like truth,
Which the ungainlier, more discordant garb,
With that symmetric soul inside my son,
The churchman's or the worldling's,—let him judge,
Our adversary who enjoys the task!
I rather chronicle the healthy rage,—
When the first moan broke from the martyr-maid
At that uncaging of the beasts,—made bare
My athlete on the instant, gave such good
Great undisguised leap over post and pale
Right into the mid-cirque, free fighting-place.
There may have been rash stripping—every rag
Went to the winds,—infringement manifold
Of laws prescribed pudicity, I fear,
In this impulsive and prompt self-display!
Ever such tax comes of the foolish youth;
Men mulct the wiser manhood, and suspect
No veritable star swims out of cloud.
Bear thou such imputation, undergo
The penalty I nowise dare relax,—
Conventional chastisement and rebuke.

But for the outcome, the brave starry birth
Conciliating earth with all that cloud,
Thank heaven as I do! Ay, such championship
Of God at first blush, such prompt cheery thud
Of glove on ground that answers ringingly
The challenge of the false knight,—watch we long,
And wait we vainly for its gallant like
From those appointed to the service, sworn
His body-guard with pay and privilege—
White-cinct, because in white walks sanctity,
Red-socked, how else proclaim fine scorn of flesh,
Unchariness of blood when blood faith begs!
Where are the men-at-arms with cross on coat?
Aloof, bewraying their attire: whilst thou
In mask and motley, pledged to dance not fight,
Sprang'st forth the hero! In thought, word, and deed,
How throughout all thy warfare thou wast pure,
I find it easy to believe: and if
At any fateful moment of the strange
Adventure, the strong passion of that strait,
Fear and surprise, may have revealed too much,—
As when a thundrous midnight, with black air
That burns, raindrops that blister, breaks a spell,
Draws out the excessive virtue of some sheathed
Shut unsuspected flower that hoards and hides
Immensity of sweetness,—so, perchance,
Might the surprise and fear release too much
The perfect beauty of the body and soul
Thou savedst in thy passion for God's sake,
He who is Pity. Was the trial sore?
Temptation sharp? Thank God a second time!
Why comes temptation but for man to meet
And master and make crouch beneath his foot,
And so be pedestalled in triumph? Pray
"Lead us into no such temptations, Lord!"
Yea, but, O Thou whose servants are the bold,

Lead such temptations by the head and hair,
Reluctant dragons, up to who dares fight,
That so he may do battle and have praise!
Do I not see the praise?—that while thy mates
Bound to deserve i' the matter, prove at need
Unprofitable through the very pains
We gave to train them well and start them fair,—
Are found too stiff, with standing ranked and ranged,
For onset in good earnest, too obtuse
Of ear, through iteration of command,
For catching quick the sense of the real cry,—
Thou, whose sword-hand was used to strike the lute,
Whose sentry-station graced some wanton's gate,
Thou didst push forward and show mettle, shame
The laggards, and retrieve the day. Well done!
Be glad thou hast let light into the world,
Through that irregular breach o' the boundary,—see
The same upon thy path and march assured,
Learning anew the use of soldiership,
Self-abnegation, freedom from all fear,
Loyalty to the life's end! Ruminate,
Deserve the initiatory spasm,—once more
Work, be unhappy but bear life, my son!

[BROWNING'S ADDRESS TO THE BRITISH PUBLIC]

(*From* Book XII)

So, British Public, who may like me yet,
  (Marry and amen!) learn one lesson hence
Of many which whatever lives should teach:
This lesson, that our human speech is naught,
Our human testimony false, our fame
And human estimation words and wind.
Why take the artistic way to prove so much?
Because, it is the glory and good of Art,

That Art remains the one way possible
Of speaking truth, to mouths like mine at least.
How look a brother in the face and say,
"Thy right is wrong, eyes hast thou yet art blind;
Thine ears are stuffed and stopped, despite their length:
And, oh, the foolishness thou countest faith!"
Say this as silverly as tongue can troll—
The anger of the man may be endured,
The shrug, the disappointed eyes of him
Are not so bad to bear—but here's the plague
That all this trouble comes of telling truth,
Which truth, by when it reaches him, looks false,
Seems to be just the thing it would supplant,
Nor recognizable by whom it left:
While falsehood would have done the work of truth.
But Art,—wherein man nowise speaks to men,
Only to mankind,—Art may tell a truth
Obliquely, do the thing shall breed the thought,
Nor wrong the thought, missing the mediate word.
So may you paint your picture, twice show truth,
Beyond mere imagery on the wall,—
So, note by note, bring music from your mind,
Deeper than ever e'en Beethoven dived,—
So write a book shall mean beyond the facts,
Suffice the eye and save the soul beside.

And save the soul! If this intent save mine,—
If the rough ore be rounded to a ring,
Render all duty which good ring should do,
And, failing grace, succeed in guardianship,—
Might mine but lie outside thine, Lyric Love,
Thy rare gold ring of verse (the poet praised)
Linking our England to his Italy!

HERVÉ RIEL

I

On the sea and at the Hogue, sixteen hundred ninety-
  two,
  Did the English fight the French,—woe to France!
And, the thirty-first of May, helter-skelter through the
  blue,
Like a crowd of frightened porpoises a shoal of sharks
  pursue,
  Came crowding ship on ship to Saint Malo on the
  Rance,
With the English fleet in view.

II

'Twas the squadron that escaped, with the victor in full
  chase;
  First and foremost of the drove, in his great ship,
  Damfreville;
    Close on him fled, great and small,
    Twenty-two good ships in all;
And they signalled to the place
"Help the winners of a race!
  Get us guidance, give us harbor, take us quick—or,
  quicker still,
  Here's the English can and will!"

III

Then the pilots of the place put out brisk and leapt on
  board;
  "Why, what hope or chance have ships like these to
  pass?" laughed they:
"Rocks to starboard, rocks to port, all the passage scarred
  and scored,
Shall the 'Formidable' here with her twelve and eighty
  guns

Think to make the river-mouth by the single narrow
  way,
Trust to enter where 'tis ticklish for a craft of twenty tons,
  And with flow at full beside?
  Now, 'tis slackest ebb of tide.
 Reach the mooring?   Rather say,
While rock stands or water runs,
 Not a ship will leave the bay!"

IV

Then was called a council straight.
Brief and bitter the debate:
"Here's the English at our heels; would you have them
  take in tow
All that's left us of the fleet, linked together stern and
  bow,
For a prize to Plymouth Sound?
Better run the ships aground!"
 (Ended Damfreville his speech).
"Not a minute more to wait!
 Let the Captains all and each
 Shove ashore, then blow up, burn the vessels on the
  beach!
France must undergo her fate.

V

"Give the word!"   But no such word
Was ever spoke or heard;
 For up stood, for out stepped, for in struck amid all
  these
—A Captain?   A Lieutenant?   A Mate—first, second,
  third?
  No such man of mark, and meet
  With his betters to compete!
  But a simple Breton sailor pressed by Tourville
  for the fleet,
A poor coasting-pilot he, Hervé Riel the Croisickese.

VI

And "What mockery or malice have we here?" cries
     Hervé Riel:
  "Are you mad, you Malouins?   Are you cowards, fools,
     or rogues?
Talk to me of rocks and shoals, me who took the sound-
     ings, tell
On my fingers every bank, every shallow, every swell
  'Twixt the offing here and Grève where the river dis-
     embogues?
Are you bought by English gold?   Is it love the lying's
     for?
     Morn and eve, night and day,
     Have I piloted your bay,
Entered free and anchored fast at the foot of Solidor.
  Burn the fleet and ruin France?   That were worse than
     fifty Hogues!
     Sirs, they know I speak the truth!   Sirs, believe me
     there's a way!
Only let me lead the line,
  Have the biggest ship to steer,
  Get this 'Formidable' clear,
Make the others follow mine,
And I lead them, most and least, by a passage I know
     well,
  Right to Solidor past Grève,
     And there lay them safe and sound;
     And if one ship misbehave,
     —Keel so much as grate the ground,
Why, I've nothing but my life,—here's my head!" cries
     Hervé Riel.

VII

Not a minute more to wait.
"Steer us in, then, small and great!
  Take the helm, lead the line, save the squadron!"
     cried its chief.

Captains, give the sailor place!
  He is Admiral, in brief.
Still the north-wind, by God's grace!
See the noble fellow's face
As the big ship, with a bound,
Clears the entry like a hound,
Keeps the passage as its inch of way were the wide sea's
    profound!
  See, safe through shoal and rock,
  How they follow in a flock,
Not a ship that misbehaves, not a keel that grates the
    ground,
  Not a spar that comes to grief!
The peril, see, is past,
All are harbored to the last,
And just as Hervé Riel hollas "Anchor!"— sure as fate,
Up the English come—too late!

VIII

So, the storm subsides to calm:
  They see the green trees wave
  On the heights o'erlooking Grève.
Hearts that bled are stanched with balm.
"Just our rapture to enhance,
  Let the English rake the bay,
Gnash their teeth and glare askance
  As they cannonade away!
'Neath rampired Solidor pleasant riding on the Rance!"
How hope succeeds despair on each Captain's counte-
    nance!
Out burst all with one accord,
  "This is Paradise for Hell!
    Let France, let France's King
    Thank the man that did the thing!"
What a shout, and all one word,
  "Hervé Riel!"

As he stepped in front once more,
 Not a symptom of surprise
 In the frank blue Breton eyes,
Just the same man as before.

IX

Then said Damfreville, "My friend,
I must speak out at the end,
 Though I find the speaking hard.
Praise is deeper than the lips:
You have saved the King his ships,
 You must name your own reward.
'Faith, our sun was near eclipse!
Demand whate'er you will,
France remains your debtor still.
Ask to heart's content and have! or my name's not
  Damfreville."

X

Then a beam of fun outbroke
On the bearded mouth that spoke,
As the honest heart laughed through
Those frank eyes of Breton blue:
"Since I needs must say my say,
 Since on board the duty's done,
 And from Malo Roads to Croisic Point, what is it but
  a run?—
Since 'tis ask and have, I may—
 Since the others go ashore—
Come! A good whole holiday!
 Leave to go and see my wife, whom I call the Belle
  Aurore!"
 That he asked and that he got,—nothing more.

XI

Name and deed alike are lost:
Not a pillar nor a post

In his Croisic keeps alive the feat as it befell;
Not a head in white and black
On a single fishing-smack,
In memory of the man but for whom had gone to wrack
    All that France saved from the fight whence England
        bore the bell.
Go to Paris: rank on rank
    Search the heroes flung pell-mell
On the Louvre, face and flank!
    You shall look long enough ere you come to Hervé
        Riel.
So, for better and for worse,
Hervé Riel, accept my verse!
In my verse, Hervé Riel, do thou once more
Save the squadron, honor France, love thy wife the
        Belle Aurore!

HELEN'S TOWER

Who hears of Helen's Tower, may dream perchance
    How the Greek Beauty from the Scæan Gate
    Gazed on old friends unanimous in hate,
Death-doom'd because of her fair countenance.

Hearts would leap otherwise, at thy advance,
    Lady, to whom this Tower is consecrate!
    Like hers, thy face once made all eyes elate,
Yet, unlike hers, was bless'd by every glance.

The Tower of Hate is outworn, far and strange:
    A transitory shame of long ago,
        It dies into the sand from which it sprang;
But thine, Love's rock-built Tower, shall fear no change:
    God's self laid stable earth's foundation so,
        When all the morning-stars together sang.

WHY I AM A LIBERAL

"Why?" Because all I haply can and do,
  All that I am now, all I hope to be,—
  Whence comes it save from fortune setting free
Body and soul the purpose to pursue,
God traced for both? If fetters, not a few,
  Of prejudice, convention, fall from me,
  These shall I bid men—each in his degree
Also God-guided—bear, and gayly, too?

But little do or can the best of us:
  That little is achieved through Liberty.
Who, then, dares hold, emancipated thus,
  His fellow shall continue bound? Not I,
Who live, love, labor freely, nor discuss
  A brother's right to freedom. That is "Why."

DEVELOPMENT

My Father was a scholar and knew Greek.
When I was five years old, I asked him once
"What do you read about?"
                         "The siege of Troy."
"What is a siege, and what is Troy?"
                         Whereat
He piled up chairs and tables for a town,
Set me a-top for Priam, called our cat
—Helen, enticed away from home (he said)
By wicked Paris, who couched somewhere close
Under the footstool, being cowardly,
But whom—since she was worth the pains, poor puss—
Towzer and Tray,—our dogs, the Atreidai,— sought
By taking Troy to get possession of
—Always when great Achilles ceased to sulk,

(My pony in the stable)—forth would prance
And put to flight Hector—our page-boy's self.
This taught me who was who and what was what:
So far I rightly understood the case
At five years old; a huge delight it proved
And still proves—thanks to that instructor sage
My Father, who knew better than turn straight
Learning's full flare on weak-eyed ignorance,
Or, worse yet, leave weak eyes to grow sand-blind,
Content with darkness and vacuity.

It happened, two or three years afterward,
That—I and playmates playing at Troy's Siege—
My Father came upon our make-believe.
"How would you like to read yourself the tale
Properly told, of which I gave you first
Merely such notion as a boy could bear?
Pope, now, would give you the precise account
Of what, some day, by dint of scholarship,
You'll hear—who knows?—from Homer's very mouth.
Learn Greek by all means, read the 'Blind Old Man,
Sweetest of Singers'—*tuphlos* which means 'blind,'
Hedistos which means 'sweetest.' Time enough!
Try, anyhow, to master him some day;
Until when, take what serves for substitute,
Read Pope, by all means!"
                                        So I ran through Pope,
Enjoyed the tale—what history so true?
Also attacked my Primer, duly drudged,
Grew fitter thus for what was promised next—
The very thing itself, the actual words,
When I could turn—say, Buttmann to account.

Time passed, I ripened somewhat: one fine day,
"Quite ready for the Iliad, nothing less?
There's Heine, where the big books block the shelf:
Don't skip a word, thumb well the Lexicon!"

I thumbed well and skipped nowise till I learned
Who was who, what was what, from Homer's tongue,
And there an end of learning. Had you asked
The all-accomplished scholar, twelve years old,
"Who was it wrote the Iliad?"—what a laugh!
"Why, Homer, all the world knows: of his life
Doubtless some facts exist: it's everywhere:
We have not settled, though, his place of birth:
He begged, for certain, and was blind beside:
Seven cities claimed him—Scio, with best right,
Thinks Byron. What he wrote? Those hymns we have.
Then there's the 'Battle of the Frogs and Mice,'
That's all—unless they dig 'Margites' up
(I'd like that) nothing more remains to know."

Thus did youth spend a comfortable time;
Until—"What's this the Germans say in fact
That Wolf found out first? It's unpleasant work
Their chop and change, unsettling one's belief:
All the same, where we live, we learn, that's sure."
So, I bent brow o'er *Prolegomena*.
And after Wolf, a dozen of his like
Proved there was never any Troy at all,
Neither Besiegers nor Besieged,—nay, worse,—
No actual Homer, no authentic text,
No warrant for the fiction I, as fact,
Had treasured in my heart and soul so long—
Ay, mark you! and as fact held still, still hold,
Spite of new knowledge, in my heart of hearts
And soul of souls, fact's essence freed and fixed
From accidental fancy's guardian sheath.
Assuredly thenceforward—thank my stars!—
However it got there, deprive who could—
Wring from the shrine my precious tenantry,
Helen, Ulysses, Hector and his Spouse,
Achilles and his Friend?—though Wolf—ah, Wolf!
Why must he needs come doubting, spoil a dream?

But then, "No dream's worth waking"—Browning
    says:
And here's the reason why I tell thus much.
I, now mature man, you anticipate,
May blame my Father justifiably
For letting me dream out my nonage thus,
And only by such slow and sure degrees
Permitting me to sift the grain from chaff,
Get truth and falsehood known and named as such.
Why did he ever let me dream at all,
Not bid me taste the story in its strength?
Suppose my childhood was scarce qualified
To rightly understand mythology,
Silence at least was in his power to keep:
I might have—somehow—correspondingly—
Well, who knows by what method, gained my gains,
Been taught, by forthrights not meanderings,
My aim should be to loathe, like Peleus' son,
A lie as Hell's Gate, love my wedded wife,
Like Hector, and so on with all the rest.
Could not I have excogitated this
Without believing such man really were?
That is—he might have put into my hand
The "Ethics"? In translation, if you please,
Exact, no pretty lying that improves,
To suit the modern taste: no more, no less—
The "Ethics:" 'tis a treatise I find hard
To read aright now that my hair is gray,
And I can manage the original.
At five years old—how ill had fared its leaves!
Now, growing double o'er the Stagirite,
At least I soil no page with bread and milk,
Nor crumple, dogs-ear and deface—boys' way.

EPILOGUE TO ASOLANDO

At the midnight in the silence of the sleep-time,
　　When you set your fancies free,
Will they pass to where—by death, fools think,
　　imprisoned—
Low he lies who once so loved you, whom you loved
　　so,
　　　　　　—Pity me?

Oh to love so, be so loved, yet so mistaken!
　　What had I on earth to do
With the slothful, with the mawkish, the unmanly?
Like the aimless, helpless, hopeless, did I drivel
　　　　　—Being—who?

One who never turned his back but marched breast
　　forward,
　　Never doubted clouds would break,
Never dreamed, though right were worsted, wrong
　　would triumph,
Held we fall to rise, are baffled to fight better,
　　　　　Sleep to wake.

No, at noonday in the bustle of man's work-time
　　Greet the unseen with a cheer!
Bid him forward, breast and back as either should be,
"Strive and thrive!" cry "Speed,—fight on, fare ever
　　　　There as here!"

NOTES ON THE POEMS

Pippa Passes. 1841. (*Bells and Pomegranates,* No. 1)

A sequence of four dramatic scenes, given a loose connection by the figure of little Pippa and her unconscious influence upon others. Pippa misconceives everything that concerns the "four happiest" individuals, yet her simple songs arouse them to action which is noble—or so regarded by the poet. The picture of Pippa, in innocence and purity of heart, passing through scenes of sordid human turpitude, oblivious of the evil about her, is a brilliant one. The first scene exhibits adultery, murder, ingratitude; the second, a vulgar practical joke by which an artist's dream is shattered; the third, the heart-breaking contrast between the purity of motive in the young political revolutionary and the motives of scheming politicians who make him their tool; the fourth, the corrupt and worldly schemes of one who is reputed a "holy man." The sheer fantastic romanticism by which the sinners are saved on the brink of their respective perditions, by the pertinence of Pippa's songs, must be accepted by the reader as poetic license of no ordinary sort. The important consideration, however, is that the youthful poet displayed in *Pippa Passes* an extraordinary ability to plumb the depths of human behavior. The realism of Browning is here early illustrated in a striking way. For a detailed and somewhat overelaborate analysis of the poem see the *Works* (Crowell ed.) vol. I, pp. 317-319. For the origin of the poem, see Griffin-Minchin *Life,* pp. 124-126; Dowden's *Life,* pp. 69-71. Compare also Ethel Colburn Mayne's *Browning's Heroines,* Chap. II.

Browning had spent four days in "delicious Asolo," on his first visit to Italy in 1838. *Pippa Passes* was written while he was finishing *Sordello,* and is an indirect product of that poem, which tells of a barefoot child, climbing the dewy hillsides of Asolo, early in the morning, and singing "to beat the lark, God's poet—." Both Pippa and Sordello are solitary, but in everything else they present contrasts—one accomplishes much unconsciously; the other, self-conscious, accomplishes nothing, and his song is fruitless.

Asolo, the scene of this drama, is a small town thirty miles west of Venice. Browning's life and work are connected with it in several ways. He visited the town in 1838, 1878, and 1889; and he named his last volume for it, *Asolando.* Curiously, it was at Asolo that his only son, Robert Wiedemann Browning, died in July 1912.

Cavalier Tunes. 1842.

I. Marching Along.
II. Give a Rouse.
III. Boot and Saddle.

These are by-products of the studies by which Browning produced *Strafford.* (See Griffin-Minchin *Life,* pp. 107-11.) They are rousing songs, as they might have been sung by stalwart, confident Cavaliers, who supported King Charles I against Parliament. Pym, Hampden, Hazelrig, Fiennes, and "Young Harry" Vane, were Parliamentarians. "Kentish Sir Byng" and Prince Rupert were supporters of Charles. "Noll's damned troopers" refers to Cromwell's own company of horse, famed for their effectiveness in battle. Compare the matter and spirit of the song for Pym at the end of the "Parleying with Charles Avison." (See *Complete Works.*)

My Last Duchess—Ferrara. 1842.

Appeared originally in the third number of *Bells and Pomegranates,* where it was called "Italy"; was published with the present title in 1863. It is one of the poet's most concentrated monologues. Fra Pandolf and Claus of Innsbruck are imaginary artists. For his Duke, Browning probably had in mind the three-times-married Vespasiano Gonzaga, Duke of Sabbioneta (a town not far from Ferrara). The Duchess of the poet may have been the Duke's first wife, a gay young Sicilian girl, Diana, daughter of Don Antonio di Cardona. It seems likely that Browning got hints for this and other poems from Ireneo Affó's life of Gonzaga (pub. 1780). See John D. Rea, "My Last Duchess," *Studies in Philology,* XXIX, 120-122. The subtle point of the whole poem is that the Duke apparently wishes to convey to the Count's envoy, and through him to the lady, his intention of demanding complete devotion and obedience from his next wife. Compare F. Bitzkat, "Robert Browning's 'My Last Duchess,' " *Zeitschrift für französische und englische Unterricht,* XXIV, 394-404.

Soliloquy of the Spanish Cloister. 1842.

The second of two poems printed under the title "Camp and Cloister" (the first was "Incident of the French Camp"). The speaker is a mean-minded and jealous Spanish monk, who can see only hypocrisy as the explanation of Brother Lawrence's simplicity and unselfishness and love of flowers. His own conception of religion is formal and ritualistic, and he can conceive of no other sort.

Browning represents him repeating perfunctorily the words of the service while his mind is filled with jealousy and hate.

Rudel to the Lady of Tripoli.   1842.

Rudel was a Provençal troubadour who lived in the 12th century. He accompanied his patron, a brother of Richard the Lion-hearted, to England, but left the English court for the Holy Land in 1162. The Crusaders returning from the East spread abroad reports of the beauty, wit, and learning of the Countess of Tripoli (a small Duchy to the north of Palestine, near the present Beirut). In the spirit of his age, Rudel fell in love with the Countess, although he had never seen her. To her he wrote some of his best songs—praising her grace, hospitality, and beauty—before he set out for the East. He became ill on the voyage to Tripoli, and died in her arms soon after reaching that port.

Cristina.   1842.

A love poem written from the point of view of the unsuccessful lover. Browning wrote many such poems. (See especially "The Last Ride Together.") Cristina, a beautiful and coquettish woman, was the daughter of Francis I, king of the two Sicilies. She married Ferdinand VII of Spain in 1829, and was made Regent after his death in 1833. The poem seems to give expression to Platonic ideas, especially in stanzas v and vi. Like others of Browning's lyrics, it expresses the lover's sense of the worth of love to the soul as the supreme gain of life.

Through the Metidja to Abd-el-Kadr.   1842.

Abd-el-Kadr ("servant of god") was born in Algeria, and became, in 1831, Emir of Mascara. He resisted the French invasions, and united the Arab tribes. In 1842 his camp was raided and his Arab troops scattered. Browning represents, in vigorous anapæstic verse, an Arab dashing through the desert called the Metidja to rejoin his chieftain. The poem was directly inspired by a gallop on the back of his Uncle Reuben's horse at New Cross, shortly after Browning had returned from a voyage which gave him glimpses of the Algerian coast.

The Pied Piper of Hamelin.   1842.

Browning was often entertained, as a child, with this well-known legend of Hamelin Town. He read it in a version by Nathaniel

Wanley (1677) and, also, in one by James Howell in the *Epistolæ Ho-Elianæ* (1643), one of Thackeray's "bedside books." A version of the Pied Piper tale, written by Browning's own father, is published in part in the Griffin-Minchin *Life* (p. 20). When Browning sought to write "a child's story" for ten-year-old Willie Macready, he very naturally turned to the theme which in childhood had delighted him. A reading of the elder Browning's version makes it clear whence the poet derived his tendency to odd rhymes and humorous prosodical effects. The date given by Howell for the legendary incident embodied in the poem is 1393. (See *Browning Society Papers*, I, 113, n.) For an important discussion of the sources of this poem, see Arthur Dickson, "Browning's Source for the 'Pied Piper of Hamelin,'" *Studies in Philology*, XXIII, 327-36.

Nationality in Drinks. 1844-5.

The first two parts, entitled "Claret" and "Tokay," first appeared in *Hood's Magazine*, 1844. The third part originally appeared in 1845 in *Dramatic Romances and Lyrics*, under the title "Here's to Nelson's Memory!"

The Flower's Name. 1844.

Originally appeared in *Hood's Magazine*, July, 1844, with another poem, under the title "Garden Fancies." It is a description of a garden by a lover whose conception of its beauty is heightened and made vital by the memories it enshrines.

Pictor Ignotus. 1845.

One of Browning's poems of failure—in this case characteristic of a monastic painter of the Renaissance. The failure of the unknown painter was due to his high conception of art—so high that he could not bear to submit pictures of real worth to the world. With his extremely sensitive disposition, he could not endure the thought of ignorant criticism by people who had no comprehension of the aim or purpose of the artist. Pictor Ignotus has chosen to sink his name in unknown service to the church. (See Pearl Hogrefe, *Browning and Italian Art and Artists*, in *University of Kansas Humanistic Studies*, no. 3, May 15, 1914.) This is the first of Browning's poems wholly devoted to a painter—in this case an imaginary one. It may be compared with the studies of real painters, "Fra Lippo Lippi" and "Andrea del Sarto." In his father's library, Browning read with delight the 1778 edition of Gerard de Lairesse's

Art of Painting in All Its Branches, and later confessed his debt to it in *Parleyings with Certain People of Importance.* Matthew Pilkington's *Dictionary of Painters* (1805 edition) was the source of most of his knowledge of the early history of art. The influence of Pilkington is traceable in his poems.

The Italian in England. 1845. (First published as "Italy in England.")

The incidents of the poem are wholly imaginary, but they present an authentic picture of the struggle of Italian liberals against Austrian oppression. Mazzini was impressed by the poem as an illustration of an Englishman's sympathetic understanding of the Italian patriots. In *Pippa Passes* Browning had earlier, in the story of Luigi and the Austrian police, given a suggestion of Italy's struggle for freedom. A few years later, in 1844, he visited Italy and wrote "The Italian in England." For a similar feeling towards Italian independence, see Mrs. Browning's *Casa Guidi Windows* (written 1848–51), and the earlier poems of Byron and Shelley.

The Lost Leader. 1845.

"The poem represents the feelings of those Liberals who were left behind when Wordsworth and others deserted the companions of their youth."—Furnivall. The poem is applicable to any popular apostasy. The "handful of silver" and "riband to stick in his coat" must not be taken too literally. This poem may well be compared with Shelley's sonnet on the same subject.

The Lost Mistress. 1845.

One of a number of poems in which Browning presents the unsuccessful lover. The title of this poem was probably suggested to Browning by that of "The Lost Leader."

Home Thoughts. 1845.

"Home Thoughts, from Abroad" expresses the nostalgia of the Englishman who remembers the beauties of the English spring. It may be compared with Rupert Brooke's "Grantchester" and Masefield's "August 1914." "Home Thoughts, from the Sea," since they were written in the neighborhood of Trafalgar and Gibraltar, concern England's naval battles and victories of the past.

The Bishop Orders His Tomb at St. Praxed's Church. 1845.

The poem was first published in *Hood's Magazine*, March, 1845, with the title, "The Tomb at St. Praxed's (Rome, 15—)." St. Praxed's, a famous Roman church, contains the tomb of Cardinal Cetive (1474), whose figure in effigy may have given Browning the hint for his Bishop. The aim of the poem is apparently to bring out some of the leading characteristics of the Renaissance, as they had an influence on the church, and on the lives of the leading ecclesiastics. Ruskin has shown how completely successful Browning was in conveying the spirit of the Renaissance in this poem. Ruskin wrote: "I know of no other piece of modern English . . . in which there is so much told, as in these lines, of the Renaissance spirit—its worldliness, inconsistency, pride, hypocrisy, ignorance of itself, love of art, of luxury, and of good Latin." (For the full quotation, a long and valuable criticism, see *Modern Painters*, vol. IV, ch. XX, sections 32 and 34.) The Bishop's address to his sons shows how fully his mind is occupied with sensuous things, even as he is dying.

The Confessional. 1845.

In a fury of indignation when she is tricked into revealing the political information confided to her by her lover, which has led to his execution, a girl denounces the teaching of the Spanish church and the priests. Imprisoned and tortured on account of her heretical denunciations of the church, she yet vows that the world shall learn from her that the priests are teaching lies. The poem is historical only in its interpretation of the spirit of the Spanish Inquisition.

The Flight of the Duchess. 1845.

This poem was inspired by a line, "Following the Queen of the gypsies, O!" in a song which the poet heard when a boy. Many students of Browning have attempted to allegorize this beautiful story; but most lovers of the poet prefer to have it remain the simple romance of the Duchess who found with the gypsies the "life" which had been denied her in the Duke's castle.

Earth's Immortalities. 1845.

Song. 1845.

Meeting at Night and *Parting at Morning*. 1845.

Supplementary pictures—the lover turns at night towards isolation with the loved one; in the morning, he turns away from this towards the business of life and men. The "him" in the next to the last line refers to the sun.

Saul. 1845–1855.

For the story upon which this poem is based see I Samuel 16: 14-23. It is probably the most popular of Browning's religious poems. The first nine sections originally appeared in *Bells and Pomegranates* VII, 1845. The remainder were written at Rome in 1853–54, and the whole was first printed in the volume entitled *Men and Women*, 1855. One of Browning's early favorites was Christopher Smart's *Song to David* (see *Parleyings with Certain People of Importance*) which may have influenced him in a general way. Edward Berdoe, in the *Browning Cyclopædia* (pp. 464 ff.) suggests a likeness with the series of tunes in Longus's *Daphnis and Chloe*. (See Smith's translation in Bohn ed., pp. 303, 332-4.) The poem, as finally concluded, might better be called "David," since Saul fades out of the picture in the later sections, and the reader is impressed with the effect on David himself—the sense of awe and solemnity with which he greets the morning. "The culminating moment in the effort of David, by which he arouses the sunken soul of the king, the moment toward which all others tend, is that in which he finds in his own nature love as God's ultimate gift." (Dowden, *Life*, Everyman ed., p. 197.)

The Glove. 1845.

This poem contains an old and oft-retold story, its ultimate source the *Essais Historiques sur Paris* of Poullain de St. Croix. Leigh Hunt's version, "The Glove and the Lions" (1836), after Schiller, is widely known. Browning developed the common story along original lines, in the interest of soul-discovery. In making Ronsard the mouthpiece for a deeper observation of the meaning of the incident he is supposed to witness than Clement Marot and the rest saw, he brings out characteristic differences between these two poets of the time, and adds to the original story an entirely new view of the lady's character, as well as criticism of the narrowness of the court and the court poets in the day of Francis I of France.

Love among the Ruins.   1855.

The lover contrasts the intense awareness of the two individuals who are meeting near the ruins with the grass-grown relics of ancient civilization itself, lying inert through the centuries. The scene is more glorified by the love of the two individuals than it had ever been in the ancient days of pomp and savage triumph—this seems to be Browning's thought. Browning's "all the mountains topped with temples" and "hundred-gated circuit of a wall" indicate that he could not have had Rome alone in mind, but rather a composite picture of Babylon and Jerusalem. (See Robert Adger Law, *Modern Language Notes*, XXXVII, 312.) See also the Bible (King James Version), I Chron. 18: 4; and compare the language, especially the use of the word "reserved." It has been suggested that "Love among the Ruins" may have been a sad reflection on David, the victorious but unhappy King of Israel.

A Lovers' Quarrel.   1855.

A picture of lovers in springtime, surrounded by all the gladness of nature. This contrasts strangely with the coldness and void at their hearts, because of a sudden word, which has unwittingly struck discord into their happy world. The speaker protests that the love which has amassed such treasuries of memory and experience cannot be blotted out by so petty a thing.

Evelyn Hope.   1855.

May be regarded as an example of Browning's investigating of all the possibilities of love. In this poem he conceives a situation which may be said to be so purely theoretical as to be almost non-existent. A man of maturity loves a young girl, too immature and virginal to realize his affection. She is dead. But in his mood of infinite tenderness and unfulfilled aspiration, the lover sees death no bar to a far-off attainment. The nature of the attainment he cannot divine; but he feels an assurance that it will be realized, and that the meaning of things obscure now will be made clear then.

Up at a Villa—Down in the City.   1855.

An impoverished Italian nobleman, condemned by circumstances to his rustic villa, sighs for the excitements of town life. Browning, who obviously does not sympathize with him, makes him suggest the beauty and charm of life in the country, even while he is describing his boredom. (See Stopford Brooke, *The Poetry of Robert Browning*, p. 322.)

A Woman's Last Word. 1855.

The poem expresses the self-surrender of a fond heart which has resisted against over-mastery. The imagery is largely derived from the Garden of Eden episodes in *Paradise Lost*. The woman speaks.

Fra Lippo Lippi. 1855.

Giorgio Vasari (*Lives of the Most Eminent Painters, Sculptors and Architects,* 1550-1558) was Browning's authority for many of the facts about Fra Filippo di Tommaso Lippi, son of a butcher, who was born in Florence at the beginning of the 15th century. Left an orphan at the age of two years, he was cared for by an aunt, and when still a mere boy placed in charge of the Carmelite friars. He stayed with the friars for twelve years, and studied at the Carmine Monastery the paintings of Tommasaccio. He left the monastery in 1432, although not renouncing his vows. Cosimo de' Medici was his patron. Further details of his interesting life may be read by the student in biographies by E. C. Strutt, A. J. Anderson, and Margaret V. Farrington, as well as in Vasari. (See edition of Blashfield and Hopkins, New York, 1923, II, 62-78. This is the most useful translation of Vasari for the modern student.)

Fra Angelico, Giovanni da Fiesole (1387–1455) held to the old mediæval ideas of painting "soul," as preached by the Prior to Fra Lippo Lippi. Tommaso Guidi, or Tommasaccio (1401–28), with his pupil, Fra Lippo Lippi, led the reaction against the romantic methods of the monastic painters. Browning makes the painter defend his realism, and justify his opposition to the Prior's artistic theories. In this poem, Browning makes the predecessor ("Hulking Tom" or Tommasaccio) the successor, as he then believed was actually the case. He follows very closely the gossipy narrative of Vasari. It is worth noting here that eleven of his poems deal with Italian painters or painting as the principal theme; thirty poems contain references to them. (See Pearl Hogrefe, *Browning and Italian Art and Artists*, pp. 45, 66.)

A Toccata of Galuppi's. 1855.

A toccata is an overture illustrating technique—a composition of indefinite form, but brilliant, fantasia-like character. Examples are to be found in the works of Bach, Schumann, and Debussy. In the character of this music as played by the Venetian composer,

Baldassare Galuppi, Browning found a parallel with the life of the Venetians, their gaiety and improvidence. Browning's theme is the transiency of happiness and gaiety, not without the thought, however, that these may have as much value in the scheme of things as the over-serious occupations of the scientists. The poem should be compared with Browning's other poems on music and musicians, such as "Abt Vogler" and "Master Hugues of Saxe-Gotha." (See Helen A. Clarke, "Musical Symbolism in Browning," *Poet-Lore*, III, 260-269; J. T. Nettleship, "Browning's Intuition, Especially in Regard to Music and the Plastic Arts," *Browning Society Papers*, I, 381-396; and Helen J. Omerod, "Some Notes on Browning's Poems Relating to Music," *Browning Society Papers*, II, 180 ff.)

By the Fireside. 1855.

A conception of old age as the crowning period of a ripe and perfect love. The allusion to the "great brow" and "spirit-small hand" clearly refer to Mrs. Browning, and give the poem autobiographical interest. The scene is a little mountain gorge near the Baths of Lucca, where the Brownings passed parts of the summers of 1849 and 1853. (See Henry James's *William Wetmore Story and His Friends*, I, 266-67, for pictures of the Brownings at the Baths of Lucca.) The ideas of the poem are amplified in "One Word More," stanzas xvi-xviii. It should be noted, however, that most of the incidents of the poem are imaginary. (See Berdoe, *Browning Cyclopædia*). For a complete analysis, see John T. Nettleship, *Robert Browning: Essays and Thoughts* (London, 1890).

Any Wife to Any Husband. 1855.

A poem expressing the poet's conception of essential differences between man's and woman's ways of loving. He is all to her; she cannot be everything to him. The speaker is a dying wife, who realizes that her husband's affections will be transferred, after she is gone, to another. He will therefore come to her in an after-life somewhat in need of pardon. She does not dare to prophesy his constancy, although she ardently desires it. The poem may be regarded as an expression of the woman's superior perception of the psychical values of constancy.

My Star. 1855.

A lyric supposed to refer to Mrs. Browning, which intimates that the soul of the loved one reveals itself fully to none but the lover.

The "angled spar" is a prism glass which breaks the sunlight into its colors.

Instans Tyrannus. 1855.

The title, suggested by lines in Horace, means "threatening tyrant." The poem is a despot's confession of one of his own experiences, which showed him the strength of the weak man who is in the right and can call to his aid the spiritual force of good. Horace's line may be translated—"The just man . . . is not to be turned aside by the . . . brow of the threatening tyrant."

"Childe Roland to the Dark Tower Came." 1855.

One of the most disputed of Browning's poems. He repeatedly declared that it was not intended as allegory. Nevertheless, it has long been one of Browning's most widely read and carefully studied poems, and has been "interpreted" over and over again for moralistic and religious ends. (See Berdoe, *Browning Cyclopædia*, pp. 102-5; see also especially *Browning Society Papers*, I, 380 ff., and T. L. Hood, "The Meaning of 'Childe Roland,'" *New England Magazine*, N. S., XLVI, 130.) None of these explanations of this poem will satisfy fully the modern student.

The poem obviously grew out of two hints; a line in Edgar's song in *King Lear*, embodied in the last line of the poem, and that derived from a picture of a sad old horse in a tapestry in Browning's home. These hints were developed by some such creative process as Professor Lowes described in his brilliant exposition of the composition of Coleridge's "Kubla Khan." (See J. L. Lowes, *The Road to Xanadu*, Boston, 1927.) When thus approached, the poem appears to be another consistent effort of Browning to express his philosophy of attainment through courageous attempt, even though the quest results in what the world calls failure. The best recent comment on the poem may be found in A. A. Brockington's *Browning and the Twentieth Century*, pp. 276-279. See also Harold Golder, "Browning's 'Childe Roland,'" *Pub. Mod. Lang. Assn.*, XXXIX, 963; and W. C. DeVane, "The Landscape of 'Childe Roland,'" *Pub. Mod. Lang. Assn.*, XL, 426 ff.

Respectability. 1855.

Two lovers who have achieved freedom by breaking away from the social conventions and usages of the "respectable world" are wandering at night in Paris, happy in their sense of life and joy.

They approach the Institute, where Guizot, who hates Montalembert, will yet receive him this night with pretended courtesy. The lovers also will make a pretense of respectability, but the man's "Put forward your best foot!" is scornfully spoken.

A Light Woman. 1855.

Mainly interesting for the poet's description of himself in the last stanza as a "writer of plays."

The Statue and the Bust. 1855.

The tradition, which Browning followed only in a general way, and modified to suit his purposes, involves the love of Ferdinand I and the wife of one Riccardi. Riccardi, so the story goes, kept his wife a closely guarded prisoner, when he found that she had conversed with the Grand Duke Ferdinand. She could see and be seen by her lover only when she appeared at the windows of the Riccardi palace. In revenge, Ferdinand is said to have erected his statue in the square in such a position as to appear to be always watching for the lady. The too-literal students of Browning have found the poem a stumbling block, because of the discrepancies between historical fact and the detail of Browning's story. But it should be remembered that the poet was only interested here in pointing a moral—the folly of not grasping love in time. The Duke and the lady lost their souls because they had not the resolution to seize the "potential moment" of love. The moral is more than this, perhaps; it is a parable of the fate of irresolute men and women everywhere, and in all ages. See Prentiss Cummings, "Browning's 'The Statue and the Bust,'" *Poet-Lore*, X, 397-416.

Love in a Life. 1855.

Life in a Love. 1855.

How It Strikes a Contemporary. 1855.

A portrait of a Spanish poet, as the unappreciative, gossiping public of his day sees him. He is thought to be an agent for the government, a spy, because he is always watching men and things. Browning pictures the mistaken notions of the Spanish folk of Valladolid, who failed to understand the true, simple greatness of the poet's life. Browning unquestionably saw himself regarded by his contemporaries much as the Spanish poet was viewed by the citizens of Valladolid.

The Last Ride Together. 1855.

It should be compared with "Love Among the Ruins," and "Two in the Campagna." Each of the poems deals with an unusual phase of love. See J. T. Nettleship's *Robert Browning: Essays and Thoughts,* pp. 18 ff.

Master Hugues of Saxe-Gotha. 1855.

A colloquy of the imaginary organist with Master Hugues, an imaginary composer of the quaint, arithmetical music, in vogue before Palestrina (died 1594) brought music back to the service of melody. The organist and speaker takes occasion, after the church service is over, and while the sexton and altar ministrants are putting things to rights, to examine one of Hugues's "mountainous fugues." The organist decides that Hugues presents in the fugue a symbol of the life of man, which begins simply with steady purpose and clear aim, becomes involved and complicated, as the man grows older, with consequent bewilderment, confusion, and uncertainty of ideals, but at last finds once more the simple and clear purpose of youth. The confusion of life, like the apparent confusion of the fugue, is finally resolved into a stately and orderly conclusion. Although Bach was the greatest composer of fugal music, Brahms, Browning's contemporary, is probably the musician whose works are most readily suggested by the imaginary Hugues.

The fugue is best understood by the non-musical reader if he remembers that the term comes from the Latin *fugere,* to flee, through the Italian *fuga.* As Browning uses it, the word suggests a fleeing of musical parts or themes, one following and answering another, until all the parts have answered, one by one, continuing their several melodies and interweaving them in one complex, progressive whole. It is characteristic of the fugue that its apparent confusion is always resolved into a well ordered ending. See A. Goodrich-Freer, "Robert Browning the Musician," *Nineteenth Century,* XLIX, 648-58.

Bishop Blougram's Apology. 1855.

It has been pointed out elsewhere that Browning frequently attempted to put himself imaginatively into the position of a person whose conduct and views of life he disapproved. It is unlikely that Browning really sympathized with the casuistry of Blougram, but he makes out an excellent case for him. Gigadibs despises the Bishop, because he believes him to be conforming to beliefs which he does not sincerely hold. The Bishop replies that since nothing can be proved, it is more useful and conducive to comfort in this life to be in practice a "believer." The Bishop shows that the arguments from expediency, instinct, and consciousness, all bear on the side of faith and convince him it is better not to let his faith and his doubts come in contact. Rewards for his way of living are of a substantial nature, says the Bishop, while Gigadibs has nothing to show for his frankness and cynicism.

Browning admitted that this poem was a portrait of Cardinal Wiseman (Nicholas Patrick Stephen Wiseman, 1802-1865, Cardinal-Archbishop of Westminster), although it cannot be accepted as a serious description of his life and aims. Wiseman, whose influence on the Oxford movement was well known, was in many respects a figure after Browning's heart—scholar, linguist, athlete, connoisseur, artist, ecclesiastical statesman. The character of Blougram is at best a poor caricature of the man. Wiseman did a great work in England (he came to this country in 1835) in giving unity and organization to the English Catholics, and in making them respected among their countrymen. (See Wilfred Ward, *Problems and Persons,* Chap. X, "The Life and Work of Cardinal Wiseman." See especially p. 326.) The Cardinal himself reviewed the volume, *Men and Women,* in which this poem appeared, in the Roman Catholic *Rambler,* in January, 1856. He evidently felt no resentment at the easily identified portrait.

Memorabilia. 1855. (Originally published with the phrase "On Seeing Shelley" included in the title.)

Reminiscent of Browning's apostrophe to Shelley in *Pauline,* lines 151 ff. ("Sun-treader, life and light be thine forever!"), the poem offers further homage to the Poet, in this case, by representing Browning's life as a blank moor, devoid of interest, save where the feather, sign of an eagle's flight, was found. All the biographers of Browning have gone astray regarding the poet's first acquaintance with Shelley's poems. The myth that Shelley's work first came to Browning's notice in a bookstall, and in the form of "Mr. Shelley's Atheistical Poem" (i.e., *Queen Mab*) was never suggested by anything that Browning himself said about it. Frederick A. Pottle, in *Shelley and Browning* (Chicago, 1923), set the matter at rest, by definitely identifying the copy of Shelley's works which first came to the youthful Browning's hands. It was a small volume obviously pirated in the main from Mrs. Shelley's edition of the *Posthumous Poems* of 1824, and containing most of Shelley's lyrics. The book was given to Browning by his cousin James Silverthorne, and bore the title *Miscellaneous Poems by Percy Bysshe Shelley,* and the publisher's date, "William Benbow, London, 1826." The volume is extant, and contains Browning's note for all the world to see, indicating that it was the "first specimen" of Shelley's poetry that came to his notice.

The important thing about this discovery is the knowledge that Browning did not make the acquaintance of Shelley through *Queen Mab,* but rather through some of the finest lyrics in the English language. After securing this volume, Browning, through an inquiry of the editor of the *Literary Gazette,* obtained all the available poems of Shelley. Their influence upon him appears in *Pauline* and *Paracelsus,* but not notably in his later work. Browning's *Essay on Shelley,* however, reveals that this early acquaintance with Shelley's poetry may have influenced his conception of the poet's mission.

Andrea del Sarto. 1855.

Browning took the bare facts of this poem regarding the faultless but soulless painter from Vasari's *Lives.* Vasari had been a pupil of Andrea del Sarto, and he does less than justice to Lucrezia. Later writers give a more favorable view of her, but the main points of the story remain undisputed. For the origin of the poem see Mrs. Andrew Crosse, "John Kenyon and His Friends," *Temple Bar Magazine,* April, 1900. The facts of the life and character of Andrea are presented fully in George Willis Cooke, *Guide-Book to the Works of Browning,* pp. 8-15; and Berdoe, *Browning Cyclopædia,* pp. 15-19. Cf. Vasari, ed. of 1923, III, 234-302.

Before. 1855.

After. 1855.

"Before" is an argument on the part of a third person in favor of having two men fight out a quarrel, on the grounds that the one who is wrong will never acknowledge his guilt, and the wronged one will never forgive as long as there is a wrong to be retaliated.

"After" reflects the feelings of the man who survives the duel. The poem should be compared with Tennyson's "Maud" for its reflections on duelling.

In Three Days.   1855.

In A Year.   1855.

Old Pictures in Florence.   1855.

Browning here defends the "rough-hewn" art of some of the so-called lesser Florentine painters, as against the polished perfection of the Greeks.   Greek art, according to Browning, by presenting unattainable ideals of material and worldly perfection, taught men to submit.   These early Christian artists, even by faultily presenting spiritual ideals, taught men to aspire.

> ". . . Paint man, man, whatever the issue!
> Make new hopes shine through the flesh they fray,
> New fears aggrandize the rags and tatters;
> To bring the invisible into full play!
> Let the visible go to the dogs—what matters?"

For the sources of many of Browning's references to painters the reader should see Giorgio Vasari's *Lives,* a book the poet frequently consulted.   Although Browning read this book in the Italian original, a convenient translation into English for the modern student is that edited by Blashfield and Hopkins.   (See note on "Fra Lippo Lippi," p. 463).   "Old Pictures in Florence" is a companion to Browning's other painter-poems, "Pictor Ignotus," "Fra Lippo Lippi," and "Andrea del Sarto."   It is important to notice that all these poems owe their origin, in one sense, to the quite incidental fact that Robert and Elizabeth Browning chose Florence (partly because of its inexpensiveness and partly because of the presence of friends) as their place of residence.   All deal with Florentine painters.

The comparison which Browning makes between Giotto's perfect O and his incomplete Campanile, like many other allusions in the poem, was drawn from the reading of Vasari.

"De Gustibus—."   1855.

"De gustibus non disputandum"—there is no disputing about tastes.   On a tablet affixed to the outer wall of the Palazzo Rezzonico in Venice, where Browning died, are the words of this poem—

> "Open my heart and you will see
> Graved inside of it, 'Italy!' "

Women and Roses. 1855.

A poem suggested by some roses sent to Mrs. Browning.

Protus. 1855.

Browning here sets in contrast the two busts and the two lives of Protus, the infant Emperor of Byzantium who was fated to obscurity, and John, the blacksmith's bastard, who usurped the throne and saved the empire with his harder hand. The persons and incidents are imaginary. Browning's interest in sculpture is well known.

Cleon. 1855.

Cleon, a learned and gifted poet from the "sprinkled isles" of Greece (probably the Sporades), a contemporary of the Apostle Paul, has received a letter from his royal patron. He writes to thank the king for his munificence in providing him with all that art and wealth can bestow, and to answer the questions asked, which lead to his confession of the failure of paganism, even in its forms of highest culture, to solve the riddle of life and answer the requirements of the human spirit.

A. W. Crawford (in "Browning's 'Cleon,' " *Journal of English and Germanic Philology*, XXVI, 485-490) expresses the opinion that "Cleon" was published as a sort of companion poem or supplement to Arnold's "Empedocles on Etna." It furnished Browning with an opportunity to show that Greek culture, at the end as at the beginning, could offer nothing but despair to the longing and inquiring spirit. By making Cleon a contemporary of the Apostle Paul, Browning was enabled to make a very striking contrast between the collapse of Greek culture and the new, rising Christian culture, with its doctrine of a future life.

Popularity. 1855.

See Keats's sonnet beginning, "Blue! 'Tis the life of heaven . . ." The elaborate figure employed by Browning implies a likeness between the discovery of the dye prized by the Phoenicians and the poetic vein of Keats, which was exploited by his successors while he was for a time neglected and forgotten. This poem, a notable tribute to Keats, written long before that poet's work had acquired its present fame, is fully interpreted in Berdoe, *Browning Cyclopædia*, p. 357.

Two in the Campagna. 1855.

The "Campagna" is an area around Rome, dotted with crumbling relics of an ancient civilization, which in the month of May becomes a rich pasturage. The elusive, melancholy quality of love—its inadequacy and incompleteness—is here given exquisite setting. Like "Evelyn Hope," this poem deals with the tragedy of love which has failed by just missing fulfillment. The perpetual elusiveness of the ideal is symbolized by the silken thread of the spider's web. Compare also "Love among the Ruins."

A Grammarian's Funeral. 1855.

This poem is not based on any historical character, but gives a symbolic representation of the thirst for knowledge, as Browning conceives it, manifested by the pioneers of the revival of learning, or Renaissance, such as Cyriac of Ancona, Filelfo, and Pierre de Maricourt. The word "grammarian" had a broader meaning then than it has now. The words of the disciples, as they bear the body of their master to the mountain top for burial, express the faith of all those seekers after truth who labor to write eternal words upon the rock of time, who attempt to advance the boundaries of human knowledge, without hope of reward or applause, except from the understanding few.

Misconceptions. 1855.

One Word More: To E. B. B. 1855.

Written in London, September 1855, and appearing in *Men and Women,* as the last poem in the volume, "One Word More" is in reality a dedication of the whole to Mrs. Browning. It may be regarded as an answer to the *Sonnets from the Portuguese,* and indicates that his affection could be as strongly expressed as hers. See comment in George Willis Cooke's *Browning Guide-Book.*

May and Death. 1857.

A personal utterance on the death of Browning's cousin, (Charles) James Silverthorne. It was first printed in *The Keepsake,* an annual, edited by Miss Power; and then included in *Dramatis Personæ,* 1864.

The Worst of It. 1864.

Although the speaker has been wronged, he takes all the blame for the woman's sins and weaknesses. The "worst of it" seems to be that he can do nothing to save her from the results of her own errors. He can take the blame; but he cannot prevent her from suffering.

Too Late. 1864.

An extraordinary study of a phase of love which Browning could comment on with force and emotion. Browning's imaginary speaker in this poem has lost his Edith, who now is dead, because he failed to seek her with resolution—was willing to take "No" for his answer. The speaker blames himself for his lack of the importunate ardor which Browning himself showed when he forcefully carried Elizabeth Barrett from a sick-chamber in Wimpole Street to happiness in Italy. This poem was written shortly after Mrs. Browning's death, and some of the poignancy of the speaker's grief is undoubtedly due to that event in the poet's recent experience.

Abt Vogler. 1864.

Georg Joseph Vogler, a Catholic priest (1749-1814), was renowned as a musician and founder of music schools. He was also famous for his organ recitals. While at Stockholm in the 1780's he invented the "Orchestrion," a "compact, portable organ with four key-boards of five octaves each, and a pedal board of thirty-six keys, with swell complete." This is the instrument on which he is represented as extemporizing in Browning's poem. Vogler brought the Orchestrion to London in 1790, and gave a series of successful concerts. Although he had many critics, some of whom regarded him as a charlatan, Vogler seems to have made a great impression on Europe in his time, both as teacher and concertist. He was especially renowned for his extemporizing. Grove's *Dictionary of Music and Musicians* gives the best account of Vogler in English, as well as a full list of his works. See also *Browning Society Papers*, I, 339-343; I, 469 ff; II, 221-236; and Berdoe, *Browning Cyclopædia*, pp. 1-4.

For the ideas presented in the poem, Browning was indebted in a general way to the idealistic philosophy of Plato, Spinoza, Hegel, and More. He follows the old idea that music is the art most capable of interpreting the spiritual world. An interesting interpretation of the poem's argument may be found in Stopford Brooke's *The Poetry of Robert Browning*, p. 149.

Rabbi Ben Ezra. 1864.

Abraham Ben Meir Ben Ezra, or Ibn Ezra, was one of the most eminent of the Jewish literati of the Middle Ages. Born at Toledo, Spain, about 1090, he led a life of restless wandering, visiting Africa, Italy, England, and France. His reputation for learning is largely based upon his commentaries on the Bible, which contain numerous contributions to the philosophy of religion. He was also noted as astronomer, physician, and poet. Neo-platonic ideas abound in his philosophical thought, a fact which probably explains Browning's interest in him. He died January 1167. A catalogue of his works (written mostly after his exile from Spain) is to be found in Fürst's *Bibliotheca Judaica* (Leipzig, 1849). Browning follows closely in his poem the thought of Ibn Ezra. For an extended explanation, see Berdoe, *Browning's Message to His Time*, pp. 157-72. Dr. M. Friedlander has devoted five volumes to an exposition of the writings of Ibn Ezra. This work is published by the Society of Hebrew Literature (by Trübner and Co., London). An interesting discussion of "Rabbi Ben Erza" may be found in *Poet-Lore*, I, 57-63. See also B. O. Flower, "Robert Browning's 'Rabbi Ben Ezra,'" *Arena*, XL, 334-341. A modern and less sympathetic view is expressed by Paul Elmer More, "Why is Browning Popular?" in *Shelburne Essays*, Third Series, 143-165.

Caliban upon Setebos; or, Natural Theology in the Island. 1864.

The motto from the Fiftieth Psalm, "Thou thoughtest that I was altogether such an one as thyself," gives the point of view of the poem. The Patagonian god Setebos is described in Richard Eden's *History of Travaile*, London, 1577, and *Purchas, His Pilgrimage*, 1613. Browning's immediate hints came, however, from Shakespeare's Caliban, the name being probably an anagram for "Cannibal." Browning here pictures the Caliban of *The Tempest*, but puts into his mouth brutish reasonings about the nature of the god Setebos. In general, Caliban creates Setebos in his own image, vaguely feeling that the god's power is limited, and subject to a higher power whom he refers to as "Quiet"—a power revealed in the remoteness and fixedness of the stars, and suggesting a calm, unalterable, passionless force. Caliban sees Setebos actuated by human motives in his creation of the world, motives no less unworthy than his own discontent, spite, envy, restlessness, and love of power. Caliban's chief philosophic idea is that it is best not to be too happy, lest Setebos be angry.

For orthodox interpretations, see Berdoe's *Browning Cyclopædia,* George Willis Cooke's *Guide-Book to Browning,* and *Browning Society Papers,* I, 489 ff.

Confessions. 1864.

The sick man indignantly repudiates the clergyman's suggestion that the world is a vale of tears. The pharmaceutical atmosphere of his sick-room, with its array of bottles, is transformed by his active imagination into the lane where lived the girl he loved, long ago.

> "How sad and bad and mad it was!—
> But then, how it was sweet!"

Prospice. 1864.

The title means "Look forward." The poem was written in the autumn following Mrs. Browning's death, and has generally been regarded as a personal expression of Browning's strong faith in immortality. It should be compared with the "Epilogue to *Asolando,*" and Tennyson's "Crossing the Bar."

Youth and Art. 1864.

Like "The Statue and the Bust," this is a poem of the failure of two who might have loved. In this case they permitted themselves to be eternally separated because he wished to make himself the equal of John Gibson (1790-1866), a sculptor, and she to rival Giulietta Grisi (born 1812), one of the distinguished operatic sopranos of the time.

Apparent Failure. 1864.

A poem written for the purpose of saving from destruction the Morgue, a small Doric building on one of the quays in Paris. Browning did his part to preserve the Morgue by writing this poem. It was inspired by a sight he had seen seven years earlier. He had visited the building in the summer of 1856, and had seen the bodies of three men who had drowned themselves, because of (1) ambition, (2) a socialist ideal, and (3) love. The poet's "optimism" here reaches its highest point, for he expresses in the closing lines of the poem his faith that "what God blessed once" can never "prove accurst." What he sees is but *apparent* failure. He declines to believe that these poor souls will not be given another chance.

The Ring and the Book.   1868–9.

Browning discovered the Old Yellow Book on a June day in 1860. (See A. K. Cook, *Commentary on The Ring and the Book*, pp. 275-278, for an interesting discussion of and evidence for this date.) It was "propped up on a booth" in the picturesque Square of San Lorenzo, in Florence; and he gave for it one lira—the equivalent of sixteen cents American currency. "Small-quarto size, part print, part manuscript," it consisted of twenty-two documents or papers, nineteen of which related to a murder trial. The fourteen "official" documents among these included "summaries" and "pleadings" of the lawyers engaged, and gave Browning a most complete picture of a murder trial held in Rome in January and February 1698. This was the most important source of Browning's poem. A less important, but still valuable, source (often referred to as the "Secondary Source") was a manuscript pamphlet entitled *The Death of the Wife-Murderer Guido Franceschini, by Beheading.* It was evidently written immediately after the execution of Guido, and came into Browning's hands in 1864. It was printed in England in the *Miscellanies* of the Philobiblion Society, XII, 1868-9, with an introduction by Sir John Simeon; and is now accessible in translation, in the Everyman's Library edition of the *Old Yellow Book*, pp. 259-266.

In the *Yellow Book* itself, the details of the story vary widely on many important points, and the Secondary Source shows other variations. It is obvious then that Browning was forced to chart his own course among the conflicting testimonies. He and Mrs. Browning went to Rome in the autumn of 1860, so that he could search for further information regarding the *cause célèbre* of 1698. They found little or nothing to be learned there. Mrs. Browning died in June 1861, and Robert returned to England. There, probably before October 1864, at his home in Warwick Crescent, the poet set to work on his great poem. (See W. P. Raymond, "Light on the Genesis of *The Ring and the Book*," *Mod. Lang. Notes*, XLIII, 357-368.)

The actual chronology of events was as follows:

Pompilia born in Rome, July 17, 1680.

Pompilia and Guido married, Sept. 6, 1693.

Removal of Comparini and Pompilia to Arezzo, Dec. 1693.

Pietro and Violante Comparini return to Rome, April 1694.

Flight of Pompilia and Caponsacchi, April 29, 1697.

Pompilia and Caponsacchi captured at Castelnuovo, May 1, 1697.

First Trial: Caponsacchi relegated to Civita Vecchia, Sept. 24, 1697.

Murder of Comparini and stabbing of Pompilia, Jan. 2, 1698.

Pompilia died, Jan. 6, 1698.

Sentence of Guido and "certain Four," Feb. 18, 1698.
Execution, Feb. 22, 1698.

Arezzo is one hundred miles from Rome; Castelnuovo fifteen. For comment and collateral reading, see especially Treves, *The Country of "The Ring and the Book"*; Harriet Gaylord, *Pompilia and Her Poet;* and A. K. Cook, *Commentary on "The Ring and the Book."* The easily obtainable translation of the *Old Yellow Book,* in the Everyman's Library edition, is indispensable to any real understanding of Browning's longest and most characteristic poem.

Hervé Riel. 1871.

Contributed to the *Cornhill Magazine* in March 1871, the poem brought Browning £100, which he turned over to the Paris Relief Fund, for food to be sent to Paris, then besieged by the Germans. It is based on an incident in the records of French naval history. Browning wrote it at Le Croisic, a small fishing village near the mouth of the Loire river, which was Hervé Riel's home. The place, Le Croisic, is mentioned elsewhere in Browning's poetry.

Helen's Tower. 1883.

Lines written on the tower erected in memory of Helen, Countess of Giffard, by her son, the Earl of Dufferin and Clandeboye. Browning was asked by the Earl to write a poem for this purpose. The poem was first printed in the *Pall Mall Gazette* of Dec. 28, 1883.

Why I Am a Liberal. 1885.

In 1885 a volume was published in London, edited by Andrew Reid, in which a number of leaders of English thought answered the question, "Why I Am a Liberal." Browning's contribution to the volume was this sonnet.

Development. 1889.

Browning seems to be telling his readers that no intellectual illusions and errors are without their educational values. "It is better that the boy should believe in the combats of Hector and Achilles as veritable facts of history, than that he should bend his brow over Wolf's *Prolegomena*." His illusions will gradually disappear. In the meantime he will have gained a genuine love of the thing learned. Philip Karl Buttmann (1764-1829) was a German philologist, famous for his *Griechische Grammatik, Ausführliche Grie-*

chische Sprachlehre, and other works. Friedrich August Wolf (1759-1824) in his *Prolegomena ad Homerum* advanced the theory that the *Iliad* and the *Odyssey* are not the work of a single and individual Homer, but a much later compilation of hymns sung and handed down by oral tradition. "The Stagirite" is, of course, Aristotle, and "the Ethics" refers to his *Nicomachean Ethics.*

Epilogue to Asolando. 1889.

Published in London, by chance, on the very day of his death in Venice (December 12, 1889), these lines summarize Browning's character and faith quite as adequately as the lines of "Crossing the Bar" do those of Tennyson. See D. G. Brinton, "The Epilogues of Browning: Their Artistic Significance," *Poet-Lore,* IV, 57-64.

Pronunciation of Some Italian Names

Agnolo (ä'nyō-lō)
Alesso (ä-lĕs'sō)
Andrea del Sarto (än'drä-ä del
            sär'tō
Angelico (än-jel'ē-kō)
Antonelli (än-tō-nel'lē)
Arezzo (ä-rĕt'sō)
Asolo (ä'sō-lō)
Baccio (bät'chō)
Baldassare (bäl-däs-sä'rä)
Baldovinetti (bäl-dō-vē-nĕt'tē)
Barberini (bär-bĕ-rē'nē)
Boccaccio (bok-kät'chō)
Bottini (bot-tē'nē)
Buonarroti (bōō-ō-när-rō'tē)
Campagna (käm-pän'yä)
Campanile (käm-pän-ē'lä)
Canova (kä-nō'vä)
Carbonari (kär-bō-nä'rē)
Caponsacchi (kä-pon-sä'kē)
Castelnuovo (käs-tĕl-nōō-ō'vō)
Cecco (chek'kō)
Cencini (chĕn-chē'nē)
Cimabue (chē-mä-bōō'ä)
Civita (chē-vē-tä')
Comparini (kom-pä-rē'nē)
Conti (kôn'tē)
Cornaro (kôr-nä'rō)
Correggio (kor-red'jō)
Duomo (dwo'mō)
Felice (fä-lē'chä)
Ferrara (fĕr-rä'rä)
Fiesole (fē-ä'sō-lä)
Foligno (fō-lēn'yō)
Francesca (frän-chĕs'kä)
Franceschini (frän-chĕs-kē'nē)
Gaddi (gäd'dē)

Gaetano (gä-ä-tä'nō)
Galuppi (gä-lōōp'pē)
Ghiberti (gē-ber'tē)
Ghirlandajo (gēr-län-dä'yō)
Giacinto (jä-chēn'tō)
Giotto (jôt'tō)
Giovacchino (jô-väk-kē'nō)
Giovambattista (jô-väm-bät-tēs'
            tä)
Giovanni (jô-vän'nē)
Giovita (jô-vē'tä)
Giuseppe (jōō-sĕp'pä)
Grisi (grē'sē)
Guido (gwē'dō)
Lapaccia (lä-pät'chä)
Lippo Lippi (lēp'pō lēp'pē)
Luigi (lwē'jē)
Maffeo (mäf-fā'ō)
Medici (mĕd'ē-chē or mä'dē-chē)
Ognissanti (ôn-yēs-sän'tē)
Orcana (or-kän'nä)
Paolo (pä-ō'lō)
Pollajolo (pōl-lä-yô'lō)
Pompilia (pom-pēl'yä)
Possagno (pōs-sän'-yō)
Pietro (pē-ä'trō)
Pippa (pēp'pä)
Prado (prä'dō)
Reni (rā'nē)
Riccardi (rēk-kär'dē)
Strozzi (strôt'sē)
Tommati (tom-mä'tē)
Trevisan (trä-vē'sän)
Uguccio (ōō-gōō'chō)
Vasari (vä-sä'rē)
Vicenza (vē-chĕnt'zä)
Violante (vē-ō-län'tä)

479

INDEX OF TITLES AND FIRST LINES

Titles are printed in italics and first lines in roman type.

Abt Vogler, 318
After, 264
Ah, did you once see Shelley plain, 254
Ah! Friends, I thank and bless you every one! 433
All's over, then: does truth sound bitter, 87
All that I know, 189
Among these latter busts we count by scores, 281
Andrea del Sarto, 255
Answer you, Sirs? Do I understand aright? 371
Any Wife to Any Husband, 185
Apparent Failure, 344
As I ride, as I ride, 65
At the midnight in the silence of the sleep-time, 453
Beautiful Evelyn Hope is dead! 155
Before, 263
Bishop Blougram's Apology, 225
Bishop Orders His Tomb at Saint Praxed's Church, The, 89
Boot and Saddle, 58
Boot, saddle, to horse, and away! 58
[Browning's Address to the British Public], 441
But do not let us quarrel any more, 255
By the Fireside, 176
Caliban upon Setebos; or, Natural Theology in the Island, 330
[Caponsacchi's Reply to the Judges], 371
[Caponsacchi's Story of the Flight], 377

Cavalier Tunes, 56

"*Childe Roland to the Dark Tower Came,*" 192

Cleon, 283

Cleon the poet (from the sprinkled isles, 283

Confessional, The, 92

Confessions, 339

[*Contents of the Yellow Book, The*], 354

Cristina, 63

Day! 3

Dear, had the world in its caprice, 199

[*Dedication to Elizabeth Barrett Browning*], 370

"*De Gustibus—,*" 278

Development, 449

Do you see this square old yellow Book, I toss, 351

Earth's Immortalities, 122

Enough of me! 354

Epilogue to Asolando, 453

Escape me? 212

Evelyn Hope, 155

Fame, 122

Fear death?—to feel the fog in my throat, 340

[*Finding of the Yellow Book, The*], 351

First of the first, 435

Flight of the Duchess, The, 95

Flower's Name, The, 78

Fra Lippo Lippi, 162

Give a Rouse, 57

Glove, The, 142

Grammarian's Funeral, A, 298

Grow old along with me! 323

Gr-r-r—there go, my heart's abhorrence! 60

Had I but plenty of money, money enough and to spare,
157

Hamelin Town's in Brunswick, 67

"Heigho," yawned one day King Francis, 142

Helen's Tower, 448

Here's the garden she walked across, 78

Here was I with my arm and heart, 314

Hervé Riel, 443

Hist, but a word, fair and soft! 220

Home-Thoughts, from Abroad, 88

Home-Thoughts, from the Sea, 88

How It Strikes a Contemporary, 213

How well I know what I mean to do, 176

I am just seventeen years and five months old, 406

I am poor brother Lippo, by your leave! 162

I could have painted pictures like that youth's, 79

I dream of a red-rose tree, 279

I know a Mount, the gracious Sun perceives, 62

I know not how the night passed: morning broke, 377

I only knew one poet in my life, 213

I said—Then, dearest, since 'tis so, 216

I wish that when you died last May, 309

I wonder do you feel today, 295

In a Year, 266

In Three Days, 265

Instans Tyrannus, 190

It is a lie—their Priests, their Pope, 92

It once might have been, once only, 341

Italian in England, The, 81

Just for a handful of silver he left us, 86

Kentish Sir Byng stood for his King, 56

King Charles, and who'll do him right now? 57

Last Ride Together, The, 216

Let's contend no more, Love, 161

Let them fight it out, friend! things have gone too far, 263

Let us begin and carry up this corpse, 298

Life in a Love, 212

Light Woman, A, 200

Lost Leader, The, 86

Lost Mistress, The, 87

Love, 122

Love among the Ruins, 148

Love in a Life, 211

Lovers' Quarrel, A, 150

Marching Along, 56

Master Hugues of Saxe-Gotha, 220

May and Death, 309

Meeting at Night, 123

Memorabilia, 254

Misconceptions, 302

My Father was a scholar and knew Greek, 449

My first thought was, he lied in every word, 192

My heart sank with our Claret-flask, 76

My Last Duchess, 58

My love, this is the bitterest, that thou, 185

My Star, 189

Nationality in Drinks, 76

Nay but you, who do not love her, 122

Never any more, 266

Nobly, nobly Cape Saint Vincent to the Northwest died away, 88

No, for I'll save it! Seven years since, 344

No more wine? then we'll push back chairs and talk, 225

O lyric Love, half angel and half bird, 370

Of the million or two, more or less, 190

Oh Galuppi, Baldassare, this is very sad to find! 173

Oh, to be in England, 88

Oh, what a dawn of day! 150

Old Pictures in Florence, 269

On the sea and at the Hogue, sixteen hundred ninety-two, 443

One Word More, 302

Parting at Morning, 123

Pictor Ignotus, 79

Pied Piper of Hamelin, The, 67

Pippa Passes, 3

[Pompilia's Gratitude to Caponsacchi—Her Death], 433

[Pompilia's Story of Her Life], 406

[Pope's Praise of Pompilia and Caponsacchi, The], 435

Popularity, 293

Prospice, 340

Protus, 281

Rabbi Ben Ezra, 323

Respectability, 199

Ring and the Book, The, 346

Room after room, 211

Round the cape of a sudden came the sea, 123

Rudel to the Lady of Tripoli, 62

Said Abner, "At last thou art come!   Ere I tell, ere thou speak, 123

Saul, 123

See, as the prettiest graves will do in time, 122

She should never have looked at me, 63

So, British Public, who may like me yet, 441

So far as our story approaches the end, 200

So, I shall see her in three days, 265

So, the year's done with! 122

Soliloquy of the Spanish Cloister, 60

Song, 122

Stand still, true poet that you are! 293
Statue and the Bust, The, 202
Take the cloak from his face, and at first, 264
That second time they hunted me, 81
That's my last Duchess painted on the wall, 58
The gray sea and the long black land, 123
The morn when first it thunders in March, 269
There's a palace in Florence, the world knows well, 202
There they are, my fifty men and women, 302
This is a spray the Bird clung to, 302
Through the Metidja to Abd-el-Kadr, 65
Toccata of Galuppi's, A, 173
Too Late, 314
Two in the Campagna, 295
Up at a Villa—Down in the City, 157
Vanity, saith the preacher, vanity! 89
What is he buzzing in my ears? 339
Where the quiet-colored end of evening smiles, 148
Who hears of Helen's Tower, may dream perchance, 448
"Why?"   Because all I haply can and do, 449
Why I am a Liberal, 449
'Will sprawl, now that the heat of day is best, 330
Women and Roses, 279
Woman's Last Word, A, 161
Worst of It, The, 310
Would it were I had been false, not you! 310
Would that the structure brave, the manifold music I
    build, 318
You're my friend, 95
Your ghost will walk, you lover of trees, 278
Youth and Art, 341

Children —

1st Chapter

Children sweeping Children
in steel mills — know man's work &
grief without their wisdom.

(Get info from Horner — ass't som
of children in factories)